Human Rights as Indivisible Rights

International Studies in Human Rights

Volume 101

Human Rights as Indivisible Rights

The Protection of Socio-Economic Demands under the European Convention on Human Rights

By
Ida Elisabeth Koch

MARTINUS
NIJHOFF
PUBLISHERS

LEIDEN • BOSTON
2009

This book is printed on acid-free paper.

Library of Congress Cataloging-in-Publication Data

Koch, Ida Elisabeth.
Human rights as indivisible rights : the protection of socio-economic demands under the European Convention on Human Rights / by Ida Elisabeth Koch.
p. cm. -- (International studies in human rights ; v. 101)
Includes bibliographical references and index.
ISBN 978-90-04-16051-4 (hardback : alk. paper) 1. Human rights--Europe. 2. Social rights--Europe. 3. European Court of Human Rights. I. Title.
KJC5132.K63 2009
341.4'8094--dc22

2009029669

ISSN 0924-4751
ISBN 978 90 04 16051 4

PRINTED IN THE NETHERLANDS

Contents

Acknowledgements

The present work has been completed during the last four years of my long employment period at the Danish Institute for Human Rights (previously the Danish Centre for Human Rights). It has been partly funded by the then Danish Social Science Research Council which has purchased me the freedom to concentrate on research for two years, during which the main part of the book was drafted. The Council also generously funded a four months' visiting scholarship in 2004 at the University of Essex, during which period the writing process was initiated. I am indebted to the Council for providing me with such good working conditions and for making it possible for me to be exempted from institutional obligations for a long period of time. I also wish to thank Professor Paul Hunt and Judith R. Bueno De Mesquita, LLM from the University of Essex for providing me with excellent working conditions and good support during my stay at the University.

Likewise I would like to thank the European Inter-University Centre for Human Right and Democratisation in Venice for granting me the possibility to work at the Centre for five weeks in the summer of 2006. Despite the humidity, heat and 'aqua alta' I recall these weeks with great pleasure, and in that context I am particularly grateful to Secretary General George Ulrich from the University Centre.

My colleagues at the Danish Institute for Human Rights have been supportive in every respect during the writing process and have taken great interest in the subject on an ongoing basis. Professional input, however, has not least been given by scholars outside the Institute. In particular I would like to thank Professor Jens Vedsted-Hansen from the University of Århus together with whom I have covered the whole range of human rights – civil, political, economic, social and cultural – in a number of works also covering the issue of justiciability of socio-economic rights and the issue of division of powers.

As to the issue of hermeneutics as a means for understanding and developing the integrated human rights approach of the European Court of Human Rights I want to thank in particular Professor Henning Koch from the University of Copenhagen and the late Professor Henrik Zahle, both of whom have provided me with constructive comments on this approach to human rights interpretation. The same applies to my former colleague Judge Marianne

Nørregaard, PhD who has shared my interest in hermeneutics and given comments of great value on several of my drafts.

With respect to the use of the tripartite obligations, to respect, protect and fulfil I am grateful for having had the privilege to know the late Katarina Tomasevski together with whom I have had interesting discussions about the expediency of the use of this terminology.

My English teacher at the Ministry of Foreign Affairs' Competence Centre Tove Lonning, MA has done a very professional job by correcting and commenting on my English for which I am most grateful. In that context I would also like to thank the Margot and Thorvald Dreyer's Foundation which has made it possible for me to pay the Competence Centre for Tove Lonning's valuable assistance.

Also, I wish to thank law student Mathias Willumsen from the Danish Institute for Human Rights for editing the manuscript. And not least the library af the Center for International Studies and Human Rights A special thanks goes to Karin Lise Thylstrup and Agnethe Olesen, Cand Scient. Bib. who have been extremy supportive during the whole process. Agnethe Olesen has in addition been indispensible as my computer advisor.

Finally I want to thank my family and good friends for encouraging me to continue the working process along the way. Like most research processes also this working process has been a lonely one and without their interest and encouragement the task would have been much harder.

Copenhagen, 12 April 2009
Ida Elisabeth Koch

Abbreviations

CAT	Convention against Torture and Other Cruel, Inhuman or Degrading Treatment or Punishment
CCDH	Steering Committee for Human Rights
CCPR	International Covenant on Civil and Political Rights
CESCR	International Covenant on Economic, Social and Cultural Rights
COE	Council of Europe
CRC	Convention on the Rights of the Child
ECHR	Convention for the Protection of Human Rights and Fundamental Freedoms
ECSR	European Committee on Social Rights
ECtHR	European Court of Human Rights
ESC	European Social Charter
ETS	European Treaty Series
CPT	European Committee for the Prevention of Torture and Inhuman or Degrading Treatment or Punishment
HRC	Human Rights Committee
ICESCR	International Committee on Economic, Social and Cultural Rights
ILO	International Labour Organisation
NOG	Non-governmental organisation
RESC	Revised European Social Charter
TRNC	Turkish Republic of Northern Cyprus
UDHR	Universal Declaration on Human Rights
UN	United Nations
WHO	World Health Organisation

Chapter 1

Background to and Purpose of the Study

1 *Introduction*

> Human Rights are [....] indivisible, interdependent and interrelated. The international community must treat human rights globally in a fair and equal manner, on the same footing and with the same emphasis [....].

Everyone working with human rights is familiar with the above passage from the Vienna Declaration and Programme of Action from 1993,[1] and the declaration is often taken for the original source for the perception of human rights as indivisible, interrelated and interdependent. However, the view that economic, social, cultural, civil and political rights are indivisible, interrelated and interdependent goes as far back as human rights themselves. Thus, a passage very much similar to the one quoted above was contained in resolution 421 (V) from 1950 by which the UN General Assembly originally decided to adopt one single covenant encompassing all rights enumerated in the Universal Declaration of Human Rights [hereinafter the UDHR].[2,3] Curiously enough, it was repeated one year later when the General Assembly in the so-called Separation Resolution decided to reverse the decision and separate the rights into two covenants, the International Covenant on Economic, Social and Cultural Rights [hereinafter the CESCR] and the International Covenant on Civil and Political Rights [hereinafter the CCPR].[4] At the European level, the

---

[1] Vienna Declaration and Programme of Action, Section 1, para. 5, 1993.

[2] Resolution 421 (V), Draft International Covenant on Human Rights and measures of implementation: future work of the Commission on Human Rights.

[3] For a very extensive analysis of the progress of the negotiations in the UN General Assembly in the years after the adoption of the UDHR, cf. *Craig Scott*, 'The Interdependence and Permeability of Human Rights Norms: Towards a Partial Fusion of the International Covenants on Human Rights' in *Osgoode Hall Law Journal*, Vol. 27, No. 4, 1989, p. 769–878.

[4] The principle of indivisibility, interrelation and interdependence is formulated in the following way in resolution 543 (VI), Draft Covenant on Human Rights and Draft Measures of Implementation: "Whereas the General Assembly affirmed, in its resolution 421 (V) of

notion of indivisibility, interdependence and interrelation lies implicit in the Preamble to the European Convention on Human Rights from 1950 [hereinafter the ECHR].[5] The Preamble initially refers to the UDHR and goes on to present the Convention as "the first steps for the collective enforcement of certain of the rights stated in the Universal Declaration." The European Social Charter from 1961[6] [hereinafter the ESC] and later the Revised European Social Charter from 1996 [hereinafter the RESC][7] cover the remaining rights – the economic, social and cultural rights. The ECHR has a strong focus on the traditional civil and political rights, and the reason for the limited scope of the Convention was explained as follows by Teitgen, the rapporteur of the Legal Committee of the Consultative Assembly of the Council of Europe (the COE) which prepared the first draft of the Convention:

> It [i.e. the Committee] considered that, for the moment, it is preferable to limit the collective guarantee to those rights and essential freedoms which are practised, after long usage and experience, in all the democratic countries. While they are the first triumph of democratic regimes, they are also the necessary condition under which they operate. Certainly, professional freedoms and social rights, which have themselves an intrinsic value, must also, in the future, be defined and protected. Everyone will, however, understand that it is necessary to begin at the beginning and to guarantee political democracy in the European Union and then to coordinate our economies, before undertaking the generalisation of social democracy.[8]

Despite the main focus on civil and political rights the perception of human rights as indivisible, interrelated and interdependent rights has come more into focus in recent years also in the COE.[9] On the other hand, the fact that human rights are indivisible, interrelated and interdependent has been repeated so often and in such a variety of human rights contexts[10] that many consider it

4 December 1950 that "the enjoyment of civic and political freedoms and of economic, social and cultural rights are interconnected and interdependent", and that "when deprived of economic, social and cultural rights, man does not represent the human person whom the Universal Declaration regards as the ideal of the free man." [....]."

[5] Convention for the Protection of Human Rights and Fundamental Freedoms, 1950, ETS No. 005.

[6] European Social Charter, 1991, ETS No. 035.

[7] The Revised European Social Charter, 1996, ETS No. 163.

[8] Council of Europe, Consultative Assembly, First Session, Reports, 1949, p. 1144.

[9] Cf. e.g. COE, Parliamentary Assembly, Recommendation 1415, Additional protocol to the European Convention on Human Rights concerning fundamental social rights, para. 2, 1999 and COE, Resolution I, Institutional and Functional Arrangements for the Protection of Human Rights at national and European Level, text adopted by the European Ministerial Conference on Human Rights on 4 November 2000, Human rights information bulletin No. 50.

[10] Cf. e.g. para. 13 of The Teheran Proclamation adopted by the International Conference on Human Rights at Teheran on 13 May 1968, General Assembly Resolutions 40/114 of

a rhetorical slogan, a sort of mantra that has to be pronounced for the sake of good order, however, having no substantial significance in itself.[11] Indeed, the passage has positive and pleasant connotations, but repeating it does not give more substance to it. As expressed by Antonio Cassese, "this convenient catch-phrase serves to dampen the debate while leaving everything the way it was."[12] Thus, it must be considered a fact that human rights are *not* in practice treated as "indivisible, interrelated and interdependent", and they are certainly not treated either "on the same footing" or "with the same emphasis." The two sets of rights are separated at the global and the regional level, and the legal protection is very far from being equal, one reason being that the complaints mechanisms for the protection of economic, social and cultural rights have been weak.

The fact that there are three quoted sub-passages: "indivisible, interrelated and interdependent", "on the same footing" and "with the same emphasis" also indicate that the understanding of the passage is far from uniform. It is often invoked as part of the strategy to strengthen socio-economic rights and to break down the hierarchy between the two sets of rights. However, human rights might be treated on the same footing and with the same emphasis and yet be separated, whereas the perception of human rights as indivisible, interdependent and interrelated seems to presuppose a kind of reciprocity; the existence of links or at least unclear boundaries between the two sets of rights.

One might also assert that indivisibility, interdependence and interrelation are three different notions and in that context, moreover, remember that the relations between the two sets of rights have been referred to in slightly different terms over the years. These differences could be subject to interpretation, and one could further discuss whether the differing versions describe a unilateral or a balanced relation between the two sets of rights. However, I see little point in pursuing such analysis. Under all circumstances, there are urgent questions to be posed and hopefully answered with regard to the relation between the two sets of rights and their mutual relationship. In the following, I will refer to this – so far relatively unexplored relation – as *the notion of indivisibility.*

---

13 December 1985, 41/117 of 4 December 1986, 42/102 of 7 December 1987, 43/113 of 8 December 1988 (all with the title "Indivisibility and interdependence of economic, social and cultural, civil and political rights") and a series of General Assembly Resolutions about International Covenants on Human Rights, cf. e.g. Resolution 60/149 of 16 December 2005.

11 As of 1 February 2009 a 'Google-search' on the phrase "human rights are indivisible" gives no less than 14.100 hits.

12 Antonio Cassese, "Are Human Rights Truly Universal?", in O. Savić (ed.), *The Politics of Human Rights*, Verso, 1999, pp. 149–165 (on p. 159).

Thus, the purpose of this book is to depart from the unclear notion of indivisibility and simply consider it a challenge to the traditional compartmentalised perception of the two sets of rights. Hence, in the present context, the indivisibility thesis is understood as asserting that it is at variance with the idea of human rights protection to uphold a categorisation in which human needs and human demands can be arranged. Human rights are there for the sake of persons; they must reflect and respect the factual conditions of human life and the complexity of human activity. The various elements of our lives are inextricably intertwined, and human experience rarely confines itself into neat categories. Human activity and human needs are 'treaty crossing'.

When discussing the notion of indivisibility as understood in the above sense one should, however, make a distinction between indivisibility as a political agenda and as a legal notion. Hardly anyone will call into question that education (as a social right) is a basic condition for making use of one's (civil) participatory rights to freedom of expression or freedom of association. Nor can it be explained away that he who suffers, because his (social) rights to a decent standard of living or to health are not respected, will die sooner or later, thus raising the question whether this should also be discussed in the context of the (civil) right to life?[13] These – and other – connections between the two sets of rights call for political consideration and coordination of the utmost importance for human rights protection, thus raising a challenge to legislative and executive bodies at the domestic level and indeed also to the international community. The fact that human needs and human activity are 'treaty crossing' must be reflected in the policy planning at the local, regional and global level.

However, in this context the focus will be on the possible *legal* implications of the notion of indivisibility. Thus, judicial bodies are not necessarily either obliged or authorised to rectify deplorable consequences of political bodies' failures to take into consideration the 'treaty crossing' character of human needs. The right to freedom of expression has not necessarily been violated because a State has not established the educational facilities necessary for citizens to learn to read and write. Nor is it evident that the right to life is violated

---

[13] The Human Rights Committee [hereinafter the HRC] deals with this connection in *General Comment No. 6*, The right to life (Article 6), 30 April 1982, para. 5 in the following way: "Moreover, the Committee has noted that the right to life has been too often narrowly interpreted. The expression 'inherent right to life' cannot properly be understood in a restrictive manner, and the protection of this right requires that States adopt positive measures. In this connection, the Committee considers that it would be desirable for States parties to take all possible measures to reduce infant mortality and to increase life expectancy, especially in adopting measures to eliminate malnutrition and epidemics."

because of unsatisfactory (administration of) health legislation. The question to be discussed in this book is therefore what are, if any, the *legal* implications of the notion of human rights as indivisible rights? To what extent are judicial bodies obliged or authorised to take into consideration the complexity of 'real life' when making assessments of human rights compliance under a specific treaty which covers only part of 'real life'?

My intention in Chapters 5–9 is to illustrate how the European Court of Human Rights [hereinafter the ECtHR] has been able to protect five different human rights under the ECHR, although these rights are traditionally categorised as socio-economic rights. The rights in question are 1) the right to health, 2) the right to housing, 3) the right to education, 4) the right to social cash benefits and 5) various work-related rights.

Before presenting the way in which I seek to pursue this aim some remarks are to be made about the classical perception of the two sets of rights. Then follows a discussion of the perception of human rights as tripartite rights (Chapter 2). Moreover, I want to present some considerations on intertextuality and permeability (Chapter 3) and, finally, I have found it useful to present some theoretical and methodological considerations (Chapter 4).

2 *The Classical Perception of Civil-Political Rights and Socio-Economic Rights*

Despite the repeated reference to the indivisibility notion, traditional theory understands civil-political rights and socio-economic[14] rights as two fairly distinct categories of rights, which cannot by their very nature be treated on the same footing and with the same emphasis as it is stated in the initially quoted passage from the Vienna Declaration. The reasons are at least three-fold. Firstly, their historical background is not identical; secondly, they are surrounded by differing ideologies; and thirdly and most importantly, their normative structure and character are differing as well. These differences are mutually interdependent and interrelated, and have in each their way had an impact on the perception of the two sets of rights leading to supervisory systems giving them an unequal protection. The differing character of the two sets of rights has been described and analysed in an endless series of works, and the following

14 I refer to the rights protected in the CESCR and the ESC/RESC interchangeably as socio-economic rights or economic, social and cultural rights. There is no authoritative classification of the rights in question under the three terms, economic, social and cultural, and the main part of my analysis will concern issues which can easily be designated as socio-economic issues.

presentation aims only at giving the necessary background to the following discussion on the indivisibility notion.[15]

As to the history of civil-political rights and socio-economic rights some authors have asserted that human rights have evolved in generations beginning with the classical first generation freedom rights emerging from the 18th century such as the United States' Constitution from 1787 and the French Declaration of the Rights of Man and Citizens from 1789: personal freedom, freedom of speech, freedom of association and assembly, freedom of religion, etc. To these were much later, in the 19th century, added a number of second generation rights emerging from Bismarck's welfare schemes for German workers and later reinforced in the beginning of the 20th century by a widespread recognition of rights to housing, health and welfare services, education, etc.[16] The phrase third generation rights refers to rights not expressly recognised by the original human rights conventions from the 1950s and 1960s and include e.g. the right to development and environmental rights. These 'solidarity rights' are often considered collective rights requiring regional and global cooperation. As most categorisations, the notion of generation of rights simplifies not only the history of human rights but also their character, and it has particularly been criticised that the categorisation seems to suggest a prioritisation of rights with economic, social and cultural rights coming in second.[17]

Secondly, the fact that the discussion on how to transform the UDHR into legally binding human rights instruments took place during the Cold War was undoubtedly one of the obstacles to the obtainment of equal protection of the two sets of rights. In the ideological battlefield of the Cold War, socio-economic rights as second generation rights were generally associated with Eastern European Communism, and this ideological battle undoubtedly had an impact on the discussions within the UN as well as the COE. As the latter at that time consisted only of Western European States it is not surprising, however, that its members chose to give priority to the classical first generation rights symbolising respect for individual liberty and capitalist enterprise.

Thirdly and most importantly, the overall scepticism towards giving socio-economic rights equal protection, both within the UN and the COE, was due

[15] Cf. e.g. Craig Scott, *Ibid.*, Asbjørn Eide & Allan Rosas, "Economic, Social and Cultural Rights: A Universal Challenge" in Asbjørn Eide et al. (eds.) *Economic, Social and Cultural Rights – A Textbook*, 2nd revised Edition, Martinus Nijhoff Publishers, 2001, pp. 3–7 (on pp. 4–5), Kitty Arambulo, *Strengthening the Supervision of the International Covenant on Economic, Social and Cultural Rights – Theoretical and Procedural Aspects*, Hart Intersentia, 1999, Chapter II and Magdalena Sepúlveda in *The Nature of the Obligations under the International Covenant on Economic, Social and Cultural Rights*, Intersentia, 2003, mainly Chapters IV and V.

[16] Cf. Karel Vasak, "A 30-year Struggle: The Sustained Efforts to Give Force of Law to the Universal Declaration of Human Rights" in *Unesco Courier*, November 1977, pp. 29–30.

[17] Cf. Asbjørn Eide & Allan Rosas, *Ibid*, with references to other authors of the textbook.

to what Craig Scott has designated as "implementation-based reasons".[18] The implementation-based reasons relate to the perception of the two sets of rights as fundamentally different in their normative character as civil and political rights are considered 'negative', precise and cost-free rights subject to immediate implementation whereas economic, social and cultural rights are regarded as 'positive', vague and resource-demanding rights subject to progressive realisation.

Proponents of this 'positive/negative' dichotomy have attached importance to the fact that economic, social and cultural rights are usually not formulated as individual rights. Rather, they often follow a 'means-and-ends-approach' in the sense that there is no link between the facts and the legal consequence but merely a relation between an end and the means supposed to lead to that end.[19] By way of example, Article 11 of the ESC on the right to protection of health states that the Contracting Parties undertake "to take appropriate measures" designed to obtain certain purposes such as the removal as far as possible of the causes of illness or the prevention of epidemic, endemic and other diseases. This has to be done "[w]ith a view to ensuring the effective exercise of the right to protection of health." It has been questioned, therefore, whether economic, social and cultural rights deserve the designation legal rights in the same way as civil and political rights which are norm rational, as there is usually a link between the facts and the legal consequences. They follow what could be described as an 'if-then-formula'. By way of example, Article 6 (3) (e) of the ECHR stipulates that ""Everyone charged with a criminal offence [....]" has the right to "free assistance of an interpreter if he cannot understand or speak the language used in court."

These differences have implications for their implementation at the domestic level. The vagueness of many economic, social and cultural rights makes it necessary for Parliaments to decide in which way and at which level they are to be implemented. As economic, social and cultural rights are, moreover, considered costly, proponents of the 'positive/negative' dichotomy are of the opinion that they are not justiciable in the sense that they can form the legal basis for individual disputes on socio-economic issues.[20]

---

18 Cf. Craig Scott, *Ibid.*

19 Amartya Sen speaks of *metarights*. He explains that "[a] *metaright* to something *x* can be defined as the right to have *policies* p *(x)* that genuinely pursue the objective of making the right to *x* realisable." The metaright e.g. to food serves the purpose of giving "a person the right to demand that policy be directed towards securing the objective of making the right to adequate means a realisable right, even if that objective cannot be immediately achieved. It is a right of a different kind: not to *x* but to p *(x)*. I propose to call a right to p *(x)* a *metaright* to *x*", Amartya Sen, "The right not to be hungry" in P. Alston et al. (eds.), *The Right to Food*, 1984, pp. 69–81 (on p. 70).

20 The notion of 'justiciability' is commonly used in the discussion of the normative character of socio-economic rights in particular with regard to the question whether or not these rights

Such considerations were decisive for the outcome of the discussions within the UN and the COE with regard to the protection of the two sets of rights. Not only was it considered most appropriate to adopt two sets of instruments for the protection of civil and political rights and economic, social and cultural rights respectively, namely the CCPR and the ECHR on the one hand and the CESCR and the ESC on the other. What is more, while individual complaint mechanisms were considered relevant to the future supervision of Member States' observance of the CCPR[21] and the ECHR, the same was not the case as regards the CESCR and the ESC.

Hence, the human rights regime has divided economic, social and cultural rights and civil and political rights into two apparently distinct categories of rights which are, until further, protected in an unequal manner. He who finds that his civil-political rights are violated has the possibility to bring claims before the ECtHR and the HRC[22], whereas the prospects for the individual who wishes to claim that his socio-economic rights are not complied with are more limited.

In principle, he can bring the matter in question before a domestic court. However, the domestic judiciary is also expected to exercise considerable self-restraint in the assessment of socio-economic claims. It is often argued that courts have no democratic legitimacy, and that an intensified examination of social issues will tend to disturb the power balance in a way which is incompatible with traditional conceptions of the division of powers in a democratic society. The domestic judicial protection under the international conventions on economic, social and cultural rights will, moreover, usually be limited due to the lack of international jurisprudence[23], and many countries do not protect socio-economic rights at constitutional level. He who finds his socio-economic rights violated enjoys a certain limited protection under the general supervisory system to the CESCR. Some will be able to invoke also the ESC or the RESC and might moreover be affected by petitions under the collective

can be enforced by judicial or quasi-judicial bodies. It does not have an unambiguous meaning and it does not appear in ordinary dictionaries over the English language. The concept of 'justiciability' is discussed by Martin Scheinin, who identifies a variety of different possible meanings; cf. Martin Scheinin, "Justiciability and the Indivisibility of Human Rights" in John Squires et al. (eds.), *The Road to a Remedy: Current Issues in the Litigation of Economic, Social and Cultural Rights*, Australian Human Rights Centre, The University of New South Wales, 2006, pp.17–26.

21 The complaints procedure is not part of the CCPR but appears in an Optional Protocol to the CCPR, also adopted in 1966.

22 Provided of course, that the State in question has ratified the mentioned Protocol to the CCPR.

23 For countries with a dualistic tradition it may also have an impact whether or not the convention in question is incorporated into domestic legislation.

complaints procedure under the ESC/RESC, which entered into force in 1998.[24] However, it would be fair to say that the legal protection offered with regard to socio-economic demands is rather poor, which makes topical the notion of indivisibility. If the notion has a legal content, one might succeed in bringing a socio-economic claim before the treaty bodies supervising the Contracting States' observance of civil and political rights claiming that human rights are indivisible, interrelated and interdependent. In this way it would be possible to give individuals access to procedures which are otherwise not open to them since the conventions on economic, social and cultural rights do not (yet) allow individual petitions.[25]

3 *Indivisibility as Protection of Socio-Economic Demands Under the ECHR*

When examining the legal implications of the notion of indivisibility it might seem most reasonable to turn to both sets of rights, civil and political rights as well as economic, social and cultural rights and analyse to which extent the two sets of rights e.g. overlap each other or presuppose one another. Nevertheless, the primary empirical basis for the following discussion will be case law from the ECtHR which is a treaty body established for the protection of what is traditionally considered civil and political rights as they are enumerated in the ECHR and its Protocols. Thus, the study of the legal implications of the notion of indivisibility will primarily take the form of an examination of the extent to which socio-economic facts are considered relevant in the assessment of the Contracting Parties' observance of the civil and political rights protected by the Convention and its Protocols, and the question to be asked is the following: Does it make sense to talk about the protection of socio-economic rights under the Convention and its Protocols?

On the face of it this approach seems awkward. Why focus on socio-economic rights protection, when the idea is to study the indivisibility thesis? And why turn to civil and political rights for answers to questions relating to socio-economic rights? Apparently, it would seem more reasonable to turn to conventions on economic, social and cultural rights for answers to socio-economic

---

[24] Additional Protocol to the European Social Charter Providing for a System of Collective Complaints, 1995, ETS No. 158. Again, the protection presupposes that the State in question is a party to the Protocol.

[25] However, the UN General Assembly has in December 2008 adopted an Optional Protocol to the CESCR providing for an individual complaints mechanism. The Protocol has however, at the time of writing (January 2009) not yet entered into force.

issues. Moreover, civil-political facts might be relevant also for the application of economic, social and cultural rights.

However, there is a deeper sense in departing from an individual protection mechanism to civil-political rights after all, which has to do with the traditional perception of the two sets of rights and the way in which they are protected domestically and internationally, cf. above in Section 2. Moreover, individual case law constitutes the most adequate basis for such analysis as the encounter between facts and law is all the more visible than in a general reporting procedure as that under the CCPR, CESCR or the ESC/RESC. In addition, the ECtHR has long since developed an *integrated approach*[26] to human rights protection which to some extent dissolves the boundaries between the two sets of rights. Thus, the ECtHR has to a considerable extent been prepared to accept social demands as relevant facts in the assessment of the Contracting Parties' observance of the rights protected under the ECHR and its Protocols. The Court has developed a case law which makes it perfectly legitimate to talk about protection of aspects of the right to health, housing, education, social cash benefits and certain work-related issues, and some of the judgments of the Court have had considerable budgetary consequences for the Contracting Parties. The HRC has adopted a similar integrated or holistic approach. However, case law from the ECtHR is far more developed and much more comprehensive, and unlike *views* from the HRC the judgments of the ECtHR are binding on the Contracting States, thus providing a solid basis for statements on the legal implications of the notion of indivisibility. Moreover, at a very early stage in my work I realised the necessity of limiting the study to one treaty body. Case law from the ECtHR is overwhelming and constantly developing, and what could be gained from including case law from the HRC in the study would hardly measure up to the disadvantages.

Admittedly, the notion of indivisibility can easily be understood as something more than protection of socio-economic demands under conventions protecting civil-political rights. It might also make sense to talk about protection of civil-political demands under instruments protecting socio-economic rights. I intend, therefore, in Chapter 11 to touch upon this issue in relation to case law under the collective complaints procedure under the ESC/RESC. However, as case law is rather sparse at the present stage, it is not possible to avoid a considerable imbalance in the analysis of the two aspects of the notion of the indivisibility of human rights. Conclusions from the European

[26] The designation *the integrated approach* was originally introduced by Martin Scheinin, cf. Martin Scheinin "Sociala rättigheter som mänskliga rättigheter" ("Social Rights as Human Rights") in *Nordisk Administrativt Tidsskrift*, 3/1994, pp. 181 ff. and most recently referred to in Martin Scheinin "Economic and Social Rights as Legal Rights" in Asbjørn Eide et al. (eds.), *Economic, Social and Cultural Rights: A Textbook*, Martinus Nijhoff, 2nd Edition, 2001, p. 29.

Committee of Social Rights [hereinafter the ECSR], however, will be referred to whenever relevant, also in the analysis of the case law under the ECHR and its Protocols. The same applies to Concluding Observations and General Comments from the International Committee on Economic, Social and Cultural Rights [hereinafter the ICESCR] and the HRC as well as similar statements from other treaty bodies. After all, the purpose is to bring to light new knowledge of human rights as indivisible rights, which makes it natural to include a number of human rights instruments all deriving from the original document in which they were listed side by side, namely the UDHR. It was not until they were separated that we began to talk about human rights as indivisible rights.

Chapter 2

Typological and Terminological Considerations

1 *Introductory Remarks*

The classical perception of human rights as dichotomous rights, referred to above in Chapter 1, has been criticised time and again as a simplification of the issue. It is counter-argued that both sets of human rights encompass a variety of obligations, and that they overlap to a certain extent. Countless are the scientific works in which the dichotomy has been pulled to pieces, and replaced by other typologies providing a more nuanced description of the two sets of rights. Thus, it is often held that civil and political rights also encompass 'positive', costly elements, and that these rights are also to some extent subject to progressive realisation. Moreover, it is often argued that economic, social and cultural rights have elements of a 'negative', cost-free character, and that they too may have to be implemented immediately.[1] The present chapter builds on some of these works and serves the purpose of providing the necessary background for the following discussion of the indivisibility notion and the integrated approach. Moreover, the chapter serves as an introduction to the terminology applied in the following, which deviates from the traditional terminology applied in works discussing the normative character of the two sets of rights.[2] Thus, I disagree with the many scholars who favour the idea of

---

[1] Cf. e.g. The Limburg Principles on the Implementation of the International Covenant on Economic, Social and Cultural Rights, UN Doc. E/CN.4/1987/17 (republished in *Human Rights Quarterly*, Vol. 9, 1987, pp. 122–135 (on p. 135)) and Theo C. van Boven et al. (eds.), *The Maastricht Guidelines on Violations of Economic, Social and Cultural Rights*, SIM Special No. 20, Netherlands Institute of Human Rights, 1998, p.19 f. Most recently the discussion has been referred to in great detail by Magdalena Sepúlveda, *The Nature of the Obligations under the International Covenant on Economic, Social and Cultural Rights*, Hart Intersentia, 2003, Chapters IV and V.

[2] In the following criticism of the tripartite typology I draw on a previous article, cf. Ida Elisabeth Koch, "Dichotomies, Trichotomies or Waves of Duties?" in *Human Rights Law Review*, Vol. 5, Issue 1, 2005, pp. 81–103.

dichotomous, tripartite, quadruple or even quintuple obligations, and I shall begin the chapter by quoting Henry Shue:

> Now, almost everyone involved in these discussions realizes that typologies are not the point. Typologies are at best abstract instruments for temporarily fending off the complexities of concrete reality that threaten to overwhelm our circuits. Be they dichotomous or trichotomous, typologies are ladders to be climbed and left behind, not monuments to be caressed or polished.[3]

2 *Trichotomies or Waves of Duties?*

2.1 *The Tripartite Typology*

The idea of a tripartite typology of State obligations with respect to basic rights was originally introduced in 1980 by Henry Shue who spoke of obligations 'to avoid depriving', 'to protect from deprivation' and 'to aid the deprived'.[4] However, it is Asbjørn Eide who has become known as the originator of the tripartite terminology as we know it today in the slightly different version of obligations to *respect*, *protect* and *fulfil*, which he originally introduced in 1987 when functioning as Special Rapporteur to the UN Sub-Commission.[5]

The introduction of the tripartite typology was motivated by a wish to do away with the 'positive/negative' dichotomy as a false and misleading description of the character and nature of human rights obligations. Asbjørn Eide argued that we cannot "make a neat distinction around the axis 'negative/positive' between civil and political rights on the one hand and economic, social and cultural rights on the other."[6] Instead he suggested that State responsibility be examined at three levels going from the predominantly cost-free and passive obligation to *respect* to the gradually more active and costly obligations to *protect* and to *fulfil*:

> The obligation to *respect* requires the State, and thereby all its organs and agents, to abstain from doing anything that violates the integrity of the individual or infringes on her or his freedom, including the freedom to use the material resources available to that individual in the way she or he finds to satisfy basic needs [....].

[3] Henry Shue, *Basic Rights: Subsistence, Affluence and U.S. Foreign Policy*, Princeton University Press, 2nd Edition, 1996, p. 160.

[4] Cf. Henry Shue, *Ibid.*, p. 52.

[5] Cf. The Right to Food as a Human Right, UN Doc. E/CN.4/Sub.2/1987/23 of 7 July 1987.

[6] Cf. Asbjørn Eide, "Realization of Social and Economic Rights and the Minimum Threshold Approach" in *Human Rights Law Journal*, 1989 Vol. 10, No. 1–2, pp. 36–51.

> The obligation to *protect* requires from the State and its agents the measures necessary to prevent other individuals or groups from violating the integrity, freedom of action or other human rights of the individual – including the prevention of infringements of his or her material resources.
>
> The obligation to *fulfil* requires the State to take the measures necessary to ensure for each person within its jurisdiction opportunities to obtain satisfaction of those needs, recognized in the human rights instruments, which cannot be secured by personal efforts.[7]

The tripartite terminology bridges the two sets of rights by illustrating that compliance with each and every human right – economic, social, cultural, civil and political – may require various measures from (passive) non-interference to (active) insurance of the satisfaction of individual needs all depending on the concrete circumstances. A social right like the right to housing can be complied with at the first or secondary level by abstaining from eviction or preventing third parties from doing that, and the tertiary level is primarily activated if there is no home to *respect* or *protect*. Likewise, the civil right to freedom of expression may require that the State abstains from interfering with the enjoyment of the right or prevents third parties from doing it, and the tertiary level only becomes relevant if other obstacles are in the way for individuals to express themselves such as lack of access to the media or – more seriously – lack of ability to express oneself due to illiteracy or disabilities.

By pointing out that economic, social and cultural rights can be complied with only by showing *respect* or providing *protection*, Asbjørn Eide deprives opponents of economic, social and cultural rights as justiciable rights of one of their primary arguments. Social rights are not entirely to be discussed within a *Welfare State paradigm* as the first two levels of the tripartite obligation *respect* and *protect* fit more naturally into a *'Rechtsstaat' paradigm*. Although neither of the two obligations can be considered entirely cost free, the expenses necessary for their implementation do not differ materially from what is needed for the implementation of civil and political rights. Moreover, by arguing that compliance with civil and political rights may also require measures of *fulfilment* – measures, which are traditionally associated with economic, social and cultural rights – he succeeds in demonstrating that the traditional 'positive/negative' dichotomy ought to be abandoned as a simplified and inadequate description of the normative character of the two sets of rights.[8]

---

7 *Ibid.*, p. 37.

8 What Asbjørn Eide does not do, however, is to provide answers to the most difficult question namely that of the justiciability of *fulfilment* rights as such, be they of a civil or social rights character, cf. on this issue, e.g. Ida Elisabeth Koch, "The Justiciability of Indivisible Rights" in *Nordic Journal of International Law*, Vol. 72, Issue 1, 2003, pp. 3–39.

In later writings Asbjørn Eide has developed his terminology by adding an obligation to *facilitate* in between the obligation to *protect* and the obligation to *fulfil*. He writes that States are required to "*facilitate* opportunities by which the rights listed can be enjoyed. It takes many forms, some of which are spelled out in the relevant instruments." As one example, he mentions Article 11(2) of the CESCR which requires States to improve measures of production, conservation and distribution of food by making full use of technical and scientific knowledge and by developing or reforming agrarian systems.[9]

Other legal scholars support the idea of quartered obligations. Thus, G.J.H. van Hoof speaks of obligations 1) to *respect*, 2) to *protect*, 3) to *ensure* and 4) to *promote*,[10] whereas Henry J. Steiner and Philip Alston are supportive of a quintuple obligation. They speak of obligations 1) to *respect rights of others*; 2) to *create institutional machinery essential to realisation of rights*; 3) to *protect rights/prevent violations*; 4) to *provide goods and services to satisfy rights* and 5) to *promote rights*.[11] A common feature is, however, that all suggestions as to the most suitable typology move along a continuum from 'negative' to more 'positive' obligations inserting an obligation to *protect* from interferences from third parties in between.[12]

The introduction of the tripartite typology to *respect*, to *protect* and to *fulfil* aimed at breaking down the hierarchy of economic, social and cultural rights and civil and political rights by showing that both sets of rights encompass what is traditionally regarded as 'negative' and 'positive' elements. The tripartite typology has relevance, therefore, not only to economic, social and cultural rights but also to civil and political rights, and case law from treaty bodies monitoring State Parties' compliance with civil and political rights is indeed illustrative of the fact that civil and political rights do encompass 'positive' elements also of a social rights character. Hence, one could have expected such bodies to take an interest in the tripartite terminology. Civil and political rights include elements of *protection* and *fulfilment*, and one could argue that the tripartite typology provides an explanation to the integrated approach by which the HRC and not least the ECtHR have read social elements into the rights covered by the civil and political rights conventions.

---

9 Cf. Asbjørn Eide, "Universalization of human rights versus globalization of economic power" in Fons Coomans et al. (eds.), *Rendering Justice to the Vulnerable:Liber Amicorum in Honour of Theo van Boven*, Kluwer Law International, 2000, pp. 99–119 (on p. 111).

10 Cf. G.J.H. van Hoof, "The Legal Nature of Economic, Social and Cultural Rights: a Rebuttal of Some Traditional Views" in P. Alston et al. (eds.), *The Right to Food*, Martinus Nijhoff Publ.,1984, pp. 97–110 (on p. 106).

11 Henry J. Steiner and Philip Alston in *International Human Rights in Context*, 2nd Edition, Oxford University Press, 2000, p. 182 ff.

12 For at more detailed description of the various suggestions, cf. Magdalena Sepúlveda, *Ibid.*, Chapters IV and V.

However, the terminology has not gained a footing among judicial and quasi-judicial bodies dealing with civil and political rights. The HRC and the ECtHR have not adopted the tripartite terminology, and nor have most NGOs dealing with civil and political rights. The terminology has primarily been adopted by individuals and bodies dealing with economic, social and cultural rights. Thus, a number of NGOs and several legal scholars have chosen to apply the terminology in human rights advocacy and scientific writings, and the ICESCR has applied the terminology since 1999.[13]

For the sake of convenience, I will take as my point of departure Asbjørn Eide's tripartite terminology in the following discussion about the adequacy of the terminology. Two issues are particularly important. Firstly, to which extent does the terminology advance the conceptual clarification of in particular economic, social and cultural rights? Secondly, is the terminology helpful in the ongoing debate about the justiciability of economic, social and cultural rights?

2.2 *Critical Considerations on the Tripartite Typology*

The tripartite typology departs from the idea that the obligation becomes ever more 'positive' and resource demanding as we move from the obligation to *respect* through the obligation to *protect* to the obligation to *fulfil*. Moreover, the presumably 'negative' features of the obligation to *respect* form part of the argumentation that socio-economic rights are justiciable rights. However, one might consider whether there is such a thing as a 'negative' obligation. One can hardly think of an obligation not to interfere which does not require *some* sort of 'positive' measure. As pointed out by Holmes and Sunstein *all* rights are 'positive' in the sense that they have budgetary implications.[14] Obligations not to interfere require that public officials are given the necessary guidance and education with regard to the legal content of the obligations in question, and at any rate the administration and monitoring of human rights compliance bear upon the economic interest of the State.[15]

---

[13] Cf. *General Comment No. 12*, The Right to Adequate Food (Article 11), 12 May 1999, E/C.12/1999/5. The ECSR monitoring States' compliance with the European Social Charter has not, however, incorporated the tripartite terminology in its vocabulary.

[14] Stephen Holmes and Cass R. Sunstein, *The Cost of Rights: Why Liberty Depends on Taxes*, W.W. Norton and Company, 1999, Chapter 1.

[15] Terence Daintith has contributed to the discussion on the indivisibility of human rights by pointing out that virtually any type of right may bear upon the economic interest of individuals and groups. Thus, freedom of speech may be construed to protect commercial advertising; freedom of press and media necessarily provides economic guarantees to the owners of such media, and freedom of movement is an essential complement to a freedom to choose one's employment, cf. Terence Daintith, "The constitutional protection of economic rights" in *International Journal of Constitutional Law*, Vol. 2, Issue I, 2004, pp. 56–90.

In fact, a 'positive' obligation to *create institutional machinery essential to the realisation of rights* is a necessary precondition at all levels, and if one were to speak of a fundamental human rights obligation this would be the one. Human rights cannot be implemented if there is no one to do it; one cannot conceive of obligations either to *respect, protect* or *fulfil* without the necessary institutional machinery. Something similar applies to the obligation to *promote* as this obligation encompasses measures such as training programmes for administrative and judicial bodies.

Moreover, non-interference may have considerable budgetary consequences even surmounting those connected with the active provision of a certain good, all depending on the circumstances. The interest of a State Party in a certain residential property may e.g. be so vital that the costs connected with abstaining from expropriation, i.e. showing r*espect* for the right to private property, exceed those of *fulfilling* the right to housing by providing accommodation to the person who becomes homeless as a consequence of the expropriation. Likewise, avoiding the use of compulsory measures towards e.g. mentally ill and drug addicts, thus respecting the right to personal liberty, may require the use of expensive treatment and therapy. Hence, non-interference may require highly 'positive' measures.

Another reason for questioning the expediency of the tripartite obligation concerns the insertion of the obligation to *protect* between the (predominantly 'negative') obligation to *respect* and the (predominantly 'positive') obligation to *fulfil*. The obligation to *protect* involves a State responsibility to regulate the behaviour of private parties such as corporations, landlords, employers, doctors etc., and to interfere if or when their behaviour is detrimental to human rights protection. The applicability of human rights – and in particular economic, social and cultural rights – in disputes between third parties is a highly complex issue, which is becoming more and more topical as privatisation increases. This issue is indeed relevant in a human rights context as it dissociates from the perception of human rights as protection only *against* States. Human rights protection has a 'positive' aspect in that it requires active measures *from* the State, and in that sense one might say that the obligation to *protect* bridges the two sets of rights.

However, the applicability of human rights in disputes between third parties seems to me to be an entirely different issue, which deserves better than being squeezed in between the obligation to *respect* and the obligation to *fulfil*. The obligation to *protect* is similar to the notion of *'Drittwirkung'*, which has been scientifically explored to a wide degree.[16] This issue is not to be discussed

[16] Cf. e.g. Andrew Clapham, "The 'Drittwirkung' of the Convention", in R. St. J. Macdonald, F. Matscher and H. Petzold (eds.), *The European System for the Protection of Human Rights*, Martinus Nijhoff Publ., 1993, pp. 163–206.

further in this context. My point here is merely to emphasise that the extension of States' obligations to private disputes is a rather complex issue with many aspects, some of which might not be addressed properly if discussed in the context of human rights typologies, cf. Chapter 3.

Moreover, there is every reason to question the assumption that the obligation to *protect* is always more 'positive' than the obligation to *respect* and always less 'positive' than the obligation to *fulfil*. Admittedly, the obligation to *protect* will have a proactive character. 'Positive' obligations will necessarily be activated in conflicts between private parties, and the notion of '*Drittwirkung*' is in fact often discussed as a sub-category of 'positive' obligations.[17] However, the obligation to *protect* does not necessarily call for steps which are naturally to be placed on a scale in between a predominantly 'negative' obligation not to interfere and a predominantly 'positive' obligation to provide. Preventing *third parties* from interfering with a certain right does not necessarily require a more active and more costly effort than preventing *public bodies* from acting in the same way. Governmental bodies are obliged to monitor the conduct of regional and municipal public bodies in the same way as they are to supervise the practices of private bodies performing (formerly) public tasks. Supervising that private prisons or private hospitals do not interfere with the rights of prisoners and patients is not necessarily less demanding than ensuring that public prisons and public hospitals comply with their human rights obligations, cf. the notion of *respect*. Such supervision presupposes the existence of institutional machinery. The obligation to *protect* seems to encompass its own continuum of increasing 'positive' obligations e.g. to *create institutional machinery essential to the realisation of rights*, to *provide goods and services to satisfy rights* and to *promote rights*.

The insertion of the obligation to *protect* between the two extremes – the obligation to *respect* and the obligation to *fulfil* – seems to me to be a terminological mixture of apples and oranges, which furthermore may leave us with only two categories in the discussion of the direct relation between the individual and the State. Thus, if we ignore non-State actors – which is in fact possible to a wide degree – the State has only two obligations in the direct relation with individuals, namely to *respect* and *fulfil*. There is nothing in between, and it seems to me that what we have achieved is only the substitution of the traditional 'positive/negative' dichotomy with another dichotomous relationship between obligations of *respect* and obligations of *fulfilment*. The added value is that both obligations apply to both sets of rights – economic, social and cultural rights and civil and political rights – but it would not be fair to claim that we have obtained a particularly nuanced description of the overall human

[17] By "Drittwirking I refer to the horisontal effect between States and private parties.

rights obligation. This might be remedied of course if one inserts further obligations as it has been suggested, cf. above in Section 2.1. However, that does not change the fact that obligations to *create institutional machinery essential to the realisation of rights*, to *provide goods and services to satisfy rights* and to *promote rights* depending on the circumstances may be as fundamental to the obligation to *respect* as they are to the obligation to *fulfil*. Human rights obligations are closely interlinked, and sometimes they defy classification.

As an abstract construction the tripartite typology has advantages, and we can easily imagine situations to which the typology applies without difficulties. However, the typology seems to lose some of its applicability when one has to decide what it takes in a concrete situation for a State party to comply with its human rights obligations. Many situations cannot be dealt with exclusively by means of one of the three levels of the tripartite obligation, and some are so complex that they require efforts belonging at all three levels, *respect*, *protection* and *fulfilment*. The relevant level is unidentifiable, and the conception of human rights obligations as a ladder one climbs step by step is not very much to the point. The adequate metaphor would rather be an unlevelled slope as the obligation imperceptibly increases for each tiny little movement uphill.[18]

2.3 *The Applicability of the Tripartite Typology to All Human Rights*

The tripartite typology supposedly applies to all human rights – economic, social, cultural, civil and political – for which reason it has been considered a useful analytical tool in the endeavours to breaking down the hierarchy between the two sets of rights. Admittedly, it might be possible to analyse the majority of human rights at each of the three levels *respect*, *protect* and *fulfil* although the task is far from simple.

However, it would be fair to say that the obligation to *fulfil* has the greatest relevance for economic, social and cultural rights, which explains why the issue of justiciability is usually discussed in relation to these rights. The case is different with regard to civil and political rights. For these rights the obligation to *respect* seems to be the primary one. Moreover, it should be recalled that there *are* rights which do not lend themselves easily to grading. Some rights are predominantly 'negative' in their nature and some are predominantly 'positive'. What does it mean, for instance, to *fulfil* the right to organise or the right to strike? It is hardly a human rights obligation to contribute financially to the operation of labour unions or to fill the strike fund. There may be a 'positive' obligation to recognise 'negative' aspects of freedom of association and right to

[18] I have previously discussed the ICESCR's application of the tripartite typology, cf. Ida Elisabeth Koch "Dichotomies, Trichotomies or Waves of Duties" in *Human Rights Law Review* 5: 1, 2005, pp. 81–105.

collective bargaining. However, most aspects of these labour rights relate to an obligation not to interfere or prevent third parties from doing it, and there is very little left for the third level, the obligation to *fulfil*.

Conversely, the right to fair trial is to a wide degree a 'positive' *fulfilment* right. The right to fair trial presupposes something, namely the existence of an "independent and impartial tribunal established by law", cf. e.g. Article 6 of the ECHR, and many of the various requirements spelt out in the provision are of a 'positive' and resource demanding character. Thus, everyone charged with a criminal offence has the right to (free) legal aid and to the free assistance of an interpreter. Something similar applies to Articles 2 and 3 of Protocol No. 7 to the ECHR about the right to review by a higher tribunal and to compensation in the event of miscarriage of justice.
These rights are predominantly construed as *fulfilment* rights.

It might be objected that interferences with the judiciary occur on a daily basis especially in undemocratic States, and that obligations e.g. to *respect* and *protect* are thereby disregarded. Thus, the requirement that the judiciary must be "independent and impartial" might be conceived of as a prohibition against interference from States or third parties. However, it seems to me somewhat strange to speak of such obligations in terms of *respect* or *protect*. What we have is a 'positive' obligation to make sure that the judiciary is in fact "independent and impartial", and when not complied with, the obligation to *fulfil* is set aside. The consequence of not considering the situation this way will be that identical measures are described either at the primary, secondary or tertiary level depending on what was the point of departure for the State in question.

These considerations are not independent let alone major objections against the applicability of the tripartite typology, but should be kept in mind when discussing the human rights continuum of obligations and the difference between the two sets of rights. One can live, of course, with the fact that some rights 'lack' a level or two. However, the examples prove that the supposition that the tripartite typology is applicable to all human rights is not entirely tenable, and that not all rights can demonstrate an equal importance on all three levels.

2.4 *The Terminology of the ECtHR*

As indicated the ECtHR applies a dichotomous terminology by recognising that the ECHR includes 'negative' as well as 'positive' elements. However, the Court seems to be increasingly aware of the fact that some obligations defy classification as either 'positive' or 'negative'. The Court is not preoccupied with the issue of fitting a certain obligation into a certain category, but rather with effective human rights protection. The following quotation from the well-known *Airey* case illustrates very well how the Court understands the relation between the two sets of rights:

> Whilst the Convention sets forth what are essentially civil and political rights, many of them have implications of a social or economic nature. The Court therefore considers [....] that the mere fact that an interpretation of the Convention may extend into the sphere of social and economic rights should not be a decisive factor against such an interpretation; there is no water-tight division separating that sphere from the field covered by the Convention.[19]

Case law in general is illustrative of the fact that the Court has a very relaxed attitude to the issue of categorisation. By way of example, in *Cyprus v. Turkey*[20] Greek-Cypriot children living in the Northern part of Cyprus had received primary school education in their own language. However, the secondary educational facilities which were formerly available to them had been abolished by the Turkish-Cypriot authorities, and restrictions imposed by these authorities prevented the children from attending schools in the southern (Greek) part of Cyprus. Accordingly, their only possibility was to continue their education at a Turkish- or English-language school in the north. The Court noted as follows:

> In the strict sense, accordingly, the Greek-Cypriot children were not *denied* the right to education, which is the primary obligation devolving on a Contracting Party under Article 2 of Protocol No. 1 [...]. Moreover, this provision does not specify the language in which education must be conducted in order for the right to be respected [author's emphasis].[21]

However, having assumed responsibility for the provision of Greek-language primary schooling, the failure of the Turkish-Cypriot authorities to make continuing provision for schooling at the secondary level had to be considered in effect to be a denial of the substance of the right at issue. Accordingly, the Court concluded that there had been a violation of Article 2 of Protocol No. 1.

The decision has the character of a prohibition against interference in a previously existing good – secondary school education in Greek language. Applying the tripartite terminology, one might say that it illustrates the legal implications of the obligation to *respect*. However, the practical implication of the decision bears upon the possibilities of the Turkish-Cypriot authorities to freely draw up their budget, and in this way a 'negative' obligation turns out to have 'positive' *fulfilment* implications after all. One might also say that *respect* requires *fulfilment* – or that a 'negative' obligation sometimes requires 'positive' measures. However, the Court does not seem to pay attention and makes no effort to explain the character of the obligation.

Cases concerning restrictions in e.g. family life, cf. Article 8 also prove the difficulties of fitting a certain measure into a certain category. In the

---

[19] *Airey v. Ireland*, Judgment of 9 October 1979, para. 26.

[20] *Cyprus v. Turkey*, Judgment of 10 May 2001.

[21] *Ibid.*, para. 277.

well-known case *López Ostra v. Spain* the Court upheld the contention of the applicant who complained about nuisance from noise, smells and polluting fumes from a plant for the treatment of liquid and solid waste situated twelve meters away from her house. She held the Spanish authorities responsible for her own and her daughter's health problems and claimed that the passive attitude of the authorities constituted a violation of her rights under Article 8 of the Convention. Thus, it took more than three years before the family was eventually offered alternative accommodation at a proper distance from the polluting plant. When considering whether the issue was to be dealt with as a 'positive' or 'negative' obligation, the Court stated as follows:

> Whether the question is analysed in terms of a positive duty on the State – to take reasonable and appropriate measures to secure the applicant's rights under paragraph 1 of Article 8 [....] or in terms of an "interference by a public authority" to be justified in accordance with paragraph 2 [....] the applicable principles are broadly similar. In both contexts regard must be had to the fair balance that has to be struck between the competing interests of the individual and the community as a whole, and in any case the State enjoys a certain margin of appreciation. Furthermore, even in relation to the positive obligations flowing from the first paragraph of Article 8 [....] in striking the required balance the aims mentioned in the second paragraph [....] may be of a certain relevance [....].[22]

The cited passage shows that the Court is perfectly aware of the fact that the 'positive' and the 'negative' are closely interlinked, and that it is hardly possible to make a distinction between the two. Instead of insisting on either category, the Court simply accepts that the obligation encompasses elements of both. In other cases the Court expresses the difficulties even more distinctly. Thus, in *Pibernik v. Croatia* about the failure of the Croatian authorities to carry out an eviction order thus preventing the applicant from living in her home for several years, the Court held as follows:

> [W]hile the essential object of Article 8 is to protect the individual against arbitrary interference by the authorities, [....] there may be positive obligations inherent in an effective respect for the applicant's rights protected under Article 8 [....]. *However, the boundaries between the State's positive and negative obligations under article 8 do not lend themselves to precise definitions* [author's emphasis].[23]

In *Stjerna v. Finland*, on the refusal of the Finnish authorities to allow the applicant to adopt a specific new surname, the Court applied the above mentioned boundary test and chose to deal with the case under Article 8 (1) as a matter of 'positive' obligations. However, in a concurring opinion Judge

---

[22] *López Ostra v. Spain*, Judgment of 9 December 1994, para. 51.

[23] *Pibernik v. Croatia*, Judgment of 4 March 2004, paras. 64 and 65.The quoted passage was used for the first time in *Keegan v. Ireland*, Judgment of 26 May 1994, para. 49.

Wildhaber made some reflections on the choice between paragraphs 1 and 2. Judge Wildhaber stated that the Court has reserved the term "interference" for facts capable of infringing the State's 'negative' obligations, and that such interference has been examined under paragraph 2. He went on as follows with regard to the distinction between the 'positive' and the 'negative':

> However, the dividing line between negative and positive obligations is not so clear-cut. In the Gaskin case, the refusal by the British authorities to grant a former child in care unrestricted access to child-care records could be considered as a negative interference, whereas a duty on the State to provide such access could arguably be viewed as a positive obligation. In the Cossey case the claim of the applicant, an operated transsexual, was that she should be issued with a fresh birth certificate showing her present sex rather than her sex at the date of birth. The refusal of the United Kingdom to carry out a modification of its system for recording civil status could be analysed either as a negative interference with the applicant's rights or as a violation of the State's positive obligation to adapt its legislation so as to take account of the applicant's situation. The Keegan case against Ireland concerned the placement of a child for adoption without the natural father's knowledge or consent, a measure permitted under Irish law. This state of affairs could be taken as a negative interference with the father's right to respect for his family life or as a failure by Ireland to fulfil a positive obligation to confer a right of guardianship on natural fathers. Again, in the instant case of Stjerna, the refusal by the Finnish authorities to allow the applicant freely to acquire the surname of his ancestors may be perceived as either a negative or a positive interference.[24]

On this basis, Judge Wildhaber found it preferable to construe the notion of interference so as to cover facts capable of breaching an obligation, whether 'positive' or 'negative'.

> Whenever a so-called positive obligation arises the Court should examine, as in the event of a so-called negative obligation, whether there has been an interference with the right to respect for private and family life under paragraph 1 of Article 8 (art. 8-1),and whether such interference was "in accordance with the law", pursued legitimate aims and was "necessary in a democratic society" within the meaning of paragraph 2 (art. 8-2).
>
> To be sure, this approach would not lead to a different result in the instant case, nor in all likelihood in the vast majority of cases of this kind. It does, however, have the advantage of making it clear that in substance there is no negative/positive dichotomy as regards the State's obligations to ensure respect for applicable private and family life, but rather a striking similarity between the applicable principles.[25]

Thus, what Judge Wildhaber suggested was that, regardless of whether the State's obligation is perceived as 'positive' or 'negative', the Court has to settle

---

[24] *Stjerna v. Finland*, Judgment of 25 November 1994, Concurring Opinion of Judge Wildhaber.

[25] Ibid.

a dispute between the individual and the community according to the requirements following from the second paragraph. The Stjerna case concerned the application of Article 8. However, it must be assumed that this is a general suggestion applying to all limitation clauses. However, the Court has only to some extent followed Judge Wildhaber's suggestion to deal with all obligations, 'positive' and 'negative', under the second paragraph in the sense that the three-fold examination stipulated in the provision actually is applied.[26]

Judge Wildhaber's in my opinion quite constructive proposal has not been fully recognised, but the cases referred to illustrate not only that the Court recognises that the Convention encompasses 'positive' and 'negative' obligations but also that the distinction between the two is blurred. However, the Court abstains from trying to define the indefinable, and the unclear boundaries between the two obligations seem to be no hindrance for the Court in its concrete decision making. On the contrary, the Court has been able to develop a case law providing for even very remarkable protection of social demands without insisting on fitting the obligatory measures into a certain category.

2.5 *Successive Waves of Duties?*

The classical dichotomous perception of human rights has not been entirely abandoned. Thus, it is still argued that judicial bodies have no say with respect to economic, social and cultural rights, and that the implementation should be left to democratically elected bodies whose subsequent regulation might be justiciable, all depending on the concrete wording. Such arguments were e.g. put forward by a number of governments in the debate as to whether it is feasible and desirable to establish an individual complaints procedure under the CESCR. Similar arguments are applied by governments against the incorporation of conventions on economic, social and cultural rights into domestic legislation.[27]

Yet, it is beyond doubt that the scholarly debate on economic, social and cultural rights as justiciable rights has developed immensely over the last 10–15 years, and the conceptual clarification of these rights has improved considerably. We have questioned the traditional understanding of social rights as programmatic rights not only in legal theory. Case law from various parts of the world confirms the increasing conception of social rights as legal rights,[28] and

[26] Cf. Ida Elisabeth Koch, *Human rights: A conflict between positive individual and collective democratic interests* in Boom Juridische uitgevers, 2008.

[27] Cf. e.g. *On the Incorporation of Human Rights Conventions in Danish Law*, Betænkning No. 1407, 2001, Chapter 9 and pp. 327 ff (English Summary).

[28] Cf. e.g. Sandra Liebenberg, "The Protection of Economic, and Social Rights in Domestic Legal Systems" in Asbjørn Eide et al. Economic, Social and Cultural Rights – A Textbook, Martinus Nijhoff Publ., 2001, pp. 55–84.

an Optional Protocol to the CESCR providing for an individual complaints mechanism may enter into force in the near future. The dialogue between scholars and law-applying bodies on the normative character of economic, social and cultural rights has gained momentum – at the national and the international level – and modern technology has provided us with valuable tools for taking this dialogue further on its way.[29]

I do not wish to draw into question the possibility that this development to some extent can be ascribed to the tripartite typology. The typology unveiled the inadequacy and simplicity of the dichotomy, and it would be fair to say that it did further the debate for a period of time. However, the justiciability issue is far from exhausted and insisting on the tripartite typology does not necessarily bring us further ahead. The debate has reached a stage where one can question the adequacy of the tripartite typology without damaging the endeavours to enhance the protection of economic, social and cultural rights. Thus, it is interesting to note that there is little disagreement in the scholarly debate with regard to the inadequacy of the 'positive/negative' dichotomy, and most of us seem to agree that economic, social and cultural rights are justiciable to some extent. Legal scholars in favour of better protection of economic, social and cultural rights have few serious contemporary opponents and tend to argue against points of view put forward many years ago.[30]

The challenge today is not to question the 'positive/negative' dichotomy but rather how to go about the fact that some human rights are more vaguely worded and more resource demanding than others. Judicial bodies such as the ECtHR and some domestic courts have responded positively to this challenge on a case by case basis and provided evidence of the fact that the protection of social demands does not depend on typologies. Admittedly, the scholarly debate is ahead of practice, which is good to keep in mind when we tend to get carried away by our own arguments. However, the issue today is not *whether* judicial bodies have a say in disputes concerning resource demanding issues but *where* to draw the line between judicial and legislative powers when the disputed measures are resource demanding and the legal basis vaguely worded. This is where we are still in deep water, and for this discussion to develop we are hardly in need of typologies. Rather, we should seek for other indicators or

---

[29] Cf. e.g. www.echr-net.org which includes a database of legal jurisprudence on economic, social and cultural rights.

[30] Cf. most recently Magdalena Sepúlveda, *Ibid.*, p. 121, where she refers to works from 1973, 1975 and 1978, namely Maurice Cranston, *What are Human Rights?* The Bodley Head, 1973, Marc Bossuyt, "La distinction entre les droits civils et politiques et les droits economiques, sociaux et culturel" in *Revue des Droits de l'Homme*, Vol. 8, No. 4, 1975 and E. W. Vierdag, "The legal nature of the rights granted by the International Covenant on Economic, Social and Cultural Rights" in *Netherlands Yearbook of International Law*, Vol. IX, 1978.

'bearing points' for how to operate in this not fully explored field. E.g. in the famous *Grootboom* case and *Treatment Action* case it was decisive for the Constitutional Court of South Africa whether the housing and health policies were *comprehensive, flexible* and *balanced*,[31] and for the ECtHR it seems to have been of importance whether the State had already engaged in a certain resource demanding activity cf. e.g. Cyprus v. Turkey, referred to above. Much is still to be said e.g. about the division of powers between legislative, administrative and judicial bodies, and the issue of minimum core rights or decency thresholds is hardly exhausted either. This is not the time and place for further considerations on the future exploration of economic, social and cultural rights.[32] Only, we are not left high and dry without the tripartite typology or any other levelled typology.

One can speak, of course, about non-interference, protection against interference, provision of goods and services, etc. Only, the classification is of little practical use because the conception of non-interference as less demanding than the provision of goods and services is untenable. In this way the fundamental idea behind the typologies has fallen apart. While intended to be helpful analytical tools typologies have rather become straitjackets or "monuments to be caressed and polished" as Henry Shue puts it.

Maybe the time has come to throw typologies overboard – be they dichotomous, trichotomous, quadruple or quintuple – and focus on what it takes to provide proper human rights protection. This should indeed not prevent the ICESCR or other treaty bodies from spelling out in General Comments and Concluding Observations what it takes for each and every human right to be implemented properly. However, this important guidance could easily be provided without the use of typologies, and Henry Shue definitely has a point when continuing the initial quotation as follows:

> Thus there is no ultimately significant question of the form, how many kinds of duties are involved in honoring rights? Three? Four? A dozen? Waldron is closer to the mark in saying "successive waves of duty."[33] How many waves? Lots – more sometimes than others.[34]

---

[31] The Constitutional Court of South Africa does apply a terminology similar to that of the ICESCR. However, it does not seem to me to have proven indispensable let alone profitable to the interpretation of the Court, c.f. e.g. *Government of the Republic of South Africa and others v. Grootboom and others, CCT 11/00 of 4 October 2000* (Constitutional Court of South Africa) and *Minister of Health and Others v. Treatment Action Campaign and Others*, CCT 8/02 of 5 July 2002 (Constitutional Court of South Africa).

[32] I will return to the issue in Chapter 10.

[33] Jeremy Waldron, "Two sides of the coin" in *Liberal Rights: Collected Papers, 1981–1991*, Cambridge University Press, 1993, p. 25.

[34] One might consider whether the wave-metaphor is the most apt way of picturing the richness of obligations we are discussing. Waves roll, and what is more important in this context, they

> The "very simple tripartite typology of duties" then, was not supposed to become a new frozen abstraction to occupy the same rigid conceptual space previously held by "negative rights" and "positive rights." The critical point was: do not let any theorist tell you that the concrete reality of rights enforcement is so simple that all the implementation of any right can usefully be summed up either as positive or negative. The constructive point was: look at what it actually takes to enable people to be secure against the standard, predictable threats to their rights – focus on the duties required to implement the right.[35]

In the following, therefore, I will abstain from the use of typologies and work from the perception of 'waves of duties'. The tripartite terminology, however, suffers from the additional disadvantage that all three expressions, *respect*, *protect* and *fulfil* have a broader meaning both in legal and colloquial language. E.g. the expression respect as applied in the ECHR has a different meaning than *respect* in the sense of the primary level of the tripartite typology. In order to avoid misunderstandings I will try, therefore, as far as possible to avoid using the three expressions in their broader meaning. Moreover, when applied in the specific sense of the tripartite typology each of the three expressions *respect*, *protect* and *fulfil* will be italicised.

Likewise, I will avoid using the terms 'positive' and negative' as far as possible, and when unavoidable illustrate my scepticism by the use of inverted commas. I will make use, of course, of terms such as 'interference', 'intervention' 'provision' and 'supply', but do not in advance give such terms a certain content. My recognition of the fact that some waves are more likely to be justiciable than others will find expression in other characteristic features such as the wording of the obligation in question and the degree to which the obligation requires resource allocation.

---

roll back. Duties, on the other hand, have a more stable character, and the presumption that retrogressive measures are in non-compliance with human rights might not be compatible with wave motions. Speaking of a 'continuum of duties' might be more to the point. However, it appears from the context that Henry Shue in the cited passage has a general perspective on human rights cf. the expression "more sometimes than others." Therefore, the message can hardly be misunderstood and the quotation expresses very well my points of view in all other respects.

35 Henry Shue, *Ibid.*, p. 160.

Chapter 3

Considerations on Intertextuality and Permeability

1 *Introductory Remarks*

The integrated approach has frequently been *described* in legal literature.[1] However, a normative *explanation* to the phenomenon has not been given, and most commentaries deal with the phenomenon only in briefness under the designation *positive obligations* often as an element in the effectiveness principle and/or as part of the obligation to protect individuals against infringements of their rights by third parties. We have not articulated clear legal principles of guidance to treaty bodies when having to decide when and to which extent social facts can be considered legally relevant under the conventions on civil and political rights. On the contrary, most legal scholars have been more concerned about the 'negative' counterpart to an integrated approach, namely that of developing legal principles of guidance to law applying bodies when having to decide whether to *abstain* from taking into consideration objectives that are usually considered under another legal instrument and maybe by another legal body.[2]

---

[1] Cf. e.g. Craig Scott, "The Interdependence and Permeability of Human Rights Norms: Towards a Partial Fusion of the International Covenants on Human Rights" in *Osgoode Hall Law Journal* Vol. 27, No. 4, 1989, pp. 769 - 878, Martin Scheinin, "Economic, Social and Cultural Rights as Legal Rights" in Asbjørn Eide et al. (eds.) *Economic, Social and Cultural Rights – A Textbook*, 2nd Revised Edition, Martinus Nijhoffs Publ., 2001, p. 29 ff., Line Ravlo, "I hvilken utstrekning er økonomiske, sosiale og kulturelle rettigheter sikret i den europæiske menneskerettighedskonvention?" ("To which extent does the ECHR encompass economic, social and cultural rights?") in *Retfærd*, Vol. 25, Issue 97, 2002, pp. 34–46 and Siri Gloppen, "Kampen for sosiale rettigheder – er rettsalen riktig arena?" ("The struggle for social rights – is the court the right arena?") in *Mennesker & Rettigheter, Nordic Journal of Human Rights*, Vol. 21, Issue 1, 2003, pp. 61–75.

[2] In domestic (Danish) administrative law the so-called *speciality principles* (in Danish: *specialitetsprincipperne*) help to decide when a legal body is to *abstain* from taking into consideration objectives that are usually considered under another legal instrument and maybe by another legal body, cf. Hans Gammeltoft-Hansen et al., *Forvaltningsret* (Administrative law), 2nd Edition, 2002, p. 333 ff. Cf. also below in Section 3 on 'ceiling effects'.

The recognition of human rights obligations as 'waves of duties' is helpful as a starting point when trying to understand the integrated approach and the legal implication of the notion of indivisibility. The wave metaphor sets free socio-economic and civil-political rights from their separated compartments. It provides a new framework for the understanding of the scope of human rights obligations, and suggests the necessity of a contextual interpretation of human rights conceivably challenging existing text-conformal interpretative traditions. The text has no life of itself; something activates the wave motions and, moreover, they take place within certain limits and according to certain rules and principles. Legal interpretation presupposes not only text and context, but also principles for the interaction between the two. However, considering the fact that the texts are listed in two different instruments – the ECHR and the ESC/RESC – the intertextual relations between the two might provide a qualified point of departure for the discussion.

2 *The Intertextuality of the Two Sets of Rights*

The assumption that human rights can be divided into two well-defined and distinct types of rights is weakened already when looking at the *wording* of the two sets of rights, in this context the ECHR and the ESC/RESC. Although the two conventions on the face of it present themselves as instruments protecting different spheres of interest, there is in fact a certain overlapping or intertextuality between the two sets of rights – both stemming from the UDHR – that might permit or even mandate an interpretation that dissolves the boundaries between the two categories. In the following I refer only to the *wording* of some human rights provisions without having any intension of *interpreting* the provisions in question.[3]

Thus, aspects of the right to family and private life and to the protection of one's home are covered by both conventions although the ESC/RESC is a great deal more specific in the descriptions of the rights and, furthermore, leaves no doubt that the Contracting Parties are obliged to provide goods and services for families and their individual members. Moreover, Article 8 of the ECHR seems to presuppose the existence of something which is worth while protecting, thus giving the immediate impression that the primary obligation is merely that of non-interference. However, the ESC/RESC is indeed focused also on

[3] I am well aware of the fact that my intention not to interpret at this stage is unrealistic. One can hardly comment on a norm without reading something into it. In that sense the interpretation has already begun, although I have no wish to make any in-depth studies in this context.

protection against interferences,[4] and the use of the term 'respect' in Article 8 of the ECHR does not exclude an interpretation reaching into the socio-economic sphere. The wording of the two sets of rights seems to indicate that each of them has an independent existence; yet at the same time there seems to be a certain common protection domain.

Something similar applies to the right of workers and employers to organise, which is protected in Articles 5 and 6 of the ESC/RESC on the one hand and Article 11 of the ECHR on the other. While there are indeed major differences in the description of the rights, the wording clearly indicates that there is a common protection domain. Thus, the idea that e.g. workers should have the right to join trade unions for the protection of their interests appears clearly from the wording of all three provisions, and it should also be noted that Article 11 (2) of the ECHR about restrictions of the right has a counterpart in Article 31 of the ESC and Article G of the RESC. Hence, both the ECHR and the ESC/RESC encompass obligations not to interfere as well as obligations to allow or even support the various endeavours of trade unions to improve conditions of employment.

Also the right to education has a treaty-crossing character in particular after the entering into force of the RESC which obliges the Contracting Parties to "take all appropriate and necessary measures designed" "to provide to children and young persons a free primary and secondary education as well as to encourage regular attendance at schools".[5] Article 2 of Protocol No. 1 to the ECHR on the other hand seems to presuppose the existence of schooling facilities when prohibiting the denial of the right to education. However, at the same time the provision expects the Contracting Parties to respect certain rights of the parents in the "exercise of any functions which it assumes in relation to education and to teaching", thus indicating a necessary link between the two conventions.

Also the right to property, which is covered by the same Protocol to the ECHR, reaches into the socio-economic sphere. The provision presupposes the existence of property and the interpretative challenge is that of defining which assets are to be recognised as possession thus activating the normative demands with regard to the justification of possible interferences. Thus, the broader the delimitation of the notion of possession the more blurred is the distinction between civil-political and socio-economic rights.

[4] Cf. e.g. Article 7 of the ESC and the RESC on the rights of children and young persons to protection against exploitation on the labour market and Article 8 of the ESC and the RESC on the rights of employed women to protection against dismissal. See also Article 17 of the RESC on the rights of children to protection from negligence, violation or exploitation and Article 31 on prevention of homelessness.

[5] Cf. Article 17 (2) of the RESC.

Another link between the two sets of rights is the prohibition against discrimination which is included both in the ECHR and the ESC/RESC[6] and, moreover, in each and every human rights instrument. Admittedly, Article 14 has an accessory character thus applicable only in conjunction with "the rights and freedoms set forth in this Convention". However, the explicit distinction between "rights and freedoms" indicates that the ECHR has to do with more than non-interference, and the other links between the ECHR and the ESC/RESC referred to above will off course have a bearing also on the scope of Article 14. In the long term Article 14 will lose importance due to the fact that Protocol No. 12 to the ECHR entered into force on 1 April 2005. Protocol No. 12 encompasses a general non-discrimination clause and, moreover, in the Preamble an equality principle, thus necessarily reaching into the socio-economic sphere.

Finally, a particular link between civil-political rights and socio-economic rights appears from the wording of para. 2 to a number of the provisions of the ECHR and its Protocols e.g. Articles 8–11. Hence, socio-economic considerations might legitimate restrictions of civil-political rights in that e.g. "the economic well-being of the country", "the protection of health or morals" or "the rights and freedoms of others" may justify restrictions of these rights if otherwise prescribed by law and necessary in a democratic society. This provision corresponds to ESC Article 31 and RESC Article G according to which restrictions or limitations aim at the protection of i.a. "the rights and freedoms of others", "public interest, national security, public health, or morals."

Hence, apparently there seems to be a certain overlapping between the two conventions as some of their provisions cover seemingly similar factual circumstances. What is more, provisions in one convention seem to apply to provisions in the other, and both conventions allow for restrictions out of consideration for interests relating to rights protected in the other convention. These intertextual relations obviously call for considerations regarding the potential as well as the limitations of the integrated approach.

3 *The Permeability of Human Rights Norms*[7]

The intertextuality between human rights treaties gives rise to a number of considerations concerning the relation between various human rights norms.

[6] The ESC does not include a separate provision prohibiting discrimination. However, the ESC refers to the principle of non-discrimination not only in the Preamble but also in some of the articles of the Convention. The RESC, however, encompasses in Article E a general accessory non-discrimination principle very much like Article 14 of the ECHR.

[7] This section draws on Ida Elisabeth Koch, "Social Rights as Components in the Civil Right to Personal Liberty" in *Netherlands Quarterly*, Vol. 20, No. 1, 2002, pp. 29–51 (on p. 35 ff.)

Is one to try to draw the exact dividing line between the two sets of rights, or is one to accept and even take advantage of the fact that the dividing line is blurred? This is an issue which has not been given much thought, which might be due to the relatively new interest among legal scholars in socio-economic rights. Some scholars, however, have considered the issue seriously.

By way of example, in 1989, Craig Scott departed from the inter-treaty textual relations when he introduced the idea of *permeability* in order to put forward a means of giving practical legal effect to the abstract doctrine of indivisibility. By permeability he means "the openness of a treaty dealing with one category of human rights to having its norms used as vehicles for the direct or indirect protection of norms from another treaty dealing with another category of human rights".[8] Craig Scott groups the three notions – indivisibility, interdependence and interrelationship – under one designation: interdependence, and suggests that this notion may be understood as having two senses: *organic* and *related interdependence.*

By organic interdependence Craig Scott understands that "one right forms a part of another right and may therefore be incorporated into that latter right." Organic rights are "inseparable or indissoluble in the sense that one right (the core right) justifies the other (the derivative right)". Organic permeability "may accordingly be seen as the direct protection of an ICESCR right because that right is incorporated into, or is part of, a particular right in the ICCPR".[9]

It has been suggested that there is an organic interdependence or an implicit overlap between the (social) right to food and health care and the (civil) right to life. The ECtHR has recognised this interdependence on a number of occasions, by way of example in *Calvelli and Ciglio v. Italy* in which the Court, while referring to Article 2 on the right to life, held that:

> [t]he aforementioned positive obligations therefore require States to make regulations compelling hospitals, whether public or private, to adopt appropriate measures for the protection of their patients' lives. They also require an effective independent judicial system to be set up so that the cause of death of patients in the care of the medical profession, whether in the public or the private sector, can be determined and those responsible made accountable.[10]

The HRC has, moreover, stated in a General Comment that:

---

[8] Craig Scott, "The Interdependence and Permeability of Human Rights Norms: Towards a Partial Fusion of the International Covenants on Human Rights" in *Osgoode Hall Law Journal*, Vol. 27, Issue 4, 1989, p 769–878 (on p. 771).

[9] *Ibid.*, p. 779 ff.

[10] *Calvelli and Ciglio v. Italy*, Judgment of 17 January 2002, para. 49. In the concrete case, however, the Court found no violation of Article 2.

> it would be desirable for States parties to take all positive measures to reduce infant mortality and to increase life expectancy, especially in adopting measures to eliminate malnutrition and epidemics.[11]

By related interdependence Craig Scott understands that the rights in question are mutually reinforcing or mutually dependent, but distinct.[12] The question is whether a right in one convention applies to a right in another convention. The right to fair trial in Article 6 of the ECHR could serve as an example. The original understanding of the Court was that the expression "civil rights and obligations" only applied to private law issues. The Court has, however, gradually dissociated itself from this understanding, and today Article 6 is considered applicable to certain social security and social welfare rights despite the fact that the public features are sometimes predominant. Protocol No. 12 on the general prohibition of discrimination is another example. Unlike Article 14 of the ECHR, the Protocol applies also to rights – such as social rights – which are not covered by the ECHR and its Protocols.[13]

The notion of permeability appears useful in the sense that it describes (some of) the ways in which the two sets of rights interact. However, the fact that the jurisprudence of treaty bodies may be captured in neat categories such as related and organic interdependence gives us only little understanding of the reasoning behind the integrated approach – its limits and future possibilities. Moreover, one may question whether all linkages between rights can actually be captured in the two categories. The right to citizenship is often a precondition for the enjoyment of other civil-political or socio-economic rights, and the right to education is indispensable for the enjoyment of participatory rights in general. These links do not seem to fit naturally into either of the categories: related and organic interdependence. Nor do they seem to capture the interrelations deriving from the permissible restriction considerations, cf. above in Section 2 about ECHR Articles 8–11 (2), ESC Article 31 and RESC Article G.

Although the doctrine of interdependence is meant to serve as a starting point for developing a general interpretative presumption for permeability, the categories as such are descriptive and cannot serve as legal explanations to the

[11] CCPR, *General Comment No. 6*, The right to life (art. 6), 30 April 1982, para. 5.

[12] Craig Scott, *Ibid.*, p. 782 f.

[13] In a later article Craig Scott seems to raise doubts as to the mutual character of the organic or related linkages. At least he underlines that in some contexts it seems analytically correct to emphasise the partial dependence of one right upon protection of another (but not *vice versa*). The above mentioned example on Article 6 of the ECHR is probably most correctly seen as one such example of partial dependence, cf. Craig Scott, "Reaching Beyond – Without Abandoning the Category of 'Economic, Social and Cultural Rights'" in *Human Rights Quarterly*, Vol. 21, Issue 3, 1999, pp. 633–660 (especially footnote 10).

jurisprudence. Nor do they provide principles to legal bodies in their decision-making. It could therefore be argued that they are of a more technical and backward-looking character and that they are of little use as practical forward-looking interpretative tools. However, one should not underestimate the value of understanding 'ways in which' human rights can interact, and the fact that the categories describe more than they explain is in my view not necessarily a reason to abandon the efforts to consider other types of relations between the two sets of rights. Such efforts will hardly result in a complete overview of relations of interdependence. However, they might contribute to the increasing awareness of the interlinks between the two sets of rights. For that reason alone they are valuable also beyond strictly academic circles.

Nevertheless, in a later work the originator, Craig Scott, has dissociated himself from the idea that the links between the various sets of rights should be expressed in (more or less well defined) categories.[14] He expresses concern as to whether the focus on technical interdependence and the inter-treaty textual relations might create *ceiling effects* in the sense that a treaty body's reference to human rights commitments in a legal instrument other than its own can be used as a means not to expand but to limit the meaning, and thus the scope, of the protection, cf. above in Section 1 about *abstention* from taking into consideration objectives which are usually considered under another legal instrument and maybe by another legal body.

This phenomenon is indeed well known. Hence, case law from the ECtHR is far from being unambiguous. In some judgments the Court refers to human rights commitments found in other legal instruments – such as the ESC/RESC – as a reason to *limit* the meaning and thus the scope of protection given to a right in the ECHR. By way of example, in earlier case law the Court referred to the ESC in its argumentation for not including the right to collective bargaining under Article 11 of the ECHR, cf. below in Chapter 9, Section 9. Moreover, the Court has only to a limited extent been willing to read a right to health care into Article 5 (1) (e) on the deprivation of liberty of mentally ill and other vulnerable groups. This is so despite the fact that individuals can be deprived of their liberty for indeterminate periods of time *because* of their need for treatment and (medical) care and despite the fact that the *duration* of the confinement will often be dependent on the existence and quality of a relevant treatment, cf. below in Chapter 5, Section 2.4. Craig Scott refers to this phenomenon as a "juridical disease", which can be called "negative textual inferentialism", and he draws the conclusion that one should be less technical and concentrate on "what is needed to make a right truly a right of everyone".[15]

[14] *Ibid.*

[15] *Ibid.*, p. 639.

I share the concern of Craig Scott about juridical diseases functioning as obstacles to effective human rights protection. However, I doubt very much that his or others' (previous) attempts to categorise some of the links between the two sets of rights are what contributes to the creation of ceiling effects. If it comes to the worst, categorisation may be considered a mere academic exercise of limited practical use, but I see no reason why awareness of categories such as related and organic interdependence could not under favourable conditions lead to "positive textual inferentialism". Later case law from the ECtHR is illustrative, cf. below in Chapter 9, Section 8 about the development of the Court's interpretation of Article 11 of the ECHR in the light of the ESC/RESC Articles 5 and 6.

However, for a coherent view on human rights to be the result of focus on textual relations some additional preconditions must be fulfilled, and I agree entirely with Craig Scott when he warns us against losing sight of the goals and values that human rights discourse should be serving: dignity, liberty, solidarity, equality, etc.[16] He emphasises the necessity of *purposive analysis* and efforts to *making rights effective*[17], and advocates the challenging of categories by looking at their "provisional", "partial" and "relational" nature.[18] As for the provisional he holds as follows:

> No one is under the illusion that the category is a timeless one. The desirability of the category is open to revision in the light of what is later discovered about it – including what has been learned about its usefulness in addressing the problems and issues that the category is presumably designed to address. Not only is the category open to revision (whether modification or wholesale replacement) but revision is even expected. This will likely occur in direct proportion to how categories emerge over time as part of an effort to understand and respond to a larger reality that defies easy understanding.[19]

Thus, Craig Scott here deals with the ability of categories to respond to altering circumstances. If not suited to deal with contemporary problems and demands, and if not reflecting contemporary perceptions of values, the categories must undergo revision. Moreover, categories have a partial nature. They are part of a whole, and as the understanding of that whole changes, so too may the categories that must cohere with that whole. Moreover:

> because of their partial nature, categories can only fully be understood "relationally." Just as a "boy" only understands himself as such in relation to what is (or is constructed to be) a "girl" and an "adult", the meaning of any given category of

---

16 *Ibid.*, p. 641.
17 *Ibid.*, p. 637.
18 *Ibid.*, p. 641.
19 *Ibid.*, p. 642.

> human rights is, to a significant extent, a function of its relation to other categories.[20]

According to Craig Scott, this conception of categories and of human rights norms both as partial and relational may "affect the interpretative processes of giving (provisional) content to those norms",[21] and the article contains a series of examples of ways in which norms may interrelate. Such interrelations have natural consequences also for institutional human rights relations at the global and regional level. Thus, Craig Scott points out that:

> imagined, or virtual, dialogues among human rights norms across received categories find their real world analogue in the institutional dialogues among the different bodies charged with interpreting various categories of human rights.[22]

Thus, Craig Scott perceives the single norm as part of a greater whole consisting in principle of the entire human rights norm system. Moreover, he imagines the monitoring bodies in mutual dialogue about how to give substance to norms which have a provisional character due to altering factual circumstances.

4 *A Possible Theory for Understanding the Notion of Indivisibility and the Integrated Approach*

The theory of permeability, as supported by the intertextuality between the two sets of rights, and the perception of human rights as waves of duties are certainly helpful analytical tools when trying to grasp the legal implications of the notion of indivisibility. Also the focus on overall values and on contextual interpretative analysis, as pointed out by Craig Scott, provides elements of an understanding. However, it might be possible to come even closer to an interpretative theory for the explanation and development of the integrated approach.

Hence, the relations between facts and norms and component parts and the unified whole, the UDHR, emphasised by Craig Scott above in Section 3, trigger some of the pivotal points in hermeneutic thinking, and it seems to me worth while considering whether a hermeneutic perspective on human rights interpretation might be profitable in the understanding – and possible development – of the integrated approach. A hermeneutic perspective might be helpful also in understanding the dynamic interpretation of the Court reflecting contemporary views on economic, social and cultural issues, cf.

---

20 *Ibid.*

21 *Ibid.*, p. 643.

22 *Ibid.*, p. 659.

above in Section 3 about Craig Scott's reflections on the provisional meaning of human rights norms. Furthermore, a hermeneutic perspective on the role of the Court as the interpreter of the Convention might shed some new light on the issue of the division of powers, which is crucial in the discussion of the normative character of economic, social and cultural rights. These issues will be discussed in further detail below e.g. in Chapter 4 and 10.

Chapter 4

Theoretical and Methodological Considerations

1 *Initial Remarks*

It has often been noticed that the Court reads the ECHR as a *living instrument*,[1] and that it has adopted an even very *dynamic style of interpretation*. The by now quite aged Convention is interpreted in the light of *present-day conditions*,[2] and limited emphasis is accordingly put on the preparatory works.[3] It is also common knowledge that the Court applies a *contextual style of interpretation*[4] in order to establish "harmony with the logic of the Convention",[5] and that the Court reads the treaty in the light of its *object and purpose*.[6] Also the principle of *effectiveness* is usually referred to when discussing the principles of interpretation of the Court indicating that the Court prefers a "practical and effective" solution to one which is "theoretical and illusory".[7] Finally, for a long time is has been generally recognised that the Convention encompasses what is called *'positive' obligations*[8] including those stemming from the notion of 'Drittwirkung' or third party effect.[9]

The above mentioned principles of interpretation correspond more or less to Articles 31 to 33 of the Vienna Convention on the Law of Treaties of 23 May 1969, and the Court has in fact positively decided to be guided by these principles.[10] Thus, the Vienna Convention states in Article 31 (1) that the terms of a treaty should be interpreted "in good faith in accordance with the ordinary

---

[1] Cf. e.g. *Sigurjonsson v. Iceland*, Judgment of 30 June 1993, para. 35.
[2] Cf. e.g. *Airey v. Ireland,* Judgment of 9 October 1979, para. 26.
[3] Cf. e.g. *Sigurjonsson v. Iceland*, para. 35.
[4] Cf. e.g. *Witold Litwa v. Poland*, Judgment of 4 April 2000, paras. 57–59.
[5] Cf. e.g. *Leander v. Sweden*, Judgment of 26 March 1987, para. 78.
[6] Cf. e.g. *Deumeland v. Germany*, Judgment of 29 May 1986, para 62.
[7] Cf. e.g. *Airey v. Ireland*, Judgment of 9 October 1979, para. 24.
[8] *Ibid*., para. 32.
[9] Cf. e.g. *López Ostra v. Spain*, Judgment of 9 December 1994.
[10] Cf. *Golder v. the United Kingdom*, Judgment of 21 February 1975, para. 29.

meaning to be given to the terms of the treaty in their context and in the light of its object and purpose", the context not only encompassing other elements of the treaty subject to interpretation such as preamble and annexes, but also "any relevant rules of international law applicable in the relations between the parties."[11] Recourse may be had to the preparatory works of the treaty and the circumstances of its conclusion, but only as a "supplementary means of interpretation."[12] Emphasis must be put on the ordinary meaning of the text, the context and the object and purpose.

Against this background, one might argue that the principles of interpretation as developed over the years by the Court in good keeping with the Vienna Convention on the Law of Treaties provide a satisfactory explanation to the integrated approach. Not least the recognition of 'positive' obligations, the effectiveness principle and the emphasis on the legal context understood also as other human rights sources than the ECHR help us a long way in the understanding of the phenomenon.

However, the Vienna Convention does not provide answers to all problems of treaty interpretation, and it might even be difficult to reconcile "the ordinary meaning" and the "object and purpose". That is particularly the case, if the classification of a certain matter in a specific legal category is left to the Contracting States. But one might go even further and ask whether or to which extent it makes sense to speak of a meaning which is "ordinary"? Also the special character of the ECHR as a treaty for the collective enforcement of *individual* human rights may be emphasised when discussing the full applicability of the Vienna Convention. The fact that the purpose of the ECHR is to protect individual human rights has as an implication that considerations of justice may supersede those of foreseeability, which is in fact also a natural consequence of the wording of the Convention in terms of principles rather than rules. As most human rights instruments the ECHR is worded in a way which necessitates interpretation, and the relevant discussion is not *whether* to interpret but *how* to interpret.

The Court has generally attached great importance to the "object and purpose" of the Convention, and although it has employed the concept of "ordinary meaning" on quite a number of occasions, the concept of "autonomous interpretion"[13] has been widely accepted implying that the Court does not entirely rely on the domestic classification of a certain matter.[14] The Court has considered that it is free to assess for itself what is the meaning of a certain

[11] Cf. Article 31 of the Vienna Convention on the Law of Treaties.

[12] Cf. Article 32 of the Vienna Convention on the Law of Treaties.

[13] Cf. e.g. *Pellegrin v. France*, Judgment of 8 December 1999, para. 63.

[14] Cf. Rolf Ryssdall, "The Coming of Age of the European Convention on Human Rights" in *European Human Rights Law Review*, Vol. 18, Issue 1, 1996, p. 18- 29 (on p. 23).

term. The Court, however, has not made general statements as to the full compatibility of the various provisions of the Vienna Convention when applied in an ECHR context. The Court has viewed the task of interpretation as a single complex operation.

Therefore, it might be worth while making a detour and devote some space for a discussion of what text interpretation is and also ought to be. Why has the Vienna Convention pointed at the above mentioned principles of interpretation and not others, and why is it that the Court has developed the above mentioned principles? Where is the line to be drawn for the integration of civil-political rights and socio-economic rights? And most importantly: What is the meaning of a text and what is the difference between text and facts? For this purpose an insight into hermeneutic thinking might be valuable not only as a supplementary explanation to the integrated approach but also as a possible guideline for further integrative steps.[15]

2 *The Hermeneutic Circle*

The designation hermeneutics derives from the Greek verb *hermeneuein*[16] meaning to understand or to interpret – in this case a text – written many years ago.[17] The hermeneutic circle expresses the idea that present understanding is determined by previous understandings, and also that the present understanding at a later stage will have an impact on future interpretations. Moreover, in hermeneutic thinking the interpretative process is conceived of as an encounter not only between past and present, but also between text and context, and the interpreter plays an active part in these encounters. These issues will be dealt with below in Sections 3–5, whereas this part discusses the central theme in hermeneutics: that the whole must be understood in terms of the detail and the detail in terms of the whole.

---

15 The following sections draw on a previous article, cf. Ida Elisabeth Koch, "Economic, Social and Cultural Rights as Components in Civil and Political Rights – A Hermeneutic Perspective" in *International Journal for Human Rights*, Vol. 10, No. 4, pp. 405–430.

16 It has also been suggested that the term hermeneutics derives from the God, Hermes, the winged messenger of Zeus.

17 The concept of hermeneutics goes way back in history and the meaning of the concept is far from being unambiguous. I do not profess a specific movement, but have been inspired by philosophers such as Hans-Georg Gadamer and not least Paul Ricoeur, whose critical approach to hermeneutics makes him a bridge-builder between traditional hermeneutics and the critique of ideologies. Moreover, I have profited from reading David R. Doublet, *Rett, Vitenskap og Fornuft*, Alma Mater 1995, and Jan Fridthjof Bernt & David R. Doublet, *Vitenskapsfilosofi for jurister – en innføring*, Fagbokforlaget Vigmostad, 1998.

This coherence between the detail and the whole has several implications in a legal context at the international as well as the domestic level. One of them relates to the issue of power balance between the three types of bodies – legislative, executive and judicial – making up together the democratic system, which is presupposed in the Preamble to the ECHR. This issue is particularly important when discussing the justiciability of the rights which are not only vaguely worded but also resource demanding. However, when trying to delineate the area of competence of each of the three powers, regard should be had to that of the two others and vice versa. It is not possible to uphold the separation between the three powers completely. A ministry has 'legislative' powers to issue departmental orders, and sometimes an executive body has the final say in legal disputes preventing the individual citizen from bringing the matter before a court of law, cf. the notion of finality clauses. The judiciary creates law – at least to some extent – and might furthermore be involved in administrative decision-making, and finally the legislature does not restrict itself entirely to legislative functions. Parliaments have administrative tasks, and they might not be totally excluded either from dealing with issues that are otherwise within the purview of the judiciary. It is an illusion to separate powers completely. When considering the tripartite division of powers each element should be considered part of a greater whole – the democratic system as such – which in turn must be understood in terms of the elements: the legislative, the executive and the judicial powers.

Moreover, the coherence between the detail and the whole is crucial for the understanding of the relations between the individual norm – and even smaller entities of the norm system in question – and the entire system of human rights norms. The component parts and the whole must be seen as coherent in the sense that the individual parts of the text must be understood exactly as parts of a greater whole, which in turn must be understood as consisting of the individual parts.

This has the obvious implication that, for example, the interpretation of Article 8 (1) of the ECHR must be considered together with Article 8 (2). If the two parts of the Article are not regarded in conjunction, we are likely to end up with very absolute results, which do not respect one of the basic ideas of the Convention, namely the weighing of individual interests against those of the public or other individuals. Relevant to the interpretation of Article 8 at a given moment is also previous interpretations as manifested in case law from the ECtHR together with other relevant sources of law including the *travaux préparatoires*.

However, Article 8 is also to be seen as part of the whole Convention, which is again part of a greater human rights norm system deriving from the UDHR – consisting of civil and political rights *and* economic, social and cultural rights. Moreover, this conception has implications for the interpretative process since "[t]he harmony of all the details with the whole is the criterion of correct understanding. The failure to achieve this harmony means that the interpretation has failed."[18] The right interpretation is accordingly the one that brings about the best possible harmony or coherence between the individual norm and the whole system of norms – in this case the entire human rights regime – and the task of the interpreter is to make sure that each end every new interpretation contributes to maintaining or even improving the coherence.[19] The component parts and the unified whole are mutually conditional, and the interpretation must be regarded as an infinite process moving back and forth between the component parts and the unified whole. This dynamic movement has been designated *the hermeneutic circle.*

The, already mentioned *Airey* case might be illustrative. Mrs. Airey wanted a separation from her abusive, alcoholic husband, and since he resisted a court decision was necessary. However, Mrs. Airey was without means and therefore unable to initiate legal proceedings before a court of law, and the question before the ECtHR was therefore, whether her right to access to court under ECHR Article 6 (1) was violated.

According to the wording of Article 6 the right to free legal aid for people without means concerns only criminal charges, not *civil right* lawsuits. Nevertheless, considering the very specific circumstances of the case, it could not be demanded of Mrs. Airey that she represented herself in court. The Court therefore chose to go beyond the wording of the Convention and held that Mrs. Airey had not enjoyed an effective right of access to court. Accordingly, there had been a breach of Article 6. The decision implies that Member States will under certain circumstances have to grant individuals free legal aid *also in civil law suits*. Free legal aid in civil law suits can be considered a social benefit, and one might say that the Court has entered the scene of redistribution of resources by reading a social element into the (civil) right to access to court. The Court justified its decision in the following way:

> The Court is aware that the further realisation of social and economic rights is largely dependent on the situation – notably financial – reigning in the State in question. On the other hand, the Convention [....] is *designed to safeguard the individual in a real and practical way* as regards those areas with which it deals [....]. Whilst the Convention sets forth what are essentially civil and political

[18] Hans-Georg Gadamer, *Truth and Method*, 2nd Revised Edition, 1989, p. 291.

[19] Craig Scott has (convincingly) argued that the right answer might sometimes even be found *between* rights and in the combined *interstitial zones* of a treaty understood as a system of values and interests, cf. Craig Scott, "Toward the Institutional Integration of the Core Human Rights Treaties" in Isfahan Merali & Valerie Oosterveld (eds.), *Giving Meaning to Economic, Social and Cultural Rights*, University of Pennsylvania Press, 2001, pp. 7–38 (on p. 30).

> rights, many of them have implications of a social or economic nature. The Court therefore considers, like the Commission, that the mere fact that an interpretation of the Convention may extend into the sphere of social and economic rights should not be a decisive factor against such an interpretation; there is no water-tight division separating that sphere from the field covered by the Convention [author's emphasis].[20]

In order for the Convention to *safeguard the individual in a real and practical way* it must be subject to an extensive interpretation reaching into the sphere of economic, social and cultural rights. This interpretation is in perfect keeping with the Vienna Convention on Law of Treaties, which states that the terms of the treaty shall be interpreted in their "context", understood also as "any relevant rules of international law applicable in the relations between the parties".[21] Thus, without referring specifically to a human rights instrument protecting socio-economic rights, notably the ESC, the Court has recognised this instrument as relevant for the interpretation of the ECHR. In other cases, however, the Court has more specifically identified the "context".

Not least in cases concerning the interpretation of Article 3 has the Court frequently referred to the European Convention for the Prevention of Torture and Inhuman or Degrading Treatment or Punishment and also to the UN Convention Against Torture [hereinafter the CAT].[22] Similarly, in the *Sigurjonsson* case on the issue of negative freedom of association, the Court referred to Article 20 (2) of the UDHR according to which "[n]o one may be compelled to belong to an association", to the ESC, the conventions of the International Labour Organisation [hereinafter the ILO] and other binding and non-binding instruments in its argumentation for an extensive interpretation of the ECHR.[23] A similar coherent view has been applied in some of the most recent cases concerning the relationship between Article 11 of the ECHR on freedom of association and Articles 5 and 6 under the ESC/RESC, which – unlike Article 11 – clearly recognise the right to organise and the right to collective bargaining. While the Court originally interpreted Article 11 of the ECHR without considering the ESC, the situation has now changed. Today, the Court has an eye to the ECSR's interpretation of the ESC (and the RESC) although there are still differences in the interpretation of the two instruments, cf. Chapter 9. The Court, however, has left open the possibility that the harmonisation of the interpretation of the two instruments may continue. E.g. in

20 *Airey v. Ireland*, Judgment of 9 October 1979, para. 26.

21 Vienna Convention on the Law of Treaties, Article 31(1) and (3)(c), 1969.

22 Cf. e.g. *Dikme v. Turkey*, Judgment of 11 July 2000 and *Selmouni v. France*, Judgment of 28 July 1999 (the UN Convention) and *Peers v. Greece*, Judgment of 19 April 2001 and *Dougoz v. Greece*, Judgment of 6 March 2001 (the COE Convention).

23 *Sigurjonsson v. Iceland*, Judgment of 30 June 1993, para. 35.

Wilson et al. v. the United Kingdom it appears that "[t]he Court has not *yet* been prepared to hold that the freedom of a trade union to make its voice heard extends to imposing on an employer an obligation to recognise a trade union" [author's emphasis].[24]

By indicating that the interpretation might change over time, the decision illustrates that the hermeneutic circle has not only a vertical but also a horizontal structure.[25] The interpretative movement – which is to establish coherence in the norm system – concerns not only the relationship between law and facts (the vertical movement) but also the relationship between past and present (the horizontal movement). The dynamics in the horizontal movement illustrate how it is possible to safeguard historical continuity and at the same time make new readings corresponding to contemporary problems and value conceptions. Only, these new readings build on previous case law; they have the character of evolutionary rather than revolutionary re-interpretations. In the vertical movement law is confronted with facts, and considering that two sets of facts are never identical, law must be seen as 'unfinished', as being in constant motion reflecting an ever-increasing part of a complex and changeable factual reality. Against this background one might say that the circle metaphor is not to the point, and several authors do instead speak of a *hermeneutic spiral*.[26] However, before elaborating further on the horizontal and the vertical aspects of the hermeneutical circle or spiral, some remarks should be made about the role of the interpreter and the notion of *pre-understanding*.

3 *About Pre-Understanding*

Hermeneutics takes as a point of departure that the interpreter is inscribed in a certain historical, social, cultural and linguistic tradition. Accordingly, he has a set of pre-understandings or prejudices, which cannot be ignored. Freeing ourselves from prejudice would be an impossible task because it would involve stepping out of our given historical situation. It is therefore a fundamental idea of hermeneutics that pre-understandings or prejudices are neither good nor bad, even though the term prejudice has a negative connotation in traditional usage.

Lawyers have pre-understandings by virtue of being members of a certain historical, social, cultural and linguistic tradition. However, lawyers also have pre-understanding by virtue of their legal training – just as other professions

---

24 *Wilson et. al. v. the United Kingdom*, Judgment of 2 July 2002, para. 44.

25 Cf. e.g. Bernt & Doublet, *Ibid.*, p. 183 ff.

26 Cf. e.g. Stig Lindholm, *Vetenskap, Verklighet och Paradigm*, Almquist & Wiksell Förlag AB, 1979, p. 117.

bring with them ideas, values, specific methodologies and specific terminologies. In order for legal argumentation to be considered valid, certain rules and principles must be complied with, and legal methodology – which can be considered part of the legal system – becomes part of our pre-understanding. Lawyers' common pre-understandings have been characterised as the *legal community's communicative qualification norm*,[27] indicating that if one wants to be taken seriously by the profession – to be recognised as a serious member of the legal community – one must play by the rules and not indulge in strictly personal preferences for a certain interpretative conclusion. My *personal* pre-understanding that economic, social and cultural rights deserve better protection is therefore not *necessarily* an element of the legal community's communicative qualification norm.

While a *global* legal community's communicative qualification norm might have a somewhat indistinct content, it is indeed possible to talk about a *domestic* and even *regional* common norm of a relatively unambiguous nature.[28] Certainly, there *are* differences among the Member States of the COE. However, case law from the ECtHR is illustrative of the fact that the Court respects the different attitudes and positions among the Member States, cf. e.g. the concept of *margin of appreciation*. A similar balancing of common values and individual interests of Member States finds expression in the EU Reform Treaty (the Lisbon Treaty)[29] with its reference to the Charter of Fundamental Rights[30] encompassing not only civil and political rights but *also* economic, social and cultural rights. It remains to be seen to what extent this reunification of civil and social rights in the Treaty – if or when in force – will contribute to the clarification of the legal notion of the indivisibility of fundamental (human) rights.

Hermeneutics presupposes an internal view assuming that there is no objective or central position, from where it is possible to decide which of our pre-understandings must be discarded as prejudices in the traditional negative meaning of the term. Thus, the idea that every prejudice can be overcome is prejudice in itself. Rather, the interpreter is *inside* the hermeneutic circle, and pre-understanding has a guiding function by enabling him to 'pose questions' to the text. Pre-understanding is considered a *precondition* for understanding although not an automatic *guarantee* for the correctness of the understanding.

---

27 Doublet, *Ibid.*, p. 26.

28 The Preamble of the ECHR speaks of "Governments of European countries which are like-minded and have a common heritage of political traditions, ideals, freedom and the rule of law [....]". Furthermore, Article 7 (2) speaks of "general principles of law recognised by civilised nations".

29 The Consolidated Version of the Treaty on European Union of 18 April 2008, Article 6, according to which the Charter shall have the same legal value as the treaty.

30 The Charter of Fundamental Rights of the European Union, adopted on 7 December 2000.

Hence, the concept of prejudice or pre-understanding must be rehabilitated, and the hermeneutic circle is not to be considered a vicious circle even though the outcome of the legal interpretation is dependent on the input. Prevailing law is not the legal norm as it appears in the Convention, but rather the cultivation of the norm in the light of other legal sources. Legal interpretation is productive rather than reproductive, and it is obvious that the recognition of the notion of pre-understanding is inconsistent with a traditional empiricist scientific criterion according to which scientific reasoning must not be circular or prejudiced. From a hermeneutic perspective the inter-subjective legal scientific practice is the only measure for the correctness of legal dogmatism.

Hence, understanding takes its point of departure in the interpreter's situation, which is surrounded by a *horizon*, a range of vision delineating the at all times existing limits for understanding. Gadamer emphasises that he who has no horizon tends to overvalue what is nearest to him. Thus, horizons may be wide or narrow, but can be expanded in encountering past horizons. This encounter is essential for the hermeneutic situation:

> In fact the horizon of the present is continually in the process of being formed because we are continually having to test all our prejudice. An important part of this testing occurs in encountering the past and in understanding the tradition from which we come. Hence the horizon of the present cannot be formed without the past. There is no more an isolated horizon of the present in itself than there are historical horizons, which have to be acquired. *Rather, understanding is always the fusion of these horizons supposedly existing by themselves.*[31]

In a human rights context it means that in order for us to understand the ECHR we must regard it in its historical context and take into consideration previous times' ideas of values, social, cultural, linguistic and other traditions and confront them with contemporary ideas and traditions. Joseph Bleicher puts it as follows:

> Both the interpreter and the part of tradition he is interested in contain their own horizon; the task consists, however, not in placing oneself within the latter, but in widening one's own horizon so that it can integrate the other. Gadamer terms the elevation of one's own particularity, and that of the 'object' onto a higher generality, the 'fusion of horizons'; this is what occurs whenever understanding takes place, i.e. our horizon is in a process of continued formation through the testing of our prejudices in the encounter with the past and the attempt to understand parts of our tradition. It is therefore inadequate to conceive of an isolated horizon of the present *since it has already been formed through the contact with the past.* This awareness of effective-history is to assist us in the controlled fusion of horizons [author's emphasis].[32]

---

[31] Gadamer, *Ibid.*, p. 306.

[32] Joseph Bleicher, *Contemporary Hermeneutics – Hermeneutics as Method, Philosophy and Critique*, Routledge & Kegan Paul, 1980, p. 112.

Thus, our present understanding is necessarily influenced by history whether we like it or not. Gadamer speaks of *The Principle of History of Effect (Wirkungsgeschichte)*[33] thereby indicating that historically affected consciousness is considered an important part of the interpretative process in that it helps us pose the right questions. In that way hermeneutics bridges the past with the present and makes it possible for us to apply the text in a meaningful way according to contemporary conditions.

However, taking our pre-understandings as our point of departure does not imply that each and every pre-understanding is legitimate, and the crucial question is of course "how to distinguish the true prejudices, by which we *understand*, from the *false* ones, by which we *misunderstand*."[34] Gadamer's answer to this question is that prejudice is exactly a judgment *before* the real judgment and not a final judgment, and that by encountering tradition (the text) we do not only become aware of our prejudices; we are also provoked. According to Gadamer, temporal distance can often solve the question of critique in hermeneutics, and the "hermeneutically trained"[35] mind will include historical consciousness. In order to understand, one must expose oneself to the text and allow it to be influential on one's prejudices. Exposing oneself to the text (to tradition) is – according to Gadamer – sufficient for one's false prejudices to become conscious and challenged.

This is where I have difficulties in following Gadamer to the full. He *does* speak of the hermeneutic significance of temporal distance,[36] and recognises that the efficient history contains within itself an element of distance. Gadamer is, however, very faithful to tradition – to the text – and I do not find it convincing that tradition alone will deal with the problem of false pre-understanding. Ricoeur's approach seems to me more persuasive since his perception of *text* allows better for a *critical* distance.

While Gadamer understands the interpretative process as a *dialogue* between interpreter and text,[37] Ricoeur conceives of text as disengaged from spoken language. The text, according to Ricoeur, is dumb; it does not respond to our questions, and the relation between writing and reading is not identical to the relation between speaking and hearing. Ricoeur prefers to see the inscription as something that gives *semantic autonomy* to the text. "[W]hat writing fix is not the event of speaking but the 'said' of speaking",[38] and the 'said' assumes greater importance than the act of speaking. When written down, the meaning

[33] Gadamer, *Ibid.*, p. 300.
[34] *Ibid.*, p. 298 f.
[35] *Ibid.*, p. 299.
[36] *Ibid.*, p. 291.
[37] *Ibid.*, p. 369.
[38] Paul Riceour, Interpretation Theory: Discourse and the Surplus of Meaning, 1976, p. 27.

of the text and the intention of the author cease to coincide. A distance between the text and its author has been established, and hermeneutics accordingly begins where the dialogue ends.[39] "Writing, in effect, assures the triple autonomy of the text which characterises it: autonomy with regard to the reader and his intentions; autonomy with regard to the initial situation of the discourse and from every social-cultural conditioning affecting that situation; and autonomy with regard to the initial hearer and the original audience. Such is the distanciation which I will call productive [....]."[40]

The meaning of the text – according to Ricoeur – is not concealed behind it. The meaning is in front of the text, in what it makes possible, and the *semantic autonomy* of the text opens up to an indefinite number of readers. "That which makes us communicate at a distance is the 'issue of the text' *(la "chose du texte")* which no longer belongs either to its author or its reader."[41] In freeing the text with regard to its initial audience the text becomes open to a whole series of re-interpretations, which re-actualise it each time in a new situation.

Hence, Ricoeur finds "that a hermeneutic of tradition can only fulfil its program if it introduces a critical distance, conceived and practiced as an integral part of the hermeneutical process."[42] On the other hand he recognises that "a critique of ideologies too can only fulfil its project if it incorporates a certain regeneration of the past, consequently, a reinterpretation of tradition."[43] In this way Ricoeur bridges hermeneutics and the critique of ideologies in a constructive manner by insisting that hermeneutics should not become blind acceptance of a meaning that might cover up e.g. political or religious ideology.

> [A] hermeneutic which would cut itself off from the regulative idea of emancipation would be no more than a hermeneutic of traditions and in these terms a form of philosophical restoration. Nostalgia for the past would drive it unpityingly towards the positions of Romanticism which it had started out to surpass.[44]

Hence, it seems to me that Ricoeur's critical approach to hermeneutics provides a better basis for making the necessary distinction between "the true prejudice, by which we *understand*, from the *false* ones, by which we *misunderstand*."[45] Furthermore, the productive distanciation to the text allows better for our pre-understandings to be challenged also by the confrontation with contemporary events.

---

[39] *Ibid.*, p. 32.

[40] Paul Ricoeur, "Ethics and Culture" in *Political and Social Essays*, collected and ed. by David Stewart and Joseph Bien, 1974, p. 259.

[41] *Ibid.*

[42] *Ibid.*, p. 257.

[43] *Ibid.*

[44] *Ibid.*, p. 269.

[45] Gadamer, *Ibid.*, p. 298 f.

Let me try to relate these observations to the notion of pre-understanding in a human rights context. Until recently, it has been the common pre-understanding among lawyers that justiciable norms consist of legal facts and legal consequences bound together by a verbal form (is, ought, shall), a perception which renders impossible the recognition of socio-economic rights as legal rights. This traditional conception is indeed still widespread, but other and more nuanced viewpoints are gradually being introduced. Case law from domestic courts accepting elements of social rights as justiciable rights is subject to intense discussions in legal literature all over the world, and the discussion at the UN level with regard to the justiciability of socio-economic rights has recently resulted in the adoption of an Optional Protocol to the CESCR. Moreover, a collective complaints mechanism under the ESC/RESC has entered into force in 1998, already providing interesting case law furthering the discussion on the normative character of economic, social and cultural rights.[46] Today one can maintain that elements of economic, social and cultural rights are justiciable and – depending of the quality of the argumentation – still be recognised as a worthy member of the legal community.

It would be fair to say that lawyers' pre-understandings are in the process of changing, and that the traditional very absolute conception of social rights as non-justiciable rights will sooner or later be considered false pre-understanding. Applying another hermeneutic expression one might say that a future *horizon* will include social rights as justiciable rights to a wider extent.

It seems to me that the explanation to this phenomenon is not (only) to be found in a series of successful confrontations with tradition but rather in contemporary events. The altering relations between East and West as a consequence of the end of the Cold War have scaled down the ideological obstacles to a meaningful discussion of the justiciability of socio-economic rights and invigorated the conception of human rights as indivisible rights. Moreover, the North-South divide has brought about an increased attention to the significance of economic, social and cultural rights as components in a rights-based approach to development. These trends are indeed reflected in the Vienna Declaration and Programme of Action from 1993 with its emphasis on the notion of indivisibility, interdependence and interrelation of human rights.[47] Moreover, an increasing conception of norms as enforceable rights might be pervasive in both hemispheres, putting the justiciability of also economic, social and cultural rights to a test.

Some might find it superfluous and even contradictory to call for a critical distance to human rights and object that human rights values and principles have a constant character. I can easily follow that way of thinking and agree, of

---

[46] Additional Protocol of 1995 providing for a system of collective complaints, ETS No. 158.

[47] Vienna Declaration and Programme of Action, 1993, Section 1, para. 5.

course, that these values should be cherished. Today, human rights protection is challenged and even threatened in a variety of ways, and there is every reason to remember why the international community in the wake of World War II found it necessary to agree on a set of fundamental rights. In this sense the confrontation with the horizon of the past may indeed expand our present horizon.

However, that does not necessarily mean that human rights should not be subject to constant consideration. An anticipation of perfection might not be more fruitful for human rights interpretation than it is for any other interpretative activity. Critical distance might on the contrary contribute to the *revitalising* of human rights by constantly questioning traditional conceptions and understandings.[48] In that way human rights might escape a destiny as frozen values not reflecting contemporary needs and demands.

4 *The Horizontal Structure of the Hermeneutic Circle*

The ECHR was adopted in a quite different historical, social, cultural and linguistic context than the one we face today, and it is more than obvious that the originators of the Convention were not able to foresee the reality we face today. The East-West divide has been replaced by a North-South divide, and globalisation and modern technology have brought about new and unforeseen problems and issues. The combat against terrorism has given rise to a whole series of issues of importance for the interpretation of the ECHR.

Likewise the large number of immigrants has brought about questions that could not possibly have been taken into account in the years after World War II. The enlargement of the COE – not least after the fall of the Berlin Wall – has made topical a series of issues, especially with regard to property rights, and so has e.g. the dissolution of the former Yugoslav Republic.

Case law from the ECtHR is illustrative of the fact that the Court has adapted the interpretation of the ECHR according to these developments. Thus, as has already been mentioned the Court applies a *dynamic* or *evolutive* style of interpretation in order for the Convention to conform to *present-day-conditions*. The interpretation of the Court adapts to new problems and situations implying that yesterday's answer to a given interpretative problem might not be applicable tomorrow. Law is in constant motion. The Convention is a *living instrument* as it has often been underlined, which of course means that limited regard should be had to the *travaux préparatoires* in good keeping with Article

48 However, widening the human rights concept too much might not be advantageous for human rights protection in the long run as it might distract attention and lead to disrespect for human rights core issues.

32 of the Vienna Convention on the Law of Treaties, which considers preparatory works merely a "supplementary means of interpretation".

The expressions, *dynamic interpretation*, *present-day-conditions* and *living instrument* fit well into the hermeneutic terminology, and the horizontal structure of the hermeneutic circle allows us to get a better understanding of case law from the ECtHR. Case law is illustrative of the notion of *fusion of horizons*. New interpretations build on previous case law, but the Convention is ever again subject to new interpretations, and the intention of the originators is not decisive for the result.

By way of example, the sex roles were different in many ways at the time of the adoption of the Convention, and the concept of a family has changed completely from being a matter of married couples with common children born or adopted in wedlock to being a variety of social relations between people in several generations with or without children in common. These changes have had a clear impact on the Court's interpretation of Article 8. Even cohabitation between a sex-change-operated male, his female cohabitant and her child, conceived by artificial insemination, has been recognised as family life under Article 8 of the ECHR because of the social ties between the parties.[49] Moreover, today, gay and lesbian relations are protected under Article 8 as private life together with transsexuals' demands for recognition of their change of sex in relation to registration in public files.[50] In this context it is important to note that *even if* the originators of the Convention *had* been able to predict for example today's conception of family and private life, it is far from certain that they would have wanted Article 8 to apply equally to gays and lesbians or even less likely to transvestites and transsexuals.

Also, the – already referred to – *Sigurjonsson* case on the issue of 'negative' freedom of association illustrates how interpretation can develop over time. According to the *travaux préparatoires* a general rule that no one may be compelled to belong to an association had *deliberately* been omitted from the Convention. Nevertheless, the Court chose to disregard the original intention and paid more attention to the fact that "[a] growing measure of common ground has emerged in this area also at the international level."[51]

Also the *Winterwerp* case about detention of "persons of unsound mind" deserves mentioning in this context. As Article 5 (1) e of the ECHR does not define this concept the Court concluded as follows:

> This term is not one that can be given a definitive interpretation: as was pointed out by the Commission, the Government and the applicant, it is a term whose

[49] *X, Y and Z v. the United Kingdom*, Judgment of 22 April 1997.

[50] Cf. e.g. *Christine Goodwin v. the United Kingdom*, Judgment of 11 July 2002.

[51] *Sigurjonsson v. Iceland*, Judgment of 30 June 1993, para. 35.

> meaning is continually evolving as research in psychiatry progresses, an increasing flexibility in treatment is developing and society's attitude to mental illness changes, in particular so that a greater understanding of the problems of mental patients is becoming more wide-spread.[52]

Thus, the interpretation should not seek to reconstruct the original *intention*, but rather to reconstruct the *situation* – the context – that caused the adoption of the provision and confront it with our contemporary context. Gadamer puts it like this:

> A law does not exist in order to be understood historically, but to be concretized in its legal validity by being interpreted. Similarly the gospel does not exist in order to be understood as a merely historical document, but to be taken in such a way that it exercises its saving effect. This implies that the text, whether law or gospel, if it is to be understood properly – i.e., according to the claim it makes – must be understood at every moment in every concrete situation, in a new and different way. *Understanding here is always application* [author's emphasis].[53]

5 *The Vertical Structure of the Hermeneutic Circle*

The last part of the Gadamer quotation – "[u]nderstanding here is always application" – illustrates that the context has a decisive role to play also in the vertical contemporary interpretative movement. It is not possible to perform a proper interpretation without having an *interest* in applying it for the solution of a concrete legal problem, and understanding therefore has a productive rather than a reproductive character. A legal provision does not refer to an endless series of concrete facts to which it is meant to apply. It rather refers to a certain legislative context, and the legal meaning of the provision unveils in the encounter with each and every concrete individual situation. This means that "discovering the meaning of a legal text and discovering how to apply it in a particular legal instance are not two separate actions, but one unitary process."[54]

Thus, Article 8 of the ECHR does not refer to the nuclear family, the extended family or any other family, but rather to the fact that people organise themselves in various structures because of love, for practical or economic reasons, etc. The ways in which people choose to tie themselves together are many; they change over time and according to cultural traditions, practical purposes, fashion, etc., and the role of the interpreter is to facilitate the encounter between

[52] *Winterwerp v. the Netherlands*, Judgment of 24 October 1979, para. 37.

[53] Gadamer, *Ibid.*, p. 309.

[54] *Ibid.*, p. 310.

the legal provision and the facts. This implies that the legal text has limited meaning outside a context.

This amalgamation of facts and law may seem excessive. However, linguistic philosophy has realised that the meaning of a certain linguistic utterance is not necessarily linked referentially to matters of fact. Rather, the meaning of linguistic expressions is located in the *function* of these expressions when applied by people or professions sharing a certain interest or form of life – lawyers, by way of example. According to Ludwig Wittgenstein, "the speaking of a language is part of an activity, or a form of life",[55] and a *language game* accordingly defined as the perceptive linguistic activity between people who belong to a certain community. The players in the *language game of law* are those who master the legal language, just as any other game requires that the players know the rules of the game. Thus, the ability to 'play' is achieved by training, not congenital, and one's conception of language is "largely determined by the language of the community to which one belongs."[56]

The meaning of a linguistic expression is *the way in which it is applied* in the language game rather than what is referred to. Meaning is not intrinsic but created by application. Thus, if we want to define the meaning of a certain word, we must look at how it is used as an instrument of language. Words have no "ordinary meaning" as presumed in the Vienna Convention and Law of Treaties, cf. above in Section 1.

Words have more than one signification when they are considered outside of their use in a determinate context, cf. the notion of *polysemy*. The word *hearts* have different meanings depending on whether we talk about food, feelings, Christmas decorations or card games,[57] and the meaning of legal terms is also to be regarded in their factual context. Moreover, the meaning of words may change according to changes in the circumstances and scene of the language game. In principle, the evolution of the meaning of the word in question is a never ending process, and "the rules of the game evolve while it is being played."[58] E.g. it is a common perception that the expulsion of sick aliens is not to be subsumed under the notion of inhuman or degrading treatment in Article 3 of the ECHR. However, the factual circumstances might be so

---

[55] Ludwig Wittgenstein, *Philosophical Investigations*, translated by G. E. M. Anscombe, 1953, 3rd edition (1967), § 23.

[56] Cf. Peter Hulsen, "Back to Basis: A Theory of the Emergence of Institutional Facts" in *Law and Philosophy* Vol. 17, Issue 3, 1998, pp. 271–299 (on p. 274).

[57] Cf. Jesper Gulddal and Martin Møller "Fra filologi til filosofi – introduktion til den moderne hermeneutik" in *Hermeneutik. En antologi om forståelse* ("From philology to philosohpy – Introduction to modern hermeneutics" in Hermeneutics, An anthology on understanding), Jesper Gulddal and Martin Møller, Gyldendal 1999, p. 19.

[58] Peter Hulsen, *Ibid.*, p. 275.

exceptional that the provision applies after all, cf. the case *D. v. the United Kingdom*,[59] referred to in greater detail in Chapter 5. Moreover, it is a common perception that children of minorities do not have a right to receive education in their own language under Article 2 of Protocol No. 1. However, depending on the concrete circumstances, they may have such a right after all, cf. *Cyprus v. Turkey*, referred to in greater detail in Chapter 7.[60] Similarly, case law illustrates that the perception of what should be considered "possession" under Article 1 of Protocol No. 1 and "civil rights" under Article 6 has been highly dependent on the concrete circumstances, and both concepts are constantly developing cf. e.g. Chapter 8.

Hence, the Court's case law illustrates that new content is added to the various human rights provisions of the Covenant in the encounter with the complexity of facts. The traditional distinction between law and facts is rooted in the conviction that what happens in everyday life reflects something which already exists in the legal discourse. However, law does not mirror reality. Law can never exhaustively stipulate or predict the range of application and cannot be fully known apart from the contextual concretisation. Fred Dallmayr puts it this way:

> For, one may ask, how can the law or its content be fully known apart from any contextual concretization – given that the law can never exhaustively stipulate its range of application? Moreover, how can the 'sameness' of the rule of the sameness of its application be grasped apart from interpretation – given that the individuals and concrete situations are never entirely identical or exchangeable.[61]

This means that the deeply rooted distinction between law and facts, grounded into every law student from day one at law school, must be revised. Facts are not merely to be subsumed under the legal text when it has been properly interpreted without consideration being had to the facts which make the interpretation topical. Thus, it makes limited sense to talk about abstract interpretation and concrete subsumption. Gadamer sees:

> an essential connection between legal hermeneutics and legal dogmatics, and in it hermeneutics has the more important place. For the idea of a perfect legal dogmatics, which would make every judgment a mere act of subsumption, is untenable.[62]

Rather, *interpretation is always application*, and if the factual circumstances call for an interpretation that reaches into what is traditionally regarded as the

[59] *D v. the United Kingdom*, Judgment of 2 May 1997.

[60] *Cyprus v. Turkey*, Judgment of 10 May 2001.

[61] Fred Dallmayr, "Hermeneutics and the Rule of Law" in Drucilla Cornell et al. (eds.), *Deconstruction and the Possibility of Justice*, 1992, p. 293.

[62] Gadamer, *Ibid.*, p. 330.

sphere of economic, social and cultural rights, the boundaries between the two sets of rights must be dissolved. In this way 'context' refers not only to the factual circumstances of the concrete case which makes the interpretation of the general norm topical, but also to the legal 'context' as referred to in the Vienna Convention on the Law of Treaties.

Thus, a given norm is necessarily 'unfinished' in that it is never to be confronted with the full range of possible contexts to which it refers. Moreover, altering pre-understandings will make contexts topical which are not at present considered relevant to the norm which is subject to interpretation, and others will lose their topicality. The horizon of the interpreter is not a constant factor the implication being that we can only grasp law as a segment of a greater possible whole. Certainly, previous case law does have a guiding character in that each and every new interpretation is based on previous interpretations. However, something is always to be added and something else to be taken away.

6 *The Added Value of Hermeneutics*

Hermeneutics in the Gadamerian version wants to explore what understanding *is* rather than what it *ought* to be. He has an ontological perspective which treats understanding as an event, and he repeats that the title of his book *Truth and Method* was never to be understood as if the hermeneutic circle provides a certain methodology.[63] As expressed by Ricoeur the title indicates the dilemma that "either we have the methodological attitude and lose the ontological density of the reality under study or we have the attitude of truth and must give up the objectivity of human sciences."[64] Thus, it seems that it would be perfectly consistent with Gadamer's thinking if the interpreter were not to be aware of the concept of hermeneutics, its many aspects and its many ramifications.

Nevertheless, Gadamer does speak of "consciousness of the hermeneutic *situation*"[65] and makes a number of remarks as to how interpretation should be performed; he speaks about hermeneutical rules.[66] What is more, his energetic insistence that hermeneutics has nothing to do with methodology has indeed not prevented others from applying hermeneutics as methodology. Several writers recognise the value of hermeneutics also as a methodological instrument, and as appears from the analysis given above, hermeneutics reflects very well the principles of interpretation developed by the ECtHR – in harmony

---

63 Gadamer, *Ibid.*, p. 293.

64 Paul Ricoeur in "The Hermeneutical Function of Distanciation" in *Philosophy Today*, Vol XVII, Issue 2–4,1973, p. 129.

65 Gadamer, *Ibid.*, p. 301.

66 *Ibid.*, p. 291.

with the Vienna Convention on the Law of Treaties. One might therefore say that hermeneutics provides a framework of understanding for the overall discussion of well-known legal concepts and interpretative traditions.

However, one might also consider whether consciousness of hermeneutic thinking could bring the integration between the two sets of human rights further on its way exactly because it arranges in an ordered whole a series of interpretative principles developed in legal theory and practice. I will return to this issue in Chapter 12.

7 *Methodological Considerations*

The case law of the ECtHR is overwhelming, and it is almost impossible to follow the development. Each month the Court pronounces a great number of judgments, and reading them all is not realistic. This circumstance gives rise to methodological considerations, in particular when the aim is to study the protection of socio-economic demands. Thus, the HUDOC database – however useful suited it is in other respects – is of little use for the identification of cases in which the Court has read socio-economic elements into the civil-political rights protected by the ECHR. One cannot search on 'the right to housing' or 'the right to health' and words such as 'health', 'housing', 'work' and 'social benefits' appear in an overwhelming number of cases which are totally irrelevant to this study.

Nor has it been possible to restrict the study to a limited number of articles. The integrated approach has been applied in a variety of cases involving not all, but a great number of articles. Moreover, it has not been possible in advance to identify which articles were the most relevant. It comes as no surprise that e.g. Article 8 contains a potential for the protection of socio-economic rights. However, the fact that Article 10 would be relevant for the protection of the right to health was not to foresee, and neither is it evident that Article 6 is highly relevant for the protection of a number of socio-economic rights.

Accordingly, I have not been able to exclude one or more articles from the empirical analysis, which would not have been a very hermeneutic approach either, as several of them are to be seen in conjunction, cf. above in Section 2 about the hermeneutic circle. I have not been able either to identify the relevant cases by means of HUDOC, and I have not even considered the possibility of reading the total number of cases. To settle for case law from a certain time period would indeed have been a possibility, but not a very hermeneutic one either considering the relevance of the horizontal structure of the hermeneutic circle, cf. above in Section 4.

What I have chosen to do is to turn to the résumés of judgments as they have been published in Yearbook of the European Convention on Human Rights from 1960–1998 and Information Notes on the case law of the Court from 1998–2008 (both years included). Thus, in principle I have read the total number of résumés published, many of them, however, in great haste, as they were obviously of no interest to my research project. The material has been overwhelming, and I may have missed some judgments which would have been relevant to mention. However, my efforts have been directed towards giving as complete as possible a picture of the Court's protection of five selected socio-economic rights.

Case law from the ECSR, however, is so far of a manageable size and I have read the total amount of cases, cf. Chapter 11.

Thus, in the next five chapters I intend to illustrate how the ECtHR has been able to protect five different human rights under the ECHR, although these rights are traditionally categorised as socio-economic rights. The rights in question are 1) the right to housing, 2) the right to social cash benefits, 3) the right to health, 4) the right to education and 5) various work-related rights. In doing this I will relate to hermeneutics hoping to be able to illustrate the added value of hermeneutic thinking in the interpretation of the ECHR.

In Chapter 11 I will consider the reverse question i.e. how the ECSR has dealt with civil political demands under the ESC/RESC.

Chapter 5

The Right to Health Under the ECHR

1 *Health as a Cross-Cutting Issue*

Unlike the right to education and the right to organise – both rights appearing in ESC/RESC and ECHR – the right to health[1] is traditionally considered a right exclusively belonging to the category of social rights. This does not mean, however, that health issues are not closely related to other human rights, economic, social and cultural rights as well as civil and political rights.

The enjoyment of health is one of the fundamental preconditions for the enjoyment of other rights belonging in the category of economic, social and cultural rights. Thus, children whose state of health is not taken care of are less likely to profit from educational measures, which again bears upon their future possibilities to provide for themselves as adults. Their prospects on the labour market are less favourable, and the inability to work due to bad health conditions bears upon a number of other rights belonging in the same category. He who cannot provide for himself and his family because of untreated sickness is dependent on social security and welfare and – dependent on the level of social benefits – often exposed to a risk of social exclusion, not to mention the reduced quality of life which is often a consequence of untreated sickness. Moreover, it goes without saying that preventive health measures such as the provision of adequate sanitary facilities, access to clean water, environmental and industrial hygiene, vaccination schemes and control of diseases, etc. are of the utmost importance for the enjoyment of other economic, social and cultural rights.

---

1 In line with common usage in the human rights discourse I have chosen to use the term 'the right to health' as a shorthand expression for a number of health-related issues, such as health care services, underlying preconditions for health and procedural rights related to health issues, cf. e.g. Brigit Toebes, "The Rights to Health" in Asbjørn Eide et al. (eds.) *Economic, Social and Cultural Rights – A textbook*, 2nd Revised Edition, Martinus Nijhoff Publishers, 2001, p. 169 f.

The issue in this context is particularly the strong relations between health issues and civil and political rights. In short: The interdependence and interrelation between the right to life and the right to health is obvious. One dies sooner or later if a serious disease is not being properly treated and pregnant women without access to advice and medical check-up during their pregnancy are more apt to miscarry or to deliver stillborn babies.[2] Likewise, the lack of medical care, sanitary facilities as well as the lack of training of staff in e.g. prisons and psychiatric hospitals increases the risk of the exposition of prisoners and patients to inhuman and degrading treatment, a fact which is indeed paradoxical if the person in question – i.e. a mentally ill person – is confined *because* of his need for treatment and care. Related to this are the links between the right to health and the right to psychical integrity, including the right to private life. Finally, freedom to seek information and to express one-self is of crucial importance to the possibilities and endeavours of the individual to preserve a good state of health by seeking medical advice and treatment at an early stage of an illness. This, in turn, presupposes that patients can trust that confidential information about their state of health is not passed on without their consent.

2 *The Right to Health Under the ECHR*

2.1 *Relevant Provisions*

The right to health is not specifically protected by the ECHR. However, the Court has ruled on health issues on numerous occasions and under several of the Covenant's provisions. The relation between the right to life and the right to medical assistance, mentioned above, has given rise to complaints under Article 2, and Article 3 has been invoked for a variety of reasons such as ill treatment in prisons and other institutions, expulsion to countries with inadequate health care facilities and lack of public care of neglected children.

Conditions in prisons and psychiatric institutions as well as the lack of proper institutional facilities for e.g. mentally ill and drug addicts have given rise to several complaints under Article 5 (1)(e), and also Article 8 has been invoked on numerous occasions in health-related matters. Not least has the Court decided on environmental health issues such as nuisances deriving from obnoxious smells, noise and sequelae from nuclear test explosions.

---

2 The HRC has considered that it would be desirable for States parties to take "all appropriate measures to reduce infant mortality and to increase life expectancy, especially by adopting measures to eliminate malnutrition and epidemics", cf. *General Comment No. 6*, The right to life (Art. 6), 1982, para. 5.

Articles 8 and 10 have been invoked with regard to the right to seek information in health matters as well as the right to confidentiality. Moreover, the right to freedom of expression has proved to be of relevance also in health-related issues. Finally, it is worth mentioning that Article 6 has been found applicable to various proceedings concerning health-related issues and that health-related social allowances might fall within the ambit of Article 1 of Protocol No. 1. Other provisions might be of relevance, but so far case law relates primarily to the above mentioned articles.

The following analysis does not strictly follow the Covenant's structure. The presentation concentrates on a selection of (sometimes cross-cutting) health-related issues, most of which have 'positive' and often also budgetary implications for Member States. The presentation begins with a discussion of the right to health in general and proceeds with a discussion of health issues in relation to two special groups of individuals, namely people deprived of their liberty, and children. It differs, needless to say, from most presentations of the right to health since the protection of health-related issues is not the main focus of the ECHR. He who seeks a thorough overview of the right to health will therefore have to look elsewhere.[3] A comparison with the ESC/RESC and the CESCR will not be performed either, as the result of such a comparison is doomed to be pointless.

2.2 *A General 'Positive Right' to Treatment and Care*

Not surprisingly, case law unveils only few illustrations of claims as regards health care measures of the kind one traditionally associates with socio-economic rights. The Court has only to a limited extent been presented with claims for a certain treatment or cure, the reason obviously being that the prospects of having such claims recognised under the ECHR are poor. In a COE context the right to health is first and foremost protected by the ESC/RESC.[4] The right *not* to be subject to medical care, however, clearly falls within the scope of the Convention.[5]

However, it should be mentioned that the Court has not entirely ruled out the possibility of such protection under the ECHR. In a number of cases the Court has argued that such claims might – under certain circumstances – raise issues under the ECHR, and in that way once again illustrated the relevance of the vertical structure of the hermeneutic circle. In *Powell v. the United Kingdom*

---

[3] Cf. e.g. Brigit Toebes, *The Right to Health as a Human Right in International Law*, Intersentia – Hart, 1999.

[4] Cf. Article 11 of the ESC/RESC.

[5] Cf. e.g. *Glass v. the United Kingdom*, Judgment of 9 March 2004 in which the Court found a violation of Article 8 because medical authorities in the absence of authorisation by a court had overridden a mother's objection to a proposed treatment of her child.

about a boy who died allegedly because a seldom – but curable – disease was not diagnosed in time the Court stated that Article 2 enjoins Member States not only to refrain from the intentional and unlawful taking of life, but also *to take appropriate steps*[6] to safeguard the lives of those within its jurisdiction. The Court declared the case inadmissible but would not exclude that the acts and omissions of the authorities in the field of health care policy may in certain circumstances engage their responsibility under Article 2.[7]

In *Erikson v. Italy* – another inadmissible case concerning alleged medical malpractice – the Court read into Article 2 "the requirement for hospitals to have regulations for the protection of their patients' lives and also the obligation to establish an effective judicial system for establishing the cause of a death which occurs in hospitals and any liability on the part of the medical practitioners concerned."[8] And in *Calvelli and Others v. Italy* the Court held that:

> [t]he aforementioned positive obligations therefore require States to make regulations compelling hospitals, whether public or private, to adopt appropriate measures for the protection of their patients' lives. They also require an effective independent judicial system to be set up so that the cause of death of patients in the care of the medical profession, whether in the public or the private sector, can be determined and those responsible made accountable.[9]

The Court, however, found no violation of Article 2.[10]

In this context it would be relevant to mention that Article 6 has been invoked successfully in a variety of health-related issues such as compensation for alleged medical negligence,[11] HIV infection following from blood transfusion[12] and exposure to radioactive emissions.[13] Rights to sickness allowances under a health insurance scheme,[14] industrial-accident insurance benefits,[15] disability allowances and invalidity pensions[16] have also been recognised as

[6] Cf. the similar usage in the CESCR Article 2 and in Part 1 to the ESC/RESC.

[7] Cf. *Powell v. the United Kingdom*, Admissibility decision of 4 May 2000. Cf. also *Tysiac v. Poland*, Judgment of 20 March 2007 in which the Court found a violation because the applicant had been denied the right to a therapeutic abortion despite risks of serious deterioration of her eyesight.

[8] Cf. *Erikson v. Italy*, Admissibility decision of 26 October 1999.

[9] *Calvelli and Others v. Italy*, Judgment of 17 January 2002, para. 49.

[10] Cf. also *Vo v. France*, Judgment of 8 July 2004, para. 89.

[11] Cf. e.g. *H. v. France*, Judgment of 24 October 1989.

[12] Cf. e.g. *X v. France*, Judgment of 31 March 1992.

[13] Cf. e.g. *Burdov v. Russia*, Judgment of 7 May 2002.

[14] Cf. e.g. *Feldbrügge v. the Netherlands*, Judgment of 29 May 1986.

[15] Cf. e.g. *Deumeland v. Germany*, Judgment of 29 May 1986.

[16] Cf. e.g. *Francesco Lombardo v. Italy*, Judgment of 26 November 1992, *Giancarlo Lombardo v. Italy*, Judgment of 26 November 1992, *Massa v. Italy*, Judgment of 24 August 1993, *Schuler-Zgraggen v. Switzerland*, Judgment of 24 June 1993 and *Paskhalidis v. Greece*, Judgment of 19 March 1997.

'civil rights' in the sense of Article 6, and so have allowances under a national health service programme, see Chapter 8 for a discussion of the development in case law concerning the notion of 'civil right'.

In *Nitecki v. Poland* the applicant claimed that the refusal to refund the full price of a life-saving drug violated his right to life under Article 2 of the ECHR. The Court referred to the aforementioned statements about the obligations of Member States with regard to health care measures – i.e. would not entirely rule out that the right to a life-saving drug might be protected under the ECHR. However, the Court attached importance to the fact that the Polish State did in fact refund 70% of the cost of the drug and concluded as follows:

> Bearing in mind the medical treatment and facilities provided to the applicant, including a refund of the greater part of the cost of the required drug, the Court considers that the respondent State cannot be said in the special circumstances of the present case, to have failed to discharge its obligations under Article 2 by not paying the remaining 30% of the drug price.

The complaint was accordingly considered manifestly ill found.[17] The applicant Government in *Cyprus v. Turkey* claimed that the Greek-Cypriots living in the northern part of Cyprus were denied the right to avail themselves of medical services in the southern part of Cyprus, and that the facilities in the north were inadequate. The Court again observed that "an issue may arise under Article 2 of the Convention where it is shown that the authorities of a Contracting State put an individual's life at risk through the denial of health care which they have undertaken to make available to the population generally." The Court, however, found no violation of Article 2. The Court took note of the fact that the Commission had not been able to establish on the evidence that the Turkish authorities (the "TRNC" authorities) "deliberately withheld medical treatment from the population concerned or adopted a practice of delaying the processing of requests of patients to receive medical treatment in the south."[18] The Court observed that during the period under consideration medical visits were indeed hampered on account of restrictions imposed by the 'TRNC' authorities, and that in certain cases delays did occur. However, it had not been established that the lives of any patients were put in danger on account of delay in individual cases, and the Court attached importance to the fact that neither the Greek-Cypriot nor Maronite populations were prevented from availing themselves of medical services including hospitals in the north.

As to the applicant Government's critique of the level of health care available in the north, the Court did "not consider it necessary to examine in this case the extent to which Article 2 of the Convention may impose an obligation on a

17 *Nitecki v. Poland*, Admissibility decision of 21 March 2002, The law, para. 1.

18 *Cyprus v. Turkey*, Judgment of 10 May 2001, para. 219.

Contracting State to make available a certain standard of health care."[19] The last part of the passage from the judgment might be interpreted as if the Court in principle recognises the notion of a *minimum core right* to health services. The information available as to the level of health care services in the north, however, did not in the view of the Court require such an examination. That the Court under different circumstances might be willing to undertake such examination – which is indeed a difficult one[20] – might, however, be understood, cf. the use of the term *necessary*. Certainly, it is most unlikely that the Court would be willing to take upon itself to define in 'positive' terms the content of a minimum core right. That should, however, not prevent – and has not prevented – the Court from stating in 'negative' terms that a given level is unacceptable.[21]

In this context it is also relevant to mention the case *D. v. the United Kingdom*[22] although – or maybe exactly because – the circumstances were special. Considering the notion of *polysemy*, referred to in detail in Chapter 4, Section 5, the content of the concept of inhuman treatment is dependent on the context. In the concrete case the Court found that the removal of a dying AIDS patient to St. Kitts in the Caribbean after his serving a prison sentence would amount to inhuman treatment because of his risk of dying under the most distressing circumstances. The patient had undergone treatment and care in a hospital in the United Kingdom and the Court concluded as follows:

> Against this background the Court emphasises that aliens who have served their prison sentences and are subject to expulsion cannot *in principle* claim any entitlement to remain in the territory of a Contracting State in order to continue to benefit from medical, social or other forms of assistance provided by the expelling State during their stay in prison.
>
> However, in the very *exceptional circumstances* of this case and given the compelling humanitarian considerations at stake, it must be concluded that the implementation of the decision to remove the applicant would be a violation of Article 3 [....][23] [author's emphasis].

The Court found that the notion of inhuman treatment had a specific meaning due to the very *exceptional circumstances* of the case, but underlined that an

19 Ibid.

20 Cf. e.g. Audrey R. Chapman, "Core obligations related to the right to health" in Audrey Chapman et al. (eds) in *Core Obligations: Building a Framework for Economic, Social and Cultural Rights*, Intersentia, 2002, pp. 185–215.

21 Cf. *Khokhlich v. Ukraine, Kuznetsov v. Ukraine* and *Poltoratskiy v. Ukraine*, Judgments of 29 April 2003, paras. 181, 128 and 148. The judgments are referred to in further detail below in Section 2.5.

22 *D. v. the United Kingdom*, Judgment of 2 May 1997.

23 *Ibid*,. para. 54.

entitlement to care and treatment could not *in principle* be invoked. Inhuman treatment would mean something else under different circumstances, and the Court has in fact on several occasions found that the expulsion of sick foreigners to their countries of origin was in keeping with Article 3 even though the prospects of the applicants in regard to treatment were more than poor.[24]

Nevertheless, the judgment might also be understood as an acceptance of the notion of minimum core rights to health care even though it apparently concerned the issue of removal and only indirectly the issue of hospital treatment.[25] However, what motivated the Court was the prospect of no treatment, and the consequence of the judgment was that the United Kingdom would have to bear the costs of comforting and treating the patient in the time period he had yet to live. Consequently, one might argue that the Court has established a – not very well defined – minimum core right to treatment for dying patients without anyone to take care of them.[26] *D v. the United Kingdom*, however, is a single example and a series of cases concerning expulsion of ill people have been declared inadmissible. In *N. v. the United Kingdom* the Court held that:

> [t]he Court does not exclude that there may be other very exceptional cases where the humanitarian considerations are equally compelling. However, it considers that it should maintain the high threshold set in D. v. the United Kingdom and applied in its subsequent case-law, which it regards as correct in principle, given that in such cases the alleged future harm would emanate not from the intentional acts or omissions of public authorities or non-State bodies, but instead from a naturally occurring illness and the lack of sufficient resources to deal with it in the receiving country.[27]

---

[24] *Bensaid v. the United Kingdom*, Judgment of 6 February 2001 (expulsion of schizophrenic to Algiers), *Arcila Henao v. the Netherlands*, Admissibility decision of 24 June 2003 (expulsion of HIV-infected patient to Columbia), *Nasimi v. Sweden*, Admissibility decision of 16 March 2004 (expulsion to Iran of purported political activist in poor health), *Ndangoya v. Sweden*, Admissibility decision of 22 June 2004 (expulsion to Tanzania following conviction for spreading HIV), *Salkic and Others v. Sweden*, Admissibility decision of 22 June 2004 (expulsion to Bosnia of a family suffering from post traumatic stress syndrome).

[25] About the implications of *D v. the United Kingdom* cf. Stephanie Palmer, "AIDS, Expulsion and Article 3 of the European Convention on Human Rights" in *European Human Rights Law Review*, Issue 5, 2005 pp. 533–540.

[26] Cf. also *Nasri v. France*, Judgment of 13 July 1995 in which case the fact that the applicant was born deaf and dumb played a decisive role in the assesment of whether a deportation to the country of origin would infringe his rights under Article 8. The Court held that "the accumulation of special circumstances, notably his situation as a deaf and dumb person, capable of achieving a minimum psychological and social equilibrium only within his family, the majority of whose members are French with no close ties to Algeria, the decision to deport the applicant, if executed, would not be proportionate to the legitimate aim pursued", cf. para 46.

[27] *N. v. the United Kingdom*, Judgment of 27 May 2008, para. 43.

The Court, furthermore, made it clear that:

> [w]hile it is necessary, given the fundamental importance of Article 3 in the Convention system, for the Court to retain a degree of flexibility to prevent expulsion in very exceptional cases, Article 3 does not place an obligation on the Contracting State to alleviate such disparities through the provision of free and unlimited health care to all aliens without a right to stay within its jurisdiction. A finding to the contrary would place too great a burden on the Contracting States.

Whether this means that the Court has in fact regretted *D. v. the United Kingdom* is not entirely clear. However, the Court maintains that the circumstances in *D. v. the United Kingdom* differed from those in later cases, and the Court has in no way dissociated itself from that decision.

2.3 *Environmental Health – Striking a Fair Balance*

The Court has recognised the obligations of Member States to "take appropriate steps to safeguard the lives of those within its jurisdiction."[28] The content of this obligation has been clarified in a series of judgments about environmental health issues such as noise nuisance and industrial waste recognising a 'positive' role of the State in the safeguarding of people's health whether or not the State itself is the polluter. In this section I will deal with the issue of striking a fair balance between the conflicting interests of the individual and the community in the context of environmental nuisance. In Section 2.7 below some other aspects of environmental health will be dealt with.

In *Powell and Rayner v. the United Kingdom* – the first of several cases about noise nuisance from Heathrow Airport – the Court held as follows:

> In each case [....] the quality of the applicant's private life and the scope for enjoying the amenities of his home have been adversely affected by the noise generated by aircraft using Heathrow Airport [....]. Article 8 is therefore a material provision in relation to both Mr. Powell and Mr. Rayner.[29]

The formulation reflects that the issue before the Court was not whether Article 8 as such had been violated but whether the two applicants had an arguable claim in the sense of Article 13 of the Convention. However, the judgment is worth mentioning also because the Court laid down the general principles to be applied in subsequent cases on environmental health issues. The Court used the following by now well-known passage:

> Whether the present case is to be analysed in terms of a positive duty on the State to take reasonable and appropriate measures to secure the applicants' rights under

[28] Cf. the case law referred to in Section 2.2 and e.g. *L.B.C v. the United Kingdom*, Judgment of 9 June 1998, para. 36.

[29] *Powell and Rayner v. the United Kingdom*, Judgment of 21 February 1990, para. 40.

> paragraph 1 of Article 8 [....] or in terms of an "interference by a public authority" to be justified in accordance with paragraph 2 [....] the applicable principles are broadly similar. In both contexts regard must be had to *the fair balance that has to be struck between the competing interests of the individual and of the community as a whole*; and in both contexts the State enjoys a certain margin of appreciation in determining the steps to be taken to ensure compliance with the Convention [....] [author's emphasis].[30]

This *fair balance that has to be struck between the competing interests of the individual and the community as a whole* illustrates yet another aspect of the hermeneutic circle according to which the detail must be considered in terms of the whole and *vice versa*. In some of the cases the margin of appreciation allows for *the whole* – the interest of the community – to be decisive, and in others the Court has held that the detail – the individual interest – must overshadow that of the community.

In *Powell and Rayner* the Court held that the United Kingdom "cannot arguably be said to have exceeded the margin of appreciation afforded to them or upset the fair balance required to be struck under Article 8."[31] In the case *López Ostra v. Spain*, however, the Court upheld the contention of the applicant who complained about nuisance from noise, smells and polluting fumes from a plant for the treatment of liquid and solid waste situated twelve metres away from her house. She held the Spanish authorities responsible for her own and her daughter's health problems and claimed that the passive attitude of the authorities constituted a violation of her rights under Article 8 of the Convention. Thus, it took more than three years before the family was eventually offered alternative accommodation at a proper distance from the polluting plant. Before the Court she furthermore argued that the plant operated without a required license from the municipal authorities.

The Court held that severe environmental pollution "[n]aturally [....] may affect individuals' well-being and prevent them from enjoying their homes in such a way as to affect their private and family life adversely, without, however, seriously endangering their health."[32] The Court went on by referring to the principles adopted in the case *Powell and Rayner*, and after having assessed the situation as a whole, the Court stated that "it need only establish whether the national authorities took the measures necessary for protecting the applicant's right to respect for her home and for her private and family life [....]."[33] The Court concluded as follows:

---

30 *Ibid.*, para. 41.

31 *Ibid.*, para. 45.

32 *López Ostra v. Spain*, Judgment of 9 December 1994, para. 51.

33 *Ibid.*, para. 55.

> The Court notes, however, that the family had to bear the nuisance caused by the plant for over three years before moving house with all the attendant inconveniences. They moved only when it became apparent that the situation could continue indefinitely and when Mrs López Ostra's daughter's paediatrician recommended that they do so [....]. Under these circumstances, the municipality's offer could not afford complete redress for the nuisance and inconveniences to which they had been subjected.
>
> Having regard to the foregoing, and despite the margin of appreciation left to the respondent State, the Court considers that the State did not succeed in striking a fair balance between the interest of the town's economic well-being – that of having a waste-treatment plant – and the applicant's effective enjoyment of her right to respect for her home and her private and family life.[34]

Accordingly, the Court found a violation of Article 8.

Some years later a group of citizens living nearby Heathrow Airport alleged a violation of Article 8 by virtue of the increase in the level of noise caused at their homes by aircraft using the airport at night after the introduction in 1993 of a quota system of night flying restrictions, the stated aim of which was to reduce noise at Heathrow Airport among others, 'the 1993 Scheme'.

Their complaint was originally considered in 2001 by the Court, sitting as a Chamber, which departed from the principles adopted in the case Powell and Rayner quoted above and added:

> It considers that States are required to minimise, as far as possible, the interference with these rights, by trying to find alternative solutions and by generally seeking to achieve their aims in the least onerous way as regards human rights.[35]

The Court went on to establish that the overall level of noise during night time had in fact increased under the 1993 Scheme, and held that the importance of night flying to the national economy had never been assessed critically.[36] Moreover, the Court attached importance to the fact that the 1993 Scheme was based on a 'Sleep Study' limited to *sleep disturbance* without mentioning of the problem of *sleep prevention* – i.e. the difficulties encountered by those who have been woken in falling asleep again. The Court did recognise that steps had been taken at improving the night noise climate, but concluded even so as follows:

> However, the Court does not accept that these modest steps at improving the night noise climate are capable of constituting "the measures necessary" to protect the applicants' position. In particular, in the absence of any serious attempt to evaluate the extent or impact of the interferences with the applicants' sleep patterns, and generally in the absence of a prior specific and complete study with the

[34] *Ibid.*, paras. 57 and 58.

[35] *Hatton and Others v. the United Kingdom*, Judgment of 2 October 2001, para. 97.

[36] *Ibid.*, paras. 98 and 102.

> aim of finding the least onerous solution as regards human rights, it is not possible to agree that in weighing the interferences against the economic interest of the country – which itself had not been quantified – the Government struck the right balance in setting up the 1993 Scheme.
>
> Having regard to the foregoing and *despite the margin of appreciation* left to the respondent State, the Court considers that in implementing the 1993 Scheme the State failed to strike a fair balance between the United Kingdom's economic well-being and the applicants' effective enjoyment of their right to respect for their homes and their private and family life [author's emphasis].[37]

The Court reached its conclusion on a five to two vote. The dissenting judges agreed in dissociating themselves from the understanding of the majority of the margin of appreciation. Moreover, they asserted that the Court deviated from its previous conception of the notion in other planning and environmental cases by introducing a requirement to minimise, as far as possible, the interference with Article 8 rights by trying to find alternative solutions and by generally seeking to achieve their aims in the least onerous way as regards human rights.

Subsequently, the Government's request that the case be referred to the Grand Chamber was accepted, and sitting as a Grand Chamber the Court found no violation of Article 8. The Court emphasised "the fundamentally subsidiary role of the Convention"[38] and underlined that "it would not be appropriate for the Court to adopt a special approach in this respect by reference to a special status of environmental human rights."[39] The Court would not take as its basis that the 1993 Scheme had in fact led to a deterioration of the night noise climate, and attached importance to the fact that there was no element of domestic irregularity. The policy on night flights was found to be compatible with domestic law, and the situation therefore differed from that of *López Ostra*.[40] Moreover, the Court found it "reasonable to assume"[41] that the controversial night flights contributed to the general economy and noted that the applicants had not contested the Government's claim that house prices in the areas in which they lived had not been adversely affected by the night noise:

> Where a limited number of people in an area (2 to 3 % of the affected population, according to the 1992 Sleep Study) are particularly affected by a general measure, the fact that they can, if they choose, move elsewhere without financial loss must be significant to the overall reasonableness of the general measure.[42]

---

37 *Ibid.*, paras. 106 and 107.

38 *Hatton and Others v. the United Kingdom*, Judgment of 8 July 2003, para. 97.

39 *Ibid.*, para. 122.

40 And from that in *Guerra et al. v. Italy*, Judgment of 19 February 1998. This judgment is referred to below in Section 2.7.

41 *Hatton and Others v. the United Kingdom*, Judgment of 8 July 2003, para. 126.

42 *Ibid.*, para. 127.

Finally, the Court found that the Government had monitored the situation consistently and concluded – on a twelve to five vote – that the margin of appreciation had not been overstepped.

The strongly worded joint dissenting opinion of five judges is worth mentioning for more than one reason. It criticises the judgment for taking a step backwards by giving precedence to economic considerations over basic health conditions and holds that the Court is turning against the global and the European current as regards the concern over the need for environmental protection. The dissenting judges recalled that the Convention is a living instrument and saw no contradiction between the first *Hatton judgment* and previous case law on environmental health. They criticised that the judgment downgrades the discomfort of all the residents who are exposed to aircraft noise to a subjective element of a small minority of people being more likely than others to be awoken or otherwise disturbed in their sleep and called to mind that one of the important functions of human rights is exactly to protect small minorities whose 'subjective element' makes them different from the majority.[43] They underlined the fundamental nature of the right to sleep and referred to guidelines from the World Health Organisation [hereinafter WHO] according to which measurable effects of noise on sleep start at levels *way below* the levels disputed in the *Hatton case* repeating that the 1992 Sleep Study was limited to sleep disturbances. In the same breath the dissenting judges noted that the Government's claims in respect of the country's economic well- being were based on reports prepared by the aviation industry.

Whether one agrees with the majority or the minority, it is fair to say that the protection of environmental human rights did not improve by the Grand Chamber judgment. Admittedly, the economic interests at issue in the *Hatton case* were different from previous cases since they related to the entire country's well-being and not (only) to the interest of a single region of the country in question. Still, the margin of appreciation allowed in the second *Hatton judgment* seems to be much wider than in previous environmental health cases, and much more is required from the applicants in proof of their allegation than is required from the State. While the Court finds it "reasonable to assume" that the controversial night flights contributed to the general economy, the applicants' claim that the 1992 Sleep Study was inadequate was ignored and their sleeping difficulties downgraded to subjective problems.

It seems to me that the hermeneutic circle has assumed a slightly distorted form, and that the conception of the importance of the detail for the understanding of the whole has been reduced. The whole – the economic well-being of the country – overshadows the individual interest. Personally – as probably

[43] *Ibid.*, Joint dissenting opinion of Judges Costa, Ress, Türmen, Zupančič and Steiner, para. 14.

appears from my presentation – I find the judgment disappointing and tend to go along with the dissenting judges whose argumentation is *as* convincing as – if not *more* convincing than – that of the majority.

In *Kyrtatos v. Greece* the Court made use of the opportunity to clarify the scope of Article 8 with regard to environmental issues. The applicants contended that urban development in the south-eastern part of Tinos had led to the destruction of their physical environment and had affected their life quality. The applicants complained that urban development had destroyed a swamp which was adjacent to their property and that their home area had lost all of its scenic beauty. Moreover, they complained about the environmental pollution caused by the noises and night-lights emanating from the activities of the firms operating in the area.

With regard to the first limb of the applicants' complaint, the Court noted that:

> the crucial element which must be present in determining whether, in the circumstances of a case, environmental pollution has adversely affected one of the rights safeguarded by paragraph 1 of Article 8 is the existence of a harmful effect on a person's private or family sphere and not simply the general deterioration of the environment. Neither Article 8 nor any of the other Articles of the Convention are specifically designed to provide general protection of the environment as such; to that effect, other international instruments and domestic legislation are more pertinent in dealing with this particular aspect."[44]

The Court went on as follows:

> In the present case, even assuming that the environment has been severely damaged by the urban development of the area, the applicants have not brought forward any convincing arguments showing that the alleged damage to the birds and other protected species living in the swamp was of such a nature as to directly affect their own rights under Article 8 § 1 of the Convention. It might have been otherwise if, for instance, the environmental deterioration complained of had consisted in the destruction of a forest area in the vicinity of the applicants' house, a situation which could have affected more directly the applicants' own well-being. To conclude, the Court cannot accept that the interference with the conditions of animal life in the swamp constitutes an attack on the private or family life of the applicants.[45]

It follows that there is no right to environmental protection unless the environmental issues can be discussed within the context of private and family life. There is no right to nature preservation. Moreover, the disturbances must reach a sufficient degree of seriousness to be taken into account for the purposes of Article 8, which was not the case in *Kyrtatos v. Greece*. Accordingly, no violation was found.

---

44 *Kyrtatos v. Greece*, Judgment of 22 May 2003, para. 52.

45 *Ibid.*, para. 53.

In *Fadeyeva v. Russia*, however, the Court found a violation of Article 8 because of Russia's failure to regulate private industry, in casu a severely polluting steel plant. The Court concluded as follows:

> The State authorised the operation of a polluting enterprise in the middle of a densely populated town. Since the toxic emissions from this enterprise exceeded the safe limits established by the domestic legislation and might endanger the health of those living nearby, the State established that a certain territory around the plant should be free of any dwelling. However, these legislative measures were not implemented in practice.
>
> It would be going too far to state that the State or the polluting enterprise were under an obligation to provide the applicant with free housing, and, in any event, it is not the Court's role to dictate precise measures which should be adopted by the States in order to comply with their positive duties under Article 8 of the Convention. In the present case, however, although the situation around the plant called for a special treatment of those living within the zone, the State did not offer the applicant any effective solution to help her move from the dangerous area. Furthermore, although the polluting enterprise at issue operated in breach of domestic environmental standards, there is no information that the State designed or applied effective measures which would take into account the interests of the local population, affected by the pollution, and which would be capable of reducing the industrial pollution to acceptable levels.[46]

Accordingly, the Court concluded that, despite the wide margin of appreciation left to the respondent State, it had failed to strike a fair balance between the interests of the community and the applicant's effective enjoyment of her right to respect for her home and her private life.

The case *Moreno Gómez v. Spain* also concerned public authorities' failure to take action towards third parties. Despite the fact that the Valencia City Council had adopted measures which should have been adequate to secure respect for family and private life, the Council allowed licensed premises such as bars and discotheques to open in the vicinity of the applicant's home, making it impossible for people in the areas to sleep. The City authorities had already designated the area in which the applicant lived an acoustically saturated zone, which meant an area in which local residents are exposed to high noise levels which cause them serious disturbance. The fact that the maximum permitted noise levels had been exceeded had been confirmed on a number of occasions by council staff. Consequently, there appeared to be no need to require a person from an acoustically saturated zone to adduce evidence of a fact of which the municipal authority was already officially aware. The Court therefore concluded that "[i]n view of the volume of the noise – at night and beyond the permitted levels – and the fact that it continued over a number of years, the

[46] *Fadeyeva v. Russia*, Judgment of 30 November 2005, paras. 132–133.

Court finds that there has been a breach of the rights protected by Article 8." With regard to the adopted measures which should have been adequate to secure respect for family and private life the Court reiterated that "the Convention is intended to protect effective rights, not illusory ones."[47]

In *Taskin and Others v. Turkey*[48] the lack of procedural safeguards was decisive. In this case the applicants asserted that the domestic authorities' permit to use a cyanidation operation process in a gold mine had given rise to a violation of their rights under Article 8. The Court began its examination by repeating that States have a wide margin of appreciation in cases concerning environmental issues. However, an examination of the material aspects of the case was unnecessary because the Turkish authorities' decision to issue an operating permit for the gold mine was annulled by the Supreme Administrative Court. The Court therefore chose to focus on the procedural safeguards afforded by the Turkish legislation and found them to be in breach of Article 8 among other things due to the fact that the annulment of the permit was not enforced for a long period of time.[49] That was similarly the case in e.g. *Lemke v Turkey*.[50]

In conclusion, in order to raise an issue under Article 8 the interference must affect the applicant directly, and the adverse effects of environmental pollution must attain a certain minimum level if they are to fall within the scope of Article 8. In the assessment of evidence the general principle is to apply the standard of proof "beyond reasonable doubt". However, the Court allows flexibility and realises that in certain instances "solely the respondent Government have access to information capable of corroborating or refuting the applicant's allegations; consequently, a rigorous application of the principle *affirmanti, non neganti, incumbit probatio* is impossible [the burden of proof lies upon him who affirms, not upon him who denies, author's translation]."[51] In all cases in which environmental questions gave rise to violations of the Convention, the national authorities had failed to comply with some aspects of the domestic legal regime.

In the assessment of whether or not the respondent Government have struck a fair balance between individual interests and the interests of the community as a whole the Court allows a wide margin of appreciation to the national authorities. The complexity of the issues involved with regard to environmental

---

[47] *Moreno Gómez v. Spain*, Judgment of 16 November 2004, paras. 60–61.

[48] *Taskin and Others v. Turkey*, Judgment of 10 November 2004.

[49] The case *Okyay and Others v. Turkey* also concerned the national authorities' failure to implement the domestic courts' orders to shut down polluting (thermal-power) plants. This case, however, was decided under Article 6, cf. *Okyay and Others v. Turkey*, Judgment of 12 July 2005.

[50] *Lemke v. Turkey*, Judgment of 5 June 2007.

[51] *Fadeyeva v. Russia*, para. 79.

protection renders the Court's role primarily a subsidiary one, and the Court has held that its role is not "to substitute for the national authorities any other assessment of what might be best policy in this difficult technical and social sphere. This is an area where the Contracting Parties are to be recognised as enjoying a wide margin of appreciation [....]."[52]However, it still remains open to the Court to conclude that a fair balance has not been struck, and the Court has made use of this possibility on several occasions.

2.4 *Deprivation of Liberty for Purposes of Treatment – Rights and Duties*[53]

2.4.1 *A Right to Compulsory Treatment?*

Case law under the ECHR includes a number of complaints from mentally ill persons who want to be released from their involuntary placement in psychiatric hospitals. Most of these cases will be passed over in silence. Of interest in this context are the 'positive' aspects of involuntary confinement i.e. the extent to which one can make claims with regard to the placement and the content of the involuntary treatment. Is their a coherence between rights and duties in the sense that one can claim a right to a certain (compulsory) treatment? The issue is not as impracticable as it might seem at first.

On a number of occasions the Court has been presented with a problem which is – unfortunately – all too widespread in the COE Member States, namely that (convicted) persons with mental diseases or addiction problems are not placed where they ought to be placed i.e. in mental hospitals or social institutions. Instead they are often confined in prisons or other – in this respect inappropriate – institutions awaiting transfer to the relevant hospital or social institution. The problem has proved to be of a highly complex character involving subparagraphs (a) and (e) of Article 5:

> 1. Everyone has the right to liberty and security of person. No one shall be deprived of his liberty save in the following cases and in accordance with a procedure prescribed by law.
>
> (a) the lawful detention of a person after conviction by a competent court
>
> [....]
>
> (e) the lawful detention of persons for the prevention of the spreading of infectious diseases, of persons of unsound mind, alcoholics or drug addicts or vagrants.

While other sub-paragraphs of Article 5 (1) affect groups that are fairly well defined, Article 5 (1)(e) brings together a diverse group of people. The provision

[52] *Ibid.*, para.104.

[53] I have previously dealt with this issue, cf. "Social Rights as Components in the Civil Right to Personal Liberty: Another Step forward in the Integrated Human Rights Approach" in *Netherlands Quarterly*, Vol 20, No. 1, 2002, pp. 29–51.

unveils nothing as to the purpose of such confinement except as regards infectious diseases. Case law, however, sheds some light over the issue. In the case *Guzzardi v. Italy* the Court stated that "[t]he reason why the Convention allows the latter individuals, all of whom are socially maladjusted, to be deprived of their liberty is not only that they have to be considered as occasionally dangerous for public safety but also that their own interests may necessitate their detention."[54] In the case of *Hutchison Reid v. the United Kingdom* the Court furthermore stated that "[s]uch confinement may be necessary not only where a person needs therapy, medication or other clinical treatment to cure or alleviate his condition, but also where the person needs control and supervision to prevent him, for example, causing harm to himself or other persons [....]."[55]

Thus, the group of people, mentioned in sub-paragraph (e) are often deprived of their liberty *because* of their need for treatment and cure, and the *duration* of their confinement is therefore likely to depend on whether or to which extent they are offered medical and social assistance. Confinement under Article 5 (1)(e) is often indeterminate for the very reason that it is difficult to assess exactly for how long the person in question will need a certain treatment or cure or for how long he will remain a danger to society without such treatment. Accordingly, it is relevant to ask whether the lawfulness of the confinement as such can be considered without also considering the conditions during the confinement with respect to health care, social services, etc.

However, the Court has been very reluctant to read a 'positive' right to treatment into Article 5 (1)(e), which is indeed notable considering the fact that the deprivation of liberty is a very serious intervention.

The first case in which the Court expressed an opinion on the issue of the right to treatment during confinement was the case *Winterwerp v. the Netherlands*. Winterwerp was confined for reasons of mental illness in a psychiatric hospital for several years and argued before the Court that sub-paragraph (e) entails the right to appropriate treatment to ensure that a mentally ill person is not confined longer than is absolutely necessary. The Court, however, dealt with this argument very briefly by stating that "a mental patient's right to treatment appropriate to his condition cannot as such be derived from Article 5 para. 1 (e) [....]."[56]

In *Ashingdane v. the United Kingdom* the Court explained and developed its view in further detail. Ashingdane, who suffered from paranoid schizophrenia, was convicted by a court of dangerous driving and unlawful possession of firearms. Because of his illness the court made a hospital order under the Mental

---

[54] *Guzzardi v. Italy*, Judgment of 6 November 1980, para. 98.

[55] *Hutchison Reid v. the United Kingdom*, Judgment of 20 February 2003, para. 52.

[56] *Winterwerp v. the Netherlands*, Judgment of 24 October 1979, para. 51.

Health Act together with an order restricting his discharge without limit of time. He was subsequently detained in a mental hospital, Broadmore Hospital, with a very strict regime. Accordingly, his case was to be considered under Article 5 (1)(e) and (e) only despite the fact that he was convicted of criminal offences, cf. subparagraph (a).

After several years of confinement psychiatrists agreed that the regime at Broadmore had adverse effects on Ashingdane's mental condition. They found that a transfer to a less strict regime at Oakwood Hospital would be "an essential step" in his recovery and that his continued detention in Broadmore had "an adverse effect on his mental health".[57] The Home Secretary consented to the transfer, but Oakwood Hospital refused to admit Ashingdane, the reason being that the nursing staff was operating a total ban on the admission of offender patients due to a shortage of adequate resources. The authorities did not insist on the transfer – to Oakwood Hospital or another similar hospital – and Ashingdane therefore remained at Broadmore Hospital for another two years.

Ashingdane argued before the Court that his compulsory confinement at Broadmore Hospital after he had been declared fit for transfer to the less restrictive regime at Oakwood was contrary to the Convention. He claimed that he was detained for purposes of preserving industrial peace rather than treatment and social protection, and that his release into society had been extended beyond what was required by the needs of society. Moreover, he argued that the authority to detain mental patients carried with it a minimal obligation to deploy available resources to protect them from discernible harm.

The Court referred to its previous statement in the *Winterwerp judgment* that Article 5 "is not in principle concerned with suitable treatment or conditions". However, the Court added that:

> there must be some relationship between the ground of permitted deprivation of liberty relied on and the place and conditions of detention. In principle the 'detention' of a person as a mental health patient will only be 'lawful' for the purpose of sub-paragraph (e) [....] if effected in a hospital, clinic or other *appropriate* institution *authorised* for that purpose [author's emphasis].[58]

The Court attached importance to the fact that Broadmore was a psychiatric hospital and even though the regimes at the two hospitals were very different "they were not such as to change the character of his deprivation of liberty as a mental patient."[59] Accordingly, the Court found no violation of Article 5 (1)(e) despite the fact that the regime at Broadmore Hospital according to specialists was not at all *appropriate* under the circumstances.

---

57 *Ashingdane v. the United Kingdom*, Judgment of 28 May 1985, para. 20.

58 *Ibid.*, para. 44.

59 *Ibid.*, para. 47.

Ashingdane's mental health deteriorated while he was waiting for transfer, and it appeared from the case that he *did* in fact recover after the transfer eventually took place. The Court, however, seems to be of the opinion that the mere *authorisation* of an institution for a certain purpose is sufficient to make it *appropriate*, and the obvious relation between the duration of detention of a mental patient and the conditions during detention was not taken into consideration.

The interpretation of the Court is – in my opinion – unnecessarily restricted and not at all contextual. What prevented the transfer was the concrete threat of a strike or industrial action, and it was undisputed that a transfer would have had a positive impact on Ashingdane's mental health. The Court could have held that Article 5 had been violated under these very specific circumstances without having to involve itself with complicated issues such as defining minimum core standards for the treatment of mentally ill persons, etc. Besides, as the dissenting judge Petitti pointed out, Oakwood was not the only institution of this kind, and the authorities did nothing to arrange for a transfer to another appropriate hospital.

A somewhat different problem was raised in the case *Johnson v. the United Kingdom*.[60] Johnson was found guilty of causing actual bodily harm to a pregnant woman. However, since he was diagnosed as a schizophrenic he was placed by court order in a mental hospital and made subject to a restriction order without time limit. After some years he recovered, and a Tribunal ordered his discharge. However, since he was also diagnosed as an alcoholic the discharge was subject to the condition that he took up residence in a hostel where he could be supervised by a psychiatrist and a social worker. Johnson was, however, not discharged. None of the – rather few – hostels in the area would agree to admit him because of his history of alcohol abuse, and the Tribunal deferred his discharge time and again. After four years of unsuccessful negotiations with the social authorities the Tribunal eventually decided to discharge him unconditionally.

Before the Court, Johnson claimed that his detention had been in non-compliance with Article 5 (1)(e) as from the day the Tribunal found him no longer suffering from mental illness. The Court upheld his contention by referring to the 'Winterwerp requirements' according to which:

> an individual cannot be considered to be of 'unsound mind' and deprived of his liberty unless the following three minimum conditions are satisfied: firstly, he must reliably be shown to be of unsound mind; secondly, the mental disorder must be of a kind or degree warranting compulsory confinement; thirdly and of

[60] *Johnson v. the United Kingdom*, Judgment of 24 October 1997.

> sole relevance to the case at issue, the validity of continued confinement depends upon the persistence of such a disorder [....].[61]

The Court had no objections to a conditional discharge and rejected the applicant's claim that he should be discharged immediately. The Court recognised the need of the authorities to locate a hostel which best suited the applicant's needs and which could provide him with the most appropriate conditions for his successful rehabilitation. However, the Court attached importance to the fact that the Tribunal lacked the powers to ensure that a placement could be secured within a reasonable time. The Tribunal was unable to overcome the difficulties because the competence to admit Johnson to a hostel rested with the social authorities, and since the hostel residence condition deferred the discharge for more than three years, the Court concluded that the continued detention constituted a violation of Article 5 (1)(e).

What was at stake was a classical matter of legal security. Johnson wanted to be free of interference, and he was not the least interested in undergoing treatment for alcoholism. In fact, he was anything but co-operative with the social authorities. However, there might be other patients who have not only agreed, but positively applied for a stay in hostel in order to facilitate the transition from confinement to a normal life in society. If the individual and the prison authorities have the same interest, as it often happens, legal security in the classical 'State governed by law' sense is not sufficient. If the patient in question – in compliance with the wish of the authorities – requests assistance from e.g. social welfare authorities, it is of course not satisfactory to be discharged without such assistance even though continued confinement is inconsistent with Article 5 (1)(e). When considering whether a mental patient is to be discharged the answer is not always either *yes* or no. Conditional discharge is in fact very common, but sometimes the conditions cannot be fulfilled because of a lack of social institutions, staff or other resources. Thus, it does indeed occur that mental patients remain detained solely because of inadequate facilities in the social sector.[62]

The Court has not yet had to deal with such circumstances, which do not relate solely to a 'State governed by law' paradigm.[63] The hypothetical situation

---

[61] *Ibid.*, para. 60.

[62] Cf. *Aerts v. Belgium*, Judgment of 30 July 1998. See also Ida Elisabeth Koch, *Behandling som alternativ til frihedsstraf – samspillet mellem kriminalretten og social- og sundhedsretten* (Treatment as an alternative to imprisonment – the interlink between criminal law and social and health law), JØP Publ.,1995.

[63] The case *Aerts v. Belgium* concerns a related issue. The same applies to *Brand v. the Netherlands* and *Morsink v. the Netherlands*, Judgments of 11 May 2004. These cases will be referred to in further detail below. In all three cases, however, it was part of the judicial decision that the offenders should be placed in treatment institutions deprived of their liberty.

just mentioned refers to the 'Welfare State' paradigm as well, since it has to do with 'positive' elements of social rights and services. Of course we can interpret the decision in the *Johnson case* as an indirect request or encouragement to the Member States to establish the necessary links between various sectors. However, we cannot conclude that the Court would be willing to state this explicitly if the situation were to occur.

What distinguishes the *Johnson case* from the *Ashingdane case* is that Johnson was about to be *discharged* – although conditionally – whereas Ashingdane was to be transferred to a less restrict regime of *continued confinement.* Although continued confinement in a relaxed environment is very often applied as a transitional solution between confinement and discharge, the approach of the Court to the two sets of facts differs completely. What can be learned from *Johnson v. the United Kingdom* is that social mental health authorities will have to adjust their demands as regards conditions for discharge according to the offers actually available. The imposition of unrealistic conditions endangers the right to personal liberty and hampers the compliance with the third Winterwerp requirement according to which the validity of continued confinement depends upon the persistence of a disorder. However, the obvious interest of a mental patient – such as Ashingdane – in transfer to an environment of treatment which is beneficial to his mental health and therefore likely to accelerate the final discharge seems to be of no relevance to the interpretation of Article 5 (1)(e) as long as the institutional frame is a psychiatric hospital.

If, however, a mental patient, who is declared not criminally responsible, is detained in a prison instead of a relevant institution, the situation is different. That was the case in *Aerts v. Belgium* concerning a man suffering from severe mental disturbance who had attacked his ex-wife with a hammer. Pending his detention in a relevant institution which was to be designated by the competent health board he was placed provisionally in the psychiatric wing of a prison, the Lantin Prison. A few months later the relevant institution – the Paifve Social Protection Centre – was designated by the Mental Health Board. Due to a shortage of places, however, it took seven months before the applicant was at last transferred to the centre.

The Court concluded that the proper relationship between the aim of the detention – treatment – and the conditions in which it took place was deficient. This conclusion was reached on the basis of comprehensive reports and observations of the conditions in the psychiatric wing of the Lantin Prison. Thus, inquiries had been made by the President of the Liege Court of First Instance, who on other occasions had dealt with the problems arising from the continued detention in the psychiatric wing of Lantin Prison; the European Committee for the Prevention of Torture and Inhuman or Degrading Treatment or Punishment [hereinafter the CPT] had reported on the conditions in the psychiatric wing, and also the Belgian Government had provided information on the situation. The Court found that these reports and observations "show sufficiently clearly that the Lantin psychiatric wing could not be regarded as an institution *appropriate* for the detention of persons of unsound mind, the latter not receiving either regular medical attention or a therapeutic environment [author's emphasis]." Moreover, the Mental Health Board had expressed the view "that the situation was harmful to the applicant, who was not receiving the treatment required by the condition that had given rise to the detention."[64]

What is worth noticing is that the Court – in contrast to the *Ashingdane case* – was prepared to make an assessment of its own as to whether the institutional facilities were *appropriate* or not. The decision is so much more interesting, since delayed transfer from prisons to the Paifve Social Protection Centre constituted a *general* problem, which had been dealt with previously by the Belgian judiciary. It was a question of capacity, of resource allocation, and by holding that Belgium had been in breach of Article 5 (1)(e) the Court indirectly interferes with what is traditionally considered a matter of general social policy.

However, the decision is very concrete, and the Court does not entirely rule out that the detention of a mentally ill person, who is found not to be criminally responsible in a psychiatric prison could be consistent with Article 5 (1)(e) if the conditions were more favourable. In this respect the Court's interpretation of Article 5 (1)(e) is not necessarily consistent with Article 12 (1) of the European Prison Rules according to which "[p]ersons who are suffering from mental illness and whose state of mental health is incompatible with detention in a prison should be detained in an establishment specially designed for the purpose."[65] The European Prison Rules recognise that some mental problems can be dealt with within prisons and have taken into account that psychiatric hospitals are sometimes reluctant with regard to admitting mentally ill offenders. Thus, the rules proceed in the following way in Article 12 (2):

> If such persons are nevertheless exceptionally held in prison there shall be special regulations that take account of their status and needs.[66]

---

[64] *Aerts v. Belgium*, para. 49.

[65] Recommendation Rec (2006) 2 of the Committee of Ministers to member states on the European Prison Rules.

[66] The requirement has been relaxed compared to the previous prison rules. Article 100 (1) of the 1987 prison rules had the following wording: "Persons who are found to be insane should not be detained in prisons and arrangements shall be made to move them to appropriate establishments for the mentally ill as soon as possible", cf. Recommendation No. R (87) 3 of the Committee of Ministers to member states on the European Prison Rules.

Nevertheless, the prison rules recognise that mental illness and imprisonment may be incompatible and that Member States are obliged to take the necessary measures to make sure that the patients in question can be admitted to psychiatric hospitals. This is worth emphasising considering the fact that offender mental patients generally are considered troublesome, and many mental institutions are reluctant to admit these patients out of consideration for other patients – as was the case in *Ashingdane*. One cannot rule out that some psychiatric prisons are able to offer treatment and care of a quality very much similar to that provided by psychiatric hospitals. However, if the notion of lack of criminal responsibility is to be taken seriously, it would indeed be logical to insist at the very least that offenders who are found not to be responsible for their acts be confined in institutions designed for purposes of treatment rather than punishment. However, as it will be argued below in Section 2.4.2 it seems to me more appropriate to attach importance to what specialists in psychiatry, psychology or social treatment recommend in regard to placement of the person in question.

The question of resource allocation was similarly at stake in two Dutch cases, *Brand v. the Netherlands* and *Morsink v. the Netherlands*. The cases concerned offenders who had been sentenced to fifteen months imprisonment in combination with an order for their confinement in a custodial clinic, a 'TBS order' (*Terbeschikkingstelling*). Neither of the two were, however, transferred on the day the TBS order took effect, but were held in pre-placement detention in remand centres while waiting for place in the custodial clinic selected for them for respectively six months (Brand) and 15 months (Morsink). The reason for the delays was in both cases lack of capacity in the custodial clinics, a problem which had existed for decades. The Dutch Government had made some efforts to overcome the problem and, furthermore, made amendments to the legislation in order to legalise continued stay in remand centres after the TBS order had taken effect. Under the rules in force prior to 1997 a six-month delay was acceptable. Under the rules in force as from 1997 the six-month period could be extended by further periods of three months – in principle indefinitely – under the observation of certain procedural requirements. Pursuant to this legislation the Dutch authorities had considered respectively the first six (Brand) and 15 months (Morsink) of pre-placement detention to be lawful.

Both applicants claimed before the Court that the prolonged detention in remand centres was in non-compliance with Article 5 (1)(e) as from the day the TBS order took effect. They took the view that as from that day there was no relationship between the placement in a remand centre and the objective of the deprivation of liberty – namely treatment.

The Court found that the detention of the two applicants fell within both subparagraphs (a) and (e) as from the day the TBS order took effect, but could not accept the argument that the failure to admit the applicants to custodial clinics on that exact date was unlawful under Article 5 (1)(e). The Court stated that "it cannot as such, be regarded as contrary to Article 5 § 1 of the Convention to commence the procedure for selecting the most appropriate custodial clinic [....] only after the TBS order has taken effect." The Court, moreover, stated that:

> it would be unrealistic and too rigid an approach to expect the authorities to ensure that a place is immediately available in the selected custodial clinic. It accepts that, for reasons linked to the efficient management of public funds, a certain friction between available and needed capacity in custodial clinics is inevitable and must be regarded as acceptable.

However, the Court went on as follows:

> Consequently, a reasonable balance must be struck between the competing interests involved. On this point, reiterating the importance of Article 5 in the Convention system, the Court is of the opinion that in striking this balance particular weight should be given to the applicant's right to liberty. A significant delay in admission to a custodial clinic and thus the beginning of the treatment of the person concerned will obviously affect the prospects of the treatment's success within the statutory two-year time-frame, for the initial validity of the TBS order. Moreover the chances of having to prolong the validity of the TBS order will, correspondingly, be increased.
>
> The Court cannot find that, in the circumstances of the present case, a reasonable balance was struck. Bearing in mind that the problem of a lack of capacity in custodial clinics had been identified by the Netherlands authorities as early as 1986 and having found no indication in the instant case that, at the material time, the authorities were faced with an exceptional and unforeseen situation, the Court is of the opinion that even a delay of six months in the admission of a person to a custodial clinic cannot be regarded as acceptable. To hold otherwise would entail a serious weakening of the fundamental right to liberty to the detriment of the person concerned and thus impair the very essence of the right protected by Article 5 of the Convention.[67]

Not surprisingly, the Court is primarily preoccupied with the issue of respect of liberty. However, the quotation illustrates that the Court is increasingly aware of the strong link between the existence of treatment and the duration of detention. The Court recognises that the right to liberty has a social as well as a civil element, and is accordingly prepared once again to interfere with the resource allocation of domestic authorities, the likely result of the case being that the Netherlands will have to speed up the establishment of more custodial clinics.[68]

---

[67] *Ibid.*, paras. 65 and 66 (*Brand*) and similarly (*Morsink*) paras. 68 and 69.

[68] In *Kolanis v. the United Kingdom* about the conditional discharge of a mentally ill woman from a hospital the Court found no violation of Article 5 (1). The decision to discharge the

2.4.2 *The Choice Between Article 5 (1)(a) and Article 5 (1)(e)*

If a court or a competent administrative authority decides – on the basis of opinions made by specialists in psychiatry, psychology or social treatment – that an offender is to be placed in a hospital or another institution designed for purposes of treatment, it would be fair to assume that subparagraph (e) is of relevance regardless of the circumstances in other respects. A hermeneutic contextual interpretation of Article 5 (1) would take into account the actual need for treatment, a need which surmounts the need for punishment, and this need for treatment is not necessarily depending on the legal basis for the confinement.

Sometimes mentally ill offenders are declared not criminally responsible. They are therefore acquitted and if need be placed in a psychiatric hospital for treatment. Placement in a psychiatric hospital or a social institution might, however, also replace confinement in a prison if – after conviction – the domestic court finds that treatment is a more appropriate solution. Furthermore, imprisonment and treatment can be combined – as in the cases *Brand* and *Morsink*. One can serve a prison sentence in an institution designed for purposes of treatment if prison authorities find it appropriate. Some develop mental illness during a term of imprisonment and are therefore transferred to a mental hospital temporarily, and others are transferred as a transition to (conditional) release. Very often crime and health are closely interconnected. Drug addicts commit crime in order to be able to buy drugs, and the mentally ill often lose control to an extent which does not qualify for lack of criminal responsibility. One can think of many situations, and criminal law in COE Member States does not deal with the issue in the exact same way. A common feature is, however, that criminal law provides for the possibility of choosing treatment as an alternative to imprisonment, and the punitive purpose thereby gives way to treatment purposes.

The Court has dealt with aspects of this issue on a number of occasions. Case law, however, is not entirely transparent, and the need for treatment has not always been decisive for the choice between subparagraphs (a) and (e). In the case *X v. the United Kingdom* the applicant was convicted of crime but sentenced to medical treatment in a hospital instead of punishment due to severe mental illness. The Court found that the applicant was 'convicted' in the sense of subparagraph (a) because he was found guilty of crime. However, since the domestic court had chosen to confine him in a mental hospital also

applicant conditionally was not implemented due to the fact that no psychiatrist was willing to give her ambulatory treatment. The Court, however, found a violation of Article 5 (4), cf. Judgment of 21 June 2005. In *Mocarska v. Poland*, Judgment of 6 November 2007 the Court found a delay of 8 months in the admission of a person to a psychiatric hospital as contravening Article 5 (1).

subparagraph (e) applied.[69] Moreover, the Court suggested – but left open – the possibility that the continued applicability of subparagraph (a) might be doubtful in a situation where a conditionally released person has enjoyed a lengthy period of liberty before being re-detained in a mental health institution.[70] That the applicability of subparagraph (a) might be dependent on the stage of the treatment also appears from the *Johnson case* concerning an offender who was also placed by a court order in a mental hospital subject to a restriction order without time limit. The Court stated that it "had not been disputed that the lawfulness of the applicant's detention [....] falls to be determined on the basis of Article 5 § 1 (e) to the exclusion of Article 5 § 1 (a)"[71] as from the day the Tribunal found him no longer suffering from mental illness, cf. above under Section 2.4.1.

In the case *Silva Rocha v. Portugal*, the domestic court had found that "the established facts constituted the offences, of which the applicant had been accused, namely aggravated homicide and unlawful possession of arms."[72] It also found that the applicant, who was suffering from mental disturbance, could not be held criminally responsible for his actions. These circumstances led the Court to hold that the decision of the domestic court was "both a 'conviction by a competent Court' within the meaning of Article 5 para. 1 (a) [....] and a security measure taken in relation to a person of unsound mind within the meaning of Article 5 para. 1 (e) [....]."[73]

In the case *Aerts v. Belgium*, however, the Court would not recognise the relevance of subparagraph (a). The Court attached importance to the fact that:

> [a]lthough the Committal Chamber of the Liège Court of First Instance found that Mr. Aerts had committed acts of violence, it ordered his detention on the ground that at the material time and when he appeared in court he had been severely mentally disturbed, to the point where he was incapable of controlling his actions [....]. *As he was not criminally responsible*, there could be no "conviction" within the meaning of paragraph 1 (a) of Article 5 [....] [author's emphasis].[74]

The fact that Aerts was not criminally responsible should not in principle hinder the application of subparagraph (a). However, Aerts *was* never convicted. He was detained pursuant to a provision in the Belgian Social Protection Act according to which "the detention of an *accused* who has committed a

---

[69] *X v. the United Kingdom*, Judgment of 5 November 1981, para. 39.

[70] Ibid.

[71] *Johnson v. the United Kingdom*, para. 58.

[72] *Silva Rocha v. Portugal*, Judgment of 15 November 1996, para. 26.

[73] *Ibid.*, para. 27.

[74] *Aerts v. Belgium*, para. 45.

serious crime" and is suffering from a mental disorder making him incapable of controlling his actions may take place in a special institution [author's emphasis]. That explains better than the reference to the lack of criminal responsibility why subparagraph (a) was not applicable.

As indicated above, one can think of a substantial number of ways in which treatment and other reactions to crime can be combined, and decisions can be taken on the subject by courts and administrative bodies in a variety of ways, some of which have been dealt with by the Court. The Court has found that both subparagraphs apply when a person is sentenced to imprisonment and placement at the disposal of the government with committal to a psychiatric institution.[75] Unanswered, however, is the question whether subparagraph (e) will also apply, if such later placement is not part of the sentence, but deemed necessary by the prison authorities because the prisoner has developed a mental illness during his detention and transfer to a psychiatric hospital is delayed or hindered due to the health authorities. If a mentally ill prisoner's continued stay in a prison is to be assessed under subparagraph (e), it is fair to claim that there is no longer a satisfactory relation between ground and placement. Moreover one can think of a variety of conditions requiring social, psychiatric or psychological treatment. The need of a social client for treatment for alcoholism or drug abuse is not necessarily less urgent than that of a mentally ill person.

The case *Bizzotto v. Greece*[76] illustrates aspects of this issue. Bizzotto, who was a drug addict, was sentenced to six years of imprisonment for drug trafficking. Greek legislation prescribed the existence of special drug addiction units and prisons with medical facilities, and the national court ordered his placement in an appropriate prison or in a State hospital where he could receive treatment for drug addiction. However, Bizotto was never admitted to such an institution for the simple reason that they were non-existent. He served his sentence in an ordinary prison without any special medical facilities. Bizzotto argued before the Court that his detention was not lawful because there was an obvious contrast between the conditions in which the Greek courts had ordered him to be detained and those in which he was in fact held. He further argued that the lack of treatment affected the duration of the detention since a conditional release was dependent on whether he had undergone treatment for his drug dependence.

The Court reiterated its statement from the *Ashingdane* case, namely that there must be some relationship between the grounds of permitted deprivation of liberty relied on and the place and conditions of detention. However,

75 Cf. *Erkalo v. the Netherlands*, Judgment of 2 September 1998, para. 51.

76 *Bizzotto v. Greece*, Judgment of 15 November 1996.

the Court avoided Bizzotto's (in my opinion highly relevant) argument by stating that the detention should be considered in the light of subparagraph (a), and (a) only, since the ground of the detention was drug trafficking (the offence) rather than drug addiction (the state of health). Accordingly the 'Ashingdane requirement' regarding the relation between grounds and placement did not apply.

The Court added that it recognised the humanitarian nature of the Greek legislation (although inoperative) but underlined that the relevant provisions "lay down merely the arrangements for implementing sentences. Although such arrangements may sometimes be caught by the Convention – in particular where they are incompatible with Article 3 [....] – they cannot, in principle, have any bearing on the 'lawfulness' of a deprivation of liberty."[77]

This way of reasoning – which gives little legal security to the convicted person – does not seem consistent. In previous case law the Court has found both subparagraphs to be applicable, if a person is convicted of criminal offences but placed in a mental institution as a preferable solution to punishment.[78] The difference between *Bizzotto v. Greece* and the previously mentioned cases where both subparagraphs applied is that Bizzotto was a drug addict, whereas the other applicants were mentally ill. Moreover, Bizzotto was sentenced to imprisonment to be served in a special institution, and the sentence was fixed to six years of imprisonment. There was no indeterminate element. Furthermore, the Court left it to the authorities to decide whether he should be placed in "an appropriate prison or in a State Hospital where he can receive treatment for drug addiction." The applicants in the cases previously mentioned were not sentenced to imprisonment. They were to be placed by court order in psychiatric hospitals or other appropriate institutions.

However, subparagraph (e) lists drug addicts on line with mentally ill persons, and it seems to me to be of little importance whether the fixing of a sentence to imprisonment is inserted between the conviction and the decision to place the offender in an institution designed for purposes of treatment. The need for treatment is the same, and the fact that criminal law in the COE Member States is not designed in the exact same way should in my opinion not be decisive. That Bizzotto could have served his sentence in "an appropriate prison" does not justify the differential treatment either. The treatment should nevertheless be determined by the Ministry of Health, Welfare and Social Security[79], and what seems to me important is that the appropriate facilities were not in place in the prison system nor elsewhere.

---

77 *Ibid.*, para. 34.

78 Cf. e.g. *X v. the United Kingdom, Johnson v. the United Kingdom and Silva Rocha v. Portugal.*

79 *Bizzotto v. Greece*, para. 15.

It is of course a fact that Bizzotto was convicted by a competent court. However, he was also deemed to be a drug addict, and the domestic court considered it appropriate that he be treated for his drug addiction. Against this background it does not seem self-evident to me that the Court had to make a choice between the two subparagraphs. The right answer lies between the two subparagraphs.[80] If both provisions had applied, the Court would have had to consider also the relationship between the drug addiction and the actual placement. As the detention was based on subparagraph (a) alone, because Bizzotto was considered a drug trafficker rather than a drug addict in need of treatment, an ordinary prison without special health facilities would suffice. If, on the other hand, the *Bizzotto case* were also to be considered under subparagraph (e), the 'Ashingdane requirement' would apply, and the assessment would probably turn out differently, since the prison in which he served his sentence could only provide him with sleeping tablets.[81]

The Commission took a similar position by stating that it was "incumbent on the State to provide the infrastructure to meet the requirements in Law no. 1729/1987" on the prevention of drug trafficking and the protection of young persons"[82] and drew a parallel to the *Bouamar* case.[83] Subsequent reference could also be made to the case *D. G. v. Ireland*,[84] to the *Aerts* case and to the cases *Brand* and *Morsink* referred to above.

Considering the strong links between drug addiction and (drug related) crime, the decision in the *Bizzotto* case seems discouraging to me. Moreover, treatment programmes for drug addiction are much more developed today than was the case when the Convention was adopted, and I see no reason why the Court in this case – as in so many other cases – could not take a more coherent and contemporary approach to the issue by focusing on the contextual circumstances of the case and on the need of Bizzotto to undergo treatment.

2.4.3 *Forward-Looking Observations on Deprivation of Liberty for Purposes of Treatment*

On the basis of existing case law I must conclude that a person who is detained because of his mental or social condition can claim very few 'positive' rights

---

80 Craig Scott has (convincingly) argued that the right answer might sometimes be found between rights and in the combined interstitial zones of a treaty understood as a system of values and interests, cf. Craig Scott, "Towards the Institutional Integration of the Core Human Rights Treaties" in *Giving Meaning to Economic, Social and Cultural Rights*, Isfahan Merali & Valerie Oosterveld (eds.), University of Pennsylvania Press, 2001, pp. 7–38 (on p. 30).

81 *Bizzotto v. Greece*, para. 29.

82 *Ibid.*

83 *Bouamar v. Belgium*, Judgment of 29 February 1988.

84 *D.G. v. Ireland*, Judgment of 16 May 2002.

regarding treatment. Article 5 (1) is interpreted as a provision permitting the deprivation of liberty because of social or mental instability for indeterminate periods of time. However, the Court finds very few corresponding obligations to give the detainee a right to treatment even though treatment will often be the means that can bring the detention to an end. The Court has been willing to accept the need for medical and social care as an *argument* for even very drastic measures, but the Court has only to a limited degree been willing to recognise an *obligation* to provide for the medical and social care that is likely to shorten the duration of these very drastic measures.

One can say that the Court in its interpretation of Article 5 (1) has focused mainly on the 'negative' obligation. A person may be deprived of his liberty, when a social or mental disorder has been proven if certain procedural rules are followed, and if there is a *relation* between the ground for the confinement and the actual placement. If a person is lucky to recover with or without treatment, the confinement can and should be brought to an end.[85] Demanding a relation between ground and placement may of course have 'positive' and resource-demanding implications, but what the Court requires is primarily an institutional framework. What happens inside the institution is irrelevant to the interpretation of Article 5 (1), but can of course be covered by Article 3, cf. Section 2.5.

A contextual and coherent interpretation of Article 5 (1) would take into consideration the strong link between inappropriate treatment and (extended) confinement and read into the provision a *minimum core right* to treatment without which confinement cannot be considered proportional. The right of Member States to deprive people of their liberty ought to bear upon the rights of the detained person or *vice versa*; the duty to tolerate confinement requires a corresponding duty of Member States to provide for treatment.

One could object to this conception by claiming that the purpose of confinement is not exclusively that of treatment out of consideration for the detainee. In this respect subparagraph (e) is not as clear as subparagraph (d), which speaks of "the purpose of educational supervision". Detention pursuant to subparagraph (e) often serves the purpose of protecting society from dangerous and violent persons, some of whom might never recover to a state of health where they do not pose a threat to society. Article 5 (1)(e) brings together a very diverse group of people, who might have little in common, and from a contemporary view one could ask why minors have their own subparagraph while other vulnerable groups are crowded together in a common subparagraph. It is very much to the point when van Dijk and van Hoof wrote that it

[85] Cf. *Winterwerp v. the Netherlands.*

seems "as if they were all infected by a disease from which society has to be protected [....]."[86]

This protective purpose of Article 5 (1)(e) might have an impact on the interpretation of the Court and explain the reluctance to read 'positive' minimum core rights to treatment into the provision. However, it can still be maintained that the protective purpose should not have appreciable significance. One could claim that other detainees as well as staff inside the institution are part of society as well. They too can claim protection, and if adequate treatment is not provided, the only means of protection is to isolate and subdue the violent patient in potential contravention with Article 3. Furthermore, this patient has a right to personal liberty, which becomes hollow if it is reduced to a procedural right. Detaining a person for indeterminate periods of time without offering 'positive' and qualified medical and social assistance will sooner or later be out of proportion to the purpose, depending of course on the circumstances. Treating the untreatable can hardly be considered a human rights obligation. The obligation in this situation must be to provide as much comfort as possible for the individual who will have to spend his (entire) life deprived of his liberty.[87] A principle to be discerned from case law is exactly that of maintaining a proper balance between the general and the individual interest, and one might question whether this balance can be upheld without accepting a 'positive' minimum core right to treatment under Article 5 (1)(e). That would be a proper hermeneutic interpretation of the situation.

One can discuss how far it is possible to go and how far one should go, but I believe that some re-interpretation is possible and desirable. The purpose of protection of society has probably remained unchanged since the adoption of the Convention. The conception of rights of mentally ill, drug addicts and other vulnerable groups has, however, changed over the years, and so have the social and medical measures suitable for their reintegration into society. The mentally ill e.g. are no longer to be confined in closed institutions, and the tendency in all COE Member States has been to de-institutionalise and provide for their treatment as integrated members of society. Moreover, measures for the treatment of other vulnerable groups such as drug addicts have been developed as part of institutional regimes within prisons and other closed or

---

86 Cf. P. van Dijk and G.J.H van Hoof, *Theory and Practice of the European Convention on Human Rights*, Kluwer Law International, 3rd Edition, 1998, p. 360.

87 Cf. *Hutchison Reid v. the United Kingdom* in which the applicant claimed that detention in a hospital under subparagraph (e) requires that the condition is susceptible to treatment. It was pointed out, however, by the authorities that the applicant derived benefit from the hospital environment and that his symptoms became worse outside the supportive structure. The Court accordingly found a sufficient relationship between the grounds of the detention and place and conditions of detention.

open institutions. It seems to me fair to ask whether this altering attitude towards vulnerable groups should not have an impact on the interpretation of Article 5 (1)(e).

A hermeneutic interpretation of Article 5 (1) (e) will take into consideration the altered perception of treatment of mentally ill persons and abusers and indeed also the purpose of detention according to subparagraph (e). A re-interpretation will of course have to be performed in the light of the division of powers, cf. Chapter 10, and will not be pursued in detail in this context. A minimum core right to treatment or comfort of detained people might initially have to be established according to the Constitutional Court of South Africa's 'reasonableness test'.[88] However, that should not keep the Court from cautiously increasing the protection on a case by case basis and thereby gradually develop legal principles for the assessment of social and health-related issues related to the right to personal liberty. Today the 'positive' right to compulsory treatment consists of a requirement as to the placement in the sense that the institution must be 'authorised' for the purpose of the detention. What happens inside the authorised institution is, however, irrelevant to Article 5 and must be assessed under Article 3 solely.

How far Article 3 reaches with respect to 'positive' requirements as regards health care in (psychiatric) hospitals and other institutions authorised for purposes of treatment remains to be seen.

The Court has only to a limited degree dealt with this issue, cf., however, below on health conditions in prisons.

2.5 *Health Conditions in Prisons*

2.5.1 *General Prison Conditions*

It is a commonly recognised principle that imprisonment should merely entail depriving a person of his freedom of movement, and that all other fundamental rights remain intact during detention. This principle is reflected in the European Prison Rules[89] and in CCPR Article 10 according to which all persons deprived of their liberty shall be treated with humanity and with respect for the inherent dignity of the human person. Moreover, the penitentiary system shall comprise treatment of prisoners the essential aim of which shall be their reformation and social rehabilitation. A similar provision is not contained

[88] Cf. *Government of the Republic of South Africa and Others v. Grootboom and Others*, CCT 11/00 of 4 October 2000 (Constitutional Court of South Africa) and *Minister of Health and Others v. Treatment Action Campaign and Others*, CCT 8/02 of 5 July 2002 (Constitutional Court of South Africa).

[89] Recommendation Rec (2006) 2 of the Committee of Ministers to member states on the European Prison Rules, paras. 39–48.

in the ECHR. However, it would be fair to say that particularly Article 3 of the ECHR has been interpreted as covering not only 'negative' but also 'positive' obligations with respect to health and well-being, and the absence of a provision similar to CCPR Article 10 hardly has as an implication that the protection under the ECHR is poorer. Thus, the Court has held on several occasions that:

> under this provision the State must ensure that a person is detained in conditions which are compatible with respect for his human dignity, that the manner and method of the execution of the measure do not subject him to distress or hardship of an intensity exceeding the unavoidable level of suffering inherent in detention and that, given the practical demands of imprisonment, his health and well-being are adequately secured by, among other things, providing him with the requisite medical assistance.[90]

This does not necessarily imply that detention centres have an obligation to establish medical facilities comparable to those available for people who are not detained. In *Khudobin v. Russia* the Court puts it as follows:

> The Court accepts that the medical assistance available in prison hospitals may not always be at the same level as in *the best medical institutions* for the general public. Nevertheless, the State must ensure that the health and well-being of detainees are adequately secured by, among other things, providing them with the requisite medical assistance [....] [author's emphasis].[91]

By emphasising that the relevant standard of comparison is *the best medical institutions*, the Court more than suggests that a certain minimum of health care is required. Moreover, it is also incumbent on States to give detained persons access to clean drinking water, adequate food, fresh air, exercise, sanitation and other facilities which are considered necessary for the prevention of sickness. In addition, considering the fact that a detention centre cannot cope with all aspects of mental and psychical health, the prohibition against inhuman and degrading treatment might – depending on the context – entail an obligation to transfer him to another environment which will be able to deal with the situation in an appropriate manner.[92] It follows that the Court presupposes that there is a general (human) right to medical assistance *outside* the detention centre.

The normative content of ECHR Article 3 has been tested on several occasions, and something general can be said as regards the minimum requirements under this provision even though the assessment of the minimum level is relative. "[I]t depends on all the circumstances of the case, such as the

[90] Cf. e.g. *Kudla v. Poland*, Judgment of 26 October 2000, para. 94.
[91] *Khudobin v. Russia*, Judgment of 26 October 2006, para. 93.
[92] Cf. e.g. *Ibid.*, para. 92.

duration of the treatment, its physical and mental effects and, in some cases, the sex, age and state of health of the victim [....]".[93] The quotation suggests that the Court has abandoned its original approach by which it considered each issue *per se* and not as a part of a bigger picture.[94] The Court now favours another criterion according to which Article 3 can be violated by the *cumulative* effect of various factors each of which would not necessarily amount to ill-treatment. This criterion of the cumulative effects of various forms of ill-treatment fits very well into hermeneutic conception of the relationship between the detail and the whole, just as the evolution of case law over the years makes up a very good illustration of the horizontal movement of the hermeneutic circle.

In early case law the Court stated that inhuman ill-treatment had to be deliberate for it to run contrary to Article 3. However, this perception of the provision has been abandoned, as the Court now states that the absence of a 'positive' intention of humiliating or debasing a detained person cannot rule out a finding of a violation of Article 3. What is decisive is whether the treatment *objectively* must be considered inhuman or degrading, and an omission to improve e.g. sanitary facilities might amount to a violation. In *Peers v. Greece* "the applicant had to spend a considerable part of each 24-hour period practically confined to his bed in a cell with no ventilation and no window, which would at times become unbearably hot. He also had to use the toilet in the presence of another inmate and be present while the toilet was being used by his cell mate."[95] And in the case *Dougoz v. Greece* the applicant allegedly was "confined in an overcrowded and dirty cell with insufficient sanitary and sleeping facilities, scarce hot water, no fresh air or natural daylight and no yard in which to exercise. It was even impossible for him to read a book because his cell was so overcrowded."[96] In both cases did the Court find that the conditions amounted to a violation of Article 3. Also in *Ahmet Öskan and Others v. Turkey*[97] did the Court find a violation of Article 3 because the conditions in which the applicants had been held in detention in two unfurnished rooms in the basement of the gendarme station, for periods of between six and thirteen days, had had detrimental effects on their health and well-being.[98]

---

93 Cf. e.g. *Peers v. Greece*, Judgment of 19 April 2001, para. 67.

94 Cf. the lengthy description in Antonio Cassese, "Prohibition of Torture" in R.St.J. Macdonal et al. (eds.) *The European System for the Protection of Human Rights*, Martinus Nijhoff Publ., 1993, pp. 225–261.

95 *Ibid.*, para. 75.

96 *Dougoz v. Greece*, Judgment of 6 March 2001, para. 45.

97 *Ahmet Öskan and Others v. Turkey*, Judgment of 6 April 2004, para. 354.

98 Solitary confinement for almost a year, however, has not been considered in violation of Article 3, cf. *Rohde v. Denmark*, Judgment of 21 October 2005.

In *Kalashnikov v. Russia*[99] the Court found a violation of Article 3 because the applicant spent close to five years in a cell so overcrowded that the detainees had to take sleep turns. In addition, there was no adequate ventilation, the cell was infested with pests causing various skin diseases and fungal infections, and he was detained on occasions with persons suffering from syphilis and tuberculosis. Moreover, the applicant had to use the toilet in the presence of other inmates and be present while the toilet was being used by his cellmates.

The Russian Government acknowledged that conditions of detention in Russia – for economic reasons – were very unsatisfactory compared to requirements set for penitentiary establishments in other COE Member States. So did the Ukrainian Government in three later cases from 2003 concerning prison conditions very much similar to those described in the *Kalashnikov* case. This gave rise to the following comment from the Court:

> The Court has also borne in mind, when considering the material conditions in which the applicant was detained and the activities offered to him that Ukraine encountered serious socio-economic problems in the course of its systemic transition and that prior to the summer of 1998 the prison authorities were both struggling under difficult economic conditions and occupied with the implementation of new national legislation and related regulations. *However, the Court observes that lack of resources cannot in principle justify prison conditions which are so poor as to reach the threshold of treatment contrary to Article 3 of the Convention* [author's emphasis].[100]

The statement is very much similar to that made by the HRC in General Comment No. 21 on CCPR Article 10 according to which "the application of this rule, as a minimum, cannot be dependent on the material resources available in the State party [….]."[101] Moreover, it indicates that the Court – and the HRC – recognise the concepts of *minimum core rights* or *decency thresholds*, which are otherwise developed by the ICESCR and the ECSR in relation to the reporting procedures under the CESCR and ESC/RESC. The language used by the Court resembles that of the ICESCR in General Comment No. 3:

> In order for a State Party to be able to attribute its failure to meet at least its minimum core obligations to a lack of available resources it must demonstrate that every effort has been made to use all resources that are at its disposition in an effort to satisfy, as a matter of priority, those minimum obligations.[102]

---

99 *Kalashnikov v. Russia*, Judgment of 15 July 2002.

100 *Khokhlich v. Ukraine*, *Kuznetsov v. Ukraine* and *Poltoratskiy v.* Ukraine, Judgments of 29 April 2003, paras. 181, 128 and 148. Similar language is applied e.g. in *Dybeku v. Albania*, Judgment of 18 December 2007, para. 50.

101 CCPR *General Comment No. 21*, Humane Treatment of Persons Deprived of Liberty (Art. 10):.10/04/92, para. 4.

102 CESCR *General Comment No. 3*, The Nature of States parties obligations (Article 2, para 1):.14/12/90, para. 10 and L. Samuel, *Fundamental Social Rights: Case law of The European*

On the face of it, the acceptance of a positive minimum core right under Article 3 of the ECHR seems notable. However, Article 3 is a rule from which no derogation is allowed, not even in time of war or other public emergency threatening the life of the nation, cf. Article 15 (2), and given the fact that the Court has long ago recognised the notion of 'positive' obligations also under Article 3, one could argue that this recognition bears with it the recognition of the notion of minimum core obligations or decency thresholds.

Finally, what is characteristic of many of the above-mentioned judgments and also of some mentioned above in Section 2.4 and below in Section 2.5.2[103] is that the Court leans on investigations carried out by the CPT. The Court often refers to the Committee's statements not as its primary legal basis, but as "relevant international material", thereby indicating that the European Convention for the Prevention of Torture and Inhuman or Degrading Treatment or Punishment is a relevant source in the interpretation of Article 3 of the ECHR.[104] This practise confirms once again the relevance of discussing the Court's interpretation of the Convention as a hermeneutic interpretation involving not only the ECHR but also other human rights instruments.[105]

2.5.2 *Prisoners with Special Needs*

The cases referred to above primarily concern the interpretation of Article 3 when applied to prisoners with no special needs. A few judgments, however, illustrate how the needs of particularly vulnerable groups might influence the interpretation of Article 3; cf. the hermeneutic conception of interpretation as application.

The Court has time and again stated that deprivation of liberty involves an inevitable element of suffering or humiliation and has distanced itself from the view that Article 3 lays down a general obligation to release a detainee on health grounds or to place him in a civil hospital to enable him to obtain a particular kind of treatment:

Social Charter 78, Council of Europe, 1997. See also Scott Leckie, "Violations of Economic, Social and Cultural Rights" in Theo C. van Boven et al. (eds.), *The Maastricht Guidelines on Violations of Economic, Social and Cultural Rights*, SIM Special No. 20, Netherlands Institute of Human Rights, 1998, pp. 35–86.

103 Cf. e.g. *Peers v. Greece, Dougoz v. Greece, Kuznetsov v.Ukraine, Poltoratskiy v. Ukraine, Khokhlich v. Ukraine, Brand v. the Netherlands and Morsink v. the Netherlands.*

104 That is also the case in *Elci and Others v. Turkey* about torture and ill-treatment of Kurds in Turkish prisons, cf. Judgment of 13 November 2003.

105 For violation of Article 3 due to lack of medical and hygiene facilities in prisons cf. also *Melnik v. the United Kingdom*, Judgment of 28 March 2006, *Popov v. Russia*, Judgment of 13 July 2006 and *Boicenco v. Moldova*, Judgment of 11 July 2006.

> Nevertheless, under this provision the State must ensure that a person is detained in conditions which are compatible with respect for his human dignity, that the manner and method of the execution of the measure do not subject him to distress or hardship of an intensity exceeding the unavoidable level of suffering inherent in detention and that, given the practical demands of imprisonment, his health and well-being are adequately secured by, among other things, providing him with the requisite medical assistance.[106]

It is obvious that some prisoners are more likely than others to be subject to distress or hardship, and conditions must be tailored to the needs and interests of particularly vulnerable groups. A healthy person requires less comfort and care than a sick or disabled person and these differences are reflected in case law. In *Price v. the United Kingdom* the applicant was four-limb deficient as a result of phocomelia due to thalidomide[107] and suffered from problems with her kidneys. In the course of civil proceedings she refused to answer questions put to her concerning her financial situation and was committed to prison for seven days (which in practise meant three and a half) for contempt of court. The sentencing judge took no steps to ascertain where she would be detained or to ensure that it would be possible to provide facilities adequate to cope with her severe level of disability. It later proved that the police and prison authorities were in fact unable to cope with the special needs of the applicant. During the first night of detention her kidney problems worsened because the cell was too cold, and since she was unable to use the bed she had to sleep in her wheel chair. Even though she was transferred the following day to a health care centre in a prison, her misery continued since she was unable to use the toilet, and she had to tolerate being lifted on and off the toilet by male prison officers. The applicant consumed very little fluid, and by the time of her release she had to be catheterised because of the lack of fluid intake and problems in getting to the toilet had caused her to retain urine. The Court concluded as follows:

> There is no evidence in this case of any positive intention to humiliate or debase the applicant. However, the Court considers that to detain a severely disabled person in conditions where she is dangerously cold, risks developing sores because her bed is too hard or unreachable, and is unable to go to the toilet or keep clean without the greatest of difficulty, constitutes degrading treatment contrary to Article 3 of the Convention. It therefore finds a violation of this provision *in the present case* [author's emphasis].[108]

Even though no one could possibly doubt that the Court's finding refers to *the present case*, the Court might have wanted to underline – as it often does – that

---

106 Cf. e.g. *Kudla v. Poland*, Judgment of 26 October 2000, para. 94.

107 A birth defect in which the hands and feet are attached to abbreviated arms and legs.

108 *Price v. the United Kingdom*, Judgment of 10 July 2001, para. 30.

the finding of a violation of Article 3 was due to the very exceptional circumstances and that little can be derived from the judgment as to the general content of Article 3. The legal content of Article 3 is dependent on the context.

The argumentation in *Mouisel v. France* is worth mentioning in the same breath. Mouisel was sentenced to fifteen years of imprisonment in 1996. However, in 1999 he was diagnosed with leukaemia and began cancer treatment in the form of chemotherapy sessions at the prison hospital. After some time, however, he withdrew his consent to the treatment because he found the conditions unsatisfactory and humiliating for the reason among others that he was handcuffed during transport to and from the hospital. A medical report stated that the cancer treatment was "scarcely compatible with imprisonment"[109] and concluded that he should be looked after in a specialist unit. Subsequently the applicant was transferred to Muret Prison (so that he would be nearer to Toulouse University Hospital), and he was given a cell of his own. After some time he resumed treatment at Toulouse University Hospital. However, his condition had deteriorated.

During the course of events he applied several times for a pardon on medical ground, but his applications were refused. Eventually – in 2001 – he was granted parole.

In its assessment of the events the Court attached importance to the fact that the applicant's health was found to be giving more and more cause for concern and to be increasingly incompatible with detention. The Court, moreover, drew attention to the applicant's psychological situation, which had been aggravated by the stress of being ill and had affected his life expectancy and caused his health to decline. The Court concluded as follows:

> All those factors show that the applicant's illness was progressing and that the prison was scarcely equipped to deal with it, yet no special measures were taken by the prison authorities. Such measures could have included admitting the applicant to hospital or transferring him to any other institution where he could be monitored and kept under supervision, particularly at night.[110]

In its final conclusion – that there had been a violation of Article 3 – the Court furthermore took into consideration the conditions under which he had received his treatment. The Court stated that although handcuffing does not normally give rise to an issue under Article 3, the use of handcuffs was nevertheless disproportionate to the needs of security, having regard to the applicant's physical weakness and to the discomfort of undergoing a chemotherapy session. Thus, there was no significant danger of the applicant's absconding or resorting to violence. In this context the Court – once again – referred to the

---

[109] *Mouisel v. France*, Judgment of 14 November 2002, para. 17.

[110] *Ibid.*, para. 45.

recommendations given by the CPT, and also to soft law instruments from the COE Committee of Ministers concerning ethical aspects of health care in prisons. In conclusion, the Court did not find that the authorities took sufficient care of the applicant's health, and that his continued detention undermined his dignity and entailed particularly acute hardship that caused suffering beyond that inevitably associated with a prison sentence and treatment for cancer.[111]

Lack of attention to the special needs of a prisoner was similarly the matter in *McGlinchey and Others v. the United Kingdom* about an asthmatic intravenous heroin addict, who suffered from withdrawal symptoms during her detention. She was constantly vomiting, and her weight was recorded as dropping from 50 to 40 kg within five days. During that time her condition was monitored by the prison health care staff. On the seventh day, however, her situation deteriorated dramatically, and she was brought to hospital where she died after a couple of weeks.

The evidence before the Court revealed that the prison scales were inaccurate, and that there had been gaps in the monitoring by the prison health care staff. The Court concluded as follows:

> Having regard to the responsibility to provide the requisite medical care for detained persons, the Court finds that in the present case there was a failure to meet the standards imposed by Article 3 of the Convention. It notes in this context the failure of the prison authorities to provide accurate means of establishing Judith McGlinchey's weight loss, which was a factor that should have alerted the prison to the seriousness of her condition, but was largely discounted due to the discrepancy of the scales. There was a gap in the monitoring of her condition by a doctor over the weekend when there was a further significant drop in weight and a failure of the prison to take more effective steps to treat Judith McGlinchey's condition, such as her admission to hospital to ensure the intake of medication and fluids intravenously, or to obtain more expert assistance in controlling the vomiting.[112]

The applicant's son in *Tarariyeva v. Russia* was diagnosed as having a perforated duodenal ulcer and peritonitis and was operated at Apsheronsk public hospital. Later he was diagnosed with a breakdown of sutures in the duodenum, duodenal fistula and peritonitis. Nevertheless, he was discharged from the hospital and transported to a prison hospital, the Khadyzhensk colony. After undergoing further surgery he died. After having examined the case, the Court held as follows:

> For more than two years preceding his death Mr Tarariyev had been in detention and the custodial authorities had been fully aware of his health problems. There was no consistency in his medical records, most of which were either mislaid or

[111] *Ibid.*, paras. 47 and 48.

[112] *McGlinchey and Others v. the United Kingdom*, Judgment of 29 April 2003, para. 57.

> incomplete. At the Khadyzhensk colony he was not properly examined and did not receive any medical treatment. Although he was promptly transferred to a public hospital, the surgery performed was defective. The doctors of the Apsheronsk hospital authorised his discharge to the prison hospital in full knowledge of the post-operative complications requiring immediate further surgery. They also withheld crucial details of Mr Tarariyev's surgery and developing complications. The prison hospital staff treated him as an ordinary post-operative patient rather than an emergency case with the consequence that surgery was performed too late. Furthermore, the prison hospital was not adequately equipped for dealing with massive blood loss.[113]

The Court accordingly concluded that there had been a violation of Article 2. The Court also found a violation of Article 3 due to the fact that Mr. Taraiyeva who was "unfit for transport"[114] had been transported 120 km between the two hospitals in a standard-issue prison vehicle. In the final analysis, the Court considers that the national authorities failed to take sufficient care of the applicant's health to ensure that he did not suffer treatment contrary to Article 3 of the Convention, at least until his transfer to an external haematological hospital on 8 February 2008.[115]

The above-mentioned cases illustrate in each their way what might lead to a violation of Articles 2 and 3, although they do not delineate what is the proper conduct of prison staff. Nor do they reveal which medical facilities one can demand when detained in a prison in serious need of treatment and care. However, they do indeed confirm that Articles 2 and 3 have a 'positive' content as regards health care which should be taken into consideration by prison authorities at the domestic level, and I cannot but endorse the Court's conclusions in the above-mentioned cases.[116] The cases in question all concerned somatic treatment. The question is whether the Court applies a similar approach when it comes to prisoners in dire need of *psychiatric treatment*.

---

[113] *Tarariyeva v. Russia*, Judgment of 14 December 2007, para. 88.

[114] *Ibid*., para. 36.

[115] Cf. also *Aleksanyan v. Russia*, Judgment of 22 December 2008 concerning the treatment of an AIDS patient in a Russian prison. The Court found that the stay in prison without adequate care undermined his dignity and entailed particularly acute hardship, causing suffering beyond that inevitably associated with a prison sentence and the illnesses he suffered from. This amounted to inhuman and degrading treatment, and there had therefore been a violation of Article 3 of the Convention.

[116] Cf. also *Khudobin v. Russia*, Judgment of 26 October 2006 in which the Court found a violation of Article 3 because the applicant who suffered from a variety of serious diseases was denied the right to medical assistance. Similarly, in *Hüseyin Yilderim v. Turkey*, Judgment of 3 May 2007, the Court found a violation of Article 3 because of the prison conditions offered to a severely disabled man. Cf. also e.g. *Gorodnichev v. Russia*, Judgment of 24 May 2007 and *Yakovenko v. Ukraine*, Judgment of 25 October 2007.

In *Aerts v. Belgium* the applicant was suffering from a severe mental disturbance which made the Court decide that he should be transferred to an institution to be designated by the competent Mental Health Board. As mentioned above in Section 2.4.1 he was, however, not transferred and spent more than nine month in the psychiatric wing of a prison under conditions which were unsatisfactory and not conducive to the effective treatment of the inmates. The CPT had considered the standard of care to fall below the minimum acceptable from an ethical and humanitarian point of view, and that prolonging the detention of people awaiting transfer to an appropriate institution carried an undeniable risk of deterioration of their mental health. A prison psychiatrist had declared that:

> it would seem that he urgently requires the full benefits of an institution better equipped to calm the constant anxiety he feels at the moment. It is therefore an urgent matter for him to be able to leave the psychiatric wing of Lantin Prison.[117]

Finally, the Mental Health Board had stated that "the failure of administration on the part of the responsible authorities is harmful to the person concerned, who is not getting the treatment required by the conditions which led to his detention."[118] The Court nevertheless found no violation of Article 3. The Court attached importance to the fact that:

> [....] there is no proof of a deterioration of Mr Aert's mental health. The living conditions on the psychiatric wing at Lantin do not seem to have had such serious effect on his mental health as would bring them within the scope of Article 3. Admittedly, it is unreasonable to expect a severely mentally disturbed person to give a detailed or coherent description of what he has suffered during his detention. However, even if it is accepted that the applicant's state of anxiety, described by the psychiatrist [....] was caused by the conditions of detention in Lantin, and even allowing for the difficulty Mr Aerts may have had in describing how these had affected him, it had not been conclusively established that the applicant suffered treatment that could be classified as inhuman or degrading.[119]

Considering the fact that the applicant had to endure for *nine* month an institutional regime which was not at all conducive to his recovery, and taking into consideration the strong recommendation from psychiatric experts, it seems to me that the Court places (too) much emphasis on the lack of evidence as regards a deterioration of the applicant's health. The general conditions were objectively described as unsatisfactory and unethical, and experts had strongly criticised the delayed transfer in the concrete case. Against this background it seems to me less important that the applicant himself might not have been able

---

[117] *Aerts v. Belgium*, para. 9.

[118] *Ibid.*, para. 12.

[119] *Ibid.*, para. 66.

to describe his suffering in great detail. Nor does it seem to me to be crucial that the lack of treatment did not seem to have a lasting effect. It might have been intolerable while it lasted.[120]

Nor did the Court find a violation of Article 3 in *Kudla v. Poland* concerning a detained person suffering from disorders such as depression, sleep disturbances, tension and difficulty in concentrating. He was attended by medical staff on a regular basis and given medical treatment of various sorts. During his detention he twice attempted suicide and was subsequently transferred to the psychiatric ward of the prison hospital for closer observation and treatment. It appears from the case that the prison authorities considered the second suicide attempt to be of an "attention-seeking nature". At the request of the Court, the applicant was examined by psychiatrists from a university in Cracow, who concluded as follows:

> These disorders are not psychotic in nature but further suicide attempts will prove to be a real threat to his health. For this reason, we also consider that if the legal proceedings require that the defendant spend a further period in prison, he should be sent to a hospital ward and be supervised by specialist staff. He should also be guaranteed access to a psychiatrist and a psychologist.[121]

The Court – wisely – refrained from expressing a view on whether the second suicide attempt was "attention-seeking"[122], but did not find anything to show that the authorities could be held responsible for what happened. The Court accepted that:

> the very nature of the applicant's psychological condition made him more vulnerable than the average detainee and that his detention may have exacerbated to a certain extent his feelings of distress, anguish and fear. It also takes note of the fact that [....] continuing detention could jeopardise his life because of a likelihood of attempted suicide [....] However, on the basis of the evidence before it and assessing the relevant facts as a whole, the Court does not find it established that the applicant was subjected to ill-treatment that attained a sufficient level of severity to come within the scope of Article 3 of the Convention.[123]

The Court's explanation is rather vague, and one might wonder why it does not pay closer attention to the recommendations in the psychiatric report. The Court seems to accept the risk of another attempted suicide as long as the authorities do what can reasonably be expected within the institutional

120 With regard to treatment of psychiatric patients cf. also e.g. *Kucheruk v. Ukraine*, Judgment of 6 September 2007.

121 *Kudla v. Poland*, para. 40.

122 *Ibid.*, para. 97. One might argue, however, that even *if* the suicide attempt was in fact "attention-seeking", the dramatic way of seeking this attention does in itself call for serious concern.

123 *Ibid.*, para. 99.

framework available. The point, however, seems to be that the institutional framework available was inappropriate, since the staff were not qualified to deal with the applicant's mental disorder. It is of little help to the psychiatric patient in question that staff take great effort to alleviate pain and suffering if the fundamental problem is that they are not trained to provide what the situation requires.

The situation in *Keenan v. the United Kingdom* was different. Keenan was suffering from paranoid schizophrenia and died from suffocation (asphyxia) caused by self-suspension whilst he was serving a sentence of four months' imprisonment. During his detention he was segregated and later subject to disciplinary punishment. The Court found no violation of Article 2, and in the examination under Article 3 the Court stated that "it is not possible to distinguish with any certainty to what extent his symptoms [....] or indeed his death, resulted from the conditions of his detention imposed by the authorities."[124] The Court, however, considered that this difficulty was not determinative and attached importance to the absence of notes concerning his mental condition, and to the fact that a prison doctor, unqualified in psychiatry, had made changes in his medication without consulting a psychiatrist. The Court concluded as follows:

> The lack of effective monitoring of Mark Keenan's condition and the lack of informed psychiatric input into his assessment and treatment disclose significant defects in the medical care provided to a mentally ill person known to be a suicide risk. The belated imposition on him *in those circumstances* of a serious disciplinary punishment – seven days' segregation in the punishment block and an additional twenty-eight days to his sentence imposed two weeks after the event and only nine days before his expected date of release – which may well have threatened his physical and moral resistance, is not compatible with the standard of treatment required in respect of a mentally ill person. It must be regarded as constituting inhuman and degrading treatment and punishment within the meaning of Article 3 of the Convention [author's emphasis].[125]

Thus, it was not the psychiatric treatment alone that led to a violation of Article 3. Rather, it was the imposition of segregation and disciplinary punishment *in those circumstances* that were determinative, and the judgment does not tell anything specific with regard to the required standard of mental health care in prisons. It remains to be seen whether or not the Court makes stronger demands for the production of evidence with regard to psychiatric patients detained in prisons than is the case with regard to other patients. However, neither the wording of – nor the preparatory works to – Article 3[126] would prevent an

124 *Keenan v. the United Kingdom*, Judgment of 3 April 2001, para. 112.

125 *Ibid.*, para. 116.

126 Cf. Antonio Cassese who describes how the drafters of Article 3 "wisely favoured the old maxim *omnis definitio periculosa est*", *Ibid.*, pp. 225–261 (on p. 227).

interpretation paying more attention to the needs of the mentally ill, and in that context more use could be made of the European Prison Rules as a legal source. The European Prison Rules constitute a valuable set of standards very much in line with *modern* conceptions of appropriate treatment of prisoners[127], and would in many ways – as minimum standards – provide an excellent yardstick in the assessment of whether or not Article 3 has been complied with.

2.6 *Protection of Neglected Children*

Article 8 of the ECHR allows for children to be removed from their family and taken into public care if that is necessary for the protection of their rights. Thus, Article 8 (2) speaks of "the rights and freedoms of others" without, however, mentioning which rights. It would be fair to assume that the rights referred to are not only the ones protected by the ECHR, cf. the distinction between "rights and freedoms". On the basis of case law one must assume that the rights referred to in Article 8 (2) also encompass economic, social and cultural rights, since numerous cases accept the necessity of interference in family life because parents have not been able to provide for their children's upbringing, education, clothing, nutrition and need for treatment and care. Moreover, Article 8 (2) speaks of the "protection of health and morals".

However, the content of such a right is not defined, and it is implied that social welfare authorities actually provide for the treatment, care and education of children who have been removed from their family. In that way, the situation resembles that concerning Article 5 (1) (d) and (e), and seen from the perspective of the child at least some removals would be covered both by Article 5 (1)(d) and Article 8 (2). It would seem meaningless to remove children from their parents for reasons of lack of care, if it were not incumbent upon States to provide exactly that which caused the interference in family life – namely lack of care. As a minimum, one might argue, there must be a relationship between the grounds of the removal of the child and the actual placement, cf. the Ashingdane requirement referred to above in Section 2.4. Thus, it might raise an issue under Article 8 (2) if a child is removed from his family without consent and placed in an environment which is not at all prepared to meet its special needs. The situation is not impractical, cf. e.g. *Scozzari and Giunta v. Italy* about placement in a controversial community 'Il Forteto'. The Court did not express an opinion as regards the adequacy of the community as such, but attached importance to the fact that two of the principal

[127] The present European Prison Rules have replaced a previous set of rules from 1987 for the exact reason that those rules were out of date, cf. the Preamble to Recommendation Rec (2006) 2 of the Committee of Ministers to member states on the European Prison Rules.

leaders were convicted of ill treatment and sexual abuse of three handicapped people previously staying in the community.[128] There is no reason to believe that children in foster care are always guaranteed either their civil and political rights or their economic, social and cultural rights, and the absence of specific 'positive' requirements once again illustrates how inappropriate it is to uphold the distinction between the two sets of rights. Human rights are – *or ought to be* – indivisible, interdependent and interrelated. However, the situation has not been dealt with in case law in a way which allows for many comments let alone conclusions, and since it very much resembles the one discussed above in Section 2.4, it shall not be pursued further in this context.

Instead two other issues will be discussed. One is the interest of the child in being taken into public care if a continued stay with the parents puts its physical and psychological development at risk. The other is the mutual interest of the family – the child and the parents – in social assistance appropriate for the prevention of the child being removed in the first place or – if a removal has been deemed necessary – to shorten the period in which the child is in foster care. I will begin with social welfare authorities' obligation to take measures if parents are not for one reason or the other able to cope with the situation themselves.

The Court has dealt with this issue of protection on a number of occasions. In *A v. the United Kingdom* the Court stated that Article 3 requires States to take measures designed to ensure that individuals within their jurisdiction are not subjected to ill treatment, including such ill treatment administered by third parties.[129] With reference to the Convention on the Rights of the Child [hereinafter the CRC] Articles 19 and 37 the Court recalled that also children are entitled to such protection.[130]

In *Z and Others v. the United Kingdom* four children had been neglected and abused by their parents to an extent which reached the threshold of inhuman and degrading treatment. The treatment had been brought to the attention of the local authorities who were under the statutory duty to protect children and had a range of powers to do so, including the removal of the children from their home. Nevertheless, the children in question had been subject

[128] *Scozzari and Giunta v. Italy*, Judgment of 13 July 2000 paras. 204–208.

[129] *A v. the United Kingdom*, Judgment of 23 September 1998, para. 22.

[130] The case concerned a nine-year-old boy who had been beaten with a garden cane by his stepfather, an event which led to the stepfather's charge with assault occasioning actual bodily harm. The stepfather was, however, acquitted by the domestic court who did not find that the punishment went beyond what was reasonable according to domestic law. The Court found that the treatment reached the level of severity prohibited by Article 3, and considering that the domestic court had acquitted the stepfather, the Court concluded that the law did not provide adequate protection against treatment or punishment contrary to Article 3.

to appalling neglect over an extended period and suffered severe physical and psychological injury. The Court acknowledged the difficult and sensitive decisions facing social services and the important principle of respecting and preserving family life. The Court concluded, however, that the present case "leaves no doubt as to the failure of the system to protect these applicant children from serious, long-term neglect and abuse."[131]

The Court did not point out which measures should have been taken, and the judiciary as such is hardly the right body to decide on such issues, at least not in the first instance. What can be learnt from the decision is only that *something* should have been done, and this something is likely to change as the situation in the family changes over time. At an early stage help and guidance might be sufficient. However, as the situation deteriorates, the demands as to which measures are appropriate increases accordingly. The last recource – which is also the most demanding – the removal of the children from their home, is mentioned in the judgment as one out of a variety of not specified possibilities. However, considering the horrific experience to which the children had been subjected, it can hardly be doubted that the proper measure in the abovementioned case eventually was the removal of the children from their home. Thus, once again the Court has indirectly dictated the domestic resource allocation and delineated the way in which to handle future similar cases.

The case *E and Others v. the United Kingdom* illustrates a similar failure of the social service authorities to intervene in family affairs to the detriment of the right to psychical and psychological health of children. Four grown-up siblings claimed to have been sexually abused by their stepfather when they were children and asserted that the social welfare authorities should have intervened. The stepfather had previously been convicted of sexual abuse of two of the children and sentenced to two years of probation. The probation officer had made it clear to him that due to the character of the offence he could no longer cohabitate with the children's mother. However, this condition was not respected, and it appeared from the case that the social welfare authorities suspected this to be the case. Moreover, the social records revealed that some of the children had shown serious levels of distress and disturbance, they had ran away from home, taken overdoses of pills etc. Yet, the authorities did not cooperate in taking the steps necessary to discover the exact extent of the problem and, potentially, to prevent further abuse from taking place.

The Court held that the authorities should have been aware that the children remained at potential risk and concluded as follows:

> The Court is satisfied that the pattern of lack of investigation, communication and co-operation by the relevant authorities disclosed in this case must be regarded as

[131] *Z and Others v. the United Kingdom*, Judgment of 10 May 2001, para. 74.

> having had a significant influence on the course of events and that a proper and effective management of their responsibilities might, judged reasonably, have been expected to avoid, or at least, minimise the risk or the damage suffered.[132]

The cases referred to above illustrate the resource demanding obligation of authorities to take measures to protect children's physical and mental health from abuse from third parties. Under certain circumstances – i.e. if the neglect is serious enough – children have a right to be taken care of by public authorities if their parents for one reason or the other are not able to provide secure and considerate surroundings. From the perspective of Article 8 (2) one might say that the right of authorities to interfere with family life for the protection of health turns into a duty if children's health is seriously threatened cf. the passage "for the protection of health [....] or the protection of the rights and freedoms of others".

However, one might also ask whether or to which extent public authorities have an obligation to take measures with the view to *reuniting* the families that have been broken up. The ECHR builds on the presumption of the family as a unity, and family life does not cease to exist because children are placed in foster care.[133] Such measures would include help towards the solution of the problems that led to the forcible removal of the child in the first place and could encompass treatment for drug or alcohol addiction, various forms of therapy and social assistance and services in general. Moreover, one could ask whether the right to family life also requires the existence of similar measures for the *prevention* of families' disintegration. In other words, do parents have a right under the ECHR to social and medical assistance if such assistance is necessary for the prevention of the disintegration of the family?

Case law does not provide much of an answer. However, such obligations might be incumbent on Member States under very specific circumstances. If parents' endeavours to hold together their threatened family or to reunite a family that has already been broken up are not supported or even opposed by social authorities, such behaviour might raise an issue under Article 8. Moreover, if authorities at an early stage of family disintegration choose to remove a child instead of providing appropriate help, the removal of the child might be considered out of proportion to the aim.[134] Similarly, a total denial of the existence

---

132 *E and Others v. the United Kingdom*, Judgment of 26 November 2002, para. 100 and *D.P. and J.C. v. the United Kingdom*, Judgment of 10 October 2002. However, the Court did not find that the authorities could be regarded as having failed in any 'positive' obligation to take effective steps to protect the children from abuse.

133 Cf. also the Preamble to the CRC and Articles 18 and 19 of the CRC.

134 Cf. e.g. *Haase v. Germany*, Judgment of 8 April 2004 about the removal of a new-born baby depriving the baby of close contact with its natural mother and of the advantages of breastfeeding.

of family ties between parents and a child placed in foster care would be likely to raise an issue under Article 8.

In the case *Olsson v. Sweden* the separation of three children and the placement of two of them at a long distance from the home of the applicants together with restricted visiting rights were considered a violation of Article 8, since it ran counter to the ultimate aim of the reunification of the family.[135] The separation of the children was partly due to shortage of foster families, and one might interpret the decision in the sense that a justification of interference in family life presupposes the existence of appropriate institutions or foster homes. In fact, the Court has often stated that Article 8 "includes a right for the natural parent to have measures taken with a view to their being reunited with their children [....] and an obligation for the national authorities to take such measures."[136] However, most cases concern restrictions in the rights of parents to keep up contact with the children or opposition to the reunification on the part of foster parents, both issues of significance to the reunification of parents and children.[137] A child who stays for a very long time in a foster home with no or little contact to its natural parents is likely to develop a stronger affiliation with the foster parents. Even though the restriction of visiting rights might have been in non-compliance with Article 8, the interest of the child in not having its family situation changed once again may override that of the natural parents in reunification.[138] Thus, the time factor is crucial, and if the aim is to reunify a disintegrated family measures towards the rehabilitation of natural parents should start on day one.

The issue of getting the natural family back on its feet by 'positive' social measures has not been dealt with by the Court. Delineating the character and the extent of such an obligation is therefore hardly possible on the basis of existing case law. From a sociological perspective the indivisibility, interdependence and interrelation between family life and active social measures is evident. From a legal perspective, however, these relations between Article 8 and social rights have not yet been established. All one can say is therefore that the full extent of Article 8 remains to be developed, and that future encounters between facts and law will gradually contribute to a more comprehensive understanding of the provision.

---

135 *Olsson v. Sweden (I)*, Judgment of 24 March 1988.

136 *Olsson v. Sweden (II)*, Judgment of 27 November 1992, para. 90.

137 *Olsson v. Sweden (II)*, Judgment of 27 November 1992, para. 90. Cf. e.g. *Margareta and Roger Andersson v. Sweden*, Judgment of 25 February 1992 (violation) and *Hokkanen v. Finland*, Judgment of 23 September 1994 (violation).

138 Cf. e.g. *Rieme v. Sweden*, Judgment of 22 April 1992, *Hokkanen v. Finland* and *K and T v. Finland*, Judgment of 12 July 2001.

2.7 *Information, Professional Secrecy and Freedom of Expression in Health Issues*

Since *Gaskin v. the United Kingdom*[139] it has been recognised that confidential information in personal files – in this particular case records compiled by social services – may relate to "private and family life" in such a way that a question of access thereto falls within the ambit of Article 8.

Gaskin wished to obtain information about his childhood with foster parents in order to be able to overcome his problems and learn about his past, but access to personal records can be important for a variety of reasons. A person whose social situation or state of health is recorded in a file does, however, not have unlimited access. A balance will have to be struck between the interest of the individual and other interests. Likewise, an individual does not have an unlimited right that such information be kept confidential. However, the Court has held as follows:

> [R]especting the confidentiality of health data is a vital principle in the legal systems of all the Contracting parties to the Convention. It is crucial not only to respect the sense of privacy of a patient but also to preserve his or her confidence in the medical profession and in the health services in general.
>
> Without such protection, those in need of medical assistance may be deterred from revealing such information of a personal and intimate nature as may be necessary in order to receive appropriate treatment and, even, from seeking such assistance, thereby endangering their own health and, in the case of transmissible diseases, that of the community.[140]

As important for the right to health is the right to receive information about health issues. Without access to existing information about e.g. occupational health risks, environmental pollution, contagious diseases, etc. one cannot protect oneself from contracting diseases. Moreover, the prospects of curing already contracted diseases are less favourable. Prevention and early medical care are considered pivotal for a well-functioning health service. This issue has been brought before the Court on a few occasions, and several of the Convention's provisions have been invoked.

In the case *Guerra et al. v. Italy*[141] inhabitants in a town, Manfredonia, claimed that the authorities had failed to inform about the risk of pollution from a neighbouring chemical factory and about the procedures to be followed in the event of a major accident. The factory in question was classified as a 'high risk' factory, and accidents had in fact occurred on previous occasions.

---

[139] *Gaskin v. the United Kingdom*, Judgment of 7 July 1989.

[140] *Z v. Finland*, Judgment of 25 February 1997, para. 95.

[141] *Guerra et al. v. Italy*, Judgment of 19 February 1998.

The applicants claimed that pursuant to Article 10 States are obliged to take the initiative to provide such information to the public.

The fact of the matter was that the Italian authorities had been slow in deciding what safety measures should be taken, and what procedures should be followed in the event of an accident. There was no emergency plan to communicate to the public. The Commission, nevertheless, took the stand that an obligation to "collect, process and disseminate" could in fact be derived from Article 10. The Court, however, held that freedom to receive information "cannot be construed as imposing on a State, in circumstances such as those of the present case, positive obligations to collect and disseminate information of its own motion."[142] Article 10 was accordingly not applicable.

Since the toxic emissions from the factory had a direct effect on the applicants' right to respect for their private and family life, Article 8, however, was applicable even though there was no question of "interference" in the traditional sense. What the applicants complained about was that Italy had *failed* to provide information about emergency measures. The Court, however, held that Article 8 had been violated because the applicants had waited in vain for the essential information that would have enabled them to make their own assessments as to whether they would continue living in Manfredonia. The case constitutes a good illustration of the difficulties of making a distinction between the 'positive and the 'negative'.

In *L.C.B v. the United Kingdom*, referred to briefly above in Section 2.3, the applicant claimed that the fact that she suffered from leukaemia was due to her father's exposure to radiation when he participated in nuclear tests and a clean-up programme following the tests on the Christmas Island in 1957–58. It was her opinion that the British authorities had exposed her father to radiation deliberately for experimental purposes, and that the authorities had possessed the necessary information about the genetic effects of radiation. Furthermore, she asserted that her father's unmonitored exposure to radiation was the probable cause of her childhood leukaemia, and claimed that if the United Kingdom had provided her parents with information regarding the extent of her father's exposure to radiation and the risks which this engendered, it would have been possible to diagnose her leukaemia earlier and to provide her with treatment which could have alleviated the risk to her life.

The United Kingdom did not recognise the competence of the Commission to receive individual complaints and the jurisdiction of the Court until 1966. The applicant was diagnosed in 1970. The question before the Court was, therefore, whether the United Kingdom in this period had done all that could have been required to prevent the applicant's life from being avoidably put at risk.

---

142 *Ibid.*, para. 53.

The Court recognised that Article 2 (1) enjoins the State not only to refrain from the intentional and unlawful taking of life, but also to "take appropriate steps to safeguard the lives of those within its jurisdiction."[143] The Court, however, found it uncertain whether the applicant's father had in fact been dangerously eradiated. The Court chose, nevertheless, to examine the question whether, in the event that there was information available to the authorities which should have given them cause to fear that the applicant's father had been exposed to radiation, they could reasonably have been expected, during the period in question, to provide advice to the applicant's parents and to monitor her health.

Based on expert evidence from 1993 doubting such a causal link the Court found conclusively that it could not reasonably hold that "in the late 1960s, the United Kingdom authorities could or should, on the basis of this unsubstantiated link, have taken action in respect of the applicant."[144] Accordingly, the Court found no violation of Articles 2 or 3.[145]

In this context, however, the important lesson to learn is that the Court in principle is prepared to examine whether or not a State has in fact made information about health risks available to those who are likely to be affected. Moreover, the Court recognised the existence of a far from budgetary neutral obligation to "take appropriate steps to safeguard the lives of those within its jurisdiction", cf. Article 2.

Finally, in *I v. Finland*[146] the Court found that insufficient protection of medical records of a HIV-infected nurse constituted a violation of Article 8.

The case Open Door and Dublin Well Women hardly had any budgetary consequences, but provides a good illustration of how *understanding is always application*, cf. Chapter 4.[147] According to Irish criminal law abortion is illegal, and the Irish Constitution protects the right to life of the unborn child from the moment of conception onwards. Nevertheless, Open Door and Public Well Women – both non-profit organisations engaged in counseling pregnant women in Ireland – complained of an injunction imposed by Irish courts to restrain them from providing certain information to pregnant women concerning abortion facilities outside the jurisdiction of Ireland.

The issue before the ECtHR was whether the injunction violated the two organisations' rights under Article 10 (2) of the ECHR according to which the right to freedom of expression may be subject to restrictions only if prescribed

---

143 *L.C.B. v. the United Kingdom*, para. 36.

144 *Ibid.*, para. 39.

145 Cf. CCPR *General Comment No. 14*, Nuclear weapons and the right to life (Art. 6), 1984.

146 *I v. Finland*, Judgment of 17 July 2008.

147 *Open Door and Dublin Well Women v. Ireland*, Judgment of 29 October 1992.

by law and if necessary in a democratic society on one of the grounds specified – one of which is moral.

The Court found that the injunction was prescribed by law, and that it had a legitimate aim – that of the protection of morals. In Ireland, the right to life of the unborn is one aspect of the protection of morals. When having to decide whether the restriction was necessary in a democratic society, the Court furthermore recognised that the Member States have a wide margin of appreciation, *especially* in moral issues. However, the margin is not unlimited. In the determination of whether there existed *a pressing social need*, and whether the restriction complained of was *proportionate to the legitimate aim pursued* the Court attached importance to the very absolute nature of the injunction which imposed a perpetual restraint on the provision on information concerning abortion facilities abroad *regardless of age, state of health or the pregnant women's reason for seeking counseling on the termination of pregnancy*. In addition, the Court attached importance to the fact that the information was available elsewhere in magazines and telephone directories, however, in a manner which was not supervised by qualified personnel and thus less protective of women's health. Moreover, the Court found that the injunction had not prevented large numbers of Irish women from continuing to obtain abortions abroad.

In sum, the Court found that the injunction had created a risk to the health of the women who would have to seek abortions at a later stage in their pregnancy, due to lack of proper counselling, and who did not avail themselves of customary medical supervision after the abortion had taken place. Finally the Court found that the injunction might have had more adverse effects on e.g. women who did not have the necessary level of education to have access to alternative sources of information.[148]

---

[148] In this context mention could also briefly be made of two cases concerning bans imposed on a researcher with a degree in technical sciences and an ophthalmologist respectively. In the first case the ban was imposed on account of the applicant's publication of an article claiming a possible connection between food prepared in microwave ovens and certain pathological disorders that could be seen as the beginning of cancerous conditions. The article had been blown up by the media out of all proportion to the detriment of the producers of microwave ovens. In its assessment of the extent of the margin of appreciation, the Court, however, noted that what was at stake was not "a given individual's purely "commercial" statements, but his participation in a debate affecting the general interest, for example over public health; in the instant case, it cannot be denied that such a debate existed." The issue of public health was, however, not the main focus, and the citation might have had limited importance for the Courts conclusion that the ban was not necessary in a democratic society, cf. *Hertel v. Switzerland*, Judgment of 25 August 1998, para. 51. The other case arose from an interview given by an ophthalmologist to a newspaper about a laser technique with which he – contrary to German rules of professional conduct – had treated more than 400 patients.

The decision illustrates that it makes limited sense to talk about an abstract interpretation of Article 10 of the ECHR. The provision is incomplete as it presents itself to us, and its full legal content is only unveiled in the encounter with real life's concrete events. Article 10 does not only protect freedom of expression for the sake of the expression as such, and the fact that the expression concerns acts which are punishable under domestic law is not necessarily of decisive importance. A hermeneutic understanding of the provision takes into account the purpose of the expression even if this purpose – the protection of women's health – extends into the sphere of economic, social and cultural rights. This interpretation is at the same time the one that brings Article 10 of the ECHR in the greatest possible harmony with the overall human rights norm system, as it derives from the UDHR, and it elucidates the relations between the right to health, the right to education and the right to freedom of expression. Hermeneutics supports the teleological tradition of contextual legal interpretation with its emphasis on effectiveness as it has been developed over the years in case law from the Court.

3 *Future Prospects*

The case law of the ECtHR with regard to the right to health is much diversified, and it is difficult to make general predictions concerning future case law. Noteworthy, however, is the fact that the Court in several connections has recognised that lack of resources is not an acceptable reason not to provide adequate health care, and the right to health is to some extent covered by the ECHR. The protection under the ECHR is absolutely not as comprehensive as that under the ESC/RESC and the CESCR. However, it is demonstrated that case law makes heavy demands on Member States also with regard to resource allocation, and the protection of the right to health has indeed increased over the years. As appeals I have raised criticism towards several of the judgments referred to. However, and more importantly, there is reason to believe that the Court in its future encounter with health-related facts will consider carefully whether it is possible to increase the protection, and one cannot exclude the

What was at stake in this case was the public interest in prohibiting such interviews for "the protection of health and the interests of other medical practitioners and the applicant's right to freedom of expression and the vital role of the press." Since the interview gave a balanced explanation of the techniques, the Court did not find that the interference achieved a fair balance between the competing interests. Accordingly, the applicant's rights under Article 10 had been violated, cf. *Stambuk v. Germany*, Judgment of 17 October 2002.

possibility that more aspects of the right to health will fall within the ambit of the Convention.[149] At least the potential of the Convention with regard to health-related issues is far from exhausted.

Moreover, case law confirms the relevance of having a hermeneutic perspective on the interpretation of the Convention, and that the notion of abstract interpretation has limited meaning. Interpretation is always application.

[149] With regard to health-related social cash benefits, cf. Chapter 8.

Chapter 6

The Right to Housing Under the ECHR

1 *Housing as a Cross Cutting Issue*

The right to housing – like any human right – cannot be viewed in isolation. It is integrally linked to other human rights and fundamental freedoms as they derive from the UDHR, i.e. not only other economic, social and cultural rights but also civil and political rights. Homelessness and poverty are inextricably linked because it is difficult to obtain and maintain a job without a place to live, and education is often impeded for the very same reasons. Street children receive little if any education. Moreover, without facilities for cooking, heating, light, sanitation, washing, sleeping, etc. the risk of contracting diseases increases and lack of security, loneliness and despair are not conducive to health either.

In a modern society, he who has no permanent address from where he can be contacted and make contact is often prevented from exercising his participatory rights including his right to freedom of expression. Moreover, his right not to be subjected to arbitrary interference with his private and family life is threatened, just as he is a more likely victim of violence and other kinds of crime.

Finally, homelessness increases inequality in most aspects of human life and leads to indignity in that everyday behavior for the satisfaction of basic needs and demands is turned into complicated and often illegal action. Cooking, urinating, washing and sleeping are often prohibited in public places, and the homeless person must spend considerable amounts of time searching for places where these basic actions can be performed without interference. Waldron argues that "a rule against performing an act in a public place amounts *in effect* to a *comprehensive* ban on that action so far as the homeless are concerned."[1] What we are dealing with here "is not just 'the problem of homelessness', but a million or more *persons* whose activity, dignity and freedom are at stake."[2]

---

[1] Jeremy Waldron, "Homelessness and the issue of freedom" in *Liberal Rights, Collected Papers 1981–1991*, Cambridge University Press, 1993, p. 332.

[2] *Ibid.*, p. 338.

2 The Relevant Provisions

The right to housing is specifically protected by Article 11 (1) of the CESCR and Article 31 of the RESC.[3] The ECHR, however, does not include a general right to housing which is not surprising as this Convention primarily protects rights which are traditionally considered civil and political rights. The only specific mention of housing rights in the Convention is Article 8 which requires respect for "home".[4] This respect for home is undoubtedly primarily of interest to those who already have a home. As will appear from the following analysis Article 8 might, however, have a wider and more obliging content. On the other hand, the restriction clause in Article 8 (2) allows for interferences serving e.g. "the economic well-being of the country" or "the protection of the rights and freedoms of others" the implication being that e.g. a tenant may have his tenancy terminated or miss out on the opportunity to have his housing situation improved, cf. e.g. *Velosa Barreto v. Portugal* below in Section 5.2. However, such interference may indirectly provide protection within the field of housing to other individuals than the right holder.

Whereas Article 8 applies equally to tenants and holders of real estate, Article 1 of Protocol No. 1 has relevance primarily to those who are already the owners of residential property. There is no right to obtain property. On the contrary, the right to property can be restricted in the same way as the right to respect for "home" if it happens in the "public" or "general" interest, cf. Article 1 (1) and (2). A deliberate and targeted housing policy will often serve the public or general interest, and in this way the provision may provide an indirect protection e.g. of tenancy rights.

The following analysis is not strictly structured under the two substantial provisions of the ECHR referred to. The presentation concentrates on a selection of housing-related issues some of which appear more often and with greater intensity in times of war or conflict. For reasons of clarity I have chosen to separate the 'everyday' housing issues from the 'times of war and conflict' issues although they have been dealt with under the same two provisions.

---

3 The ESC merely provides protection to certain groups such as families (Article 16), migrant workers (Article 19 (4) and elderly persons (Article 4 of the Additional Protocol to the ESC from 1987).

4 The concept of "home" is interpreted rather broadly. In the *Gillow case* the applicants had lived in their house for two years and rented it out for eighteen. The house was, nevertheless, recognised as "home" in the sense of Article 8 due to evidence of a strong continuing link with the house, cf. *Gillow v. the United Kingdom*, Judgment of 24 November 1986. In *Niemietz v. Germany* the business premises of a professional person was recognised as home, cf. Judgment of 16 December 1992. In *Buckley v. the United Kingdom*, a caravan site used as home without planning permission was recognised, cf. e.g. Judgment of 25 September 1996 and in *Demades v. Turkey*, the Court recognised a holiday house as "home", cf. Judgment of 31 July 2003.

Moreover, there is a difference between the rights of tenants and owners to protection from arbitrary and destructive interferences such as eviction from or illegal occupation of a home and having to tolerate interferences as a consequence of a general, deliberate and targeted housing policy of a State Party aiming at the protection e.g. of secure tenure.

Needless to say, the presentation differs from most other presentations of the right to housing. The aim it not to give a thorough overview of housing rights, but merely to prove that it makes sense to talk about *aspects* of the right to housing under the ECHR. The presentation begins with a quite lengthy discussion of a possible State obligation to provide for (lawful) housing under the Convention and goes on to discuss the potential of the principle of non-discrimination in Article 14 with regard to the right to housing. The chapter proceeds with an analysis of judgments in which housing policy considerations have motivated interferences primarily in property rights and thereby indirectly had an impact on the housing situation of other individuals than the right holder. Subsequently follows a discussion of two problems which have frequently occurred in times of war and conflict: demolition of houses and eviction from, illegal occupation of and denied access to residential property or rented homes.

3 *A State Obligation to Provide for (lawful) Housing?*

According to the *wording* of Article 8 the primary focus is the respect of already existing homes, whereas he who has no home apparently enjoys no protection under the ECHR. Similarly, according to the *wording* of Article 1 of Protocol No. 1 the provision protects already acquired possessions, whereas he who has no possessions apparently enjoys no protection. The ECHR primarily aims at preserving already existing positions, and he who wants to obtain a certain good – in this case a place to live – must normally seek elsewhere for the solution to his housing problem.

However, as will appear from the following discussion the Court has stated on numerous occasions that Article 8 and Article 1 of Protocol No. 1 also contain a 'positive obligation' to protect the individual from interferences from third parties. Moreover, the Court has not entirely ruled out that Article 8 might oblige Member States to provide a citizen with a home. Thus in *Marzari v. Italy* the applicant, a severely disabled person, complained that the local administrative authorities had failed to provide him with adequate accommodation. He was in fact offered an apartment for rent but asserted that a previous apartment – from which he had been evicted – was more suitable for his special needs. The Court considered that:

> although Article 8 does not guarantee the right to have one's housing problem solved by the authorities, a refusal of the authorities to provide assistance in this respect to an individual suffering from a severe disease might *in certain circumstances* raise an issue under Article 8 of the Convention because of the impact of such refusal on the private life of the individual [author's emphasis].[5]

However, the Court took note of the fact that the local authorities were willing to carry out further work in the apartment offered to the applicant for rent and make it adequate for his condition. The Court therefore considered "that no positive obligation for the local authorities can be inferred from Article 8 to provide the applicant with a *specific* apartment [author's emphasis]." Accordingly, the application was declared inadmissible.[6] The Court does not rule out, however, that the assessment might have been different had the applicant not been offered this apartment.[7]

The conception that the ECHR in principle may encompass also elements of a more proactive character within the field of housing has, until now, only been translated into practice to a very limited degree. However, in several cases the applicant has claimed that the right to respect for home under Article 8 encompasses also the right to receive a 'residence licence', if such licence is required by the authorities. In *Gillow v. the United Kingdom*[8] the applicants had built a house – "Whitenights" – on Guernsey in which they lived from 1958 to 1960. At that time they had so-called residence qualifications entitling them to live on the island without a licence. In 1960, they left the island to work abroad and let the house to people approved by the housing authorities. When returning after more than eighteen years with the intention of living in the house, they had, however, lost their residence qualifications by virtue of legislation adopted during their absence. They did not fulfil the strict requirements for obtaining a licence to re-occupy their house and were prosecuted for unlawful occupation.

The Court considered that although the applicants had been absent from Guernsey for more than eighteen years, "Whitenights" could still be considered their home in the sense of Article 8. The applicants had not established a home elsewhere, they had always intended to return, and they had kept their furniture in the house. Moreover, the refusal of the licence applied for, the

---

5 *Marzari v. Italy*, Admissibility decision of 4 May 1999.

6 Cf. also *Peter O'Rourke v. the United Kingdom*, Admissibility decision of 26 June 2001.

7 I have chosen to discuss the case *López Ostra v. Spain*, Judgment of 9 December 1994 in the chapter about The Right to Health, cf. Chapter 5, Section 2.3. However, the case does indeed include a housing element, and one might interpret the judgment as recognising a right to alternative adequate housing if the economic well-being of a town requires the existence of a polluting plant.

8 *Gillow v. the United Kingdom*.

institution of criminal proceedings and the conviction of one of the applicants for unlawful occupation constituted interferences with the exercise of their right to respect for home.[9]

The refusal was based on a rather restrictive system of licences for the occupation of houses which was introduced to keep the population within acceptable limits. As Guernsey was in fact a very densely populated island the Court considered that the legislation had a legitimate aim, and that the Guernsey legislature was in a better place to assess the effects of any relaxation of the housing controls. Moreover, when considering whether to grant a licence the authorities could exercise their discretion so as to avoid any disproportionality in a particular case. The statutory obligation imposed on the applicants to seek a licence to live in their home could therefore not be regarded as disproportionate to the legitimate aim pursued.[10]

However, the Court did not find that the manner in which the authorities had exercised their discretion in the applicant's case corresponded to a pressing social need and, in particular, was proportionate to the legitimate aim pursued. The Court took note of the fact that the population of the island had declined – although marginally – and that the availability of houses had not suffered any significant deterioration. Against this background the Court considered that insufficient weight was given to the particular circumstances of the case – as referred to above – and regretted that the authorities had taken steps to prosecute the applicants for illegal occupation. In the Court's view this "did not materially alleviate Mr. and Mrs. Gillow's already precarious situation."[11] The Court therefore concluded that the decision to refuse the applicant's licences to occupy "Whitenights" as well as the conviction and fining of one of the applicants constituted a violation of Article 8.

The decision is very *concrete*, and little can be derived from it with regard to a *general* right to obtain the permission necessary for making one's occupation of a home lawful. The circumstances were unusual and particular, and the

[9] The applicants had also invoked Article 1 of Protocol No. 1. However, at a very late stage of the proceedings the Government informed the Court that the United Kingdom had not extended the application of the Protocol to the island of Guernsey. Accordingly it was not applicable. Article 1 of Protocol No. 1 may, however, be applicable also in cases of refusal of necessary residential permits, cf. Arjen van Rijn (rev.) in P. van Dijk et al. (eds.) *Theory and Practice of the European Convention on Human Rights*, 4td Edition, Kluwer Law International, Intersentia, 2006, p. 872 with reference to *Wiggins v. the United Kingdom*, Admissibility decision of 8 February 1978 also concerning the refusal of a housing licence to the applicant to live in his house. (This case also concerned Guernsey. However, the British Government did not at that time draw attention to the fact that the application of the Protocol did not extend to the island.)

[10] *Gillow v. the United Kingdom*, para. 56.

[11] *Ibid.*, para. 57.

general consequences of this narrowing of the margin of appreciation must be considered limited if at all existent. Thus, the case was very much unlike a series of later cases about Gypsies claiming their right to live in caravans on land acquired for residential purposes, cases in which the Court found no violations of the Covenant.

In the first case *Buckley v. the United Kingdom* the applicant was denied a planning permission to live on her own land and was left to apply for a pitch at an official site for Gypsies nearby. She claimed, however, that the official site was unsuitable for a single woman with children and that her right to respect for home outweighed the public interest in preservation of the environment.

The Court recognised that respect for home could be engaged even though the home in question had been established unlawfully. However, the Court recalled its previous practice to admit the national authorities a wide margin of appreciation in the choice and implementation of planning policies, and held that "the procedural safeguards provided for in the regulatory framework were [....] such as to afford due respect to the applicant's interests under Article 8 [....]."[12] As to the suitability of the official site the Court merely stated that "Article 8 [....] does not necessarily go so far as to allow individuals' preferences as to their place of residence to override the general interests."[13] The Court concluded – on a four-to-three vote – that:

> proper regard was had to the applicant's predicament both under the terms of the regulatory framework, which contained adequate procedural safeguards protecting her interests under Article 8 [....] and by the responsible planning authorities when exercising their discretion in relation to the particular circumstances of her case.[14]

Accordingly, the interference was considered "necessary in a democratic society".

The disagreement in the *Buckley case* between the judges was followed up in 2001 in altogether five very similar cases in which seven out of 17 Grand Chamber judges expressed their common dissenting opinion in quite strong language. In the leading case, *Chapman v. the United Kingdom*, the applicant bought a piece of land in a district without an official Gypsy site. Her application for planning permission was, however, rejected and she was advised to apply for a pitch at sites outside the district. Whether or not such application would have been complied with was most uncertain since overall statistics proved a lack of sites for Gypsy caravans.

The approach of the Court was in many ways similar to that followed in the *Buckley case*, and the Court stated that "it is in the interests of legal certainty,

---

12 *Buckley v. the United Kingdom*, Judgment of 25 September 1996, para. 79.

13 *Ibid.*, para. 81.

14 *Ibid.*, para. 84.

foreseeability and equality before the law that it should not depart without good reason from precedents laid down in previous cases."[15] However, at the same time "the Court must [....] have regard to the changing conditions in Contracting States and respond, for example, to any emerging consensus as to the standards to be achieved [....]."[16] In this context it is worth noticing that the Court as relevant international material chose to list a number of instruments most of which were not adopted or in force at the time when the *Buckley case* was pending. Among the instruments in question was the COE Framework Convention for the Protection of National Minorities from 1995. The Court, however, did not agree with the applicant that the framework convention would narrow the margin of appreciation of Member States. The Court was:

> *not persuaded* that the consensus is sufficiently concrete for it to derive as any guidance as to the conduct or standards which contracting States consider desirable in any particular situation. The framework convention, for example, sets out general principles and goals but the signatory States were unable to agree on means of implementation. This reinforced the Court's view that the complexity and sensitivity of the issues involved in policies balancing the interests of the general population, in particular with regard to environmental protection, and the interests of a minority with possibly conflicting requirements renders the Court's role a strictly supervisory one [author's emphasis].[17]

Moreover, the Court held that it would raise substantial problems under Article 14 to accord to a Gypsy who has unlawfully stationed a caravan at a particular place different treatment from that accorded to non-Gypsies.

The Court *did* find that there is an obligation to facilitate the Gypsy way of life. However, the Court could not accept the argument that, because statistically the number of Gypsies was greater than the number of places available on authorised Gypsy sites, the decision not to allow the applicant Gypsy family to occupy land where they wished in order to install their caravan in itself, and without more, constituted a violation of Article 8:

> This would be tantamount to imposing on the United Kingdom, as on all the other contracting States, an obligation by virtue of Article 8 to make available to the Gypsy community an adequate number of suitably equipped sites. The Court is not *convinced*, despite the undoubted evolution that has taken place in both international law, as evidenced by the framework convention, and domestic legislation in regard to protection of minorities, that Article 8 can be interpreted as implying for States such a far-reaching positive obligation of general social policy [....].
>
> It is important to recall that Article 8 does not in terms recognise a right to be provided with a home. Nor does any of the jurisprudence of the Court

[15] *Chapman v. the United Kingdom*, Judgment of 18 January 2001, para. 70.
[16] *Ibid.*
[17] *Ibid.*, para. 94.

> acknowledge such a right. While it is clearly desirable that every human being have a place where he or she can live in dignity and which he or she can call home, there are unfortunately in the Contracting States many persons who have no home. Whether the State provides funds to enable everyone to have a home is a matter for political not judicial decision [author's emphasis].[18]

The Court recalled that the issue to be determined by the Court was not the acceptability of the general situation, however deplorable, but whether or not the particular circumstances disclosed a violation of the applicant's rights. In this context the Court further held that it would be of relevance to the assessment of the proportionality of the interference whether or not the home was established unlawfully and whether or not alternative accommodation would be available elsewhere.

When applying the above-mentioned general principles to the concrete facts the Court reached the conclusion that Article 8 had not been violated. The Court held that the authorities had given consideration to the applicant's arguments and to her personal circumstances. As to the issue whether alternative accommodation was available elsewhere – outside the county – the Court stated that:

> [n]otwithstanding that the statistics show that there is a shortfall of local authority sites available for Gypsies in the country as a whole, it may be noted that many Gypsy families still live an itinerant life without recourse to official sites and it cannot be doubted that vacancies of official sites arise periodically.[19]

The Court moreover held that there were in fact ordinary caravan sites with planning permission available, and that it was for the applicant to adduce evidence as to what was required of a site to make it suitable, and whether or not she could afford that. Since the applicant had not placed before the Court any information as to her financial situation or as to the qualities a site must have before it would be locationally suitable for her, the Court was "*not persuaded* that there were no alternatives available to the applicant [....][author's emphasis]."[20] However, even if the applicant had demonstrated a financial inability, it would not have helped her. The Court went on to say that "[i]f the applicant's problem arises through lack of money, then she is in the same unfortunate situation as many others who are not able to afford to continue to reside on sites or in houses attractive to them."[21]

As appears from above, the Court several times used the phrase *not convinced* or *not persuaded*, and given the fact that a large minority of seven judges gave a joint and strongly worded dissenting opinion, one cannot conclude that

---

18 *Ibid.*, paras. 98–99.

19 *Ibid.*, para. 111.

20 *Ibid.*, para. 113.

21 *Ibid.*

the legal position of Gypsies as regards planning permissions is definitive. A brief mention of the very comprehensive dissenting opinion might therefore be appropriate.

The dissenting judges' principal disagreement with the majority concerned the assessment that the interference was "necessary in a democratic society". They held that there is in fact an emerging and *sufficiently concrete consensus* among the Member States of the COE recognising the special needs of minorities, and that this consensus includes a recognition that the protection of the rights of minorities such as Gypsies requires that Contracting States take steps to improve their situation through, for example, legislation or specific programmes. The dissenting judges attached importance to the fact that it could not be taken for granted that vacancies existed or were available elsewhere, and that the burden placed on the applicant to prove very special circumstances was extremely high, if not insuperable. It was the opinion of the dissenting judges that "where the planning authorities have not made any finding that there is available to the Gypsy any alternative, lawful site to which he or she can reasonably be expected to move, there must exist compelling reasons for the measures concerned."[22]

Moreover, the dissenting judges could not recognise that the environmental arguments put forward by the Government were of such a nature as to disclose a "pressing social need". They attached importance to the fact that little had been done to increase the number of sites, and that local authorities had disregarded their statutory duty to improve the situation for Gypsies. The dissenting judges (wisely) abstained from suggesting how to solve the problem of long-term failure of local authorities to make effective provisions for Gypsies in their planning policies, but concluded that it was disproportionate to take steps to evict a Gypsy family from their home on their own land in circumstances where there had not been shown to be any other lawful, alternative site reasonably open to them.[23] In this context the dissenting judges noted that Gypsies are not welcome on private residential sites which are in any event often prohibitively expensive, and that the options available to Gypsies were severely limited if existent at all.

The dissenting judges recalled that it is *not* the Court's case-law that a right to be provided with a home is totally outside the ambit of Article 8, cf. the quotation above from para. 99 of the judgment. In the *Marzari case* the Court *did* in principle accept that Article 8 may under certain circumstances oblige authorities to provide housing assistance. Moreover, in the present case the applicant had a home in her own caravan on her own land. Only, she was

[22] *Ibid.*, Joint dissenting opinion, para. 3.

[23] *Ibid.*, paras. 4–5.

prevented from settling there. In this context, the dissenting judges also expressed their disagreement with the majority as regards the issue of discrimination in the case of special treatment of Gypsies. They stated that:

> in this case the applicant's lifestyle as a Gypsy widens the scope to Article 8, which would not necessarily be the case for a person who lives in conventional housing the supply of which is subject to fewer constraints. The situations would not be likely to be analogous. On the contrary, discrimination may arise where States, without objective and reasonable justification, fail to treat differently persons whose situations are significantly different.[24]

The dissenting judges concluded by calling to mind that it would not be a necessary consequence of finding a violation in the case that Gypsies could freely take up residence on any land in the country. Where there were shown to be other sites available, the balance between the interests of protecting the environmental value of the site and the interests of the Gypsy family in residing on it would tip more strongly towards the former.[25] Accordingly, the consequences of finding a violation would not be insurmountable.[26]

It remains to be seen whether the dissenting judges' conception of the issue of *sufficiently concrete consensus* will prevail in the future. Similar cases about obtainment of planning permission have not been brought before the Court. However, in *Connors v. the United Kingdom* about the *withdrawal* of licence and subsequent eviction of a Gypsy family from a local authority site the Court did find a violation of the right to respect for home as the legal framework did not provide the applicant with sufficient procedural protection of his rights.[27] Strictly speaking, the case does not belong in this section having to do with the *withdrawal* of a license. However, the issue is closely related to the one discussed above, and as the Court made a great but in my opinion not quite successful effort to distinguish the case from the previous Gypsy cases, a certain disorder has to be tolerated.[28]

The applicant and his family were evicted from their plot at a Gypsy site where they had lived for thirteen years. A written warning had been given to the applicant because of alleged misbehaviour. However, the eviction was

---

[24] *Ibid.*, para. 8.

[25] *Ibid.*, para. 9.

[26] Cf. also *Beard v. the United Kingdom, Coster v. the United Kingdom, Lee v. the United Kingdom and Jane Smith v. the United Kingdom*, all Judgments of 18 January 2001.

[27] *Connors v. the United Kingdom*, Judgment of 27 May 2004.

[28] The disorder stemming from dealing with *withdrawals* in the context of *provision* illustrates how difficult it is to graduate the human rights obligation into reasonable categories, and that neither the 'positive/negative' dichotomy nor the tripartite obligation to *respect*, *protect* and *fulfil* provides a satisfactory classification reflecting practical situations of everyday life, cf. Chapter 2.

enforced on the basis of a provision permitting the local authorities to give 28 days' notice before regaining summary possession *without* having to prove any breach of licence.

The Government claimed that the provision in question served the purpose of catering for the special needs of Gypsies who live a nomadic life, and that it was necessary in order to address anti-social behaviour on sites. For reasons of flexibility in the management it was therefore considered necessary to exempt Gypsy sites from security of tenure that apply in other areas of accommodation in the United Kingdom. Moreover, to require local authorities to justify their management decisions would add significantly to their administrative burden and would reduce the flexibility intended by the framework.[29]

The Court, however, attached importance to the fact that a substantial majority of Gypsies no longer travel and that most sites are residential in character. Moreover, the mere fact that anti-social behaviour occurs on local authority sites did not in the Court's opinion justify a summary power of eviction since such problems also occur in other local authority housing estates. Accordingly, the Court was not persuaded that there were any particular features about local authority Gypsy sites which would render their management unworkable if they were required to establish reasons for evicting long-standing occupants.

The Court did recognise the complexity of the situation being enhanced by the apparent shift in habit in the Gypsy population remaining "nomadic in spirit if not in actual or constant practice"[30] However, the Court was:

> not persuaded that the necessity for a statutory scheme which permitted the summary eviction of the applicant and his family has been sufficiently demonstrated by the Government. The power to evict without the burden of giving reasons liable to be examined as to their merits by an independent tribunal has not been convincingly shown to respond to any specific goal or to provide any specific benefit to members of the gypsy community.[31]

Consequently, the Court did not find that the interference could be regarded as justified by a "pressing social need" or proportionate to the legitimate aim being pursued. There had, accordingly, been a violation of Article 8.

In all the 'Gypsy cases' referred to, the Court emphasised that the vulnerable situation of Gypsies as a minority means that special consideration should be given to their needs and their particular lifestyle both in the relevant regulatory framework and in reaching decisions in particular cases. "To this extent, there is a positive obligation imposed on the Contracting States by virtue of

[29] *Ibid.*, para. 79.
[30] *Ibid.*, para. 93.
[31] *Ibid.*, para. 94.

Article 8 to facilitate the gypsy way of life."[32] However, only in *Connors* did the Court narrow the margin of appreciation by referring to the seriousness of the interference even though the other applicants were as seriously affected. They were all homeless or about to be homeless, and the fact that their situation stemmed from differing events hardly make any appreciable difference.

The Court distinguished the *Conners case* from *Chapman v. the United Kingdom* by referring to the fact that the present case was "not concerned with matters of general planning or economic policy but with the much narrower issue of procedural protection for a particular category of persons."[33] In addition, Chapman had breached planning law in taking up occupation of land without licence, whereas Connors was lawfully on the site.[34]

It seems to me, however, that both arguments are slightly feeble. Firstly, the *reason* for the lack of procedural protection granted to Connors was according to the Government the need for flexibility in the management of local authority sites, which is a somewhat broader issue than "the policy of procedural protection for a particular category". Secondly, while it is true that Connors was *originally* lawfully on the site the case only began as his presence was no longer in accordance with the law, and because he refused to vacate the plot. Considering the fact that the case concerned the issue of whether the domestic legal framework provided the applicant with sufficient legal protection, it seems to me a bit strained to attach much importance to whether or not the applicant had originally complied with a legal provision, when this provision is later on overruled as not being in keeping with the Convention. There is of course a difference between not having a licence to begin with and not complying with the later withdrawal of one originally enjoyed lawfully. However, the distinction hardly justifies a very differential treatment, and in any case it is not the applicant's respect for domestic statutory law which is to be assessed but rather the State's respect for international human rights.

Despite the efforts to distinguish the cases from one another, one might ask whether the Court in *Connors* began making cautious concessions to the dissenting judges in *Chapman* and the other previous cases. It seems to me at least that the Court in *Connors* shows a more nuanced understanding of the Gypsy life style than was the case in previous cases. One cannot entirely rule out that pre-understanding as regards the treatment of Gypsies might be undergoing a change, and what can be said for the time being is only that nothing in either of the judgments would prevent the Court from deviating from the line set out in

[32] *Ibid.*, para. 84 with reference to *Buckley v. the United Kingdom* and *Chapman v. the United Kingdom*.

[33] *Ibid.*, para. 86.

[34] *Ibid.*

Buckley, *Chapman* and the other four cases from 2001 if or when similar cases in the future are brought before the Court. New and slightly different facts might add to the legal content of Article 8 the interpretation of which might also be revised due to altering conceptions as regards the treatment of minorities. However, until now it has to be concluded that an obligation to provide for (lawful) housing under the ECHR has only been suggested in an even very cautious way and primarily with regard to exceptional circumstances or very vulnerable groups. It has, however, been suggested, and one cannot exclude that the examination of future cases will add to the legal content of Article 8.

4 *The Right to Housing and the Principle of Non-Discrimination*

It has been recognised on more than one occasion that the right to housing falls within the ambit of Article 8. If or when applied in conjunction with Article 14, Article 8 might therefore lead to a quite comprehensive protection of the right to housing depending of course on the circumstances in the COE Member States as regards housing policy and legislation. The same applies to Article 1 of Protocol No. 1 if the property in question is residential.

In *Larkos v. Cyprus*[35] the applicant, a retired civil servant, had rented a house from the Cypriot State in which he had lived together with his family for many years. When he retired the authorities terminated the lease asserting that the premises had been allocated to him by administrative order because of his position in the civil service. The applicant, however, contended that he had been unlawfully discriminated against in the enjoyment of his right to respect for his home on account of the fact that he – unlike a tenant renting from a private landlord – was not protected from eviction.

The Court found that the fact relied on fell within the ambit of Article 8 and noted that the lease made no reference to the fact that the house was let to the applicant in his capacity of civil servant, and it did not mention either that the subsistence of the lease was dependent on his continued employment in the civil service. There was no mention either of the consequences resulting from his retirement or resignation from the civil service. Moreover, the terms of the lease in general indicated clearly that the State let out the property in a private-law capacity. The Court therefore considered that the applicant could claim to be in a similar situation to that of other private tenants who rent from private landlords.

As to the possible justification of the differential treatment the Court considered that "in the instant case the Government have not provided any

[35] *Larkos v. Cyprus*, Judgment of 18 February 1999.

convincing explanation of how the general interest will be served by evicting the applicant".[36] Accordingly, there had been a violation of Article 8 in conjunction with Article 14.

Larkos v. Cyprus is illustrative of the fact that the listing of criteria in Article 14 is not exhaustive, cf. the expression "[....] or other status". The same applies to *Karner v. Austria*[37] about the right of a homosexual man to succeed to the tenancy after the death of his partner. They had lived together for a number of years as a couple and shared the outgoings on the flat. The applicant had nursed his partner while he was sick with AIDS and was designated as his heir.

After his death the landlord, however, brought proceedings against the applicant for termination of the tenancy. According to Section 14 of the Austrian Rent Act "a life companion" is entitled to succeed to the tenancy under certain conditions. However, the domestic Constitutional Court found that the legislature's intention in 1974 – when the Rent Act was adopted – was not to include persons of the same sex.

The Court found that the subject matter of the case fell within the ambit of Article 8 since the differential treatment adversely had affected the applicant's enjoyment of his right to respect for home. It held that "very weighty reasons would have to be put forward before the Court could regard a difference in treatment based exclusively on the ground of sex as compatible with the Convention."[38] Such reasons were not put forward by the Austrian Constitutional Court which had merely referred to the legislature's original intention to exclude homosexuals. The Government had, however, supplemented the – very 'unhermeneutic' – perception of the Constitutional Court and submitted that the aim of the provision was the protection of the traditional family unit.

The Court did accept that the protection of the family in the traditional sense might, in principle, justify a difference in treatment, but went on as follows:

> The aim of protecting the family in the traditional sense is rather abstract and a broad variety of concrete measures may be used to implement it. In cases in which the margin of appreciation afforded to Member States is narrow, as the position where there is a difference in treatment based on sex or sexual orientation, the principle of proportionality does not merely require that the measure chosen is in principle suited for realising the aim sought. It must also be shown that it was necessary to exclude persons living in homosexual relationships from the scope of application of Section 14 of the Rent Act in order to achieve that aim. The Court cannot se that the Government had advanced any arguments that would allow of such a conclusion.[39]

---

[36] *Ibid.*, para. 31.

[37] *Karner v. Austria*, Judgment of 24 July 2003.

[38] *Ibid.*, para. 37.

[39] *Ibid.*, para. 41.

There had therefore been a violation of Article 14 taken in conjunction with Article 8.[40]

In both cases the applicants were already living in the flats in question and terminologically the situations must be construed as examples of an obligation not to interfere. However, depending on the circumstances the two provisions taken in conjunction may very well apply also to claims concerning an obligation to provide. In *Petrovic v. Austria* the Court recognised that the right to paid parental leave for fathers fell within the ambit of Article 8.[41] Against this background it seems natural to assume that some benefits and advantages in the field of housing may likewise fall within the ambit of Article 8. If for instance domestic legislation concerning access to housing, rent allowance, rent control or secure tenure exempts certain groups from benefiting, an issue may very well arise under the ECHR.

Moreover, the Court has previously recognised that the ECHR may encompass 'inverted discrimination' or affirmative action towards certain groups.[42] Thus, the minority judges in *Chapman* suggested that a failure to treat Gypsies differently from the rest of the population might in certain circumstances amount to discrimination. The scope of the protection of the two articles taken in conjunction is therefore in principle quite wide and far from budgetary neutral.

5 *Protection of Housing Rights by Means of Restriction of Other's Rights*[43]

5.1 *Initial Remarks*

So far the analysis has dealt with the rights holders' direct enjoyment of housing rights under Article 8 and Article 1 of Protocol No. 1. However, a number of judgments primarily about property rights illustrate the fact that

---

40 The applicant died in the course of the proceedings and there were no heirs. Nevertheless, the Court chose to continue its examination of the case due to the common interest in elucidating, safeguarding and developing the standards of protection under the Convention with regard to the treatment of homosexuals.

41 *Petrovic v. Austria*, Judgment of 27 March 1998.

42 Cf. *Thlimmenos v. Greece*, Judgment of 6 April 2000 about a member of Jehova's Witnesses who was denied employment after having served a prison sentence for conscientious objection. The Court held a violation of Article 14 in conjunction with Article 9 as the Greek authorities had not made a distinction between those who had been convicted of 'ordinary crime' and those who were sentenced because they had refused to do military service for religious reasons.

43 I have dealt with aspects of this issue on a previous occasion in "Boligrettigheder – Beskyttelse af sociale rettigheder gennem indgreb i civile rettigheder" (Housing Rights – Protection of Social Rights by means of Interferences in Civil Rights) in *MENNESKER & RETTIGHEDER, Nordic Journal for Human Rights*, No. 4, 2001.

interferences may have an indirect impact on the housing situation of *other* individuals than the right holder. From a societal point of view the interest in e.g. secure tenure might overtrump the right to peaceful enjoyment of possession thereby giving tenants an indirect or derived protection. An interesting question in a social rights context is therefore to what extent Member States may interfere with private property rights in order to enhance a certain housing policy to the benefit of the population as such or to the benefit of certain individuals. On the other hand, the right to respect for property rights may contribute to the realisation of the owner's right to housing if the property in question is a residential property and the owner himself wants to use it for habitation. In this situation a competition may arise between owner and tenant, and only one of them will have a satisfactory solution to his problem.[44] How strong is therefore the right to peaceful enjoyment of possession?

A somewhat similar question may arise in connection with Article 8 on the right to respect for home, private and family life. Thus, a number of public and also private interests enumerated in Article 8 (2) allow for interferences if in accordance with the law and if necessary in a democratic society. Thus, both provisions may serve as a guarantee that owners and tenants can enjoy their residential rights. However, at the same time they allow for interferences with the aim of giving third parties protection within the field of housing.

It has been clear from the outset, that the Court leaves an even very wide margin of appreciation to Member States in the field of housing. Thus, in several cases about interferences with property rights the Court has held that:

> [i]n spheres such as housing, which plays a central role in the welfare and economic policies of modern societies, the Court will respect the legislature's judgment as to what is in the general interest unless that judgment is manifestly without reasonable foundation [....].[45]

However, it would be fair to ask whether the scope of the margin of appreciation left to Member States when applying the two provisions in matters of housing policy is the same? While the right to respect for peaceful enjoyment of possession might indeed be of vital importance to the individual, the rights protected under Article 8 very often concern matters belonging to the personal sphere of the individual in question. One could therefore expect a more critical and intensive examination of interferences under Article 8 when affecting the right of an individual to respect for his home. On the other hand, if the property in question is used as "home" for the owner there is no reason to expect a different and more reluctant approach, and the applicant, who can, will often invoke both provisions. Against this background it would be more fair to make

[44] With regard to tenants, cf. *Stretch v. the United Kingdom*, Judgment of 24 June 2003.

[45] Cf. e.g. *Immobiliare Saffi v. Italy*, Judgment of 28 July 1999, para. 49.

a distinction between cases in which no social consideration is to be paid to the owner and cases in which the relative strength between the parties is more even.

5.2 *Case Law Under Article 8 and Article 1 of Protocol No. 1.*

The first case in which owners and tenants had conflicting interests was *James and Others v. the United Kingdom.*[46] The case concerned the enactment of new legislation affecting the formerly widely applied system of 'long leaseholds' under which a leaseholder typically purchases a long lease of property for a capital sum and subsequently pays a more or less nominal rent for it. The new legislation in question provided 'long leaseholders' with the right to purchase the 'freehold' of the house under certain conditions and repealed the former rule according to which the landlord received the property at the end of the lease contract without compensation to the leaseholder. As the leaseholder had quite comprehensive obligations with regard to maintenance and reparation the original system was held as unfair against the leaseholder.

A large group of long leaseholders in London made use of the opportunity to purchase the freehold the consequence, however, being that the landlords suffered a considerable loss. Accordingly, they claimed before the Court that the compulsory sale violated their rights under Article 1 of Protocol No. 1.

The Court took for its basis that the applicants had in fact been deprived of their possessions but – giving a wide margin of appreciation – held that the taking of property in pursuance of a policy calculated to enhance social justice within the community could properly be described as being "in the public interest". As to the relationship between the public interest and the derived interest of individuals the Court held that:

> [i]n particular, the fairness of a system of law governing the contractual or property rights of private parties is a matter of public concern and therefore legislative measures intended to bring about such fairness are capable of being "in the public interest", even if they involve the compulsory transfer of property from one individual to another.[47]

The Court went as far as to say that "a taking of property effected in pursuance of a legitimate social, economic, or other policies may be "in the public interest", even if the community at large has no direct use or enjoyment of the property taken."[48] However, "a deprivation of property effected for no reason other than to confer a private benefit on a private party cannot be "in the public

[46] *James and Others v. the United Kingdom*, Judgment of 21 February 1986.

[47] *Ibid.*, para. 41.

[48] *Ibid.*, para. 45.

interest" ".[49] In other words, a deprivation of property might very well be in the "public interest" even if it is to the benefit of only one individual, as long as this individual favour is desirable and necessary from a societal point of view.

The aim of the legislation in question was to right the injustice which was felt to be caused to occupying tenants by the operation of the long leasehold system of tenure, and the Court therefore held that:

> [e]liminating what are judged to be social injustice is an example of the functions of a democratic legislature. More especially, modern societies consider housing of the population to be a prime social need, the regulation of which cannot entirely be left to the play of market forces. The margin of appreciation is wide enough to cover legislation aimed at securing greater social justice in the sphere of people's homes, even where such legislation interferes with existing contractual relations between private parties and confers no direct benefit on the State or the community at large.[50]

Accordingly, the aim pursued was considered a legitimate one, and as the Court found a reasonable relationship of proportionality between the means employed and the aim sought to be realised, there was no violation of the Protocol.

The case *Mellacher v. Austria*[51] also concerned conflicting interests between letters and tenants who had availed themselves of provisions in the newly enacted Austrian Rent Act pursuant to which tenants could apply for the rent to be reduced considerably. The letters complained that the Austrian authorities had interfered with their freedom of contract and deprived them of a substantial proportion of their future rental income.

The Court found that the contested measures amounted to a control of the use of property but attached importance to the fact that:

> [t]he 1981 Rent Act was intended to reduce excessive and unjustified disparities between rents for equivalent apartments and to combat property speculation. Through these means the Act also had the aims of making accommodation more easily available at reasonable prices to less affluent members of the population, while at the same time providing incentives for the improvement of substandard properties.[52]

Accordingly, the Court found that the Rent Act had a legitimate aim in the general interest[53] and observed that "in particular in the field of rent control"[54]

---

[49] *Ibid.*, para. 40.

[50] *Ibid.*, para. 47.

[51] *Mellacher and others v. Austria*, Judgment of 19 December 1989.

[52] *Ibid.*, para. 47.

[53] Article 1(1) applies the expression "public interest" whereas Article 1 (2) speaks of "general" interest. However, the two expressions are presumably synonymous, cf. Katarina Krause, 'The Right to Property' in Asbjørn Eide et al. (eds) *Economic, Social and Cultural Rights – A Textbook*, 2nd. Revised Edition, 2001, p. 202.

[54] *Mellacher and Others v. Austria*, para. 51.

it must be open to the legislature to take measures affecting the further execution of previously concluded contracts in order to attain the aim pursued. The Court admitted that "the rent reductions are striking in their amount", but found nevertheless – by twelve votes to five[55] – that they could not be considered "so inappropriate or disproportionate as to take them outside the State's margin of appreciation." "The fact that the original rents were agreed upon and corresponded to the then prevailing market conditions does not mean that the legislature could not reasonably decide as a matter of policy that they were unacceptable from the point of view of social justice."[56]

Both the *James case* and the *Mellacher case* concerned relations between tenants and financially strong owners without an interest in inhabiting the apartments in question. They illustrate how it is possible for Member States to redistribute resources to the benefit of tenants who are supposedly in a less fortunate financial position without violating Article 1 of Protocol No. 1. However, even if the relative strength between the parties is more even, and even if the owner has expressed the wish to inhabit the property himself the assessment of the Court might very well favour the tenant, and the Court seems more than willing to accept even radical limitations of property rights if these limitations serve the purpose of pursuing a certain housing policy.

The *Velosa Barreto v. Portugal* case is illustrative of the fact that the right to property is easily outdone by housing policy considerations even if the relative strength between the owner and the tenant seems even. The case was, however, primarily pleaded under Article 8 and does not seem to confirm an assumption of a narrower margin of appreciation in matters concerning the personal sphere.

The applicant, Mr. Velosa Barreto, his wife and their son lived together with Ms. Barreto's parents in a house consisting of four bedrooms, a kitchen, a living-cum-dining room and a basement. Having inherited a house let for residential use to a couple the applicant wanted to establish a home of his own with a view to enlarging the family with another child and initiated proceedings against the tenants with a view to having the tenancy terminated.

Pursuant to Portuguese legislation a landlord may seek termination of a tenancy contract when he "needs" the property in order to live there. However, the applicant did not succeed in convincing the Portuguese judiciary that they really needed the house for themselves. The domestic courts applied a very restrictive interpretation of the word "needs" and attached importance to the fact that both couples and the son could have each their bedroom in the house

55 The minority – and the Commission – found that in two cases the interference did not satisfy the proportionality requirement. In these cases the rent had been reduced to respectively 17.6 and 20 percent of the original amount.

56 *Ibid.*, paras. 55–56.

of the parents-in-law and that the applicant had not proved that there were tensions making it intolerable for them to live there. Moreover, the domestic courts took account of the fact that the house previously had been inhabited by three additional persons – two aunts and a brother – leaving more room for the applicant's household. Subsequently, the applicant claimed before the Court that their rights under Article 8 had been violated. The Court held that Article 8:

> does not go as far as to place the State under an obligation to give a landlord the right to recover possession of a rented house on request and in all circumstances.
>
> [....] the Court considers that the legislation applied in this case pursues a legitimate aim, namely the social protection of tenants, and that it thus tends to promote the economic well-being of the country and the protection of the rights of others.[57]

In the assessment of the balancing of the respective interests the Court relied entirely on the Portuguese courts and their very restrictive interpretation of the word "needs". As the Portuguese courts had not acted arbitrarily or unreasonably[58] the Court did not find that they had failed to strike a fair balance between the competing interests. The Court did not find either – and for similar reasons – that the applicant's rights under Article 1 of Protocol No. 1 had been violated.

The case illustrates how easily not only property rights but also family rights are outdone in competition with the economic well-being of the country and the protection of the rights of others, cf. the notion of *Drittwirkung*. The Barreto family was an ordinary family with an understandable wish to live a family life of their own under conditions providing room enough for a family increase. Moreover, it was disputed whether a housing shortage did in fact exist in the town in question and the environments at the house of the parents-in-law were far from luxurious.[59]

That social housing considerations may take precedence over property rights is also illustrated in *Spadea and Scalobrino*, the first in a series of cases about the Italian long-lasting tradition of intervening in residential tenancy legislation

[57] *Velosa Barreto v. Portugal*, Judgment of 21 November 1995, paras. 24 and 25.

[58] *Ibid.*, para 30.

[59] One judge expressed his dissenting opinion that both provisions had been violated. He found that "the possibility for the applicant and his family to occupy living space separate from the rooms or space where his wife's parents live is a substantive element of family life" and added that the Court did not attach sufficient weight to the suggested wish of the applicant to increasing the size of the family. He did not find either that the domestic courts had succeeding in striking a fair balance between the directly protected property right of the applicant and the right of the tenant, cf. Dissenting opinion of Judge Gotchev, paras. 1–2.

with the aim of controlling rents. This has been achieved by rent freezes, by the statutory extension of all current leases and by the postponement, suspension or staggering of evictions.[60]

The case concerned a couple who bought two adjacent apartments with the aim of making their home there. The apartments in question were, however, let out to two elderly women of modest means who refused to vacate the apartments when given notice. The applicants' efforts to have them evicted were prevented or hampered due to the above-mentioned legislation giving tenants very far-reaching protection against eviction. Only after more than six years did the applicants gain possession of one of the flats, not because the authorities took the initiative to enforce the eviction order, but simply because the tenant died. In the meantime the applicants had felt compelled to buy another flat and claimed that the wretched state of affairs was due to an unsuccessful housing policy.

The Court found – in this and later cases – that the legislation suspending evictions amounted to control of the use of property, and observed that the legislation in question was prompted by the need to deal with a large number of leases which expired at the material time and by the concern to enable the tenants affected to find acceptable new homes or obtain subsidised housing.[61] Italian society suffered from considerable housing shortage, and it would undoubtedly have led to considerable social tension if all evictions were to be enforced at the same time. Therefore, the Italian Government had considered it necessary to resort to emergency provisions to postpone, suspend or stagger the enforcement of court orders requiring tenants to vacate the premises they occupied. These measures did provide for exceptions under which, among other things, landlords who urgently needed to recover their property or who were entitled to arrears of rent could obtain police assistance to enforce eviction.[62]

When considering the balancing of interests, the Court attached importance to the fact that none of the exceptions applied to the applicants, and that the tenants were two elderly ladies of modest means. The Court did admit that the applicants had to buy another flat. However, regard being had to the legitimate aim pursued the Court did not find that the legislative measures could be considered disproportionate in view of the wide margin of appreciation which is admitted in matters of housing policy.

It appears from the above mentioned cases that the Court has proved more than willing to accept even radical limitations of property rights and rights

---

[60] *Spadea and Scalabrino v. Italy*, Judgment of 28 September 1995.

[61] *Ibid.*, para. 31.

[62] *Ibid.*, para. 37.

under Article 8 if these restrictions serve the purpose of pursuing a certain housing policy. That is not only the case in (domestic) disputes between financially strong owners cf. the cases *James* and *Mellacher*, but also in disputes in which the relative strength between the parties has been more even cf. the *Velosa Barreto case* and the *Spadea and Scalabrino case*. There is a limit, however, which is illustrated in later Italian cases concerning the consequences of the long Italian tradition of statutory extension of all current leases and by the postponement, suspension or staggering of evictions.

Scollo v. Italy[63] concerned the difficulties of the owner in gaining possession of a flat in Rome. Since he wanted to inhabit the flat himself he gave the tenant notice to quit when the lease expired on 31 December 1983. However, due to the suspension and staggering of eviction orders he had to wait for twelve years before he eventually obtained possession of the house.

The Court observed that the measures were prompted by need of the Government to deal with a large number of leases which expired in 1982 and 1983 and by the concern to enable the tenants affected to find acceptable new homes or obtain subsidised housing. However, the Court attached importance to the fact that the Italian authorities had paid no attention whatsoever to two 'declarations of necessity' submitted by the applicant's lawyer explaining that the applicant had no job, that he was 71 % disabled, and that the tenant had not paid the full rent. The Court concluded that "the restriction on Mr. Scollo's use of his flat resulting from the competent authorities' failure to apply those provisions [the above mentioned exemptions, author's insertion] was contrary to the requirements of the second paragraph of Article 1 of Protocol No. 1 [....]."[64]

Cases concerning later amendments to the Italian housing legislation also illustrate that there are limits to the margin of appreciation. The amendments provided that requests for police assistance in enforcing orders for possession would be dealt with in order of priority. As of 1990 priority was particularly given to landlords urgently requiring the premises as accommodation for themselves or their family the consequence, however, being that non-urgent orders were never enforced, cf. *Immobiliare Saffi v. Italy* in which the Court observed:

> that the Italian system suffered from a degree of inflexibility: by providing that cases in which the lease has been terminated on the ground that the landlord urgently needs to recover the apartment for himself or his family should always be given priority, it automatically made the enforcement of non-urgent orders for possession dependent on their being no requests warranting priority treatment. It followed that, since there was always a large number of priority

---

[63] *Scollo v. Italy*, Judgment of 28 September 1995.

[64] *Ibid.*, para. 40. Cf. also *Schirmer v. Poland*, Judgment of 21 December 2004, in which the Court also found to the benefit of the owner.

requests outstanding, non-urgent orders were in practice never enforced after January 1990.[65]

The administration of this legislation has subsequently more or less consistently been considered in non-compliance with Article 1 of Protocol No. 1 irrespective of the social situation of the parties, cf. e.g. *A. O. v Italy*.[66] In this case the tenant – an elderly sick lady – had inhabited the apartment for many years, and the owner deserved no special social protection. He complained of the financial burden resulting from the impossibility of raising the rent and had apparently no intention of using the apartment himself for residential purposes. Moreover, it appeared from the eviction report that the tenant had been bedridden for two years, and that she had to be transferred by ambulance to a council flat which was allocated to her by the Municipality of Rome on the very same day. The Court, however, attached more importance to the fact that the applicant had been left in a state of uncertainty for approximately six years and held that an excessive burden was imposed on the applicant. The Court accordingly found that Article 1 of Protocol No. 1 had been violated.[67]

The situation of the tenant was dealt with as follows:

> It is true that the tenant was elderly and sick and therefore deserved special protection. Even assuming that this was the reason for not granting the applicant police assistance, the Court is of the opinion that this circumstance could not in itself justify the lengthy restriction of the applicant's use of his apartment. Indeed, on the very same day of the eviction the authorities managed to allocate to the tenant a subsidised apartment: the Court has not been provided with any information as to why this could not be done earlier, nor as to whether the authorities made any efforts to allocate at all to her such an apartment prior to the date of the eviction.[68]

The Italian system of staggering eviction orders leaves the owner with very limited legal safeguards thus exceeding the margin of appreciation left to Member States. The cases referred to prove that little can be said with regard to an abstract interpretation of Article 1 of Protocol No. 1, and that the legal content of the provision only reveals in the encounter with concrete facts, cf. the vertical structure of the hermeneutic circle. This hermeneutic approach is confirmed in a later case *Pincová and Pinc v. the Czech Republic*[69] concerning a dispute between the original owner and a later purchaser of a forester's house. The house in question had been confiscated in 1948, and the first applicant and

[65] *Immobiliare Saffi v. Italy*, Judgment of 28 July 1999, para. 54.

[66] *A. O. v. Italy*, Judgment of 30 May 2000.

[67] Cf. also e.g. *Lunari v. Italy*, Judgment of 11 January 2001, *Bellini v. Italy*, Judgment of 29 January 2004 and *Antonio Siena v. Italy*, Judgment of 11 March 2004.

[68] Cf. *A. O. v. Italy*, para. 29.

[69] *Pincová and Pinc v. the Czech Republic*, Judgment of 5 November 2002.

in 1967 her husband had purchased the house, which they had rented since 1953. After the death of the first applicant's husband the second applicant – her son – became the co-owner of the forester's house. However, after the entry into force in 1992 of legislation providing for the return of formerly confiscated property under certain preconditions the title to the disputed property was transferred to the original owner. The applicants in turn received compensation corresponding to the price they had paid for the purchase in 1967 and claimed before the Court that they had been deprived of possessions they had acquired in good faith and in accordance with domestic legislation, alleging that they had not received adequate compensation.

The Court accepted that the general objective of the restitution laws, namely to attenuate the consequences of certain infringements of property rights caused by the communist regime, is a legitimate aim and a means of safeguarding the lawfulness of legal transactions and protecting the country's socio-economic development:[70]

> However, it considers it necessary to ensure that the attenuation of those old injuries does not create disproportionate new wrongs. To that end, the legislation should make it possible to take into account the particular circumstances of each case, so that persons who acquired their possessions in good faith are not to bear the burden of responsibility which is rightfully that of the State which once confiscated those possessions.[71]

In the assessment of the factual circumstances the Court found that the applicants had acquired the house in good faith and that the purchase price, which was given back to the applicants, could not reasonably be related to its value thirty years later. Moreover, the applicants had lived in the house for 42 years, 28 of those as its owners, and they were in a difficult social situation not able to buy somewhere else to live. The Government had accepted that it was impossible to assert a right to alternative accommodation in the courts, and it appeared that the new owner took advantage of his position of strength vis-à-vis the applicants by demanding a monthly rent even though they had no tenancy agreement. The Court therefore concluded that:

> the 'compensation' awarded to the applicants did not take account of their personal and social situation and that they were not awarded any sum for the non-pecuniary damage they sustained as a result of being deprived of their only property. In addition, they have still not obtained reimbursement of the costs reasonably incurred for the upkeep of the house, even though a period of seven and a half years has elapsed since [....] the day when the judgment of the Prague regional Court confirming the transfer of the title to the son of the former owners became final.

---

70 *Ibid.*, para. 58.

71 *Ibid.*

> The applicants have thus had to bear an individual and excessive burden which has upset the fair balance that should be maintained between the demands of the general interest on the one hand and protection of the right to peaceful enjoyment of possession on the other. There has therefore been a violation of Article 1 of Protocol No. 1.[72]

The applicants were accordingly awarded compensation which would enable them to buy a house of their own.[73]

5.3 *Margin of Appreciation – Article 8 and Article 1 of Protocol No. 1*

The cases referred to above illustrate that interferences in the right to property are acceptable from a human rights point of view to a very large degree if motivated in social and economic considerations. The Court has given Member States an even very wide margin of appreciation and digs down its heels only in situations – such as the later Italian cases and *Pincová and Pinc* – where the applicant has had to bear a "disproportionate burden" disrupting the balance between the competing interest between societal interests and the requirements of fundamental rights.[74] It has to be concluded that the right to property is a rather weak right when interfered with in 'everyday' situations as an effect of deliberate and targeted social and economic policy considerations. The Court has adopted an even very cautious approach to such issues presumably for the very same reasons that restrict domestic courts from performing a thorough examination of social and economic issues in general.

On the basis of the *Velosa Barreto case* one could be tempted to draw a similar conclusion as regards interferences in Article 8 if motivated in housing policy considerations. *Buckley* and *Chapman*, mentioned above in Section 3, point in the same direction. However, such conclusion would probably be too hasty. Member States are without any doubt left with a wide margin of appreciation in the field of housing especially when it comes to resource-demanding obligations. However, the scope of the margin of appreciation will always be dependent on the context, and dramatic interferences into the personal sphere will tend to narrow the margin. Thus, in *Connors v. the United Kingdom* the Court did find a violation of the right to respect for home as the legal

---

72 *Ibid.*, paras. 63–64. Cf. also *Brumarescu v. Romania*, Judgments of 28 October 1999 and 23 January 2001, *Străin and Others v. Romania*, Judgment of 21 July 2005 and *Velikovi and Others v. Bulgaria*, Judgment of 9 July 2007.

73 Cf. also *Hutten-Czapska v. Poland*, Judgment of 19 June 2006, a pilot case in which the Court – sitting as a Grand Chamber – found that a landlord's property rights had been violated because she – due to Polish rent control schemes – had never entered into any freely negotiated lease agreement with her tenants.

74 Cf. also e.g. *Prodan v. Moldova*, Judgment of 18 May 2004 (non-enforcement of eviction order due to lack of accomodation).

framework applicable to the occupation of pitches on local authority Gypsy sites did not provide the applicant with sufficient procedural protection of his rights. *Gillows v. the United Kingdom* illustrates a similar narrowing of the margin.

One should not jump to conclusions on the basis of a few cases and especially not on the basis of very special cases such as *Connors* and *Gillows*. The whole issue is highly complex, and decisions are made on the basis of a variety of considerations over the nature, intensity and also specificity of interferences, the character and reasonableness of the regulation and probably also the frequency with which a certain kind of interference is likely to occur. Thus, the more specific the concrete circumstances are, the less likely is the holding of a violation to imply an unjustified intervention in the internal social affairs of Member States. Interferences in housing rights under Article 8 are probably a field where law is only beginning to take shape, and the provision is awaiting the encounter with facts in order for more to be said about the legal content. I would leave open, therefore, whether the margin of appreciation left to Member States when dealing with radical interferences in the personal sphere under Article 8 is in fact narrower than when it comes to interferences with property rights under Article 1 of Protocol No. l.

The discussion will be continued in Sections 6 and 7 although in another context. The cases in this section concerned the 'everyday' interferences, whereas the following sections deal with similar – and other – issues typically occurring in times of war and conflict. Thus, as already mentioned above in Section 2 there is a distinct difference between interferences in Article 8 and Article 1 of Protocol No. 1 for the purpose of pursuing a certain deliberate and targeted housing policy and interferences with the intention of driving away an ethnic group from a certain area or a certain country even if the houses left behind may contribute to the solution of a housing problem for another ethnic group. Although in particular Section 7 has a wider scope, I have chosen to deal with the two situations separately.

5.4 *The Character of the Derivative Protection Under Article 8 and Article 1 of Protocol No. 1*

Before proceeding with the presentation, a few remarks should be made on the character of the indirect protection of housing rights that may follow from interferences or limitations of rights under Article 8 or Article 1 of Protocol No. 1. As illustrated in Section 5.3 both provisions allow for quite radical interferences to the detriment of the right holder. On the other hand, such interference will often be to the advantage of third parties, and the societal interest in this advantage is what justifies the interference. Thus, both provisions allow for reallocation of resources and material comforts, and the individual who benefits from such reallocation is left in a *factual* position similar to that of someone whose legal claim to housing has been complied with.

However, the factual position of third parties who benefit from interferences in e.g. property rights is not necessarily the result of State compliance with human rights. In the field of housing a third party will traditionally not be in a position from where he can argue that his human rights are violated without such interference.[75] The protection which falls to the share of a third party is an indirect or derived protection, which is only made topical if preconditions for interfering with someone else's rights are met. There is no independent right to claim such interferences, and the protection is fundamentally different from that of the primary right holder.

One might talk about respect for (domestic) tenancy rights and about protection against arbitrary terminations of tenancies. However, we have to do with a phenomenon which falls outside the traditional perception of State Parties' obligations under the human rights conventions in that State Parties themselves decide which measures to take within the field of housing. State Parties may choose to adopt a housing policy which considers the interests of tenants to the detriment of owners of residential property. However, they are not necessarily obliged to do so, and if they are, this housing policy is primarily to be evaluated under the conventions on economic, social and cultural rights. The individual whose housing situation is threatened can only make relatively few claims under the ECHR, cf. Section 3. However, with regard to discrimination in housing issues, cf. Section 4, the situation is different.

Nevertheless, the phenomenon is indeed interesting from a social point of view as it confirms the perception of human rights as indivisible rights. What is traditionally considered civil and political rights encompass elements of a social rights nature, and one may even say that the phenomenon tampers with the perception of civil rights as highest in a hierarchical order of rights. The limitation clauses recognise that social considerations must sometimes be given a greater weight, and in that context it is of less importance that State Parties themselves are given the powers to decide when the civil right has to give way.

6. *Demolition of Homes*[76]

That e.g. the deliberate burning of houses with the intention of driving away an ethnic group constitutes a violation of the Convention is rather obvious, and the production of evidence for State responsibility has been the major issue in

---

75 That may, however, be the case in other fields such as forcible removal of neglected children if an omission amounts to a violation of Article 3, cf. Chapter 5 on The Right to Health under the ECHR.

76 I see no reason to deal with this issue as an 'everyday' issue. Fortunately, people's homes are rarely demolished in times of peace cf., however, the very specific circumstances in *Allard*

such cases. Thus, since 1996 the Court and the Commission have scrutinised evidence for a series of allegations that Turkish state security forces have brutally evicted Kurdish citizens in the South-East of Turkey and destroyed their homes. Once the alleged events have been proven, the Court has not hesitated to hold a breach of the Convention either as a violation of Article 8 or Article 1 of Protocol No. 1 depending on the circumstances. In some cases both provisions have been considered violated.[77]

In *Akdivar and Others v. Turkey* the Court – on the basis of the findings of the Commission – found that it was established that security forces were responsible for the burning of the applicants' houses, and that the loss of their homes caused them to leave their village and move elsewhere. The Court sitting as a Grand Chamber held as follows:

> The Court is of the opinion that there can be no doubt that the deliberate burning of the applicants' homes and their contents constitutes at the same time a serious interference with the right to respect for their family lives and homes and with the peaceful enjoyment of their possessions. No justification for these interferences having been proffered by the respondent Government – which have confined their response to denying involvement of the security forces in the incident – the Court must conclude that there has been a violation of both Article 8 of the Convention [....] and Article 1 of Protocol No. 1 [....].[78]

In *Mentes and Others v. Turkey* the Court – also sitting as a Grand Chamber – agreed with the Commission that similar facts "disclose a particularly grave interference with the [....] right to respect for private life, family and home as guaranteed by Article 8 and that the measure was devoid of justification."[79] Similar expressions are used in e.g. *Selçuk and Asker v. Turkey,*[80] *Dulas v. Turkey*[81]and *Orhan v. Turkey.*[82]

In some of the cases the applicants further claimed a violation of Article 3 because of the way in which the destruction took place or because the destruction affected them in a particularly serious manner. Thus, in *Selçuk* and *Asker* the Court attached importance to the applicants' age (54 and 60 respectively) and to the fact that they had to stand and watch the burning of their house. Moreover, the Court took account of the fact that inadequate precautions were

---

v. Sweden, Judgment of 24 June 2003 in which the applicant's house – built on jointly owned land without the consent of the joint owners – was demolished. The Court found that the authorities had failed to strike a fair balance between the applicant's interests and that of the other owners.

77 Cf. e.g *Doğan and others v. Turkey*, Judgment of 29 June 2004.

78 *Akdivar and Others v. Turkey*, Judgment of 16 September 1996, para. 88.

79 *Mentes and Others v. Turkey*, Judgment of 28 November 1997, para. 73.

80 *Selçuk and Asker v. Turkey*, Judgment of 24 April 1998, para. 86.

81 *Dulas v. Turkey*, Judgment of 30 January 2001, para. 60.

82 *Orhan v. Turkey*, Judgment of 18 June 2002, para. 379.

taken to secure the applicants' safety and of the fact that they had been deprived of their livelihoods without any assistance being provided to them afterwards. The Court found that these facts amounted to a violation of Article 3.[83] The facts in *Bilgin v. Turkey*[84] and *Dulas v. Turkey* were very much similar, and the Court held that Article 3 had been violated. However, in *Orhan v. Turkey*, the Court sitting as a Grand Chamber, disagreed with the applicant that Article 3 had been infringed. The Court, in particular, did "not find in the present case distinctive elements concerning the age or health of the applicant or the Orhans or specific conduct of the soldiers vis-à-vis either of those persons which could lead to a conclusion that they had suffered treatment contrary to Article 3 of the Convention [....]".[85]

The differing conclusions in the cases illustrate once again the notion of *polysemy* with regard to inhuman treatment; cf. similarly the case *D. v. the United Kingdom*, mentioned in Chapter 5, Section 2.2. It makes limited sense to talk about an abstract interpretation of Article 3. The notion of inhuman treatment must be considered in its determinate context, and the fact that the applicants in the *Orhan case* had been subject to a "particularly grave interference" of their rights under Article 8 did not suffice also to a violation of Article 3.

The destruction of Croatian houses during the war has likewise led to cases before the Court. The cases have, however, had a different course due to the fact that the ECHR did not enter into force until November 1997. The demolitions took place several years before. Moreover, the cases involved newly enacted legislation about actions in respect of damage hampering civil lawsuits. In *Kutic v. Croatia* e.g. the applicant's house, a storage room and a shed were destroyed as a result of explosions, and in *Acimovic v. Croatia* the applicant found his cottage devastated and his possessions removed after the Croatian Army had used the house for their military needs.

In 1996 the Croatian Parliament had introduced an amendment to the Civil Obligations Act which provided that all proceedings concerning actions in respect of damage resulting from *terrorist acts* were to be stayed pending the enactment of new legislation on the subject. Before the enactment of such new legislation damages for terrorist acts could not be sought. Moreover, in 1999 Parliament introduced an amendment to the Civil Obligations Act to the effect that all proceedings concerning actions for damages resulting from *acts of members of the Croatian army and police* when acting in their official capacity during the Homeland War in Croatia were to be stayed. However, such legislation was not enacted until 2003.

[83] *Selçuk and Asker v. Turkey*, para. 77–80.

[84] *Bilgin v. Turkey*, Judgment of 16 November 2000.

[85] *Orhan v. Turkey*, para. 362.

Both applicants alleged violations of Article 6 because the domestic courts had stayed the proceedings pursuant to the legislative amendments to the Civil Obligations Act. In *Kutic v. Croatia* proceedings had been stayed for over six years, more than four of which had been after the Convention entered into force, and in *Acimovic v. Croatia* the applicant was prevented from having his claim decided by a Court for three years and eight months. The Court found that the long period during which both applicants had been prevented from having their civil claims determined by a domestic court as a consequence of legislative measures entailed a violation of Article 6.[86] Some later similar cases have been struck out of the list after the applicant's acceptance of a proposal for friendly settlement. In *Freimann v. Croatia*, however, the Court again found a violation of Article 6 because the applicant had been prevented for more than seven years from having her claim decided by the domestic courts.[87]

7. *Eviction and Illegal Occupation of Homes*

7.1 *Examples from Cyprus*

In the cases referred to above homes were demolished in a way which made them more or less unfit for habitation. Something similar has happened in many other areas affected with conflicts between various ethnic groups.[88] The eviction of one ethnic group for the purpose of using their homes as accommodation for another ethnic group is, however, as widespread and gives rise to a number of problems not only for the original occupant but also for the – often distressed – individual or family who are offered a flat or a house for (temporary) residence maybe after having been evicted from the original home in another area or in another country. Turkish and Greek Cypriots residing in each their part of the divided Cyprus have been prevented from the peaceful enjoyment of their property situated on the 'wrong' side of the boundary; and during the war in the former Yugoslavia a great number of refugees and displaced persons competed with the original population over a limited number of houses and flats. This situation has been compared to the game *musical*

[86] *Kutic v. Croatia*, Judgment of 1 March 2002 and *Acimovic v. Croatia*, Judgment of 9 October 2003.

[87] *Freimann v. Croatia*, Judgment of 24 June 2004. Cf. also e.g. *Varićak v. Croatia, Marinković v. Croatia*, Judgments of 21 October 2004.

[88] Case law provides only few cases about eviction in peacetime, cf. e.g. *Prokopovich v. Russia*, Judgment of 18 November 2004, in which the Court found a violation of Article 8 because the eviction did not take place "in accordance with the law", cf. para. 45.

chairs[89] in which players go round a row of chairs (one fewer than the number of players) until the music stops. The one who finds no chair to sit on has to leave the game.[90]

The situation in Cyprus has been dealt with on several occasions beginning with *Loizidou v. Turkey* concerning a Cypriot woman from Nicosia, who was the owner of a number of plots in Kyrenia in Northern Cyprus. Since 1974 she had been refused access to the land by the 'TRNC' authorities [Turkish Republic of Northern Cyprus] and consequently effectively lost the control over her property as well as all possibilities to use and enjoy it. The Court did not doubt that the facts fell within the meaning of Article 1 of Protocol No. 1 and stated as follows:

> Such an interference cannot, in the exceptional circumstance of the present case to which the applicant and the Cypriot Government have referred [....] be regarded as either as deprivation of property or a control of use within the meaning of the first and second paragraph of Article 1 [....]. However, it clearly falls within the meaning of the first sentence of that provision [....] as an interference with the peaceful enjoyment of possessions [....].
>
> Apart from a passing reference to the doctrine of necessity a justification for the acts of the "TRNC" and to the fact that property rights were the subject of intercommunal talks, the Turkish Government have not sought to make submissions justifying the above interference with the applicant's property rights which is imputable to Turkey.
>
> It has not, however, been explained how the need to rehouse Turkish Cypriot refugees in the years following the Turkish intervention in the island in 1974 could justify the complete negation of the applicant's property rights in the form of a total and continuous denial of access and a purported expropriation without compensation.
>
> Nor can the fact that property rights were the subject of intercommunal talks involving both communities in Cyprus provide a justification for this situation under the Convention.[91]

The Court accordingly found that there had been and continued to be a breach of Article 1 of Protocol No. 1. The Court, however, did not agree with the applicant that there had also been a breach of Article 8 due to the fact that she had intended to build a house for residential purposes on one of the plots. The Court held that it would:

[89] *Special Report: Musical Chairs, Property Problems in Bosnia and Herzegovina*, OSCE, July 1996 and Antoine Buyse, *Post-Conflict Housing Restitution. The European Human Rights Perspective, with a Case Study on Bosnia and Herzegovina*, Intersentia, 2008.

[90] Cf. *Oxford Advanced Learner's Dictionary of Current English*, A.P. Cowie (Chief Editor), Oxford University Press, 1989, 4th Edition.

[91] *Loizidou v. Turkey*, Judgment of 18 December 1996, paras. 63–64.

> strain the meaning of the notion "home" in Article 8 [....] to extend it to comprise property on which it is planned to build a house for residential purposes. Nor can that term be interpreted to cover an area of a State where one has grown up and where the family has its roots but where one no longer lives.

The result in *Loizidou v. Turkey* was followed up in the inter-state case *Cyprus v. Turkey*. A great number of displaced Greek-Cypriots were prevented from returning to their homes in the northern part of Cyprus, and the applicant Government claimed that the continuing refusal to permit the return of the displaced persons not only prevented them from having access to their property there but also from using, selling, bequeathing, mortgaging, developing and enjoying it.[92] Moreover, the applicant Government alleged that property of Greek Cypriots still living in the northern part of Cyprus could not be bequeathed by them on death, and that it passed to the 'TRNC' authorities as abandoned property. Finally, the applicant Government claimed that the continuing refusal of the 'TRNC' authorities to allow the displaced persons to return violated not only the right to respect for their homes but also the right to respect for their family life.

Recalling the *Loizidou case* the Court found that there had been a continuing violation of Protocol No. 1 by virtue of the fact that Greek-Cypriot owners of property in northern Cyprus had been denied access to and control, use and enjoyment of their property as well as any compensation for the interference with their property rights.[93] Moreover, the Court found a violation of Article 1 of Protocol No. 1 in respect of Greek Cypriots living in northern Cyprus in that their right to the peaceful enjoyment of their possession was not secured in case of their permanent departure from the territory and in that, in case of death, inheritance rights of relatives living in southern Cyprus were not recognised.[94] Finally, the Court found a violation of Article 8 because of the refusal to allow the return of any Greek-Cypriot displaced persons to their homes in northern Cyprus. The Court held that the denial had no basis in law within the meaning of Article 8 (2), and that the inter-communal talks could not be invoked in order to legitimise a violation of the Convention.[95]

A similar approach was taken in *Demades v. Turkey* in which the Court also applied an extended interpretation of the notion of "home" in Article 8. The applicant in question lived in Nicosia but had used a fully furnished and completely equipped house in Kyrenia as a holiday home and for providing hospitality and entertainment to relatives, friends and persons associated with the applicant's business activities. Since 1974, however, the applicant had been

---

92 *Cyprus v. Turkey*, Judgment of 10 May 2001, paras. 165–166 and 178.

93 *Ibid.*, para. 198.

94 *Ibid.*, paras. 269–270.

95 *Ibid.*, para. 175.

prevented from having access to the house which was occupied by officers and/or other members of the Turkish armed forces. The Court argued that it may not always be possible to draw precise distinctions since a person may divide his time between two houses or form strong emotional ties with a second house, treating it as a home. A narrow interpretation of the notion of "home" could give rise to inequality of treatment, and a contemporary interpretation would encompass the house in question. The Court found violations of both Article 8 and Article 1 of Protocol No. 1 for the very same reasons as in *Loizidou v. Turkey* and *Cyprus v. Turkey*.[96]

The cases differ from the ones referred to in Section 5.2 in that the Court rather quickly refuses the respondent government's arguments concerning inter-communal talks and the need to re-house displaced Turkish Cypriot refugees in the years following the intervention in the island in 1974. The argumentation is very brief, and the Court omits the traditional exercise regarding factors widening and narrowing the margin of appreciation respectively.

7.2 *Examples from Croatia*

The situation in Croatia is dealt with in a number of judgments, however, in a somewhat different manner due to the fact that the ECHR did not enter into force until November 1997. The Court has therefore been prevented from taking a stand on many of the housing issues that arose during the war and not least in the wake of Operation Storm (Oluja) on 5 August 1995. A great number of complaints have been declared inadmissible *ratione temporis*. However, some have been decided on the merits.

Some cases concern the difficulties of tenants in regaining possession of their flats due to the staggering of eviction orders. In *Cvijetic v. Croatia*[97] the applicant, who was the holder of a specially protected tenancy on a flat in Split was evicted by a third party in February 1994. She immediately filed an action against the person in question and quickly obtained a judgment from the Municipal court in Split declaring her the sole holder of the flat. Not until November, however, did the Court order the intruder to vacate the flat, and this decision was not final until February 1995. The intruder, however, did not comply with the court's order to vacate the flat, and the applicant had to ask the court for an eviction order. The eviction was scheduled for 26 November 1995, but not executed, apparently because another person was now occupying the flat. The applicant subsequently had to ask the court for a new eviction order which was not scheduled until October 1996. This eviction was adjourned

[96] *Demades v. Turkey*, Judgment of 31 July 2003, paras. 37 and 46.

[97] *Cvijetic v. Croatia*, Judgment of 26 February 2004.

because the applicant did not appear. In November 1998 the applicant again asked the court to enforce the eviction order which was scheduled for October 2000, but not executed this time either. The Association of the Homeland War Invalids and the Ministry of the Homeland War Veterans had asked the court to adjourn it, and a number of war veterans obstructed the (half-hearted?) attempt which was in fact made to carry out the eviction. Another attempt in June 2001 to evict the occupant failed because a physician invited to assist did not appear, and the applicant did not regain possession over the flat – which she had bought in the meantime – until March 2002.

The Court held that the execution of final decisions given by any court must be regarded as an integral part of the "trial" for the purposes of Article 6 and noted that the proceedings had lasted *more than eight years* of which a period of *more than four years* fell to be examined by the Court. Since the responsibility for the long duration of the proceedings primarily rested with the domestic authorities, the Court found a breach of Article 6. Moreover, the Court found a violation also of Article 8 because the authorities had not undertaken their 'positive' obligations under this provision. Thus, the failure to act had prevented the applicant from living in her home for a period of more than four years after the Convention entered into force in respect of Croatia. The circumstances in *Pibernik v. Croatia*[98] were very much similar. The eviction procedure lasted seven and a half years of which a period of almost five and a half years fell to be examined by the Court. The Court found that both Articles 6 and Article 8 had been violated.

7.3 *Margin of Appreciation – Article 8 and Article 1 of Protocol No. 1*

The Court has repeatedly stated that the margin of appreciation within the field of housing is wide. However, the Court contributed to an answer with regard to the question raised above in Section 5.1 namely whether the scope of the margin of appreciation left to Member States when applying Article 8 and Article 1 of Protocol No. 1 in matters of housing policy is the same. The Court has held as follows:

> [I]n spheres such as housing, which plays a central role in the welfare and economic policies of modern societies, the Court will respect the legislature's judgment as to what is in the general interest unless that judgment is manifestly without reasonable foundation.[99]

However, the hermeneutic perception of the Convention as a whole does in my view not necessarily lead to the conclusion that the margin of appreciation applied in the field of housing has to be uniform. There is indeed a difference

---

98 *Pibernik v. Croatia*, Judgment of 4 March 2004.

99 Cf. e.g. *Immobiliare Saffi v. Italy*, para. 49.

between being deprived of property not used for one's own housing needs and being deprived of one's home, and it seems difficult to reconcile the perception with the traditional interpretation of the phrase 'necessary in a democratic society' as encompassing what has to be considered a 'pressing social need'.

One might also make reflections about whether the different wording of the limitation clauses has any importance for the indirect protection of housing rights. It might make a difference that Article 8 speaks of "the economic well-being of the country" and "the rights and freedoms of others" whereas Article 1 of Protocol No. 1 speaks of the "public interest" and the "general interest". Moreover, one could as well consider the differences of the two provisions as regards the description of the domestic legal basis and the competence to perform the 'necessity test', cf. Article 1(2) which seems to leave it entirely to the domestic bodies.

However, I have chosen not to do so as I do not expect the result to bear comparison with the efforts. Moreover, such an analysis would be in the periphery of my analysis. My primary interest is the protection of housing rights under the ECHR rather than the 'division' of the protection between two provisions.

8 *Future Prospects*

The case law of the ECtHR only encompasses aspects of the right to housing, and there is indeed a difference between the case law of the Court and that of the ECSR and the ICESCR.[100] Nevertheless, the Court's case law is interesting also from a social point of view, and one can far from exclude that it will develop in the future for the benefit of those who are in need of (protection of) a home. However, in a commentary to the ECHR on the *Velosa Barreto* case it has been suggested that:

> [i]t is likely that this rather marginal test [of 'arbitrariness or unreasonableness', author's insertion] is influenced, on the one hand, by the broad concept of 'economic well-being of the country' as a ground of restriction invoked in this particular case, and on the other hand by the 'social right' nature of the right at issue: the right to a home. Interference in this matter could easily lead the Court into the thicket of judging upon social and economic issues of housing policies. The absence of a clear emergency situation on the part of the applicant may also explain and justify this approach in this particular case.[101]

---

100 For a comprehensive coverage of the right to housing, cf. e.g. Rachel G. Bratt, Michael E. Stone and Chester Hartman (eds.), *A right to housing: foundation for a new social agenda*, Philadelphia, PA : Temple University Press, 2006.

101 Aaat Willem Heringa and Leo Zwaak (rev.) in P. van Dijk et al. (eds.), *Theory and Practice of the European Convention on Human Rights*, 4th Edition, Intersentia, 2006, p. 725.

The commentary goes on to say that the recognition of a right to a decent home would amount to a considerable socialisation of Article 8. "The Court may be expected to only recognise a positive obligation as to housing in circumstances in which there is a finding of a serious infringement of one's personal life as well as a disproportional balancing (arbitrariness, unreasonableness) of the conflicting interests".[102] It has furthermore been suggested that "the approach adopted by the Court in balancing the competing interests might leave some room for a gradual expansion of Article 8 by allowing for social rights elements to be included, while taking one step at a time."[103]

The *Velosa Barreto* case is indeed not a case in which such a step has been taken despite the fact that it seems quite radical to deny the Barreto family the right to take up residence in a house of their own the general circumstances taken into consideration. Something similar can be said about the cases concerning gypsies' right to planning permission, cf. eg. *Chapman v. the United Kingdom.*[104] On the other hand, none of the judgments were unanimous, and in the cases concerning gypsies applying for planning permission the dissenting opinion was quite strong. One can not exclude, therefore, that the Court in the future will take steps to develop the protection of the right to housing thereby harmonising the interpretation of the ECHR with the ESC/RESC.[105]

[102] *Ibid.*

[103] *Ibid.*

[104] *Chapman v. the United Kingdom.*

[105] Cf. e.g. Complaint No. 39/2006, *European Federation of National Organisations Working with the Homeless (FEANTSA) v. France*, Decision of 5 December 2007. The complaint related to Article 31 (the right to housing) of the RESC. The ECSR concluded that there was a violation of Articles 31 §§1 and 2 and Article 31 §3 in conjunction with Article E of the RESC.

Chapter 7

The Right to Education Under the ECHR

1 *Education as a Cross-Cutting Issue*

When asking why a holistic approach to human rights in general is necessary, the right to education provides much of an answer. Not only is the right to education a human right in itself. The right to education also has an important role to play as a linkage and as a key to the unlocking of other human rights – economic, social and cultural as well as civil and political ones. Education is an indispensable means of realising human rights in general,[1] and the following quotation from the famous American judgment, *Brown v. Board of Education* is very much to the point:

> Today, education is perhaps the most important function of state and local governments. Compulsory school attendance laws and the great expenditures for education both demonstrate our recognition of the importance of education to our democratic society. It is required in the performance of our most basic public responsibilities, even service in the armed forces. It is the very foundation of good citizenship. Today it is a principal instrument in awakening the child to cultural values, in preparing him for later professional training, and in helping him to adjust normally to his environment. In these days, it is doubtful that any child may reasonably be expected to succeed in life if he is denied the opportunity of an education. Such an opportunity, where the state has undertaken to provide it, is a right which must be made available to all on equal terms.[2]

Free and compulsory education until a certain age functions as a protective measure against economic exploitation of children either by parents or by employers. Hence, a fixed minimum age for admission to employment corresponding to the age for the completion of compulsory education is likely to support other endeavours to protect children against child labour and trafficking. Not only does education protect children from entering the labour market

[1] Cf. CESCR *General Comment No. 13*, The right to education (Art. 13), 1999, para. 1.

[2] *Brown v. Board of Education*, 347 U.S. 483 (1954).

at too early an age. An increasing number of jobs require skills and knowledge, and education increases the opportunities of obtaining a well-paid job, this again having a number of consequences e.g. for social security and old-age security.

The link between education and health has likewise been emphasised on several occasions. In recent years focus has been attached to the importance of information about how to protect oneself against HIV-infection, but the linkage between the right to education and the right to health is of a much more general character. Article 24(2)(e) of the CRC lists education as an appropriate measure to ensure the popularisation of existing knowledge on nutrition, advantages of breast-feeding, hygiene, environmental sanitation and prevention of accidents.

The impact of education is not only on economic, social and cultural rights but reaches into the sphere of civil and political rights. Most conspicuous is the impact of education on participation rights in general. Education has an impact on the full enjoyment of the right to vote and for political representation and is therefore of vital importance for the development and for the functioning of democracy. Illiterate persons are rarely – if ever – elected to political bodies, and the elected representatives usually belong to the best-educated part of the population. Furthermore, a minimum level of education including literacy is necessary for the seeking and receiving of information and for the freedom of expression, assembly and association. These rights have little substance and meaning for the illiterate.

Finally, illiterate persons and persons without basic education make up a regrettably large percentage of the prison population thereby proving the intimate link between the right to education and the right to personal liberty.

2 *The Right to Education in Three Generations*

The cross-cutting nature of the right to education explains the difficulties as to the classifying of the right to education as a first, second or third generation right.[3] Most often, the right to education is classified as a second generation right, although it is disputed whether it belongs in

[3] Civil and political rights are often referred to as *first generation rights*, economic, social and cultural rights as *second generation rights*, whereas the right to development and other solidarity rights are refereed to as *third generation rights*, cf. e.g. Asbjørn Eide & Allan Rosas in Asbjørn Eide et al. (eds.) *Economic, Social and Cultural Rights – A Textbook*, Martinus Nijhoff Publ., The Hague, 2001, p. 4 with reference to Karel Vasak.

the sub-category of economic, social or cultural rights. The assignment of the right to education to the category of economic, social and cultural rights is due to the fact that *the full realisation* of the right to education requires active and resource-demanding State action.

However, the right to education can easily be described as a classical freedom right obliging the State to refrain from interferences in choices as regards education because of religious and philosophical convictions. This respect of the liberty of parents fits most naturally into the category of first generation rights. The fact that the right to education has links also with third generation rights, however, is pointed out among others by Manfred Nowak[4] – who refers to provisions in the CESCR and the CRC obliging States to co-operate within the field of education.[5] In this co-operation particular account must be taken of the needs of developing countries.

Accordingly, the right to education *is* in fact included in human rights conventions belonging to all categories, and while some might find it somewhat unusual to discuss the right to e.g. health and housing under the ECHR, hardly anyone would deny the relevance of discussing the right to education under this Convention. In contrast to most other rights that are traditionally considered economic, social and cultural rights, the right to education *is* specifically protected under the ECHR.

3 *The Right to Education Under the ECHR*

3.1 *Relevant Provisions*

The extended introduction given above serves as an attempt to explain why it would be meaningful to include a provision on the right to education in a convention which primarily appears to protect civil and political rights. However, the inclusion of a right to education in the ECHR is not necessarily due to such integrative considerations, and the following analysis seeks to explore whether or to which extent an integrated approach to the right to education and other human rights is actually reflected in the ECHR. A few introductory remarks are appropriate.

The right to education is specifically protected by Article 2 of Protocol No. 1 to the ECHR. The provision runs as follows:

> No person shall be denied the right to education. In the exercise of any functions which it assumes in relation to education and to teaching, the State shall respect

---

[4] Cf. Manfred Nowak in "The Right to Education" in Asbjørn Eide et al., *Ibid.*, p. 252 ff.

[5] Cf. ICESCR Article 15(4) and CRC Article 28(3).

> the right of parents to ensure such education and teaching in conformity with their own religious and philosophical convictions.

Article 2 of the First Protocol contains a primary right to education and a secondary right to be educated in accordance with parental convictions. However, as the ECtHR has pointed out on a number of occasions "Article 2 [....] constitutes a whole that is dominated by its first sentence. "The right set out in the second sentence of Article 2 [....] is an adjunct of this fundamental right to education."[6] This statement reflects a holistic – one could say hermeneutic – perspective on human rights protection, and the Court even goes on to state that the two sentences should be read not only in the light of each other "but also, in particular of Articles 8, 9 and 10 [....] of the Convention which proclaim the right of everyone, including parents and children to 'respect for his private and family life', to 'freedom of thought, conscience and religion' and to 'freedom....to receive and impart information and ideas.'"[7]

Moreover, aspects of the right to education might also be included in other of the Convention's rights. That is the case as regards Article 3 and Article 5 (1) (e), and links between the right to education and other articles of the Convention might also be established. This is the case as regards Article 6[8] on the right to fair trial and Article 11 on freedom of association. Moreover, even though Article 2 of Protocol No. 1 as such includes aspects of non-discrimination cf. the expression "*no person* shall be denied the right to education [author's emphasis]", Article 14 has been invoked on a number of occasions in regard to educational matters.

In this context it is, however, particularly interesting whether the integrative approach of the Court does also go beyond the scope of the ECHR. The following analysis serves exactly this purpose, and has no intention of covering all aspects of the right to education under the Protocol. Accordingly, the chapter does not provide an extensive overview of case law, and it avoids any attempt to define the content of expressions such as "religious and philosophical convictions". He who seeks a thorough analysis of case law under the ECHR should therefore look elsewhere. Moreover, the analysis cuts across the first and second sentence of Article 2 of Protocol No. 1 – in good compliance with the conception of the Court of the two sentences as interlinked – in search of the 'positive' elements of the provision as such. In addition to the analysis of case law under Protocol No. 1 special attention is given to case law under Article 5

[6] Cf. *Kjeldsen, Busk Madsen and Pedersen v. Denmark*, para. 52 and *Campbell and Cosans v. the United Kingdom*, Judgment of 25 February 1982, para. 40.

[7] *Kjeldsen, Busk Madsen and Pedersen v. Denmark*, para. 52.

[8] As for the question whether educational matters can be regarded as "civil rights and obligations", cf. e.g. Anthony Bradley, The Convention Right to Education and the Human Rights Act 1998 in *European Human Rights Law Review*, 1999, Issue 4, p. 406 f.

(1)(e) under the ECHR, cf. below in Section 3.2.5, whereas aspects of the right to education under other articles of the Convention are only dealt with sporadically on the way if or where it seems apt.

3.2 *'Positive' Rights to Primary Education Under Article 2 of Protocol No. 1*

3.2.1 *Article 2 of Protocol No. 1 and Other Provisions on the Right to Education*

When talking about the right to education under Article 2 of Protocol No. 1 a relevant question – in this specific context – is whether the provision only includes what is traditionally regarded as a freedom right or whether it also encompasses active obligations. Is the right to education divided between the two sets of treaties in accordance with the traditional 'positive/negative' dichotomy, or is Article 2 of Protocol No. 1 to be read in conformity and/or in conjunction with the provisions on the right to education in the conventions on economic, social and cultural rights, the ESC, the RESC, the CESCR and with the CRC?[9] Relevant questions in this context are whether the right to education under Protocol No. 1 is to be considered *compulsory* and available *free of charge*, and whether it makes sense to talk about *minimum core rights* to education. Even though Protocol No. 1 covers the field of education more broadly I will restrict myself to dealing with primary and secondary education.[10] Most of the case law concerns these issues and the issue of 'positive' rights is most essential in regard to basic schooling.

The ESC is of limited interest in this context since it only provides for vocational guidance and training and seems to presuppose the existence of educational facilities for children.[11] Thus, the right to primary education is only mentioned indirectly in Article 7 (3) according to which persons who are still subject to compulsory education must not be employed in such work that would deprive them of the full benefit of the education.[12] A provision on (compulsory) education is, however, missing in the ESC,[13] and the RESC applies the traditional means-and-ends approach in Article 17 (2) by obliging States Parties to "take all appropriate and necessary measures designed" "to provide

---

[9] Mention could also be made of CCPR Article 18 (4) which – together with CESCR Article 13 (3) – is the UN counterpart of the second sentence of Article 2 of ECHR Protocol No. 1.

[10] About the right to education of an adult, cf. e.g. *Mürsel Eren v. Turkey*, Judgment of 7 February 2006.

[11] ESC, Articles 9 and 10.

[12] Cf. also ESC Article 7 (4) on working hours of people under the age of 18.

[13] Alledgedly because the right to education was not considered a matter of social policy, cf. Donna Gomien et al., *Law and practice of the European Convention on Human Rights and the European Social Charter*, Council of Europe Publishing, 1996, p. 407.

to children and young persons a free primary and secondary education as well as to encourage regular attendance at schools". Article 17 (2) does not specifically mention compulsory education. However, in the Appendix to the Charter it is stated that there is no obligation to provide compulsory education up to the age of majority. The explanation to this apparent inconsistence is given in the Explanatory Report in this way: "The reason that there is no mention of compulsory education in the paragraph itself is that in some states only primary education is compulsory, whereas in others secondary education is also compulsory."[14] This must be understood as if the protection of the RESC is in fact similar to that of the CESCR even though is has found no clear expression in the treaty. A relevant question remains, however, to which rules the ESC refers. Is it the presupposed compulsory education in ESC Article 7 (3), the one which is stipulated in domestic legislation or does the provision refer to other human rights treaties such as the CESCR, the CRC *and* the ECHR? It must necessarily refer to regulation and not to facts. Education can take place without regulation, but compulsory education cannot. This question is indeed relevant, since the RESC has only been ratified by 25 Member States.[15]

The protection of the right to education in the COE has improved by the adoption of the RESC. However, the wording of the European provisions are indeed vague compared to Article 13 (2)(a) in the CESCR, which is quite clear and often pointed out as one of the justiciable provisions in the Covenant.[16] According to CESCR Article 13 (2)(a) primary education shall be *compulsory* and available *free* to all. If not free it cannot be available to those without means, and only when compulsory does the right to primary education provide an efficient protection against child labour.[17] Article 28 (1)(a) of the CRC is worded likewise also as regards secondary education which shall (only) be made generally available and accessible to all by every appropriate means, and in particular by the progressive introduction of free education, cf. CESCR Article 13 (2)(b) and CRC Article 28 (1)(b).

The Committee on economic, social and cultural rights has furthermore dealt with the issue of *minimum core obligations* in relation to the right to education in its General Comment No. 3 and found that States Parties have "a minimum core obligation to ensure the satisfaction of, at the very least,

---

[14] Explanatory Report to the RESC, para. 74.

[15] As of 20 August 2008 25 COE Member States had ratified the RESC. By the same date 27 Member States had ratified the ESC.

[16] Cf. CESCR, *General Comment No. 3*, The nature of States parties Obligations (Art. 2, par. 1):.14/12/90, para. 5

[17] The conception of CESCR Article 13 (2) (a) as a provision subject to immediate implementation is modified by Article 14. This provision addresses the situation in developing countries and has limited relevance in the COE.

minimum essential levels" of each of the rights enunciated in the Covenant, including "the most basic forms of education".[18] And in its General Comment No. 12 the Committee developed further the content of the minimum core obligation in the following way:

> In the context of article 13, this core includes an obligation: to ensure the right of access to public educational institutions and programmes on a non-discriminatory basis; to ensure that education conforms to the objectives set out in article 13 (1); to provide primary education for all in accordance with article 13 (2) (a); to adopt and implement a national educational strategy which includes provision for secondary, higher and fundamental education; and to ensure free choice of education without interference from the State or third parties, subject to conformity with "minimum educational standards" (art. 13 (3) and (4)).[19]

3.2.2 *The Travaux Préparatoire to Article 2 of Protocol No. 1*

The right to education had a "stormy genesis".[20] The negotiations in the COE lasted for almost three years (from 1949–1952), and the outcome must be characterised as somewhat of a compromise "based on a common condemnation of events from the past but not on a common policy for the future."[21] The disagreements were many,[22] and far from all of them are relevant in this context. The "common condemnation of events from the past" concerned primarily the obvious interest in preventing a repetition of the totalitarian influence of the educational system under the Nazi regime. However, also a good portion of Communist scare left its stamp on the negotiations[23] which were otherwise not at all dominated by a wish to secure the child's interest in education. What was in focus was the interest of parents – in particular the father as head of the family – and when reading the preparatory works with contemporary glasses it is difficult not to smile a little. Just one example: "The right to give education, moral and intellectual training to a child [....] rests with none other

[18] CESCR, *General Comment No. 3*, para. 10.

[19] CESCR, *General Comment No. 12*, The right to education (Art. 13):. 0/8/12/99. E/C.12/1999/10, para. 57.

[20] Cf. Torkel Opsahl, "The Convention and the right to respect for family life, particularly as regards the unity of the family and the protection of the rights of parents and guardians in the education of children" in *Privacy and Human Rights*, Manchester University Press, 1973, p. 221.

[21] *Ibid.*, p. 244.

[22] Cf. e.g. *The British Year Book of International Law 1951*, Oxford University Press, 1952, *Preparatory work on Article 2 of the Protocol to the Convention*, COE, CDH (67) 2 and *Collected Edition of the "Travaux Préparatoires" of the European Convention on Human Rights, Vol. VII*, Martinus Nijhoff Publishers, 1985.

[23] Cf. the description by Opsahl with references to the preparatory works, Torkel Opsahl, *Ibid.*, p. 236 f.

than its father. This is a matter of natural right."[24] There is little mention of a natural right of the child to receive education, and the issue is predominantly that of protecting parents from improper State interference with family and private life. In this context it is worth mentioning that the article originally was discussed as part of a group of family rights with particular focus on the principle which later found its expression in the second sentence.

It is true that the negotiations took their point of departure in Article 26 of the UDHR with its various elements.[25] According to Article 26 parents e.g. have a prior right to choose the kind of education that shall be given to their children, and (fundamental) education shall be free and compulsory. Nevertheless, the preparatory works are not very preoccupied with the rights and duties of the child but rather with the rights of parents and in particular the possible budgetary implication of the rights of parents as regards the free choice of education. What worried some Member States was whether an obligation to respect all sorts of religious and philosophical beliefs would entail an obligation to provide or subsidise education performed in accordance with such beliefs. In this context it should be mentioned that an original duty to "have regard to" had been replaced by the stronger duty to "respect". The impact of this fear eventually went beyond the provision on parental rights and affected the first sentence which has the child as its addressee.

According to the original drafting of the first sentence of Article 2 "every person has the right to education". Some States, however, raised objections to the wording fearing that "if the right to education were stated positively, it might be interpreted as imposing on the governments the obligation to take effective measures to ensure that everybody could receive the education *which he desired*" [author's emphasis].[26] Accordingly, the formulation "[n]o person shall be denied the right to education" was eventually preferred in order to underline that States themselves should have the power to decide to which extent resources are to be spent on educational purposes. No one questioned, however, that children have a right and also a duty to be educated at the expense of the Member States as long as the States themselves have the competence to decide the setting up of a public educational system. In this context is should be recalled that the COE consisted of far fewer[27] and more homogeneous

---

[24] *Preparatory work on Article 2 of the Protocol to the Convention*, COE, CDH (67) 2, p. 188 (Mr. Boggiano Pico, Italy).

[25] *Preparatory work on Article 2 of the Protocol to the Convention*, COE, CDH (67) 2, p. 1.

[26] *The British Year Book of International Law*, p. 362 ff and *Collected Edition of the "Travaux Préparatoires" of the European Convention on Human Rights, Vol. VII*, p. 201 ff. and 208 ff.

[27] At the time of the adoption of Protocol No. 1 the following States were members of the COE: Belgium, Denmark, France, Germany, Greece, Iceland, Ireland, Italy, Luxembourg, the Netherlands, Norway, Sweden, Turkey and the United Kingdom.

States[28] than is the case to day, and that all States did in fact provide compulsory primary education free of charge – in line with the requirements deriving from Article 26 of the UDHR. The wording was not really aimed at primary education but rather at other requirements which were not necessarily met in the COE Member States:

> While education is provided by the State for children, as a matter of course, in all Member States, it is not possible for them to give an unlimited guarantee to provide education, as that might be construed to apply to illiterate adults for whom no facilities exist, or to types and standards of education which the State cannot furnish for one reason or another.[29]

Thus, the right to primary education was not really the issue, it was presupposed, cf. also the expression "[i]n the exercise of any functions which it [the State, author's addition] assumes in relation to education and teaching." Whatever the State "assumes" is uncertain, but it does indeed assume something.

Against this background it *is* a relevant question whether or to which extent the right to education in Article 2 of Protocol No 1 also encompasses a right to demand a certain standard of education free of charge or – in other words – whether the provision should be interpreted in the light of other 'positive' requirements in regard to education as they derive from the UDHR. Equally relevant is the question whether the right to education is to be understood also as a duty.

These questions have never been properly answered in case law from the ECtHR, which is far from being extensive. However, aspects of the questions have been addressed also by the Commission, and the *travaux préparatoire* should be kept in mind when trying to throw light on the issue. The Court has in fact made frequent reference to the *travaux préparatoire* in its judgments concerning the right to education,[30] and one might consider whether the preparatory work to Protocol No. 1 constitutes an exception to the general (hermeneutic) assumption that the original intention of the drafters of the Convention has limited importance in a contemporary context. This question will de dealt with in further detail below.

[28] With Turkey as a possible exception.

[29] *Preparatory work on Article 2 of the Protocol to the Convention*, COE, CDH (67) 2, p. 152 (Commentary by the Secretariat-General on the draft Protocol).

[30] *Case relating to certain aspects of the laws on the use of languages in education in Belgium*, Judgment of 23 July 1968, [hereinafter the *Belgium Linguistic case*], B. Interpretation adopted by the Court., para 3., *Kjeldsen, Busk Madsen and Pedersen v. Denmark*, para. 50 and *Campbell and Cosans v. the United Kingdom*, para. 36.

3.2.3 *Case Law Under Article 2 of Protocol No. 1*

Despite the *travaux préparatoires* the Court has held from the outset that Article 2 of Protocol No. 1 *has* a 'positive' content, without, however, defining this content in great detail. In the *Belgian Linguistic* case the Court referred to the *travaux préparatoires* in the following way:

> The negative formulation indicates, as is confirmed by the "preparatory work" [....] that the Contracting Parties do not recognise such a right to education as would require them to establish at their own expense, or to subsidise, education of any particular type or at any particular level. *However, it cannot be concluded from this that the State has no positive obligation* to ensure respect for such a right as is protected by Article 2 of the Protocol [....][author's emphasis].[31]

The Court went on by noting that all Member States of the COE possessed a general and official educational system at the time when the ECHR was adopted and that there was – and is – no question of *establishing* such a system:

> but merely of guaranteeing to persons subject to the jurisdiction of the Contracting Parties the right, in principle, to avail themselves of the means of instruction existing at a given time. The Convention lays down no specific obligations concerning the extent of these means and the manner of their organisation or subsidisation.[32]

This implies without any doubt that States enjoy an even very wide – but not unlimited – discretion in regard to the educational set-up. Thus, according to the *Belgian Linguistic case* the right to education signifies at least a right to access to existing educational facilities, a right to be educated in a national language and a right to obtain official recognition of completed studies.[33] It is furthermore assumed that the right to education includes entry to nursery, primary, secondary and higher education.[34] However, little can be said as to questions such as school age, length of (compulsory) school attendance, curricula etc., and the obligations incumbent upon States as regards establishing or subsidising educational facilities for children or adults with special needs or requirements are limited. Neither is there a right of parents to demand that their children are educated at a particular school.[35] It is assumed that Article 2

31 *The Belgian Linguistic case*, B. Interpretation adopted by the Court, para. 3.

32 *Ibid.*

33 *Ibid.*, paras. 3 og 4.

34 Cf. Luzius Wildhaber, "Right to Education and Parental Rights" in R. St.J. Macdonald et al. (eds.), *The European System for the Protection of Human Rights*, Martinus Nijhoff Publ, 1993, p. 531.

35 In three cases, the Court has rejected the argument that a refusal to allow gypsies to remain on their land with their caravans due to planning measures resulted in their children effectively being denied access to satisfactory education, cf. *Coster v. the United Kingdom*, *Lee v the United Kingdom* and *Jane Smith v. the United Kingdom*, all Judgments of 18 January 2001.

prevents States from denying citizens the right to establish special educational facilities to safeguard e.g. religious convictions or for the purpose of preserving linguistic traditions. However, the respect of parents' philosophical conviction and religious belief does not imply an obligation to provide for schools to accommodate special wishes. The requirement does not go beyond what can be acknowledged within the existing school system. It is usually assumed that there is no duty to subsidise private or special schools.[36] If, however, such schools are established – and indeed if they are publicly subsidised – it is incumbent on the Member States to ensure that the rights under the Protocol are guaranteed. In sum, if the educational set up chosen by a State does not infringe on the right not to be discriminated against, cf. Article 14,[37] the discretion is even very wide.[38] As the Court has put it:

> The right to education [....] by its very nature calls for regulation by the State, regulation which may vary in time and place according to the needs and resources of the community and of individuals. It goes without saying that such regulation must never injure *the substance of the right to education* nor conflict with other rights in the Convention [author's emphasis].[39]

The last past of the quotation, however, raises the question whether this implies that Member States are absolutely free to reduce the educational standard indefinitely or whether they are obliged to maintain a certain minimum standard in order not to injure *the substance of the right to education.* There is a strong case for reading at least some substantial requirements into the Article as it makes limited sense to talk about e.g. a prohibition to discriminate if there

---

36 Cf. e.g (rev.) by Ben Vermeulen in P. van Dijk et al. (eds.) *Theory and Practice of the European Convention on Human Rights*, 4th Edition, Intersentia p. 899. The Human Rights Committee has expressed a similar view on the basis of the general non-discrimination clause in CCPR Article 26 by stating that "a State party cannot be deemed to discriminate against parents, who freely choose not to avail themselves of benefits which are generally open to all", cf. *Blom, Lindgren et al. v. Sweden*, Communication No. 191/1985 and Communication No. 298 and 299/1988.

37 Some COE Member States do in fact discriminate against Roma children, cf. Fons Coomans, "Discrimination and Stigmatisation regarding Education: The Case of the Romani Children in the Czech Republic" in Willems (ed.), *Developmental and Autonomy Rights of Children: Empowering Children, Caregivers and Communities*, Intersentia, 2002.

38 If, however, the state educational system is found to be discriminatory, it might have budgetary consequences for the State. If e.g. a State Party chooses to provide public funding to religious schools, it should make this funding available without discrimination. This means that providing funding for the schools of one religious group and not for another must be based on reasonable and objective criteria. In a concrete case the Human Rights Committee concluded that a differential treatment between the Roman Catholic faith and the author's religious denomination violated the author's rights under article 26 of the Covenant, cf. *Arieh Hollis Waldman v. Canada, Communication No. 694/1996,* View of 5 November 1999.

39 *Belgium Linguistic case, Ibid.*, para 5.

is nothing or little to be distributed. In other words, is it possible to read a *minimum core right* to education into Article 2 of the First Protocol, and in that case how is it to be defined?

There is nothing in the preparatory works that answers the question directly. One might conclude by contrast from the debate during the drafting of the provision that Member States have accepted a public responsibility for *some* resource allocation, cf. the passage that "the Contracting Parties do not recognise such a right to education as would require them to establish at their expense, or to subsidise education of any *particular* type or at any *particular* level" [author's emphasis].[40] Primary and secondary education in general can hardly be considered education either of a particular type or a particular level. A similar contrasting conclusion can be drawn from the general opinion that it is not incumbent on States to subsidise private schools. Moreover, since the right to primary education is not directly covered by the ESC – which is still the only relevant economic, social and cultural rights treaty for a number of Member States – it would indeed be paradoxical if the obligation incumbent on relatively more affluent COE Member States on the basis of regional treaties were to be less extensive than that, which can be derived from e.g. the CESCR and the CRC. Case law, however, provides only scattered fragments as regards the more precise content of such a minimum core.

The Court was for the first time confronted with the issue of active and resource demanding obligations in regard to education in the already referred to *Belgium Linguistic* case in which a group of French-speaking parents claimed that part of the Belgian legislation was inconsistent with Article 2 of Protocol No. 1 since it did not allow for French-speaking children residing in the Flemish-speaking part of Belgium to be educated in French. Only by travelling to schools at a considerable distance from their homes could the children be taught in French. The Court recognised – as indicated above – that "the right to education would be meaningless if it did not imply in favour of its beneficiaries, the right to be educated in the national language or in one of the national languages, as the case may be."[41] However, the Court did not find that Protocol No. 1 requires of States that they should respect parents' linguistic preferences, but only their religious and philosophical convictions.[42] Only in one respect did the Court find a violation of the ECHR. Some French-speaking children were prevented from having access to French-language schools in six districts ("communes") in the periphery of Brussels (which is bilingual) solely on the basis of the residence of their parents. No equivalent restriction applied to

---

40 *Belgium Linguistic case, Ibid.*, para 3.

41 *Ibid.*, para. 3.

42 *Ibid.*, para. 6.

Flemish-speaking children, and the Court – on an eight to seven vote – found a violation of the Protocol in conjunction with Article 14 of the Convention.

Considering the fact that French is one of the territorial languages in Belgium – and indeed widely spoken – the decision seems to place limited burdens on the Member States. Luzius Wildhaber – writing in his personal capacity twenty years after the judgment – finds it "too harsh to claim that the right to education 'contains in itself no linguistic requirements'" and is of the opinion that "it remains open whether a denial of a right to be educated in a language which is spoken in a State but not defined as a national language should not be considered a violation of Article 2."[43] He emphasises the intimate connection between education and language and argues that the possibility of drawing profit from an education received in a national language other than the territorial language might be arbitrarily restricted if the position in the *Belgian Linguistic* case is to be upheld. In this context one might consider why the Court chose to refer to the fact that some of the drafters of the Protocol were of the opinion that the right of parents to choose a language other than that of the country in question "concerned an aspect of the problem of ethnic minorities and that it consequently fell outside the scope of the Convention [....]."[44] That might be true. However, irrespective of how one defines an ethnic minority, the notion would hardly include French-speaking people in Belgium.

I cannot but endorse the opinion of Luzius Wildhaber and add that if the conception of 'positive' obligations as introduced in the *Belgian Linguistic* case were to be upheld today very few aspects of educational policy would be encompassed by the Protocol. The judgment merely presupposes an educational system the content of which is, however, completely blurred.

Before discussing this issue in further detail, one might draw a parallel to Article 6 about the right to a fair trial since this provision also presupposes something, namely the existence of an "independent and impartial tribunal established by law". Article 6 does not specifically impose a duty upon States to establish a (resource-demanding) judicial system, and even though especially sub-paragraph 3 specifically requires the existence of e.g. interpreters and free legal assistance in criminal cases, the basic surrounding machinery of justice – buildings, educated judges, other staff, etc. – is in principle presupposed. However, the right to a fair trial would completely lose its *raison d'être* if a judicial system had not been established, and it would be fair to say that the provision implies that it is incumbent on Member States to establish such a system, the quality of which may very well vary among the Member States depending on the resource situation in the individual State.

---

43 Luzius Wildhaver, *Ibid.*, p. 541.

44 *Belgium Linguistic case, Ibid.*, para. 7.

In fact, the right to fair trial is implemented at different levels in the COE Member States, which proves that the right to fair trial – although characterised as a civil right – is subject to progressive realisation. However, certain (European) minimum requirements must be understood with respect to the education of judges, capacity of the legal machinery, etc. By way of example, Member States must take 'positive' measures with a view to securing fair trial within a "reasonable time" and the Court has repeatedly held that a backlog of cases or a restructuring of the judicial system are not valid excuses.[45] The *Airey* case – in which the Court chose to go beyond the wording of the provision and – if necessary – include a right to legal aid also in civil law suits points in the same direction.[46]

Something similar can be argued in regard to the right to education:

> However, the exercise of the right to education, understood as a right of equal access, requires by implication the existence and the maintenance of a minimum of education provided by the State, since otherwise that right would be illusory, in particular for those who have insufficient means to maintain their own institutions. Denying a person the possibility to receive primary education has such far-reaching consequences for the development of the person and for his possibilities to enjoy the rights and freedoms of the Convention to the full that such a treatment is contrary, *if not to the letter of Article 2, at all events to the whole system of the Convention, in the light of which Article 2 has to be interpreted* [author's emphasis].[47]

This – hermeneutic – perspective on the right to education as an effective right and as a precondition to the enjoyment of other human rights is also reflected in the case *Cyprus v. Turkey* about the 'positive' right of Greek-Cypriot children to receive secondary school education in Greek language in the northern (Turkish) part of Cyprus.[48] The children in question had received primary-school education in their own language. However, the secondary educational facilities which were formerly available to the children of Greek-Cypriots had been abolished by the Turkish-Cypriot authorities, and restrictions imposed by these authorities prevented the children from attending schools in the southern (Greek) part of Cyprus. Accordingly, their only possibility was to continue their education at a Turkish- or English-language school in the north.

In the strict sense, accordingly, the Greek-Cypriot children were not *denied* the right to education, which is the primary obligation devolving on a Contracting Party under Article 2 of Protocol No. 1. Moreover, this provision does not specify the language in which education must be provided in order that the right can be respected. However, in the Court's opinion, the option available to

---

45 *Süßmann v. Germany*, Judgment of 16 September 1996, para.55.

46 *Airey v. Ireland*.

47 Ben Vermeulen, *Ibid*., p. 899.

48 *Cyprus v. Turkey*, Judgment of 10 May 2001.

Greek-Cypriot parents to continue their children's education in the north was unrealistic in view of the fact that the children in question had already received their primary education in a Greek-Cypriot school there. The Court held that the authorities must without doubt have been aware that it was the wish of Greek-Cypriot parents that the schooling of their children be completed through the medium of the Greek language. Having assumed responsibility for the provision of Greek-language primary schooling, the failure of the Turkish-Cypriot authorities to make continuing provision for it at the secondary-school level had to be considered in effect to be a denial of the substance of the right at issue. Accordingly, the Court concluded that there had been a violation of Article 2 of Protocol No. 1 in respect of Greek-Cypriots living in northern Cyprus in so far as no appropriate secondary-school facilities were available to them.

The judgment illustrates once again that the Court does not necessarily seek to avoid deciding on issues that have budgetary implications for the Member States, and it might in the long run contribute to the recognition of a minimum core right to education under the Convention. It is true, of course, that the decision has the character of a prohibition against interference in a previously existing good – secondary school education in Greek language – and in this way it differs from the *Belgian Linguistic* case. However, the practical implication of the decision bears upon the possibilities of the Turkish-Cypriot authorities to freely use their budget, and in this way a 'negative' obligation turns out to have 'positive' implications after all. The obligation might to some extent limit the manoeuvring room of Member States with respect to their disposal over resources, and one might as well argue that what the case illustrates is the 'negative' aspect of the notion of progressive realisation, i.e. the prohibition against retrogressive measures.

Even though one should be cautious in comparing cases – two sets of facts are never identical, and there *is* a difference between never establishing and discontinuing a public good – one might, nevertheless, consider whether the Court is in a process of distancing itself from its previous viewpoints in the *Belgian Linguistic case* in regard to the very restrictive inclusion of 'positive' obligations under the provision on the right to education. In this context it is interesting to note that the Court found no reason to refer to the *travaux préparatoires* in the case *Cyprus v. Turkey*, and that this decision had further budgetary implications than many previous decisions in the field of education in which the preparatory work has been mentioned.[49]

---

[49] Another question is whether States are obliged to create additional educational facilities for the benefit of those aliens having taken up residence in the territory for a considerable time who do not yet have sufficient command of the language in which education is conducted. Ben Vermeulen answers the question in the affirmative as regards elementary education, *Ibid.*, p. 909.

The Court's interpretation of the right to education under the ECHR has indeed undergone a development in the time span between the two decisions – 33 years – and the Court's incentive to accept 'positive' obligations under the Convention and its Protocols has increased to a considerable extent. The two cases – *Cyprus v. Turkey* and the *Belgian Linguistic* case – represent two different stages in the evolution of case law, and the original approach taken in the Belgian case was and had to be cautious, since it was one of the very first cases with which the Court had to deal. It could be argued that the decision has set back the development by the Strasbourg organs of the right to education. However, considering the preceding extraordinary complicated and lengthy negotiations in the COE, it could hardly be expected that the Court already in 1967 would be prepared to introduce what would probably have been considered a revolutionary interpretation. The preparatory works give good support for the view that Article 2 of Protocol No. 1 contains only an obligation not to interfere, and one might say that the Court by choosing a teleological interpretation adopted a very independent position.

When considering to which extent the Court in recent years has been willing to read active, resource-demanding elements into other of the Convention's articles, it is, however, not surprising that the Court in the *Cyprus v. Turkey* case took one step further along this road. Case law on the right to education is, however, limited. The Court has not often had the opportunity to decide on educational matters, and it is too soon to guess whether it has in fact distanced itself from its previous use of preparatory works as an obligatory and decisive legal source in the interpretation of Protocol No. 1. However, there is no doubt an ever existing wish among the Member States to avoid excessively burdensome and resource-demanding obligations, and one might say that the common referral to the *travaux préparatoires* has as much to do with the traditional – albeit decreasing – reluctance of law applying bodies towards resource-demanding issues as with a wish to applying an interpretation faithful to the original intention. In this context it is worth remembering that the Court did *not* refer to the *travaux préparatoires* in the case *Cyprus v. Turkey*.

The Court did exactly that, however, in the admissibility decision in the case *Skender v. the Former Yugoslav Republic of Macedonia* about Turkish-speaking children's right to receive education in Turkish in Macedonian schools. Under the Macedonian Constitution members of minorities have the right to receive primary and secondary education in their own language, a right which was, however, not implemented in the applicant's municipality, and his daughter was denied the right to be educated in another district.[50] When declaring most

[50] Cf. *Skender v. the Former Republic of Macedonia*, Admissibility decision of 22 November 2001.

of the complaint inadmissible the Court repeated the drafting history of the article and brought to mind that the drafting committee had "set aside a proposal put forward in this sense, several of its members having believed that it concerned an aspect of the problem of ethnic minorities and that it thus fell outside the scope of the Convention [...]."[51] In this case, however, a referral to the concern about language rights and minorities is in place considering the fact that Turks constitute only a few percentages of the Macedonian population. There is a huge difference between providing mother tongue education for an – often large – number of ethnic minority groups and providing education in Greek and French in Northern Cyprus and Belgium respectively.

Also the case *Campbell and Cosans v. the United Kingdom*[52] about corporal punishment in Scottish schools illustrates the 'positive' dimensions of Article 2 of Protocol No. 1, even though the case apparently had to do with non-interference. Parents who opposed corporal punishment could not obtain a guarantee that corporal punishment would not be applied and therefore claimed that their children were actually denied the right to education, since there was no alternative. Neither of the children in question were actually punished, but the refusal to accept punishment as such had the effect that one of the children was suspended from school and remained suspended for more than a year. The Court found this to be a violation of the rights of both children and parents.[53]

The British Government argued that a policy of gradually eliminating corporal punishment had been adopted and referred to its reservation according to which "the principle affirmed in the second sentence of Article 2 (P1–2) is accepted by the United Kingdom only so far as it is compatible with the provision of efficient instruction, and the avoidance of *unreasonable* public expenditure"[author's emphasis].[54] However, the Court – once again going back to the preparatory works – held that the original words "have regard to" in Article 2 were replaced by the existing and stronger word "respect" implying some 'positive' obligations on the States. The British policy to move gradually towards the abolition of corporal punishment was accordingly not in itself sufficient to comply with the Convention.[55] The Court accepted that:

> the establishment of a dual system whereby in each sector there would be separate schools for the children of parents objecting to corporal punishment - would be incompatible, especially in the present economic situation, with the avoidance of

51 *Ibid.*, The Law, para 3.

52 *Campbell and Cosans v. the United Kingdom.*

53 In the *Costello-Roberts case* the Court did not find that corporal punishment of a seven-year-old school boy amounted to a violation either of Article 3 or Article 8, cf. *Costello-Roberts v. the United Kingdom.*

54 *Campbell and Cosans*, para. 37.

55 *Ibid.*

> unreasonable public expenditure. However, the Court does not regard it as established that *other means* of respecting the applicants' convictions, such as a system of exemption for individual pupils in a particular school, would necessarily be incompatible with "the provision of efficient instruction and training, and the avoidance of unreasonable public expenditure". [author's emphasis][56]

Accordingly, there is a difference between *reasonable* and *unreasonable* public expenditure, and demands as regards *other means* than establishing a dual school system for those who support corporal punishment and those who do not respectively are compliant with Article 2 of Protocol No. 1. Such *other means* are to some extent resource-demanding and one cannot help asking which 'positive' obligations are incumbent upon those States which have *not* made reservation to the provision. Hardly an obligation to establish private schools to comply with all sorts of religious and philosophical convictions, but indeed something more than *other means* in the sense the expression was used in the *Campbell and Cosans case.*[57]

Certainly, the Court's decision in *Campbell and Cosans* is much bolder than the decision in the *Belgian Linguistic case*, and it is not logical that parental views on disciplinary measures in schools qualify as "philosophical convictions" whereas a linguistic preference to a language widely spoken does not. The two decisions are not necessarily consistent. However, it should once again be recalled that the *Belgium Linguistic* case was one of the first cases with which the Court had to deal, and that much experience has been gathered over the years. Moreover, what the Court seeks to do in the *Campbell and Cosans* case is not so much to find a general all-purpose definition of the notion of "philosophical conviction", but rather to regard the entire issue in a concrete context and in the light of contemporary value conceptions.

Something similar applies to the case *Kjeldsen, Busk Madsen and Pedersen v. Denmark* about sex education in Danish schools.[58] A group of parents were opposed to obligatory sex education in Danish public schools and claimed to be victims of a violation of Article 2 of Protocol No. 1. In deciding that the obligatory sex education did not constitute a failure to respect the rights of parents, the Court stated that the setting and planning of the curriculum in principle falls within the competence of the States, and that the second sentence

---

56 *Ibid.*

57 In a later case the Court has repeated its opinion in regard to 'positive' obligations, cf. *Valsamis v. Greece*, Judgment of 18 December 1996, para. 27. However, the Court did not consider it non-compliant with the Protocol that a pupil – who was the child of pacifist Jehovah's Witnesses – was obliged to participate in a school parade on a national holiday to commemorate the outbreak of the war between Greece and Italy in 1940. The facts of the case hardly raised any appreciable budgetary implication. Accordingly, it fell outside the scope of this analysis.

58 *Kjeldsen, Busk Madsen and Pedersen v. Denmark.*

of Article 2 does not prevent States from imparting through teaching or education information or knowledge of a directly or indirectly religious or philosophical kind. The crux of the matter is how it is done. *If* conveyed in an objective, critical and pluralistic manner – as was the case in Danish public schools – obligatory sex education is in compliance with Article 2 of Protocol No. 1.[59] In this respect, the Court took into consideration the fact that Danish children discover without difficulty and from several quarters the information that interests them on sexual life, and that the aim of the Danish legislator was to give the children such knowledge "more correctly, precisely, objectively and scientifically" and to warn against induced abortions, venereal diseases, etc. The Court recognised that "[t]hese considerations are indeed of a moral order, but they are very general in character and do not entail overstepping the bounds of what a democratic State may regard as the public interest." Accordingly, there was no violation of Article 2 of Protocol No.1.

The judgment illustrates the capability of the Court to keep up with the times. Obligatory sex education was hardly an issue in the late 1940s when the Convention was adopted, and even though children at that time might also have managed to find the information they wanted on sexual matters, one cannot exclude that the Court would have had a different approach, if the case had had to be decided upon in the early 1950s. The "public interest" meant something else at that time, and sexual matters were not discussed openly.

However, it should be added that the Court might have taken into consideration the fact that the law on obligatory sex education was not binding on private schools. Although the Court rejected the opinion of the Danish Government that parents could avoid such education by sending their children to heavily state subsidised private schools, two passages suggest that these circumstances might have had an impact after all on the decision. Before reaching a conclusion the Court stated as follows:

> In its investigation as to whether Article 2 (P1-2) has been violated, the Court cannot forget, however, that the functions assumed by Denmark in relation to education and to teaching include the grant of substantial assistance to private schools.[60]

And after having concluded the Court added as a kind of *obiter dicta*:

> Besides, the Danish State preserves an important expedient for parents who, in the name of their creed or opinions, wish to dissociate their children from integrated sex education; it allows parents either to entrust their children to private schools, which are bound by less strict obligations and moreover, heavily subsidised by the State [....] or to educate them or have them educated at home,

[59] *Ibid.*, paras. 53 og 54.

[60] *Ibid.*, para. 50.

> subject to suffering the undeniable sacrifices and inconveniences caused by recourse to one of those alternative solutions.[61]

Although the judgment is not directly based on the fact that the Danish State pays contributions to the defrayment of costs of private schools one cannot help asking how much weight the Court in future cases would be prepared to attach to such circumstances. The question is highly relevant in connection with the ongoing debate in COE countries as to whether Muslim girls – and female teachers for that matter – can wear head scarves in public schools, an issue which raises questions under several articles of the Convention, not least Article 9. Even though the Danish State and other COE Member States contribute to a considerable extent to the operation of private schools, the burden on parents is indeed significant. Set aside the negative consequences of a segregated school system as regards the integration of refugees and immigrants, a referral of Muslim girls to private schools would be a heavy burden on the (typically) tight budget of a refugee or immigrant family. Moreover, the possible acceptance of a partly self-financed school system brings into focus the question whether the right to education is also a duty.

Finally, the phrase "no person shall be denied the right to education" has given rise to case law about discrimination. In *Timishev v. Russia* e.g the applicant was a Russian national of Chechen ethnic origin. Since 1996 he lived in Nalchik, in the Kabardino-Balkaria Republic of Russia, as a forced migrant. He complained about the domestic authorities' refusal to secure his children's right to education on the ground that he had no registered residence in Nalchik and did not have a migrant's card. The Court held as follows on the right to education:

> This right is also to be found in similar terms in other international instruments such as the Universal Declaration of Human Rights (Article 26), the International Covenant on Economic, Social and Cultural Rights (Article 13), the International Convention on the Elimination of All Forms of Racial Discrimination (Article 5(e)(v)), and the Convention on the Rights of the Child (Article 28). There is no doubt that the right to education guarantees access to elementary education which is of primordial importance for a child's development.[62]

The statement is interesting as it seems as if the Court recognises that the legal content of Article 2 of Protocol No. 1 is similar to e.g. Article 13 of the CESCR, and it is not surprising that the Court concluded that the applicant's children's exclusion from school was incompatible with the requirements of Article 2 of Protocol No. 1.

In *D. H. and Others v. the Czech Republic* the situation was more complicated. The applicants – all of Roma origin – claimed that they had been

[61] *Ibid.*, para. 54.

[62] *Timishev v. Russia*, Judgment of 13 December 2005, para. 64.

discriminated against in the enjoyment of their right to education on account of their race, colour, association with a national minority and their ethnic origin:

> The difference in treatment consisted in their being placed in special schools without justification, where they received a substantially inferior education to that provided in ordinary primary schools, with the result that they were denied access to secondary education other than in vocational training centres. They were victims of racial segregation and had thus suffered psychological damage as a result of being branded 'stupid' or 'retarded'.

There was, however, uncertainty with regard to the question of whether the children were placed in the special schools with informed consent and the Court explained its role in the following way:

> The Court notes that the applicants' complaint under Article 14 of the Convention, taken together with Article 2 of Protocol No. 1, is based on a number of serious arguments. It also notes that several organisations, including Council of Europe bodies, have expressed concern about the arrangements whereby Roma children living in the Czech Republic are placed in special schools and about the difficulties they have in gaining access to ordinary schools. The Court points out, however, that its role is different from that of the aforementioned bodies and that, like the Czech Constitutional Court, it is not its task to assess the overall social context. Its sole task in the instant case is to examine the individual applications before it and to establish on the basis of the relevant facts whether the reason for the applicants' placement in the special schools was their ethnic or racial origin.[63]

The Court acknowledged that statistics disclose figures that are worrying and that the general situation in the Czech Republic concerning the education of Roma children is by no means perfect. However, the Court went on by stating that it could not find the measures taken against he applicants discriminatory:

> Although the applicants may have lacked information about the national education system or found themselves in a climate of mistrust, the concrete evidence before the Court in the present case does not enable it to conclude that the applicants' placement or, in some instances, continued placement, in special schools was the result of racial prejudice, as they have alleged.[64]

Accordingly, the Court did not find that a violation of Article 14 of the Convention, taken together with Article 2 of Protocol No. 1, had been established.

The Grand Chamber, however, found that the evidence submitted by the applicants showed that the number of Roma children in special schools was disproportionately high, and that it was "sufficient to give rise to a strong presumption of indirect discrimination so that the burden of proof shifted to the Government to show that the difference in the impact of the legislation was the

[63] *Ibid.*, para. 45.

[64] *Ibid.*, para. 52.

result of objective factors unrelated to ethnic origin."[65] The Court concluded that the schooling arrangements for Roma children:

> were not attended by safeguards [....] that would ensure that, in the exercise of its margin of appreciation in the education sphere, the State took into account their special needs as members of a disadvantaged class [....]. Furthermore, as a result of the arrangements the applicants were placed in schools for children with mental disabilities where a more basic curriculum was followed than in ordinary schools and where they were isolated from pupils from the wider population. As a result, they received an education which compounded their difficulties and compromised their subsequent personal development instead of tackling their real problems or helping them to integrate into the ordinary schools and develop the skills that would facilitate life among the majority population. Indeed, the Government have implicitly admitted that job opportunities are more limited for pupils from special schools.[66]

The Grand Chamber continued as follows:

> In these circumstances and while recognising the efforts made by the Czech authorities to ensure that Roma children receive schooling, the Court is not satisfied that the difference in treatment between Roma children and non-Roma children was objectively and reasonably justified and that there existed a reasonable relationship of proportionality between the means used and the aim pursued. In that connection, it notes with interest that the new legislation has abolished special schools and provides for children with special educational needs, including socially disadvantaged children, to be educated in ordinary schools.[67]

The Court concluded that it had been established that the relevant legislation as applied in practice at the material time had a disproportionately prejudicial effect on the Roma community.

Therefore, the Court considered that the applicants as members of that community necessarily suffered the same discriminatory treatment. Accordingly, it was not necessary to examine their individual cases. Consequently, there had been a violation of Article 14 of the Convention, read in conjunction with Article 2 of Protocol No. 1, as regards each of the applicants. The decision is remarkable as the Court's approach resembles that of other COE monitoring bodies such as the ECSR. Also, in *Sampanis and Others v. Greece*[68] the Court cited a number of soft law COE sources concerning the integration of Roma children in the educational system. The case concerned the authorities' failure to provide schooling for a number of Roma children during and their subsequent placement in special classes, in an annex to the main primary school building.

---

[65] *D. and H. and Others v. the Chech Republic*, Judgment of 13 November 2007, para. 195.

[66] *Ibid.* para. 207.

[67] *Ibid.* para. 208.

[68] *Sampanis and Others v. Greece*, Judgment of 6 June 2006. Available in French only.

The parents complained that their children had suffered discrimination in the enjoyment of their right to education on account of their Roma origin, and the Court concluded that, the conditions of school enrolment the children in question ultimately resulted in discrimination against them. Accordingly, there had been a violation of Article 14 of the Convention taken together with Article 2 of Protocol No. 1.

3.2.4 *Compulsory Education Free of Charge*

Even if one takes as a point of departure that it is incumbent upon States to provide primary and secondary education, it does not necessarily imply that school fees are non-compliant with the provision, and some commentaries seem to presuppose that the right to education is not necessarily to be understood as a right free of charge.[69] The question is relevant because several COE Member States do in fact charge school fees for public primary education.[70]

As to the question whether the right to primary education is also a duty, the approach of the ECHR (and also the ESC) is indeed somewhat different from that of the CESCR and probably also the RESC. While the CESCR and more indirectly also the RESC perceives of right and duty as two sides of the same coin, Article 2 of Protocol No. 1 of the ECHR does not specifically address the issue. The *Belgian Linguistic* case might conceive of compulsory education simply as interference in family and private life under Article 8 – an interference which is to some extent in keeping with the Convention[71] – and most commentaries deal with the issue of compulsory education as any other 'negative' right. It is usually argued that compulsion is not prohibited suggesting that compulsory education is not necessarily a good thing for the child. The 'positive' aspects of compulsory education are seldom highlighted, and the strong links between e.g. compulsory education and freedom from child labour, as described above in 1 are passed over in silence. The Commission, however, has indirectly addressed the issue under Article 2 of Protocol No.1 on a few occasions. E.g. the Commission has stated that education given in public nurseries, "in spite of its non-compulsory character"[72] must conform to the conditions laid down in the Protocol, and in a later case the Commission has stated as follows:

> Moreover, it is clear that Article 2 of Protocol No. 1 implies a right for the State to establish compulsory schooling, be it in State schools or private tuition of a

---

[69] Wildhaber, *Ibid.*, p. 532.

[70] Cf. e.g. Report of 15 January 2004, submitted by the Special Rapporteur on the Right to Education to the sixtieth session of the Commission on Human Rights, E/CN.4/2004/45, p. 11.

[71] *Belgium Linguistic case, Ibid.*, para. 7.

[72] Cf. *40 mothers v. Sweden*, Admissibility decision of 9 March 1977.

> satisfactory standard, and that verification and enforcement of educational standards is an integral part of that right.[73]

That compulsory education is *consistent* with the Protocol is of course not the same as stating that it is also *required* by the Protocol. However, the quoted statement might very well be understood as if the compulsion is actually an inherent element in the right to education, an interpretation which would bring ECHR into line with the RESC and the CESCR. The concrete case was about the parents of dyslectic children who claimed their right to educate the children themselves at home. The dispute arose over the issue as to whether the parents were capable of guaranteeing an acceptable educational standard or whether the children were to be educated in the public school system.

When discussing the State discretion in the set-up of the educational system Luzius Wildhaber mentions as one of these discretions "how long [....] education [should] be compulsory", possibly suggesting that a compulsory element is in fact part of the obligation.[74] Moreover, the obligation under Article 2 of Protocol No. 1 – according to the preparatory works – is to be seen in the light of the existing educational setup in the COE Member States at the time when the Protocol was adopted. Since the educational system in all Member States did in fact – and still does – include compulsory primary education, it would be fair to say that the right to education under Article 2 of Protocol No. 1 – whatever it includes in other respects – is also a duty. If not, the inclusion of the right under the convention would to a wide degree lose its *raison d'être*.

That Article 2 of Protocol No. 1 at least *presupposes* the existence of compulsory education can furthermore be derived from the second sentence of the provision, which gives parents a right of veto on the ground of their religious or philosophical convictions. Obligatory education must not be enforced contrary to parents' convictions, and the second sentence serves the purpose of protecting parents in this respect. The representative from the Netherlands expressed it in this way after two years of negotiations on the draft protocol: "As for the fundamental right of parents, all things considered, one point is only important: to make it possible for parents to refuse the compulsory education offered by the State if it is contrary to their conscience."[75]

The second sentence without any doubt has parents as its addressee and children's need of protection from parents' interferences with their education has not found a similar explicit expression in the article. However, if a parent were to prevent a child from attending school, and public authorities did

---

[73] Cf. *Family H v. the United Kingdom*, Admissibility decision of 6 March 1984.

[74] Luzius Wildhaber, *Ibid.*, p. 532.

[75] *Preparatory work on Article 2 of the Protocol to the Convention*, COE, CDH (67) 2, p. 172 (Mr. Schmal, the Netherlands).

nothing to prevent it, it is more than likely that such an issue could be dealt with under the first sentence of Article 2 of Protocol No. 1. Depending on the circumstances such a situation might also raise issues under Article 3 and 8 of the ECHR. An exemption of certain groups of children – disabled children, children of asylum seekers or children belonging to minority groups – from compulsory primary education would certainly also raise an issue under Article 2 of Protocol No. 1, a situation which is not hypothetical at all. Moreover, one might ask how the Court would react if the unthinkable should happen that a COE Member State decided to abolish the concept of compulsory education altogether and left it to parents to decide whether or not their children should receive education. It is most likely that the consequence would be that some children were in fact exempted – and maybe subjected to child labour instead – with severe consequences for their later integration and participation in societal activities, not to speak of all the other consequences such a move would have for their future prospects in general, cf. above in Section 1.

This is of course pure speculation, and the situation is not likely to occur. Moreover, all COE Member States are obliged to establish compulsory education free of charge on the basis of other conventions such as the CESCR and CRC. However, the supposition might be useful after all, and I must say that I cannot imagine that the Court would not feel prompted to find one way or the other to declare such a move contradictory to Article 2 of Protocol No.1. Surely, the State is not the one *denying* the children the right to education. The parents are. However, the obligation of the State to protect from interferences from third parties, cf. the notion of *'Drittwirkung'* can hardly be made efficient in any other way than by establishing and enforcing a compulsory (primary) educational system.

If the right to primary education under Article 2 of Protocol No. 1 is in fact also a duty, it is reasonable to claim that it must accordingly have a 'positive' content. It makes little sense to force children into something which is not there or has no 'positive' educational purpose. Moreover, one could argue that compulsion and payment in this particular respect do not go very well hand in hand, and that a prohibition against school fees accordingly should be read into Article 2 of Protocol No. 1. The former UN Special Rapporteur on the right to education has put it like this: "Imposing a requirement upon children to attend school whose cost their parents cannot afford would make compulsory education illusory."[76] It would indeed be interesting to see how the Court would handle also such a complaint.

---

[76] Progress report of the Special Rapporteur on the right to education to the Human Rights Commission of 1. February, E/CN.4/2000/6, para 50.

3.2.5 *Case Law Under Article 5 (1)(e) – Rights and Duties*[77]

The general issue of rights and duties under Article 2 of Protocol No. 1 in relation to (compulsory) primary education is dealt with above. However, a special aspect of the right and duty to receive education arises from ECHR Article 5 (1)(d) according to which deprivation of liberty for educational purposes is permitted. Article 5 (1)(d) runs as follows:

> 1. Everyone has the right to liberty and security of person. No one shall be deprived of his liberty save in the following cases and in accordance with a procedure prescribed by law:
>
> …
>
> (d) the detention of a minor by lawful order for the purpose of educational supervision or his lawful detention for the purpose of bringing him before the competent legal authority.

Deprivation of liberty is indeed a very radical interference, and the fact that the Convention allows for confinement for educational purposes illustrates that education is considered even very important in the COE. It is beyond doubt that educational purposes can legitimise confinement. That follows from Article 5 (1)(d). The crucial question is what the confined persons can require as regards education.

The Court has dealt with this issue on at least two occasions. The first case – *Bouamar v. Belgium*[78] – concerned a young boy of the age of sixteen, who was suspected of certain criminal offences and placed by order of the Juvenile Court in a remand prison nine times, for four months in total. All these measures were taken by virtue of an emergency procedure provided for in Belgian legislation, by which the detention of juveniles in remand prisons can be justified only if it is "materially impossible" to find a social institution able to accept the juvenile immediately. Under the Belgian Children's and Young Persons Welfare Act "offending acts" committed by juveniles can normally be dealt with only by means of custodial protective or educative measures and not by means of criminal sanctions. Bouamar therefore challenged the lawfulness of these decisions, and the question before the Court was whether the nine placements were justified under sub-paragraph (d).

The Court found that the nine placements taken together were not in keeping with the purpose of Article 5 (1)(d). A detention in a remand prison without the assistance of staff with educational training could not be regarded as

---

[77] I have previously dealt with this issue, cf. "Social Rights as Components in the Civil Right to Personal Liberty: Another Step forward in the Integrated Human Rights Approach", in *Netherlands Quarterly*, Vol 20, No. 1, 2002, pp. 29–51.

[78] *Bouamar v. Belgium*. Judgment of 29 February 1988.

furthering any educational aim. The Court took for its basis that Bouamar was shuttled to and fro between the remand prison and his family, and that this was not accompanied by the actual application of a regime of educational supervision in a setting designed for this purpose. The Court did recognise the liberal spirit of the Belgian legislation, but found nevertheless that the authorities were under an obligation to put in place appropriate institutional facilities, which met not only the demands of security but also the educational objectives of the national legislation in order to comply with the requirements under the Convention. Since the Belgian institutional facilities were obviously inadequate, the *series* of nine placements were not compatible with the Convention. Article 5 (1)(d) does not preclude an interim custody measure, if it is used as a preliminary to a regime of supervised education, and it is uncertain at which stage the unlawfulness precisely sets in. The Court stated that "their fruitless repetition had the effect of making them less and less lawful [...]."[79]

The second case *D.G. v. Ireland*[80] concerned a minor who was considered in serious need of educational supervision at a time when he was neither charged with nor convicted of criminal offences. He was nevertheless – although reluctantly – placed for a month in a penal institution, St. Patrick's, for the simple reason that the relevant therapeutic unit did not exist in Ireland. The Irish High Court judge, who made the decision, pointed out in his conclusion that he was:

> extremely unhappy at having to make this order [....] but of the four options available to [him] it is the one which, in [his] view, is best suited to the welfare and needs of this applicant in the short term. It is not a solution. None of the other options are a solution either. But of the four unattractive options it seems to [him] that from the welfare of this applicant it is the least offensive and in [his] view his welfare will be best served by being committed there as [he has] ordered. [author's insertions][81]

It furthermore appeared from the case that when the High Court shortly after was presented to a similar case it chose to *order* the Minister of Health to make available sufficient funding to allow for the building, opening and maintenance of a high security unit to be in operation not later than 1 October 2001.[82] By doing so the High Court anticipated events at the ECtHR in the case *D. G. v. Ireland* in which the applicant claimed that the failure to provide appropriate accommodation and care constituted a violation of Article 5 (1)(d).

Thus, the Court denied that the detention in the penal institution could be considered an interim custody measure preliminary to a regime of supervised

[79] *Ibid.*, para. 53.

[80] *D.G v. Ireland*, Judgment of 16 May 2002.

[81] *Ibid.*, para. 20.

[82] *Ibid.*, para. 54.

education and did not attach importance to the fact that the High Court had made efforts to facilitate the applicant's stay at St. Patrick's by attaching special conditions to his detention. The Court found that the Irish State – when choosing a system of educational supervision implemented through court orders to deal with juvenile delinquency – was obliged to put in place appropriate institutional facilities, which met the security and educational demands of that system in order to satisfy the requirements of Article 5 (1)(d). Accordingly the Court found that the applicant's detention in St. Patrick's was not compatible with this provision.

In both cases the Court attached great importance to the wording of sub-paragraph (d) according to which the lawfulness is to be assessed in relation to the purpose of the detention – in both cases the educational training that the two minors were in need of for social reasons. The qualitative demands for the conditions during the detention were considered an integral part of lawful detention under sub-paragraph (d) and one might consider whether the examination of the Court is more searching as regards deprivation of liberty for *educational* purposes than when it comes to medical and social treatment and care of e.g. mentally ill persons and drug addicts.[83]

However, the willingness of the Court to integrate social dimensions into the civil right to personal liberty in these cases might not differ from the interpretation in the cases *Ashingdane* and *Aerts*[84] in which the Court stated that there must be a *relation* between the ground of permitted deprivation of liberty and the place and the conditions of detention.[85] At least it is an open question whether the Court would have acted differently if the two minors had in fact been admitted to institutions administered by the social or educational system without, however, being offered any educational supervision.

In the case *D.G. v. Ireland* an assessment was indeed made as to whether the regime at St. Patrick's could in fact be considered "educational supervision". However, the point of departure was that St. Patrick's was designated as a penal institution and not an institution designed for educational purposes, and that might explain the Court's willingness to deal with this issue. It cannot necessarily be expected that the Court in future cases will feel prompted to make an assessment as to whether social institutions provide the proper educational and other facilities for minors with adjustment difficulties.

However, the fact that an institution is designed for a specific purpose – be it education or psychiatric treatment – does unfortunately not imply that adequate treatment is actually provided for, and the question as to whether the Court

[83] Cf. Chapter 5 on The Right to Health under the ECHR.

[84] *Ashingdane v. the United Kingdom* and *Aerts v. Belgium*, cf. above in Chapter 5.

[85] *Ibid.*, para. 44 (*Ashingdane*) and para. 49 (*Aerts*).

would be prepared to make an assessment of the quality of the treatment remains unanswered. Article 3, of course sets a lower limit, but considerations on proportionality might – depending on the concrete circumstances – contribute to a vague outline of a minimum core right to educational supervision. If there is nothing or little to offer the minor in need of educational supervision, the drastic measure – confinement – is hardly justified under Article 5 (1)(d). If, however, such an assessment were ever to be made, the Court would without any doubt take a very cautious approach, and the minimum core content would hardly be defined in clear terms. The margin of appreciation would require that the Member State in question and not the Court were to redefine the content.

4 *Future Prospects*

The right to education under the ECHR was born essentially as a parental right with strong 'negative' components, and it might be too soon to tell whether it is undergoing a transformation into something more 'positive' than was originally intended. The same applies to the question of whether the interest of the child is gradually coming into focus. Case law reveals some very cautious indications of such tendencies; however, too few to draw firm conclusions. Most importantly, the questions I pose have not been addressed directly by the Court or the Commission. The answers to some of them might have more academic than practical interest, since the educational set-up in most of the COE Member States probably complies with the requirements deriving from the conventions on economic, social and cultural rights. Moreover, some of the issues I have discussed concern discrimination, and there is hardly any doubt that these issues "fall within the ambit" of the ECHR provisions on educational matters. They can accordingly be dealt with under Article 14 in conjunction with the article in question.

I will restrict myself to suggesting that it might be possible to build up a legal (hermeneutic) argumentation in favour of a more 'positive' interpretation of the ECHR. Such argumentation would take into consideration the fact that the conception of the rights of children vis-à-vis the rights of parents has changed dramatically since the adoption of the Convention, and that the *natural right of the father*[86] – which was invoked during the drafting of Protocol No. 1 – is no longer in focus. The adoption and ratification of the CRC by all COE Member States[87] has undoubtedly had an impact on human rights interpretation

[86] Cf. above in 3.2.2.

[87] The CRC has been ratified by all UN Member States with the US and Somalia as the only exceptions.

in general, and also on the interpretation of the Court.[88] Moreover, the Court has in fact repeatedly held that Article 2 of Protocol No. 1 is dominated by its first sentence, and it would presumably be possible to give more substance to this conception if or when the occasion arises.

Moreover, even though the RESC has entered into force, many COE Member States have not yet ratified this convention, and children in these countries would not enjoy a regional protection of their rights as regards education, if some minimum core rights could not be read into the ECHR. It would in many ways be absurd if the relatively more affluent COE Member States were not to protect their citizens at a level equal to that of the global treaties covering a variety of countries – some of which are indeed poorer than even the least developed COE countries.

The reluctance as regards the undertaking of 'positive' obligations as it was presented during the drafting of Protocol No. 1 should of course be taken into consideration. However, it should be recalled that 'positive' obligations are in fact incumbent on the very same Member States on the basis of the CESCR and the CRC.

At least one can say that the original drafters of Protocol. No. 1 in another and contemporary context have distanced themselves from the original 'negative' parents-oriented perception of the right to education. Against this background one might argue that it would be inconsistent with the dynamic (hermeneutic) style of interpretation if the Court were to cling to preparatory works from the middle of the last century.

Moreover, there is nothing in the wording of the ECHR that prevents an interpretation pointing to a more 'positive' content of its provisions, and remembering the hermeneutic doctrine *understanding is always application*,[89] one can claim that the ECHR has only been challenged to a limited degree. The Court has not been confronted with the factual needs and demands that would require a position as regards these issues, and my humble attempt to construe some of these needs and demands hardly provides a satisfactory factual basis for a final assessment as regards these questions.

---

[88] Cf. e.g. the case *Costello-Roberts v. the United Kingdom*. In this case the Court applied the CRC as a legal source in its interpretation of the ECHR and underlined the importance of a contextual interpretation, cf. para. 27 and 35.

[89] Gadamer, *Ibid*., p. 309.

Chapter 8

The Right to Social Cash Benefits Under the ECHR[1]

1 *The Right to Social Cash Benefits as a Cross-Cutting Issue*

Consideration for people who cannot work or cannot find work whether because of old age, lack of jobs, sickness or childbirth is of the utmost importance for more than one reason. Placing people in destitution is not conducive for their ability to re-enter the labour market and recover the ability to provide for themselves and their families, and an extra burden is, moreover, placed on poor parents if they are to prevent their children from making a false start. Thus, the existence of a well-functioning social welfare system is of fundamental importance not only for the individual in question but also for society as such.

It should be recalled that having to live on social cash benefits[2] is in itself likely to marginalise the person in question. With few exceptions the recipient will have to reduce his standard of living often to a considerable extent with the risk of being socially excluded from society. It goes without saying that without a decent level for the payment of social cash benefits people are not able to care for themselves or their families with respect to the basic necessities of life such as food, clothing, housing, medical care, etc. Having to live on social cash benefits may affect the self-worth of the individual depending on when and why the ability to provide for oneself has ceased – temporarily or

[1] I have previously dealt with aspects of this issue cf. "The Right to Social Cash Benefits as Property Rights under the European Convention on Human Rights?"' in Julia Iliopoulos-Strangas and et Theunis Roux (eds.) *IACL-AIDC PUBLICATION, Association internationale de droit constitutionnel, Perspectives nationales et internationales des droits sociaux.*

[2] I have chosen to apply the term 'social cash benefits' as a shorthand expression for a number of social benefits, which are traditionally designated as e.g. social assistance, social security, welfare payments, social relief or supplementary benefits. The more specified distinction between these various benefits does not have my interest in this context. The term, 'social *cash* benefits' is chosen to distinguish these benefits from social welfare *services* such as home help, home care, placement in social institution etc.

permanently – and the level of social cash benefits is crucial for the preservation of contacts with other people and for participation in the life of society. He, who cannot afford to subscribe to a newspaper, go to the cinema not to mention theatre, runs the risk of leading a life in intellectual poverty without any incentive to exercise his civil and political participatory rights to the full.

Therefore, a missing or inadequate level of social cash benefits is likely to create indignity and inequality in so many aspects of life, not only with regard to what is traditionally considered economic, social and cultural rights but also within the field of civil and political rights.

2 *The Relevant Provisions*

On the face of it, the ECHR is not the right place to search for the right to social cash benefits, and the Convention surely does not contain specific provisions on this issue. Rather, the social counterpart to the ECHR would be the place to search cf. e.g. Articles 12 and 13 of the ESC/RESC. However, the exclusion of specific provisions concerning social cash benefits from the ECHR does not imply that such protection is entirely irrelevant to the Convention. Several articles may be of relevance.

Firstly, the ECtHR has not entirely ruled out that social demands within the field of cash benefits may be of relevance to the interpretation of Article 3 of the ECHR in the sense that Member States are obliged to provide a certain minimum protection cf. below in Section 3. Secondly, Article 6 of the ECHR has proved relevant as the Court has gradually applied a rather proactive and extended interpretation of the notion of "civil rights" which has proved relevant not only for the procedural but also for the substantial protection of demands concerning social cash benefits, cf. below in Section 4. Thirdly, the Court has held on several occasions that social demands within the field of social cash benefits may fall within the ambit of private and family life, cf. below in Section 5. Finally, the notion of "possession" in Article 1 of Protocol No. 1 encompasses some social cash benefits, one of the implications being that the Court may examine allegations concerning discrimination within that field, cf. Article 14 in conjunction with Article 1 of Protocol No. 1, cf. below in Section 6. The following presentation will be limited to the above-mentioned four topics, and I have no ambition to claim that the right to social cash benefits as such is protected under the ECHR. The purpose of the chapter is to prove that it makes sense to talk about *aspects* of the right to social security and social assistance under the ECHR, even though the issue is much more broadly covered under e.g. the ESC/RESC. However, considering the relative strength between the two conventions and their control mechanisms, it is of practical and theoretical interest to explore the issue.

3 *A Minimum Core Right to Social Cash Benefits?*

He who wishes to claim a right to social cash benefits will usually have a very bad case under the ECHR, and it is not surprising that very few such claims have been submitted to the Court. As a point of departure it must be considered pointless to claim that one has the right to a certain benefit or that the amount of a certain benefit which is already provided for is inadequate. However, one cannot entirely rule out that an issue could arise under Article 3, if the cash benefit complained over is absolutely insufficient in its amount.

Thus, in *Pancenco v. Latvia* the Court rejected an application concerning socio-economic problems in general by recalling "that the Convention does not guarantee, as such, socio-economic rights, including the right to charge-free dwelling, the right to work, the right to free medical assistance, or the right to claim financial assistance from a State to maintain a certain level of living."[3] However, the Court did recognise that an issue *might* in principle arise under Article 3, and gave the following concrete reason for declaring the application manifestly ill founded:

> To the extent that this part of the application relates to Article 3 of the Convention, which prohibits torture or inhuman or degrading treatment, the Court observes, on the basis of the applicant's submissions, that *her present living conditions do not attain a minimum level of severity* to amount to treatment contrary to the above provision of the Convention [....] [author's emphasis].[4]

In *Larioshina v. Russia* the Court repeated its opinion by stating that:

> a complaint about a wholly insufficient amount of pension and the other social benefits may, in principle, raise an issue under Article 3 of the Convention which prohibits inhuman or degrading treatment.[5]

However, the Court did not in this case either find any indication that:

> the amount of the applicant's pension [at the time when the applicant lodged the application she received 653 roubles per month] and the additional social benefits have caused such damage to her physical or mental health capable of attaining the minimum level of severity falling within the ambit of Article 3 of the Convention [author's insertions].[6]

Not much can be deduced from the case. If in 2001, in Russia a person receives 653 roubles per month, then equivalent to approximately € 25, she is not subject to a violation of Article 3. However, the decision says nothing about where

---

[3] *Pancenko v. Latvia*, Admissibility decision of 28 October 1999, The Law, para. 2.

[4] *Ibid.*

[5] *Larioshina v. Russia*, Admissibility decision of 23 April 2002, The Law, para. 3.

[6] *Ibid.* Cf. also *Nitecki v. Poland*, Admissibility decision of 21 March 2002.

exactly to draw the line between underpay and inhuman or degrading treatment, and of course it would all depend on the context. The purchasing power of roubles and €'s differ from region to region and from country to country, and other factors may also have to be taken into consideration. However, even without much knowledge about the purchasing power of a rouble in Russia in 2001, I believe that it would be fair to say that 653 roubles or € 25 per month is an extremely limited amount of money, and that a Russian pensioner is indeed in a very unfortunate financial position. She is actually among those more than a billion people who live in *extreme poverty*, namely on less than a dollar a day as the concept is understood by the World Bank.[7]

Since the Court in principle has acknowledged that there exists a decency threshold or minimum core right to social cash benefits under Article 3, one cannot avoid asking how small a cash payment can be without infringing the threshold. Would € 20 be ok? Would 15 or 10? The threshold is certainly not identical with what the ECSR defines as the poverty threshold in relation to social assistance and social security under the ESC/RESC, namely 50 % of the media equivalised income.[8] Poverty does not necessarily amount to inhuman and degrading treatment. However, what kind of a life can one live on 25 or less € a month, and one may ask why or whether it is less degrading and humiliating to live permanently on € 25 than having to tolerate a physical interference for an even very short period, cf. e.g. *Tyrer v. the United Kingdom* about three strokes with a birch, which were considered degrading treatment contrary to Article 3?[9]

Maybe the Court has set out on a risky journey by recognising in principle that a benefit may fall below the threshold in Article 3. One cannot exclude that the Court sooner or later will be confronted with facts within the field of social cash benefits which are so poor that they make topical this not yet applied legal content of Article 3. However, the consequences of actually holding that an infringement of Article 3 has taken place might be considerable, and the Court would run the risk of being pelted by complaints. If or when it ever happens, one must expect the concrete facts to be even very specific in order for the budgetary consequences for the Member State in question to be restricted to the one case in question or at least be manageable.

---

[7] About the poverty line, cf. e.g. *Poverty*, World Development Report 1990, Published for The World Bank by Oxford University Press, p. 27. The report employs two figures: $ 275 and $ 370 per person pr. year in constant 1985 purchasing power parity prices.

[8] Cf. e.g. *Conclusions XVIII-1, 2004* concerning Denmark's compliance with Article 13, at. Art. 13. For general remarks about the Committee's assessment of the adequacy of social assistance, cf. e.g. *Social Protection in the European Social Charter*, Human Rights, Social Charter Monograhps, No. 7, 1999, Council of Europe Publishing, p. 67.

[9] *Tyrer v. the United Kingdom*, Judgment of 25 April 1978.

4 *Social Cash Benefits as Rights Protected Under Article 6*

In *Airey v. Ireland* the Court held that the right to free legal aid also in *civil* law suits may under certain circumstances be invoked as a social element of Article 6 on the right to fair trial. The Court underlined that some of the Convention's rights have implications of a "social or economic nature" and that there is no "watertight division" between the two sets of rights.[10] This perception of Article 6 as extending into the sphere of economic and social rights is also reflected in case law concerning the expression "civil rights and obligations", which is one of the requirements for invoking the fair trial clause. Thus, in the determination of civil rights everyone is entitled to procedural protection of a quite wide-ranging character, which might even have substantial implications. If therefore, social cash benefits are to be considered "civil rights" in the sense of Article 6, another link between the two sets of rights is established, the consequence being that the protection of social cash benefits intensifies. The Court's approach to the interpretation of the notion is very well reflected in the following passage, which has been repeated in case law over the years:

> Whether or not a right is to be regarded as civil within the meaning of this expression in the Convention must be determined by reference to the *substantive content and effects* of the right – and not its legal classification – under the domestic law of the State concerned. In the exercise of its supervisory functions, the Court must also take account of the *object and purpose* of the Convention and of the national legal systems of the other Contracting States [....] [author's emphasis].[11]

Rights of a private law character are conceptually encompassed by the expression "civil rights". If, however, the right in question in domestic law is classified as a public right, the *substantive content and effects* and the *object and purpose* must be examined in order to establish whether the private law features or the public law features are predominant. Such examination was done in the first two cases in which the Court had to deal with the issue of social security, namely the cases *Feldbrugge v. the Netherlands*[12] and *Deumeland v. Germany.*[13]

In the *Feldbrugge* case the applicant was deprived of her right to sickness allowance, whereas the *Deumeland* case concerned the issue of survivor's supplementary pension. Both applicants claimed that they had been subject to violations of Article 6 (1), and the crucial question was whether the fair trial clause was applicable altogether. The two cases were related to respectively the

---

[10] *Airey v. Ireland*, para. 26. Cf. also *P., C. and S. v. the United Kingdom*, Judgment of 16 October 2002 and *Steel and Morris v. the United Kingdom*, Judgment of 15 February 2005.

[11] Cf. originally in *König v. Germany*, Judgment of 28 June 1978, para. 89.

[12] *Feldbrugge v. the Netherlands*, Judgment of 29 May 1986.

[13] *Deumeland v. Germany*, Judgment of 29 May 1986.

Dutch sickness insurance scheme and the German industrial action insurance scheme, both schemes which had public law features due to the character of the legislation, the compulsory nature of the insurance and the assumption of the State of responsibility for ensuring social protection.

However, the Court underlined that State intervention by means of a statute does not necessarily bring the asserted right within the sphere of public law. Compulsory insurance schemes occur in the field of private law as well, and the insurance schemes in question were operated by semi-public institutions thus extending the public law domain.[14] Moreover, the Court attached importance to the fact that the applicants suffered interferences with their means of subsistence and were claiming a right flowing from specific rules laid down by the legislation in force. The disputed rights were personal, economic and individual rights, which were furthermore closely linked to contracts of employment governed by private law.[15] Finally, the Court emphasised the importance of a number of similarities between the two insurance schemes and private sector insurance under ordinary law.[16] Having evaluated the relative cogency of the private and public law features the Court concluded that the private law features were predominant. Accordingly, Article 6 was applicable.

The *Feldbrugge* and the *Deumeland* cases were both about social insurance benefits with quite strong private law features. However, in 1993 the Court was to decide on the applicability of Article 6 in relation to statute-based welfare assistance which obviously had a predominantly public law character. The benefit in this case – the *Salesi* case – concerned a disability allowance, which was not dependent on the payment of individual contributions. It was entirely publicly financed.

The Court repeated what it had already stated in the *Feldbrugge* and *Deumeland* cases, namely that "there was a great diversity in the legislation and practice of the member States of the Council of Europe as regards the nature of the entitlements to insurance benefits under social security schemes."[17] Some States treat them as private law rights, some as a public law rights, and yet again some States operate a mixed system. The Court therefore held that the "development in the law that was initiated by those judgments and the principle of equality of treatment warrant taking the view that today the general rule is that Article 6 para. 1 [....] does apply in the field of social insurance."[18]

---

[14] *Cf. Feldbrugge v. the Netherlands*, paras. 32–34 and *Deumeland v. Germany*, paras. 66–68.

[15] *Ibid.*, paras. 37–38 and paras. 71–72.

[16] *Ibid.*, para. 39 and para. 73.

[17] *Salesi v. Italy*, Judgment of 26 February 1993, para. 19, *Deumeland v. Germany*, para. 63 and *Feldbrugge v. the Netherlands*, para. 30.

[18] *Salesi v. Italy*, para. 19.

The *Salesi* case, as mentioned, did not concern social insurance but welfare assistance, and the Court went on by arguing that the differences between social insurance and welfare assistance "cannot be regarded as fundamental at the present stage of development of social security law."[19] State intervention is not sufficient to establish that Article 6 is inapplicable, and the applicant was not affected in her relations with the administrative authorities as such, acting in the exercise of discretionary powers:[20]

> She suffered an interference with her means of subsistence and was claiming an individual, economic right flowing from specific rules laid down in a statute giving effect to the Constitution [....].[21]

Against this background, the Court saw no reason to distinguish between welfare benefits and social insurance benefits, and Article 6 was therefore applicable.

A quite similar reasoning was applied in *Schuler-Zgraggen v. Switzerland* about a woman who was granted disability pension because of tuberculosis. However, after having given birth she was deprived of the pension because of the Federal Insurance Court's "assumption based on experience of everyday life", namely that "many married women go out to work until their first child is born, but give up their jobs for as long as the children need full time care and upbringing." The Federal Insurance Court therefore assumed that "the applicant, even if her health had not been impaired, would have been occupied only as a housewife and mother."[22]

The Court found no violation of Article 6 taken in isolation. However, the Court noted that the Federal Insurance Court did not attempt to prove the validity of the assumption that married women give up their jobs when their first child is born. As the assumption constituted the sole basis for the reasoning, thus being decisive, it introduced a difference of treatment based on the ground of sex only. Accordingly, Article 6 was applicable in conjunction with Article 14, and the Court found no reasons for such differential treatment. There had accordingly been a breach of Article 14 taken in conjunction with Article 6.

The *Schuler-Zgraggen* case is significant in that the procedural protection under Article 6 turned out to have *substantial* implications of a far-reaching character. The protection under Article 6 is not only of a purely formal character. The Court considered it a task under the ECHR "to ascertain whether the proceedings, considered as a whole, including the way in which the evidence

[19] *Ibid.*, para. 19.
[20] *Ibid.*
[21] *Ibid.*
[22] *Schuler-Zgraggen v. Switzerland*, Judgment of 24 June 1993, para. 29.

was submitted, were fair [....]."[23] As a result of this assessment Mrs Schuler Zgraggen was brought in a legal position as advantageous as if the examination was made on the basis of Protocol No. 12 to the ECHR or Article 26 of the CCPR.

The issue of whether the scheme in question is primarily of a private law or public law nature was also decisive in the case *Schouten and Meldrum v. the Netherlands*.[24] Unlike the previously mentioned cases, which all concerned the *right* to benefits, this case concerned a legal *obligation* to pay social security contributions for employees, cf. the notion of "civil rights and obligations". The Court admitted that the approaches to benefits and to contributions were not necessarily identical, and that there:

> may exist "pecuniary obligations" vis-à-vis the State or its subordinate authorities which, for the purpose of Article 6 [....] are to be considered as belonging exclusively to the realm of public law and are accordingly not covered by the notion of "civil rights and obligations". Apart from fines imposed by way of "criminal sanctions", this will be the case, in particular, where an obligation which is pecuniary in nature derives from tax legislation or is otherwise part of normal civic duties in a democratic society.[25]

The Court, however, found that the method of analysing the various features of public and private law which was applied in the *Feldbrugge* case was appropriate nevertheless. Referring back to the analysis in this case, the Court observed three features of a public law character, namely the character of the legislation, the compulsory nature of the schemes in question and the assumption of the State of responsibility for ensuring social protection. In this context, the Court noted that "it is in the nature of things that the means resorted to by government agencies to ensure payment of compulsory contributions should bear some resemblance to the levying of taxes." The Court, however, went on to say that it "cannot be concluded from this that those contributions necessarily belong to the domain of public law."[26] As to the private law features, the Court noted that the *Schouten* case deviated from the *Feldbrugge* case with respect to the alleged "personal and economic nature" of the right in that it concerned:

> contributions for whose payment the employer is made responsible and which as a rule are not of crucial importance to his very livelihood. Although the obligations in issue are certainly "personal, economic and individual", the same may be said of all 'pecuniary' obligations vis-à-vis the State or its subordinate

[23] *Ibid.*, para. 66.
[24] *Schouten and Meldrum v. the Netherlands*, Judgment of 9 December 1994.
[25] *Ibid.*, para. 50.
[26] *Ibid.*, para. 55.

> authorities, even those which must be considered to belong exclusively to the realm of public law.[27]

However, the Court held that this factor could not be decisive. As to the link between the social- insurance schemes and the contract of employment, the Court applied the same reasoning as in the *Feldbrugge* case, and finally the Court found that greater weight should be attached to the similarities between social-security schemes and private insurance than to the differences. Notwithstanding the public law features, the Court concluded the analysis of the relative cogency between the features of private and public law by attaching greater importance to those of a private law character. Accordingly, Article 6 was applicable.

In some later judgments the Court upheld the evaluation of the relative cogency of the private and public law features.[28] However, in the most recent judgments the Court seems to have abandoned this approach, which has proven somewhat strained the unmistakable public law features of some of the contested rights taken into consideration. Today, the Court seems to concentrate on the economic nature of the claim in question, and on whether the right in question has a clear legal basis in legislation. This approach was initiated in the *Salesi* case in which the dominant public law features could not be explained away. Hence, in *Le Calvez v. France*[29] about a contested right to payment of benefits and compensation – closely bound up with a former contract of employment – the Court laid stress on the fact that the claim at issue related to "a purely economic" right, which furthermore did not in any way call into question the discretionary powers of the authorities.[30] This new way of arguing has been followed up e.g. in *Mennito v. Italy*, in which the Court specifically refers back to the *Salesi* case.[31]

By letting the applicability of Article 6 depend on the pecuniary character and the distinctness of the wording of the right in question, the Court has established a link to Article 1 of Protocol No. 1, and the gradual extension of the scope of Article 6 is likely to have a knock-on effect on Article 1 of Protocol No. 1.The scope of the two provisions is not identical. However, the dynamic and very much similar interpretation of the two provisions illustrates the endeavours of the Court to create homogeneity and integration in the human rights norm system, cf. below in Section 6.

27 *Ibid.*, para. 57.

28 Cf. e.g. *Kerojärvi v. Finland*, Judgment of 19 July 1995 and *Paskhalidis and Others v. Greece*, Judgment of 19 March 1997.

29 *Le Calvez v. France*, Judgment of 29 July 1998.

30 *Ibid.*, paras. 57–58.

31 *Mennito v. Italy*, Judgment of 5 October 2000, para. 28.

5 *Social Cash Benefits Under Article 8*

In the case *Petrovic v. Austria* about the right to parental leave allowance the Court held that "Article 8 does not impose any positive obligation on States to provide the financial assistance in question."[32] The question was, however, whether it was discriminatory towards fathers that Austrian legislation only gave mothers the entitlement to receive parental leave allowance. The question therefore arose whether the issue could be dealt with under Article 8 taken in conjunction with the non-discrimination clause in Article 14. The Court argued that a State by granting parental leave allowance demonstrates its respect for family life. The allowance is intended to promote family life because it enables one of the parents to stay at home and look after the children. Article 8 was therefore applicable in conjunction with Article 14 on non-discrimination.

Now, it is probably beyond doubt that the founding fathers of the Convention did neither have maternity leave allowances nor paternity leave allowances in mind when Article 8 was adopted. Nevertheless the Court stated that the equality of the sexes is a major goal in the COE Member States, and that "very weighty reasons" would be needed for such a difference in treatment to be regarded as compatible with the Convention.[33]

The Court did *not* find, however, that Austria had exceeded the margin of appreciation allowed. At the material time – in the late 1980s – there was no common standard in the COE Member States as regards parental leave allowance for fathers, and the Court added that "it therefore appears *difficult to criticise* the Austrian legislation [author's emphasis]",[34] an addition which conceivably suggests some doubt as to whether the decision would have looked different if the circumstances time-wise had been different. Thus, the judgment was not passed until 1998, and in the meantime Austria *had* actually changed its legislation together with a number of other European countries. The Court emphasised that there was no common ground in 1998 either with respect to paternity leave allowance. However, two dissenting judges found that it *did* amount to discrimination. They emphasised that the differential treatment could have unfortunate consequences also for mothers, and did not find the reference to the situation in other European States conclusive. Austria *had* in fact introduced parental leave allowance without being obliged to do so. Thus, when opting for a system of parental leave allowance, a State is not permitted to grant benefits in a discriminatory manner.

---

32 *Petrovic v. Austria*, Judgment of 27 March 1998, para. 26.
33 *Ibid.*, para. 37.
34 *Ibid.*, para. 41.

The view of the two dissenting judges might already today be more in keeping with the times, and despite the negative conclusion, the decision illustrates that the legal content of human rights provisions changes over time according to altering circumstances and conceptions in Member States, even if this necessitates a reading reaching into the sphere of economic, social and cultural rights. The decision illustrates that the interpretative task is not only that of going backwards to study the intention of the originator in the late 1940s when fathers typically had a much less prominent role in the care for children than today. The interpretation should not seek to reconstruct the original *intention*, but rather to reconstruct the *situation* – the context – that caused the adoption of the provision and confront it with our contemporary context, our contemporary conception of family life and the role of fathers.

The *Petrovic* case represents a major step forward by recognising that social cash benefits may fall within the ambit of Article 8 and thereby activate Article 14.[35] The case prepared the way for the *Niedzwiecki* case, in which the applicant complained that the German authorities' refusal of child benefits due to the fact that he did not fulfil a residence criterion amounted to discrimination. The Court stated as follows:

> By granting child benefits, States are able to demonstrate their respect for family life within the meaning of Article 8 of the Convention; the benefits therefore come within the scope of that provision [....]. It follows that Article 14 – taken together with Article 8 – is applicable.[36]

With regard to the issue of discrimination the Court recalled that States enjoy a certain margin of appreciation and emphasised the narrow the scope of the examination:

> The Court is not called upon to decide generally to what extent it is justified to make distinctions, in the field of social benefits, between holders of different categories of residence permits. Rather it has to limit itself to the question whether the German law on child benefits *as applied in the present case* violated the applicant's rights under the Convention [author's emphasis].[37]

In the assessment of the concrete circumstances the Court leaned on the German Federal Constitutional Court ruling on the exact same issue, and found that the legislation was incompatible with the right to equal treatment under Article 3 of the Basic Law. The Court held as follows:

---

35 The same applies to social services such as day care, foster care and other social services related to family and private life. However, as mentioned above in Section 1, the chapter is restricted to the discussion of social cash benefits.

36 *Niedzwiecki v. Germany*, Judgment of 25 October 2005, para. 31.

37 *Ibid.*, para. 33.

> Like the Federal Constitutional Court, the Court does not discern sufficient reasons justifying the different treatment with regard to child benefits of aliens who were in possession of a stable residence permit on one hand and those who were not, on the other. It follows that there has been a violation of Article 14 in conjunction with Article 8 of the Convention.[38]

Admittedly, it would have been remarkable had the Court ruled differently from the German Federal Constitutional Court, but the ruling, nevertheless, falls in line with the Court's previous case law. Social cash benefits may enjoy protection under Article 8 in conjunction with Article 14, and under special circumstances also under Article 8 taken in isolation. That was the case in *Grant v. the United Kingdom*[39] in which a male to female transsexual complained that a decision denying her retirement pension already at the age of 60, which was the pensionable age for women, violated her right to private life under Article 8.

The *Grant* case relates to *Chistine Goodwin v. the United Kingdom* about legal recognition of gender re-assignment, in which the Court concluded that there had been a failure to respect the right to private life in breach of Article 8 of the Convention.[40] Consequently, the applicant in the *Grant* case could claim to be a victim of lack of legal recognition from the moment, after the *Christine Goodwin* judgment, when the authorities refused to give effect to her claim. It followed that there had been a breach of the applicant's right to respect for private life contrary to Article 8 of the Convention.

The *Grant* case relates to *Cristine Goodwin* in which the Court concluded that there had been a failure to respect the right to private life in breach of Article 8 of the Convention. Consequently the applicant in the *Grant case* could claim to be a victim of legal recognition from the moment, after the *Christine Goodwin* judgment, when the authorities refused to give effect to her claim. It followed that there had been a breach of the applicant's rights to respect for private life contrary to Article 8 of the Convention.

6 *Social Cash Benefits as Property Rights*

6.1 *Initial Remarks*

When discussing the relation between the right to property and social cash benefits, at least two issues arise. Firstly, one may ask whether the obligation to pay contributions to various social cash benefit schemes is compatible with the

38 *Ibid.*, para. 33.

39 *Grant v. the United Kingdom*, Judgment of 23 May 2006.

40 *Christine Goodwin v. the United Kingdom*, Judgment of 11 July 2002.

right to peaceful enjoyment of possession. Secondly, recent case law makes it even more relevant to discuss social cash benefits of various kinds as "possession" in the sense of Article 1 of Protocol No. 1.

The second issue is by far the most interesting. Thus, it comes as no big surprise that Member States have the power to impose and enforce obligations to pay various contributions in pursuance of their social policy cf. the wording of Article 1 (2) which speaks of "the right of a State to enforce such laws as it deems necessary to control the use of property in accordance with the general interest or to secure the payment of taxes or other contributions [....]." Although the imposition of taxes and contributions does in fact amount to interference with property rights, treaty bodies have consistently held that the States Parties have very wide – although not unlimited – margins of appreciation.[41] Such interference seems to be permissible under Article 1 provided that it is not discriminatory[42] or disproportionate to the income by placing an excessive burden on the individual.[43] I will deal with the issue of contributions briefly below, but otherwise concentrate on the second question, whether claims concerning social cash benefits may be considered possession in the sense of Article 1 of Protocol No. 1.[44]

This question was originally seen as closely connected with the way in which the benefit in question is financed. Thus, in the Commission's case law individual contributions to a social scheme were considered necessary for the benefit in question to be regarded as possession.

Moreover, the Commission took the view that without a direct link between payment of contributions and the benefit awarded, there could be no property right. Conversely, the Commission stated on several occasions that "the making of compulsory contributions to a pension fund may, in certain circumstances, create a property right in a portion of such fund and that such right might be affected by the manner in which the fund is distributed."[45] Hence, the Commission made a distinction between social security systems based on the

41 Cf. e.g. Arjen van Rijn (rev.), "Right to the peaceful enjoyment of ones possession (Article 1 of Protocol No. 1)" in Pieter van Dijk et al. (eds.) *Theory and Practice on the European Convention on Human Rights*, 4th Edition, Intersentia, p. 891 ff.

42 Cf. e.g. *Darby v. Sweden*, Judgment of 23 October 1990 and *Van Raalte v. the Netherlands*, Judgment of 21 February 1997. The *Van Raalte* judgment is referred to below in Section 5.3.

43 Cf. e.g. *X v. the Netherlands*, Admissibility decision of 20 July 1971.

44 Martin Scheinin and Catarina Krause points out that the distinction is also decisive for the procedural protection the individual may claim under the Convention. The Strasbourg organs have consistently held that disputes concerning individual property rights enjoy the procedural protection offered by Article 6 (1) of the Convention. cf. Martin Scheinin and Catarina Krause, "Social Security as 'possessions'" in Stefaan Van den Bogaert (ed.), *Social Security, Non-Discrimination and Property*, Maklu, 1997, pp. 59–73.

45 Cf. e.g. *X v. the Netherlands, Ibid.*

principle of solidarity and systems according to which the size of the future benefit was decided on the basis of the contributions made. In order for a benefit to be considered possession it would require – according to the Commission – a "relationship between the contributions made and the pension received in the sense that the amounts paid by the insured person are accumulated with a view to covering the pension benefits accruing to him when reaching pensionable age."[46]

This view is reflected and further elaborated in a series of cases decided by the Commission, which will not be referred to in this context as the Commission's previous case law has long since been overtaken by events.[47] Previous case law is interesting from a hermeneutic perspective, of course, and reflections over the possible shift in the perception of the concept of property will be made at a later stage in the presentation, cf. below in Section 6.3.

6.2 *Social Cash Benefits and the Issue of Discrimination*

In *Gaygusuz v. Austria* the Court apparently took a view different from that of the Commission by holding that a so-called emergency assistance could be considered possession in the sense of Article 1 of Protocol No. 1.[48] The case concerned the right to a so-called emergency assistance, which was granted among others to unemployed persons who had exhausted their entitlement to unemployment benefit. This emergency benefit was financed partly from various governmental sources partly from unemployment insurance contributions. Gaygusuz had paid his contributions and fulfilled all criteria but one. He was not an Austrian but a Turkish citizen. He therefore claimed before the Court that he was a victim of discrimination based on national origin contrary to Article 14 of the Convention taken in conjunction with Article 1 of Protocol No. 1. The Court considered:

> that the right to emergency assistance – in so far as provided for in the applicable legislation – is a pecuniary right for the purposes of Article 1 of Protocol No. 1 [....]. That provision [....] is therefore applicable *without it being necessary to rely solely on the link between entitlement to emergency assistance and the obligation to pay "taxes or other contributions"* [author's emphasis].[49]

This – somewhat cryptic remark – was subsequently subject to various interpretations. Some argued that also non-contributory benefits could be considered possessions to the extent they have a clear legal basis in legislation,

---

[46] *Ibid.*

[47] Some cases are referred to by Martin Scheinin and Catarina Krause, cf. Stefaan Van den Bogaert (ed.), *Ibid.*, pp. 60–66.

[48] *Gaygusuz v. Austria*, Judgment of 16 September 1996.

[49] *Ibid.*, para. 41.

whereas others had a more cautious approach.[50] Admittedly, the Court *noted* that entitlement to emergency assistance was linked to the unemployment insurance fund, and that there was no entitlement to emergency assistance, if such contributions had not been made.[51] However, it seems as if the Court made this observation not to determine whether the emergency assistance was possession, only to ascertain that the applicant fulfilled the other conditions upon which the entitlement to the benefit depended. Accordingly, the decision may be understood as if the Court distanced itself from the view of the Commission that the matter fell within the ambit of Article 1 of Protocol No. 1 *because* of the link between contributions and benefits.

While the Court's motive for accepting that the emergency assistance fell within the ambit of Article 1 of Protocol No. 1 may seem unclear, the concrete examination under Article 14 in conjunction with Article 1 was 'done by the book'. The Court repeated the principles developed in previous case law, namely that a differential treatment is discriminatory if it has no objective and reasonable justification i.e. if it does not pursue a legitimate aim or if there is no reasonable relationship of proportionality between the means employed and the aim sought to be realised. The Court recalled that the Contracting States enjoy a certain margin of appreciation in assessing whether and to what extent differences in otherwise similar situations justify a different treatment and added that "very weighty reasons" would have to be put forward before a difference of treatment based exclusively on the ground of nationality could be considered compatible with the Convention.[52] As the reasons put forward by the Austrian Government were "unpersuasive", the Court concluded that there had been a violation of Article 14 taken in conjunction with Article 1 of Protocol No. 1.

Wessels Bergervoet v. the Netherlands[53] did not contribute to a clarification with regard to tax financed benefits as possession in the sense of Article 1 of Protocol No. 1. The case concerned an Old Age Pension Act (AOW) which provided for a general old age pension scheme for persons who had attained the age of 65. Under this scheme, all persons between the age of 15 and 65, who resided in the Netherlands were insured, and entitlement to AOW benefits was independent of whether or not contributions had been paid. It was a general social security scheme characterised by the principle of solidarity.[54] As the group of contributors was different from the group of beneficiaries, the respondent Government argued that Article 1 of Protocol No. 1 was not applicable.

---

50 Cf. e.g. several of the articles in Stefaan Van den Bogaert (ed.), *Ibid.*

51 *Gaygusuz v. Austria*, para. 39.

52 *Gaygusuz v. Austria*, para. 42.

53 *Wessels-Bergervoet v. the Netherlands*, Judgment of 4 June 2002.

54 *Ibid.*, paras. 32 and 33.

The Court, however, sidestepped the issue of the significance of contributions. The Court referred to its admissibility decision in which it noted that "it is not disputed that the applicant is entitled to an at least partial AOW pension."[55] In its admissibility decision the Court therefore accepted that the applicant's right to a pension under the AOW could be regarded as a "possession" within the meaning of Article 1 of Protocol No. 1 and that, consequently, Article 14 of the Convention was applicable.

The applicant claimed to be subject to discrimination when she was granted old age pension in 1989 after having reached the age of 65. The pension was reduced by 38 percent on the ground that she had not been insured during nine periods between 1957 and 1977 when *her husband* had been working abroad. The husband's pension had also been reduced some years earlier by the same percentage. The reduction of his pension was made pursuant to a decree issued under the AOW according to which persons residing in the Netherlands but working abroad and who were socially insured under foreign legislation were not insured under the AOW. This limitation also applied to a woman who was married to a man working abroad irrespective of whether she herself had been insured under foreign insurance legislation. The decree, however, did not contain a comparable provision in respect of married men. The relevant legal rules were changed in 1985, i.e. before the reduction in the applicant's pension in order to bring them into conformity with present-day standards of equality between men and women. However, no measures were taken to remove the discriminatory effects of the former rules.

With regard to the issue of discrimination the Court took for its basis that the reduction applied to the applicant's pension was based exclusively on the fact that she was a married woman. In line with previous case law the Court stated that very strong reasons would have to be put forward before it could regard such difference as compatible with the Convention. The respondent Government argued that at the material time – beginning in 1957 when the first period of non-insurance began – social attitudes were different in that most of the then breadwinners were married men, thus justifying the differential treatment. The Court did not entirely refuse that argument,[56] but attached importance to the fact that pre-understanding with regard to equality between men and women had in fact changed in the period between 1957 and 1989:

---

[55] *Wessels-Bergervoet v. the Netherlands*, Admissibility decision of 3 October 2000, The Law, para. 3.

[56] The Court expressed its uncertainty in the following way: "Even assuming that the Government's argument that at the material time social attitudes were different in that most of the breadwinners were married men, so that the difference in treatment was justified, were grounded, the Court considers it relevant that the Convention and Protocol No. 1 had already come into force in the Netherlands by 31 August 1954", *Wessels-Bergervoet v. the Netherlands, Judgment of 4 June 2002*, para. 51.

> The Court does not only have regard to its aim at the time the relevant provisions were enacted, but also to its effects in the concrete case concerned [....] the inequality in treatment embodied in the former legal rules materialised in 1989 when, given the prevailing social attitudes at that time, the aim pursued by the legal provisions could no longer be upheld.[57]

As no measures were taken in 1985 to remove the discriminatory effects of the former legal rules the Court concluded that the differential treatment constituted a violation of Article 1 of Protocol No. 1.

A few days later the Court once again had the opportunity to clarify the issue of social cash benefits as possession in the sense of Article 1 of Protocol No. 1. In *Willis v. the United Kingdom*[58] the applicant – a widower – claimed that he was subject to discrimination as he was not entitled to the same social cash benefits as widows. The benefits in question were paid out of the National Insurance Fund, and the funds required for paying such benefits were to be provided by means of contributions payable to the Secretary of State for Social Services by earners, employers and others together with certain additions made to the fund by Parliament.[59] Male and female earners were obliged to pay the same contributions in accordance with their status as employed earners or self-employed earners.

The applicant's late wife had been the primary breadwinner of the family and had paid full social security contributions. The applicant himself, however, had been a relatively low earner, and in 1995 he had given up work to nurse his wife, who was sick of cancer, and take care of their two children. After the death of his wife the applicant worked part-time for a short period. However, as it proved uneconomic for him, he ceased his employment to care full-time for the children. Despite all this he was not entitled to Widow's Payment and Widowed Mother's Allowance.

The Court noted that a female in the same situation would have had a right, enforceable under domestic law, to receive the two benefits. With regard to the issue of contributions the Court, however, once again sidestepped the issue with the following argumentation:

> The Court does not consider it significant that the statutory condition requiring payment of contributions into the National Insurance Fund required the contributions to have been made, not by the applicant, but by his late wife. It is therefore not necessary for the Court to address in this case the question of *whether a social security benefit must be contributory in nature in order that it can constitute a "possession"* for the purposes of Article 1 of Protocol No. 1 [author's emphasis].[60]

---

57 *Ibid.*, para. 52.

58 *Willis v. the United Kingdom*, Judgment of 11 June 2002.

59 *Ibid.*, para. 14.

60 *Ibid.*, para. 35.

The phraseology indicates that the Court has not yet made up its mind, and that it preferred to postpone the decision until it would no longer be possible to avoid taking a position. Contributions *had* been made, and the Court saw no reason to make general statements on the issue.

The *Gaygusuz* case was supported by a Chamber judgment in the case *Azinas v. Cyprus*[61] concerning the disciplinary sentence of dismissal of a public official which resulted also in the forfeiture of the applicant's retirement benefits including his pension. The pension scheme in question was not contributory in the strict sense of the word in that the applicant did not formally pay contributions to a pension fund. The pension, however, was part of the employment contract, and in the Chamber judgment from 2002 the Court argued that a pecuniary right for the purposes of Article 1 may arise "where an employer [....] has given a more general undertaking to pay a pension on conditions which can be considered to be part of the employment contract."[62] Moreover, the Court did in fact find a violation of Article 1 of Protocol No. 1, because the retrospective forfeiture of the applicant's pension could not be said to serve any commensurate purpose. The case, however, was later referred to the Grand Chamber, which decided – by twelve votes to five – to declare it inadmissible because the applicant had not exhausted domestic remedies. Nevertheless, as one of the dissenting judges pointed out:

> [....] the pension rights of public servants relate to services done by the relevant persons and are thus dependent on "contributions" in a more general way. It would be arbitrary to place the dividing line under the property aspect between those public servants who are working within a system of social security contracts where contributions are formally paid and those whose contributions are from the very beginning indirectly deducted from their salaries and thus to be paid by the State.[63]

The dissenting judge was more far-sighted than his colleagues as will appear later. However, the cases so far referred to show that the Court is inclined to restrict itself to the current facts of the case, and that it avoids indulging in considerations of a more general character. Law comes into being in the concrete context and each and every case contributes to a higher or minor degree to the creation of a legal picture which will, however, never be complete. There are always new facts ahead waiting for the encounter with the text and old conceptions of law are constantly challenged by new facts and changing pre-understandings. In this way, the facts of the case *Koua Poirrez v. France*[64] differed from the previous cases and therefore made up such challenge.

---

[61] *Azinas v. Cyprus*, Judgment of 20 June 2002.

[62] *Ibid.*, para. 34.

[63] *Azinas v. Cyprus*, Judgment of 28 April 2004, Dissenting opinion of Judge Rees, para. 2.

[64] *Koua Poirrez v. France*, Judgment of 30 September 2003.

Koua Poirrez was a physically disabled young man from the Ivory Coast who was adopted by a French citizen. Shortly after the adoption his application for a declaration of French nationality was declared inadmissible on the ground that he had been over eighteen when it was submitted. He was registered by the Occupational Counselling and Rehabilitation Board as 80 percent disabled and applied to the Family Allowances Office for an allowance for disabled adults (AAH). His application was, however, refused on the ground that he did not satisfy the condition of the Social Security Code. He was neither a French national nor a national of a country which had entered into a reciprocity agreement with France in respect of the allowance in question.

Unlike the previous cases the benefit in question was entirely tax financed, and the respondent Government claimed that such non-contributory benefits fall outside the concept of possession in Article 1 of Protocol. No.1. The Court, however recalled the *Gaygusuz* case in which Article 1 was considered applicable "without it being necessary to rely solely on the link between entitlement to emergency assistance and the obligation to pay 'taxes or other contributions'." The Court added:

> In that connection the Court considers that the fact that, in that case, the applicant had paid contributions and was thus entitled to emergency assistance [....] does not mean, by converse implication, that a non-contributory social benefit such as the AAH does not also give rise to a pecuniary right for the purposes of Article 1 of Protocol No. 1.[65]

Before concluding that the applicant *did have* a pecuniary right for the purposes of Article 1 of Protocol No. 1 the Court noted that the applicant fulfilled the other statutory conditions for receiving the benefit, and that the allowance was paid both to French nationals and to nationals of a country that had signed a reciprocity agreement with France. Moreover, the Court stated that the other circumstances of the case, including the fact that the applicant had received a minimum welfare benefit, did not in itself justify refusing him the disability allowance, and noted that as from June 1998 the applicant had in fact received that allowance as the nationality condition had then been abolished. Finally, the Court once again took a holistic approach to human rights by referring to the recommendation of the Committee of Ministers No. R (92) 8 aiming at the adoption of a policy adapted to the needs of disabled persons. Moreover, the Court referred to conclusions of the ECSR on the basis of the ESC/RESC.

Apart from the fact that the applicant fulfilled the other statutory conditions for receiving the AAH, the above considerations relate more closely to the issue of possible discrimination than to the issue of whether or not the AAH can be considered possession within the meaning of Article 1 of Protocol No. 1.

[65] *Ibid.*, para. 37.

It seems therefore as if the decision actually renders superfluous the distinction between what is traditionally considered contributory social security benefits and non-contributory social welfare assistance. The decisive factor seems rather to be whether or not the benefit in question has a clear legal basis in the sense that he who fulfils the legal criteria – except for the disputed nationality criterion – has an enforceable legal claim.[66] If that is the case, the benefit in question falls within the concept of possession contrary to benefits which are granted at the discretion of public authorities.

This interpretation was eventually supported by the admissibility decision in *Stec and Others v. the United Kingdom*. The case concerned a certain reduced earnings allowance to which the applicants – all women – had been entitled until the day they retired on a pension which was paid at a lower rate than the earnings allowance. They claimed that they were subject to discrimination because the pension age in the United Kingdom was 60 for women and 65 for men.

Sitting as a Grand Chamber the Court began its argumentation by referring to the notion of "civil rights" in Article 6 which – in the *Salesi* case – was held also to apply to a dispute over entitlement to a non-contributory welfare benefit. The Court further referred to the case *Schuler-Zgraggen v. Switzerland* in which it held that "[….] the development in the law [….] and the principle of equality of treatment warrant taking the view that today the general rule is that Article 6 § 1 does apply in the field of social insurance, including even welfare assistance".[67] The Court stressed the importance of a coherent interpretation of the Convention and continued as follows:

> The Court's approach to Article 1 of Protocol No. 1 should reflect the reality of the way in which welfare provision is currently organised within the Member States of the Council of Europe. It is clear that within those States, and within most individual States, there exists a wide range of social security benefits designed to confer entitlements which arise as of right. Benefits are funded in a large variety of ways: some are paid for by contributions to a specific fund; some depend on a claimant's contribution record; many are paid for out of general taxation on the basis of a statutorily defined status [….] Given the variety of funding methods, and the interlocking nature of benefits under most welfare systems, it appears increasingly artificial to hold that only benefits financed by contributions to a specific fund fall within the scope of Article 1 of Protocol No. 1. Moreover, to exclude benefits paid for out of general taxation would be to disregard the fact that many claimants under this latter type of system also contribute to its financing, through the payment of tax.

---

66 Paul Lemmens suggests that the Court has developed a "theory of legitimate expectations", cf. "The Gaygusuz decision situated in the case law of the European Court of Human Rights" in Stefaan Van den Bogaert (ed.), *Ibid.*, pp. 25–33 (on p. 28 ff).

67 *Stec and Others v. the United Kingdom*, Admissibility decision of 6 July 2005, para. 50.

> In the modern, democratic State, many individuals are, for all or part of their lives, completely dependent for survival on social security and welfare benefits. Many domestic legal systems recognise that such individuals require a degree of certainty and security, and provide for benefits to be paid—subject to the fulfilment of the conditions of eligibility—as of right. Where an individual has an assertable right under domestic law to a welfare benefit, the importance of that interest should also be reflected by holding Article 1 of Protocol No. 1 to be applicable.[68]

In response to the Government's contention that the recognition of a right to a non-contributory benefit as possession renders otiose the provisions of the Social Charter the Court reiterated the famous passage from the *Airey case* from 1979:

> Whilst the Convention sets forth what are essentially civil and political rights, many of them have implications of a social or economic nature. The Court therefore considers, like the Commission, that the mere fact that an interpretation of the Convention may extend into the sphere of social and economic rights should not be a decisive factor against such an interpretation; there is no water-tight division separating that sphere from the field covered by the Convention [....].[69]

Accordingly, the pension in question could be considered possession for the purposes of Article 1 of Protocol, and Article 14 of the Convention was therefore applicable. With regard to the margin of appreciation the Court stated that very weighty reasons would have to be put forward before the Court could regard a difference in treatment based exclusively on the ground of sex as compatible with the Convention. The Court, however, went on as follows:

> On the other hand, a wide margin is usually allowed to the State under the Convention when it comes to general measures of economic or social strategy [....]. Because of their direct knowledge of their society and its needs, the national authorities are in principle better placed than the international judge to appreciate what is in the public interest on social or economic grounds, and the Court will generally respect the legislature's policy choice unless it is "manifestly without reasonable foundation [....]."[70]

The Court accepted that the linking of cut-off age for the reduced earning allowance to the end of working life and entitlement to old age pension pursued a legitimate aim and were reasonably and objectively justified. The Court further noticed that the difference in treatment was originally adopted in the 1940s in order to mitigate financial inequality arising out of the woman's traditional unpaid role of caring for the family in the home. Originally, therefore,

[68] *Ibid.*, paras. 50–51.

[69] *Airey v. Ireland*, para. 26.

[70] *Stec and Others v. the United Kingdom*, Judgment of 12 April 2006, para. 52.

the differential pensionable ages were intended to correct "factual inequalities" between men and women and were therefore considered objectively justified under Article 14. The Court added:

> It follows that the difference in pensionable ages continued to be justified until such time that social conditions had changed so that women were no longer substantially prejudiced because of a shorter working life. This change, must, by its very nature, have been gradual, and it would be difficult or impossible to pinpoint any particular moment when the unfairness to men caused by differential pensionable ages began to outweigh the need to correct the disadvantaged position of women.[71]

The number of women in paid employment had indeed increased since the differential pensionable ages had been introduced in 1940s, and the United Kingdom had taken a number of initiatives to developing parity in the working lives of men and women. According to the information before the Court, the Government made a first, concrete, move towards establishing the same pensionable age for both sexes in 1991. The Court had the following comment:

> It would, no doubt, be possible to argue that this step could, or should, have been made earlier. However, as the Court has observed, the development of parity in the working lives of men and women has been a gradual process, and one which the national authorities are better placed to assess [....]. Moreover, it is significant that many of the other Contracting States still maintain a difference in the ages at which men and women become eligible for the State retirement pension [....].[72]

The Court went on to notice the slowly evolving nature of the change in women's working lives, and emphasised that there was no common standard amongst the Contracting States. Accordingly, the Court did not find that the United Kingdom could be criticised for not having started earlier on the road towards a single pensionable age. Moreover, the Court did not consider it unreasonable that the United Kingdom having once begun the move towards equality, had chosen to introduce the reform slowly and in stages. However, one of the major reasons for the Court's not finding a violation of Article 1 of Protocol No. 1 in conjunction with Article 14 may have been the following:

> Given the extremely far-reaching and serious implications, for women and for the economy in general, these are matters which clearly fall within the State's margin of appreciation.[73]

This conclusion is hardly surprising given the fact that the benefit in question was applicable to half the population of the United Kingdom. The budgetary implications were indeed far reaching compared to the *Gaugusuz* case and the

---

71 *Ibid.*, para. 62.
72 *Ibid.*, para. 63.
73 *Ibid.*, para. 65.

case of *Koua Poirrez*. However, the fact that entitlements to tax financed benefits constitute possession for the purposes of Article 1 of Protocol No. 1 has clearly been established, and the Court, once again, has brought coherence into the Convention complex. Moreover, later case law shows that the Court is not afraid of finding a violation if the domestic decision is not based on objective and reasonable justification.

That was the case in *Zeman vs. Austria* also about differential treatment between men and women with regard to survivor's pension. The Austrian Pension Act was regulated in 1986 with a view to creating equality between the sexes and full equality was to be achieved in 1995. According to the 1986 Pension Act:

> [t]he monthly instalments to which the widower or the former husband are entitled, are – from 1 August 1986 onwards the amount of one third; – from 1 January 1989 onwards the amount of two thirds; – and from 1 January 1995 onwards the full amount. If the widower or former husband is incapable of gainful employment and indigent, this restriction does not apply.[74]

However, in December the Act was changed in the way that widowers were only entitled to the full pension if "he is incapable of gainful employment and indigent [....]."[75] This requirement did not apply to women. The Court referred to the *Stec* case and remembered that:

> the Court found no violation of the Convention as it considered that the respondent State's decisions as to the precise timing and means of putting right the inequality in pension age did not exceed the wide margin of appreciation allowed in such a field and the link of eligibility for the benefits to the pension system was consistent with the purpose of the benefits.

The Court went on as follows:

> However, unlike in the Stec case, the reform towards equality between women and men in the present case was already effectively under way and the final target of equal treatment should have been reached on 1 January 1995. At this date, the applicant would have reached entitlement to a full survivor's pension in the amount of 60 % of his late wife's retirement pension.
>
> The Court finds that very strong reasons have to be put forward in order to explain the amendment in the relevant legislation in December 1994 which introduced further differentiation and thereby frustrated the planned equalisation for part of the widowers, including the applicant, at the very last moment. However, the Government have not forwarded any convincing reason why, contrary to the prior assessment expressed in the Vienna Pension Act of 1986 that equal treatment of widows and widowers should be reached by 1 January

[74] *Zeman v. Austria*, Judgment of 29 June 2006, para. 23.
[75] *Ibid.*

> 1995, a more favourable treatment of widows suddenly appeared to be justified again. Their argument that a new assessment of the pension of those persons who already received the full amount of survivor's pension before 1 January 1995 would have interfered with their existing rights, might equally well apply to persons who, until amendment of the Pension Act in December 1994, were entitled to and trusted to receive the full amount of a survivor's pension as from 1 January 1995. The Court accordingly considers that the subsequent difference in treatment between men and women as regards entitlement to survivor's pensions acquired prior to 1995 was not based on any "objective and reasonable justification".[76]

It is worth noticing that the Court reached this decision unanimously, and the lesson learned is probably that a well activated process towards equality obliges the State Party to continue unless there is a "objective and reasonable justification." That was the case in the *Stec* case,[77] but not in *Zeman*. Similarly, in *Hobbs, Richards, Walsh and Geen v. the United Kingdom*, the British Government was unable to justify why only widows were entitled to a temporary income tax reduction, the widow's bereavement allowance (WBA) after the death of their husbands. The Court gave the following explanation concerning the history of the WBA and explained its reasons for finding a violation:[78]

> WBA was introduced at a time when married couples were taxed as a single entity, with a tax allowance available to the man in respect of his wife's earnings. A widowed man could continue to claim this married man's allowance in the year following the wife's death, whereas a widowed woman received only a single person's allowance. WBA was intended to rectify this inequality, but became obsolete when independent taxation of married men and women was introduced from 1990/91 and spouses were given the choice, from 1993/94, as to how to share the married couples allowance [....]. The Government have not attempted to justify the availability of the WBA to female widows only from 1990/91 until its abolition in respect of deaths occurring after 6 April 2000. The Court does not consider that, during the period when the applicants were denied the allowance, the difference in treatment between men and women as regards the WBA was reasonably and objectively justified.[79]

In general, however, a wide margin is usually allowed to the State under the Convention when it comes to general measures of economic or social strategy and the Court has often stated as follows:

[76] *Ibid.*, paras. 39–40.

[77] Cf. also *Runkee and White v. the United Kingdom* , Judgment of 10 May 2007 concerning differential treatment of widows and widowers.

[78] Cf. also *Luczak v. Poland*, Judgment of 27 November 2007 concerning discrimination with regard to nationality.

[79] *Hobbs, Richards, Walsh and Geen v. the United Kingdom*, Judgment of 14 November 2006, para. 53.

> Because of their direct knowledge of their society and its needs, the national authorities are in principle better placed than the international judge to appreciate what is in the public interest on social or economic grounds, and the Court will generally respect the legislature's policy choice unless it is "manifestly without reasonable foundation [....]."[80]

6.3 *Social Cash Benefits as Property Rights – Further Reflections*

If one takes into consideration the differences among the States Parties to the ECHR with regard to the financing of social cash benefits, the acceptance of tax-financed benefits under Article 1 of Protocol No. 1 seems fair and logical. Some countries – such as the Nordic countries – have a long tradition of public financing of many social cash benefits with the natural consequence that the burden of taxation is much higher than in countries where cash benefits are financed completely or predominantly by private contributions. There is a huge variety in ways of financing. However, at the end of the day the citizens themselves provide the funding either directly by private contributions to various social schemes or indirectly by tax paying. If these differences were not reflected in the perception of what falls under the concept of possession it would in fact have as a consequence that e.g. a Dane would enjoy less protection under the ECHR than a person from a country with a tradition for privately-funded social cash benefit schemes. Social cash benefits deriving from not directly contributory schemes are not to be considered good deeds of generous States or generous employers. At the end of the day citizens themselves are the contributors in one way or the other, and it would indeed be arbitrary to draw the dividing line between direct and indirect contributions and payments. We do not get anything for nothing in this world. Outgoing payments from the State, from employers and from insurance companies correspond to ingoing payments, although the beneficiaries are not necessarily the same as the contributors.

On the face of it, the Court's conclusion seems far-reaching. However, it need not be. The consequences are probably manageable. First of all it should be emphasised that Article 1 of Protocol No. 1 does not guarantee the right to *acquire* possessions. Thus, in *Stec and Others* the Court emphasized:

> that the principles [....] which apply generally in cases under Article 1 of Protocol No. 1, are equally relevant when it comes to welfare benefits. In particular, the Article does not create a right to acquire property. It places no restriction on the Contracting State's freedom to decide whether or not to have in place any form of social security scheme, or to choose the type or amount of benefits to provide under any such scheme [....].[81]

---

[80] *Stec and Others v. the United Kingdom*, Judgment, para. 52.

[81] *Stec and Others v. the United Kingdom*, Admissibility decision, para. 54.

Moreover, it should be recalled that all the above-mentioned cases about Article 1 of Protocol No. 1 concerned the issue of non-discrimination with regard to social cash benefits. The Protocol merely functioned as the vehicle which could bring the issue in question within the ambit of the non-discrimination clause in Article 14, and differential treatment only amounts to discrimination if it is not objective and reasonable.

In addition, Article 1 of Protocol No. 1 does not include an indispensable obligation not to interfere with the enjoyment of property rights. The provision allows for deprivation of possessions if "in the public interest and subject to conditions provided for by law and by the general principles of international law." In matters of social policy the Court traditionally allows Member States a considerable margin of appreciation, and it must be assumed that the Court will exercise considerable self-restraint also in future assessments of the legitimacy of interference within the field of social benefits. Although not concerning non-contributory social benefits, the case *Kjartan Asmundsson v. Iceland*[82] might be illustrative of such cautiousness. The applicant had been deprived of his disability pension due to an Act altering the basis for the assessment of the right to disability pension from inability to perform the same work to work in general. The applicant was 100 percent disabled as a seaman, but did not reach a minimum level of 35 percent of capacity for work in general. Accordingly, he lost all rights to disability pension after a transitional period of five years.

It was not disputed that the termination of the applicant's disability pension amounted to an interference with his right to peaceful enjoyment of his possessions, and the Court's examination was centred round the issue of proportionality. The Court held that an important consideration in the assessment under Article 1 of Protocol No. 1 is whether the applicant's right to derive benefits from the social insurance scheme in question has been infringed in a manner resulting in the impairment of the essence of his pension rights,[83] thereby indicating that the provision cannot be interpreted as entitling the possessor to a benefit of a particular amount. The Court went on by recognising that the introduction of the new pension rules had been prompted by legitimate concerns about the need to resolve the Fund's financial difficulties. However, the Court was "struck by the fact that the applicant belonged to a small group of 54 disability pensioners [....] whose pensions were discontinued altogether [....]", whereas the vast majority of the in total 689 disability pensioners continued to receive disability pensions at the same level as before the adoption of the new rules.[84] The Court, moreover, attached importance to

[82] *Kjartan Asmundsson v. Iceland*, Judgment of 12 October 2004.
[83] *Ibid.*, para. 39 with reference to a number of previous cases.
[84] *Ibid.*, para. 43.

the fact that the applicant had received his pension for nearly 20 years, and found that he could "validly plead an individual legitimate expectation that his disability would continue to be assessed on the basis of his incapacity to perform his previous job."[85] Against this background, the Court concluded that:

> the applicant was made to bear an excessive and disproportionate burden which, even having regard to the wide margin of appreciation to be enjoyed by the State in the area of social legislation, cannot be justified by the legitimate community interests relied on by the authorities.[86]

However, it is worth noticing that the Court added that "it would have been otherwise had the applicant been obliged to endure a reasonable and commensurate reduction rather than the total deprivation of his entitlements."[87] This addition indicates that social legislation may be adjusted within reasonable limits without bringing about a conflict in relation to Article 1 of Protocol No. 1.

In the same breath it should be recalled that the right to peaceful enjoyment of property is also limited by Article 1 (2) of Protocol No. 1. According to this provision a State has the right to enforce such laws as it deems necessary to control the use of property in accordance with the general interest or to secure the payment of taxes or other contributions or penalties.

Admittedly, this right of the State to "secure the payment of taxes or other contributions" is not unlimited. Within the field of social security the limitations are well illustrated by the case *Van Raalte v. the Netherlands*[88] concerning unequal treatment in the levying of contributions under the Dutch child benefit scheme. As the case concerned the right of the State to "secure the payment of taxes or other contributions", it came within the ambit of Article 1 of Protocol No. 1, and the applicant claimed that it was discriminatory towards men that unmarried, childless women over the age of 45 unlike men in the same situation were exempted from making contributions under a child-care benefit scheme. The respondent government defended the differential treatment by claiming that sex equality with regard to the payment of contributions would "impose an unfair emotional burden"[89] on middle-aged childless women. However, the Court held that "such an objective cannot provide a justification for the gender-based difference of treatment in the present case."[90]

What can be derived from the case is that taxes and contributions must be levied in a non-discriminatory manner. Moreover, one must assume that taxes

---

85 *Ibid.*, para. 44.
86 *Ibid.*, para. 45.
87 *Ibid.*, para. 45.
88 *Van Raalte v. the Netherlands*, Judgment of 21 February 1997.
89 *Ibid.*, para. 43.
90 *Ibid.*, para. 44.

and contributions must be proportionate to the income. However, States are given a very wide margin of appreciation when it comes to the levying of taxes and other contributions. The fact that social cash benefits or contributions under a social scheme fall within the ambit of Article 1 of Protocol No. 1 does not mean that States Parties cannot pursue a flexible social policy. States Parties are not necessarily prevented from altering either the character or the size of social cash benefits if such alterations are considered necessary or appropriate in a greater political context. The margin of appreciation in social policy issues are wide, and one can imagine even very thoroughgoing amendments to social legislation within the margin.[91]

7 *Future Prospects*

In principle, one will have to maintain that social cash benefits are not protected by the ECHR. There is no provision in the Convention guaranteeing individuals the right to social cash benefits, and even though the Court has left a door open for holding that absolutely insufficient social cash benefits may raise an issue under Article 3, cf. above in Section 3, there is no case law as yet. However, the case is different if the Contracting States have introduced legislation at the domestic level providing for social cash benefits in various situations. The existence of legislation within the field of social cash benefits carries along obligations not only of a procedural character but also with regard to substance. Social cash benefits must be treated as civil rights in the sense of Article 6 provided the benefit in question has a clear legal basis, and something similar applies with respect to the acceptance of social cash benefits as possessions in the sense of Article 1 of Protocol No. 1.[92]

The entering into force of Protocol No. 12 to the ECHR will necessarily have as an implication that the protection increases, not only within the field of social cash benefits but with respect to economic, social and cultural rights as such. However, the potential of the 'old' Convention is not necessarily exhausted either. One may ask whether the recognition of social cash benefits as possession necessarily has to be restricted to rights which have a clear legal basis in legislation i.e. rights which are not granted on a discretionary basis.

---

[91] Cf. also *Adriana C. Goudswaard-van der Lans*, Admissibility decision of 22 September 2005 about reduction of a pension. The application was declared manifestly ill founded.

[92] The search for coherence between Article 6 (1) and Article 1 of Protocol No. 1 calls for a reinterpretation of Article 6 (1) with regard to tax matters. It is not logical that an obligation to pay contributions under a social security scheme is "civil" while an obligation to pay income tax is not. Such reinterpretation might be on its way, cf. *Ferrazzini v. Italy*, Judgment of 12 July 2001 in which Judge Lorenzen's dissenting opinion was joined by five other judges.

Existing case law provides a number of examples that the individual who is denied the right to a social cash benefit because of lack of nationality, because of sex or race can challenge the decision in question, provided the underlying legal provision is otherwise worded with precision i.e. not to be granted on a discretionary basis. Thus, if *the legislature* is responsible for the omission to include certain groups among the potential beneficiaries of the benefit in question, the excluded groups might be able to challenge a decision made by the executive and the judiciary according to such legislation. However, if the legislature has left open or only described in vague terms who are to be the potential beneficiaries and *the executive* and *the judiciary* chooses to apply their discretionary powers to exclude certain groups in a discriminatory way, it seems to me difficult to defend the viewpoint that these groups should not have the opportunity to challenge such decisions before the Court. Thus, it seems to me that one has to make a distinction between discretion with regard to the potential beneficiaries and discretion with regard to the measuring out of the benefit in question. While it is difficult to argue that the Court should have a say with regard to the size and the nature of the vaguely worded social benefit that seems not to be the case with regard to the exclusion of certain groups.

Chapter 9

Work-Related Rights Under the ECHR

1 *Work-Related Rights as Cross-Cutting Issues*

The international community has dealt with work or labour-related issues ever since the foundation of the International Labour Organisation [hereinafter the ILO] in 1919, and a complex and comprehensive regulation system has gradually developed not only within the ILO system but also in other international regulation systems. Thus, treaties dealing with socio-economic rights encompass a multiplicity of labour-related provisions, and so do civil and political rights treaties at the global as well as the regional level. This treaty-crossing character of labour-related rights reflects the perception of labour not only as a means for economic survival but also as a means for self-realisation and development of the human personality. Moreover, labour related issues have attracted the attention of the international community due to the fact that conditions of labour may involve "such injustice hardship and privation to large numbers of people as to produce unrest so great that the peace and harmony of the world are imperilled."[1]

Despite this three-fold aim, the general anti-revolutionary purpose of regulating labour-related issues is eclipsed by consideration for social justice and human self-realisation. He who can provide for himself by virtue of earned income has easier access to a number of human goods and services, and recognition has been accorded with regard to the protection of workers' rights not only to a healthy working environment but also to decent conditions with regard to salary, unemployment insurance, vocational training and holiday with pay. The State is the primary responsible agent for securing workers' rights. However, workers themselves safeguard their interests through a participatory process which also has the character of human rights, namely to organise, to bargain collectively and to take collective action. These participatory rights

[1] Preamble to the Constitution of the ILO, 1919, para. 2.

escape classification either as socio-economic or civil and political rights, and it is characteristic that these rights appear in both sets of conventions, thus underlining the indivisibility, interdependence and interrelation of human rights.

2 *The Relevant Provisions*

Whereas the ESC/RESC encompass an even very rich catalogue of rights related to labour issues, the protection under the ECHR seems rather poor. Thus, the ESC/RESC devote the first ten articles to the protection of various labour-related issues,[2] whereas there is no mention of a right to work in the ECHR. In fact, terms such as 'work', 'employment', 'job' or 'labour' are more or less missing in the Convention and its Protocols. Only Article 4 speaks of 'work' and 'labour' the context, however, being the exact opposite, namely the right *not* to work and the right to be protected against forced or compulsory labour. Moreover, Article 11 deals directly with another aspect of the issue, namely the right of workers to form and to join trade unions.

Against this background it is noteworthy that a number of labour-related issues have nevertheless been subject to adjudication before the ECtHR. It goes without saying that the protection under the ECHR is incommensurable in every respect with the protection under the ESC/RESC and the CESCR. However, as will appear from the following analysis of case law, several other articles than Articles 4 and 11 have appeared to be relevant for the protection of work-related issues either alone or in conjunction with Article 14. Thus, work-related issues have been adjudicated also under Articles 8, 9 and 10 of the ECHR.[3] Moreover, Article 1 of Protocol No. 1 has proved to be relevant as well. In addition, the interpretation of the expression "civil rights" in Article 6 of the Convention has undergone an interesting development especially as regards the rights of public sector employees.

---

2 The labour-related rights covered by the ESC/RESC are the following: The right to work (Article 1), the right to just conditions of work (Article 2), the right to safe and healthy working conditions (Article 3), the right to a fair remuneration (Article 4), the right to organise (Article 5), the right to bargain collectively (Article 6), the right of children and young persons to protection (Article 7), the right of employed women to protection (Article 8), the right to vocational guidance (Article 9) and the right to vocational training (Article 10). Moreover, Article 19 guarantees the right of migrant workers and their families to protection and assistance.

3 Even Article 3 deserves to be mentioned albeit only in a footnote. Thus, in a number of cases the Court has found that Article 3 was violated because of the way in which individuals were deprived of their livelihood, cf. e.g. *Selçuk and Asker v. Turkey*, Judgment of 24 April 1998, *Bilgin v. Turkey*, Judgment of 16 November 2000 and *Dulas v. Turkey*, Judgment of 30 January 2001.

The discussion under the substantive provisions of the ECHR and Protocol No. 1 relates especially to restrictions with regard to the seeking of employment and the protection against dismissal. Moreover, the chapter includes an analysis of the way in which the ECtHR and the ECSR gradually seem to coordinate their interpretations of Article 11 of the ECHR and Articles 5 and 6 of the ESC/RESC.

When discussing the scope of Article 8 with regard to labour-related issues I have chosen to leave out in this chapter the issues related to a healthy working environment. They are already dealt with in Chapter 5 on The Right to Health under the ECHR. Moreover, I have chosen not to include Article 4 of the ECHR in the analysis as my focal point is the right to work rather than the right *not* to work.[4] Finally, it goes without saying also in this context that the analysis makes no claim to be anything like an exhaustive analysis of work-related issues. The purpose is once again to illustrate that civil and political rights encompass elements of a socio-economic character, and answers to specific questions must be sought in commentaries and in the special literature about the right to work.[5]

3 *Access to Work?*

The ECHR has no general provision similar to that of Article 1 of the ESC/RESC, which obliges the Contracting States to undertake various measures with a view to ensuring the effective exercise of the right to work. The ECHR does not either include a specific provision similar to Article 25 of the CCPR according to which "every citizen shall have the right and the opportunity [....] to have access, on general terms of equality, to public service in his country." Such a provision was deliberately omitted from the ECHR.[6] This does not exclude, however, that aspects of the right to work may under certain circumstances be protected under the Convention. So far at least two judgments seem to be of interest.

---

4 However, Chapter 11 includes aspects of this issue.

5 Cf. e.g. Krzysztof Drzewicki, "The Right to Work and Rights in Work" in Asbjørn Eide et al. (eds.) *Economic, Social and Cultural Rights – A Textbook*, 2nd Revised Edition, 2001, pp. 223–243 with references to literature on the issue.

6 In fact, such a right was deliberately omitted from the Convention because of the "great difficulty of bringing before an international court the problem of recruitment and the arrangements for selection and admission, which by their very nature differ considerably in Council of Europe member States according to national tradition and the system governing the public service", cf. e.g. the joint concurring opinion by Judges Bindschelder, Robert, Pinheiro Farinha, Petteti, Walsh, Russo and Bernhardt in *Glasenapp v. Germany* and *Kosiek v. Germany*, Judgments of 28 August 1986.

In *Thlimmenos v. Greece*, the applicant sat a public examination for the appointment of twelve chartered accountants, a liberal profession in Greece. Despite the fact that he came second out of 60 candidates, the Executive Board of the Greek Institute of Chartered Accountants refused to appoint him due to the fact that he had served a four-year prison sentence. It was not considered relevant to the refusal that he, due to his religious belief as a member of Jehovah's Witnesses, was convicted of insubordination for having refused to wear the military uniform at a time of general mobilisation.

Before the ECtHR, the applicant claimed that the statutory-based exclusion of persons convicted of a serious crime from appointment to a chartered accountant's post did not distinguish between persons convicted as a result of their religious beliefs and persons convicted on other grounds. He submitted that his non-appointment was directly linked to the manifestation of his religious beliefs, and that the issue accordingly fell within the ambit of Article 9. The applicant therefore relied on Article 14 taken in conjunction with Article 9.

The Court attached importance to the fact that the applicant did not complain of the distinction that the rules governing access to the profession made between convicted and not convicted persons. Thus, the Court underlined that the applicant's argument:

> amounts to saying that he is discriminated against in his exercise of his freedom of religion, as guaranteed by Article 9 of the Convention, in that *he was treated like any other person convicted of a serious crime* although his own conviction resulted from the very exercise of this freedom. Seen in this perspective, the Court accepts that the "set of facts" complained of by the applicant – his being treated as a person convicted of a serious crime for the purposes of an appointment to a chartered accountant's post despite the fact that the offence for which he had been convicted was prompted by his religious beliefs – "falls within the ambit of a Convention provision", namely Article 9 [author's emphasis].[7]

The Court went on to remember that the traditional perception of discrimination pertains to situations in which States treat differently persons in analogous situations. However, the Court took a major step by extending the protection to situations where States without an objective and reasonable justification "fail to treat differently persons whose situations are significantly different."[8] Accordingly, Article 14 was considered relevant to the applicant's complaint.

In the concrete assessment under Article 14 the Court held that – although States have a legitimate interest to exclude some offenders from the profession of chartered accountants – the applicant's conviction could not imply any dishonesty or moral turpitude likely to undermine his ability to exercise the profession as a chartered accountant. Excluding him on the ground that he was

[7] *Thlimmenos v. Greece*, Judgment of 6 April 2000, para. 42.

[8] *Ibid*., para. 44.

an unfit person was considered unjustified as amounting in fact to imposing a further sanction. The Court therefore held the exclusion from the profession to be disproportionate and concluded that the exclusion did not pursue a legitimate aim. There had accordingly been a violation of Article 14 taken in conjunction with Article 9.

The case is indeed interesting because the applicant was not excluded from the profession because of his religious conviction. He was excluded because he had a previous conviction which happened to be closely connected to his religious beliefs. By regarding the exclusion as discriminatory the Court has in principle widened the scope of Article 14 considerably. It remains to be seen what will be the implications of the *Thlimmenos* case, but Luzius Wildhaber is indeed right in pointing out that disabled people would be an obvious category to challenge the scope of this widening of the non-discrimination principle in Article 14.[9]

Two other cases are worth mentioning in this context. *Sidabras and Džiautas v. Lituania* concerns Article 8 taken in conjunction with Article 14. These provisions were invoked by two former KGB officers who – after Lithuania's independence in 1990 – were employed as a tax inspector and a prosecutor respectively. Both applicants were dismissed from their positions because of their previous occupation with the KGB and furthermore, prevented from finding alternative employment. Thus, in 1999 the Lithuanian Parliament had adopted an Act which to a wide degree excluded former KGB officers from a large number of positions not only in the public sector but also in the private sector. The case concerned the ban on the applicants' finding employment in the private sector, which they alleged to be in non-keeping with Article 8 taken alone and in conjunction with Article 14.

The Court considered Article 14 to be applicable as the applicants had been treated differently from other persons in Lithuania who had not worked for the KGB. With respect to the applicability of Article 8, the Court initially recalled previous rulings that "private life" is a broad term not susceptible to exhaustive definition. E.g. in the case *Niemietz v. Germany* the Court made the following remarks about the scope of the notion of private life thus reflecting the remarks made above in section 1 about labour as a means for self-realisation and development of the human personality:

> [i]t would be too restrictive to limit the notion to an "inner circle" in which the individual may live his own personal life as he chooses and to exclude therefrom entirely the outside world not encompassed within that circle. Respect for private life must also comprise to a certain degree the right to establish and develop

[9] Luzius Wildhaber,, "Protection against Discrimination under the European Convention" in *Baltic Yearbook of International Law*, Vol. II, 2002, pp. 71–82 (on p. 81).

> relationships with other human beings. There appears, furthermore, to be no reason of principle why this understanding of the notion of "private life" should be taken to exclude activities of a professional or business nature since it is, after all, in the course of their working lives that the majority of people have a significant, if not the greatest, opportunity of developing relationships with the outside world.[10]

The Court remembered the *Thlimmenos* case and recalled that the right to choose a particular profession is not covered by the Convention. However, the Court went on to consider "that a far-reaching ban on taking up private-sector employment does affect private life."[11] The Court attached "particular weight in this respect to the text of Article 1 § 2 of the European Social Charter and the interpretation given by the European Committee of Social Rights [....] and to the texts adopted by the ILO [...]." Thus, the Committee has consistently held that the ESC/RESC lay down a right not to be discriminated against in employment, and the ILO Committee of Experts on the Application of Conventions and Recommendations has interpreted in particular ILO Convention No. 111 on Discrimination (Employment and Occupation) in a similar manner. The Court expressed its wish to coordinate the interpretation of the two instruments, the ECHR and the ESC by repeating the famous quotation from the *Airey case*, namely that:

> there is no watertight division separating the sphere of social and economic rights from the field covered by the Convention [....].[12]

The Court established that the ban had "created serious difficulties for them in terms of earning their living, with obvious repercussions on the enjoyment of their private lives." and found that also the "possible impediment to their leading a normal personal life" had to be taken into consideration.[13] Against this background, the Court concluded that the ban had effects on the enjoyment of the applicant's right to private life within the meaning of Article 8.

When considering the issue of discrimination, the Court recognised that the restrictions of the applicant's employment prospects pursued a legitimate aim, namely that of protecting national security, public order, the economic well-being of the country and the rights and freedoms of others. However, when considering the issue of proportionality, the Court chose to disregard the applicants' principal argument that their lack of loyalty had not been proven. The Court held that "[e]ven assuming that their lack of loyalty had been undisputed, it must be noted that the applicant's prospects were restricted not only

---

10 *Niemietz v. Germany*, Judgment of 16 December 1992, para. 29.

11 *Sidabras and Džiautas v. Lithuania*, Judgment of 27 July 2004, para. 47.

12 *Ibid.*, para. 47.

13 *Ibid.*, paras. 48–49.

in the State service but also in various branches of the private sector."[14] The Court found that such restrictions cannot be justified in the same manner as restrictions governing access to employment in the public sector. Moreover, as the Act in question did not contain a definition of the specific jobs, functions or tasks which the applicants were barred from holding, the Court concluded that:

> such a legislative scheme must be considered as lacking the necessary safeguards for avoiding discrimination and for guaranteeing adequate and appropriate judicial supervision of the imposition of such restrictions [....].[15]

The Court finally noted that the Act did not come into effect until 1999 i.e. almost a decade after Lithuania had declared its independence. Hence, the restrictions were imposed on the applicants as late as 13 years and 9 years after their departure from the KGB.

The Court concluded that the concrete ban constituted a disproportionate measure, and that there had been a violation of Article 8 taken in conjunction with Article 14. However, by disregarding the issue of the applicants' loyalty and concentrating on the broad scope and imprecise wording of the Act, the judgment has implications beyond the concrete case. In this context it is worth mentioning that the Court in its conclusion referred to conclusions pertaining to access to the public service, reached in regard to similar legislation in Latvia by the ILO Committee of Experts on the Application of Conventions and Recommendations.[16]

In the other case worth mentioning, *Rainys and Gasparavicius v. Lithuania*, the applicants' complaints were very similar, albeit wider in that they related not only to the applicants' hypothetical inability to apply for various private sector-jobs but they also concerned the applicants' actual dismissal from existing employment in that sector. However, this extra element did not "prompt the Court to depart from the reasoning developed in *Sidrabras and Džiautas*",[17] and the Court rapidly came to the conclusion that there had been a violation of Article 14 taken in conjunction with Article 8.

The cases prove that it does make sense to talk about a right to work under the ECHR although this right does not have the same scope as the right to work protected under the ESC/RESC. Admittedly, the more specific scope of this right is uncertain. Thus, the Court did not find it necessary to consider the cases under Article 8 taken on its own, and it remains to be seen whether or to which extent restrictions with regard to employment may constitute a

[14] *Ibid.*, para. 57.
[15] *Ibid.*, para. 59.
[16] *Ibid.*
[17] *Rainys and Gasparavicius v. Lithuania*, Judgment of 7 April 2005, para. 35.

violation of Article 8 in itself. That seemed to be the opinion of three of the seven judges in *Sidabras and Džiautas*, one of whom expressed his view in the following way in a partly concurring opinion:

> In my opinion, it is conclusive that the ban on seeking employment affected to an extremely significant degree the applicants' opportunity to pursue various professional activities and that there were consequential effects on the enjoyment of their right to respect for their private life within the meaning of Article 8. I agree with the majority that the fact that the applicants were prevented from seeking employment in various branches of the private sector on account of the statutory ban constituted a disproportionate measure, even having regard to the legitimacy of the aims pursued by that ban. That in itself should have been sufficient to have led the Court to a conclusion that Article 8 was violated in the applicants' case.[18]

Two dissenting judges were in disagreement with regard to the applicability of Article 14. One did not find that people who had worked for the KGB were in analogous or similar situations to those who had not, and the other did not find that "working for the KGB" could be recognised as a forbidden discrimination ground.[19] Against this background, it is notable that the Court insisted on making the laborious detour around Article 14 instead of beginning with Article 8. The "detour-approach" is typically chosen when "in view of the nature of the allegations, it is appropriate to examine the case first from the perspective of the non-discrimination clause."[20] However, as the dissenting judge pointed out, it is not crystal clear that "working for the KGB" deserves the recognition of a forbidden discriminatory ground under Article 14. Nevertheless, the recognition of "private life" as also encompassing employment restrictions does indeed represent a major step forward in the integrated approach, and the Court may have wanted to take a step-by-step approach to the issue. Hence, it is indeed possible to imagine restrictions which do not encompass any element of discrimination let alone differential treatment, and a further development cannot be excluded.[21]

4 *Protection Against Dismissal*

4.1 *Initial Remarks*

The cases referred to in Section 3 illustrate that the ECHR provides some – although limited – protection with regard to access to employment. Those who have succeeded in achieving a job are, however, also protected by the

---

[18] *Sidabras and Džiautas v. Lithuania*, partly concurring opinion of Judge Mularoni.
[19] *Ibid.*, Partly dissention opinions by Judge Thomassen.
[20] Cf. Luzius Wildhaber, *Ibid.*, p. 77.

Convention. Dismissal may be inconsistent with the Convention if carried out on account of certain grounds. Thus, respect for private life, for the right to freedom of religion, freedom of speech and expression or freedom of association, cf. ECHR Articles 8, 9, 10 and 11 may – either alone or in conjunction with Article 14 – involve certain limitations in employers' rights with respect to the discharge of employees.

4.2 *Homosexuality and the Right to Work*

Some British cases illustrate the scope of Article 8 with respect to the discharge of homosexuals from authorities under the Ministry of Defence. The cases concerned the British policy according to which homosexuality was considered incompatible with service in the armed forces. Thus, it was argued that this policy was necessary for the maintenance of the morale of service personnel and, consequently, for the fighting power and the operational effectiveness of the armed forces. In the first two cases from 1999, *Lustig-Prean and Beckett* and *Smith and Grady*,[22] the applicants had been discharged from their jobs on the sole ground of their sexual orientation, which was considered by the Court to be an interference with their right to private life under Article 8 of the Convention.

The Court noted that the policy was given statutory recognition, and that it was designed with a view to ensuring the operational effectiveness of the armed forces. Moreover, the Court underlined that States enjoy a certain margin of appreciation when the core of the national security aim pursued is the operational effectiveness of the armed forces. Only, assertions as to a risk to operational effectiveness must be "substantiated by specific examples."[23]

When assessing the concrete cases the Court attached importance to the fact that the administrative discharges of the applicants had "a profound effect on their careers and prospects"[24] one of the reasons being that military qualifications and experience are not easily transferable to civilian life. With regard to the alleged concrete risk to the operation of the armed forces the Court was not convinced by the general arguments put forward by the Government concerning security, morale and effectiveness and concluded that "convincing and

---

[21] About a statutory obligation for Freemasons to declare their membership when applying for regional authority posts, cf. *Grande Oriente d'Italia di Palazzo Giustiniano*, Judgment of 31 May 2007 (violation) and *Alexandridis v. Greece*, Judgment of 21 February 2008 about an applicant who was forced to disclose that he was not a member of the Orthodox Church when being sworn in as a lawyer (violation).

[22] *Lustig-Prean and Beckett v. the United Kingdom* and *Smith and Grady v. the United Kingdom*, Judgments of 27 September 1999.

[23] *Ibid.*, paras. 82 and 89.

[24] *Ibid.*, paras. 85 and 92.

weighty reasons have not been offered [....] to justify the policy against homosexuals in the armed forces or, therefore, the consequent discharge of the applicants from those forces."[25]

It should be noted that the Court reached its conclusions on the basis of Article 8 alone, and that it saw no need to decide on the applicants' invocation of Article 14 in conjunction with Article 8.[26] The Court considered that the two allegations amounted in effect to the same, and in this way the cases illustrate the wide scope of Article 8. Thus, some grounds of differential treatment can be captured by the main provision without it being necessary to include the accessory non-discrimination clause in the assessment.

When the Court was to decide on the issue of pecuniary damage, it recalled the effect on the careers of the applicants of the discharge and "referred to the applicants' "relatively successful service careers in their particular field", to their length of service, to their rank on discharge and to their "very positive" service records prior to and after discharge."[27] Against this background, the Court awarded compensation on a discretionary basis for past and future loss of earnings and for loss of the benefit of a non-contributory service pension scheme. A contention for reinstatement, put forward by one of the applicants, was, however, not upheld.

Comparable factual circumstances gave rise to the cases *Perkins and R. v. the United Kingdom* and *Beck, Copp and Bazely v. the United Kingdom*. In 2002, the Court adjudicated these cases in a similar manner.[28] The four British cases concerning discharge of homosexuals from the armed forces provide excellent illustration of the fact that the perception of homosexuality has changed radically over the years, cf. the horizontal structure of the hermeneutic circle. The tolerant approach, which is reflected in the four cases mentioned, does indeed deviate from previous case law from the Commission in which it was accepted that homosexuality was considered a particular risk to order within the armed forces. Thus, in a case from 1983 the Commission declared a similar case inadmissible as manifestly ill-founded by leaning on the following statement from the Ministry of Defence on the conditions within the Armed forces:

> Such conditions, and the need for absolute trust and confidence both within and between all ranks require that the potentially disruptive influence of homosexual

---

[25] *Ibid.*, paras. 98 and 105.

[26] Thus, in these cases the Court followed a different approach than in *Sidabras and Džiautas v. Lithuania*, cf. above in 3. However, it is undisputed that sexual orientation – unlike "working for the KGB" – is generally recognised as a forbidden discrimination ground.

[27] *Lustig-Prean and Beckett v. the United Kingdom* and *Smith and Grady v. the United Kingdom*, paras. 24 and 20.

[28] *Perkins and R. v. the United Kingdom* and *Beck, Copp and Bazeley v. the United Kingdom*, Judgments of 22 October 2002.

> practices should be excluded. It is also necessary to ensure that those in authority over younger or junior men do not use their positions to coerce or persuade those in their charge to perform acts in which they would not otherwise engage. A member of the armed forces engaging in homosexual activity would also be liable to blackmail and as such present a security risk.[29]

The passage suggests that homosexual people – unlike heterosexuals – are sex-starved people unable to control themselves, and that they are potential sex criminals. The passage reflects an outdated, condemnatory and discriminatory attitude towards homosexuals. Pre-understanding has indeed changed in the time period between the Commission's decisions and the Court's decision in the four contemporary cases referred to above, and this alteration is reflected in the interpretation of the notion of respect for private life.

4.3 *Freedom of Speech, Association, Religion and the Right to Work*

That the ECHR is relevant to employment issues is also reflected in other cases about claims concerning (continued) employment. Thus in the case *Vogt v. Germany* Article 10 was invoked by a school teacher who was dismissed from her teaching job in a State secondary school on the sole ground that she was a member of the Communist Party. The Court took for its basis that although the ECHR – unlike the UDHR and the CCPR[30] – does not include a right to equal access to public service, civil servants do not fall outside the scope of the Convention. As the applicant was dismissed because of her political activities, the Court – sitting as a Grand Chamber – considered there to be an interference with the exercise of the right to freedom of expression.

The interference was prescribed by German legislation, and the Court did also find that the interference had a legitimate aim. An obligation was imposed on German civil servants to bear witness to and uphold the free democratic constitutional system, and the notion of civil service was considered to have a special importance in Germany. Thus, the Court referred to "that country's experience under the Weimar Republic, which, when the Federal Republic was founded after the nightmare of Nazism, led to its constitution being based on the principle of a "democracy capable of defending itself [....]".[31]

In the assessment of whether the interference was also necessary in a democratic society the Court initially noted the very absolute character of the loyalty requirement and pointed out that a similar strict duty had not been

[29] *B v. the United Kingdom*, Admissibility decision of 12 October 1983, The Facts.

[30] Article 21 (2) of the UDHR speaks of "equal access to public service" and Article 25 of the CCPR guarantees that "every citizen shall have the right and the opportunity [....] to have access, on general terms of equality, to public service in his country."

[31] *Vogt v. Germany*, Judgment of 26 September 1995, para. 51.

imposed by any other Member State in the COE. As to the concrete dismissal of the applicant the Court emphasised the severe nature of the measure because of the loss of livelihood and possible difficulties in finding another job as a teacher. Thus, the Court noted that in Germany teaching posts outside the civil service were scarce. The Court went on to note that the security risk was not intrinsic as the applicant was a teacher of German and French,[32] and that her work had been considered wholly satisfactory. Moreover, the Court emphasised that there was no evidence that the applicant even outside her work made anti-constitutional statements or personally adopted an anti-constitutional stance. The Court finally remembered that the Communist Party had not been banned by the Federal Constitutional Court, and that the applicant's activities were entirely lawful.[33]Against this background the Court concluded – by the votes ten to nine – that the dismissal was disproportionate, and that there had accordingly been a violation of Article 10.[34]

The decision differs from the one the Court had reached a decade earlier in the cases *Kosiek v. Germany* and *Glasenapp v. Germany*[35] in which the applicants held *probationary* appointments as university lecturer and school teacher respectively. Both applicants were denied the status of permanent civil servants and dismissed from their temporary positions, Kosiek because of his ultra right-wing activities, Glasenapp because of her ultra left-wing activities. Both claimed before the Court that there had been an interference with their rights under Article 10. The Court, however, did not recognise that the cases concerned *dismissals* from civil service. The Court held that the claims concerned *access* to civil service, a matter that was deliberately omitted from the Convention. The German authorities had not found that either of the two applicants fulfilled the conditions required by German legislation namely that of upholding the free democratic system. The Court saw no reason to review the correctness of their findings and concluded that there had been no interference with the exercise of the rights protected under Article 10.[36]

---

[32] In this sense the Vogt case differs from *Ahmed and Others v. the United Kingdom*, Judgment of 2 September 1998 concerning legislative measures designed to limit the involvement of certain categories of local government officials in political activities. The issue was not whether membership of a political party was compatible with employment by local authorities, but rather whether certain types of pronounced political activity were compatible with working closely to the political process. In this case the Court found no violation of either Articles 10 or 11.

[33] *Vogt v. Germany*, para. 60.

[34] A friendly settlement was later reached between the German Government and the applicant concerning her claims for pecuniary damage, cf. *Vogt. v. Germany*, Judgment of 2 September 1996.

[35] *Kosiek v. Germany* and *Glasenapp v. Germany*.

[36] *Ibid.*, paras. 38–39 and 52–53.

The Court considered that the *Vogt* case was to be distinguished from the cases of *Glasenapp* and *Kosiek* because the applicant had been a permanent civil servant for a number of years. However, Glasenapp and Kosiek did also have their appointments annulled, and one could argue that the difference between the cases is modest. Vogt had a permanent position whereas Glasenapp and Kosiek held temporary positions. However, they did indeed lose their jobs because of their political sympathies, and one might question whether the differences justify that Vogt had her dismissal examined under Article 10 (2) whereas Kosiek and Glasenapp did not.[37]

In the *Vogt* case the Court came to the conclusion that also Article 11 had been violated since the applicant was dismissed from her teaching job because of her membership of the Communist Party. When reaching this conclusion, the Court referred to its considerations under Article 10 of the Convention. The Court could, moreover, have analysed the case also in light of the special provision in Article 11 (2) according to which the Article "shall not prevent the imposition of lawful restrictions on the exercise of these rights by members of the armed forces, of the police or of the administration of the State." The Court, however, sidestepped the issue by agreeing with the Commission that the notion "administration of the State" should be interpreted narrowly. The Court added that "even if teachers are to be regarded as being part of the "administration of the State [....] Mrs. Vogt's dismissal was [....] disproportionate to the legitimate aim pursued.[38] Thus, the judgment gives the impression that the Court is of the opinion that interferences in public sector employees' rights under Article 11 are subject to the ordinary requirements of the first sentence of Article 11 (2).

Case law from the Court also provides examples of dismissal on account of religious belief. Thus, in *Ivanova v. Bulgaria* the applicant claimed that the applicant's right to freedom of religion had been violated because her employment as a non-academic school staff member had been terminated on account of her religious beliefs (she was a member of a Christian Evangelical Group, which pursued clandestine activities because the authorities refused to register them). The official reason for her dismissal was that she did not meet the requirements for the job. The Court, however, reached the conclusion that the real reason for her dismissal was her religious beliefs. Accordingly the Court found a violation of Article 9 of the Convention.[39]

---

[37] Judge Cremona expressed similar considerations in his concurring opinion. So did Judge Spielmann in his diverging opinion, cf. paras. 16–17 in which he also referred to the opinion of the Commission. Cf. also *Leander v. Sweden,* Judgment of 26 March 1987, in which the Court argued in a similar way.

[38] *Vogt. v. Germany*, paras. 67–68.

[39] *Ivanova* v. Bulgaria, Judgment of 12 April 2007.

5 The Rights of the Self-Employed

The ECHR does not only provide protection to wage earners in the private and public sector. Also the self-employed may enjoy a certain protection e.g. as possessors of property from where they gain their livelihood. Thus, interferences with property rights may affect all kinds of self-employed persons in the way they earn their living, from the wealthy businessman to the poor smallholder, and case law from the ECtHR is illustrative of the fact that the protection of Article 1 of Protocol 1 applies to all categories. Moreover, the self-employed person who does not own the assets which form the basis for his income may enjoy some protection under Article 1 of Protocol No. 1 due to the very extensive interpretation of the notion of 'possession' as also encompassing some rights of disposal, goodwill, etc.[40] Likewise, Article 8 may provide some protection to the self-employed person who uses his home also as his workplace.

By way of example Turkey has been held responsible on a number of occasions for the destruction by security forces of villagers' tobacco crop, barns, mills, sheds with winter feed for animals or other sources of income thus depriving the applicants of their livelihood.[41] Something similar happened during the war in Croatia although the Court has only been able to deal with certain aspects of these cases due to the fact that the ECHR did not enter into force for Croatia until 1997, cf. Chapter 6, Section 7.2 on the Right to Housing.

Also *Bruncrona v. Finland*[42] illustrates how a right to make a living may be protected under Article 1 of Protocol No. 1. In this case the applicants claimed ownership in the form of a right to permanent usufruct in respect of islands and waters surrounding their property in a village. The applicants and their ancestors had made undisturbed use of the islands and the surrounding water for 300 years in return for an annual levy, later replaced by payment of a wealth tax to the State. In 1984 fishing rights were, however, granted by the State to a third party without the consent of the applicants, who were, moreover, in 1998 requested to leave the property.

The Court did not find that the applicants had been "deprived of their possessions" within the meaning of the second sentence of Article 1 of Protocol No. 1.

---

[40] Cf. e.g. *Tre Traktörer Aktiebolag v. Sweden*, Judgment of 7 July 1989 (revocation of licence to sell alcoholic beverage), *Fredin v. Sweden*, Judgment of 18 February 1991 (revocation of permit to exploit gravel), *Matos e Silva v. Portugal*, Judgment of 16 September 1996 (interference with concession rights to salt extraction) and *Posti and Rahko v. Finland*, Judgment of 24 September 2002 (restriction of lease-based right to engage in certain types of fishing in State-owned waters).

[41] Cf. e.g. *Mentes and Others v. Turkey*, Judgment of 28 November 1997, *Selçuk and Asker v. Turkey*, *Bilgin v. Turkey*, Judgment of 16 November 2000 and *Dulas v. Turkey*, Judgment of 30 January 2001.

[42] *Bruncrona v. Finland*, Judgment of 16 November 2004.

Notwithstanding, the Court found that the applicants had been granted a proprietary interest, which was classified as a lease, and that the interference should therefore be analysed in the light of the general rule in the first sentence of Article 1 of Protocol No. 1. Whereas the Court recognised the Government's legitimate interest in upholding the principles of real-property law and in clarifying that the State had ownership of the land in question, it did not find that there had been a fair balance as regards the manner in which the applicant's lease had been terminated. A letter received by the applicants requesting them to vacate the property was not considered an acceptable means of terminating a right which the applicants had enjoyed for over 300 years. The Court noted that the applicants could have reasonably expected at the very least to have been informed of the date of the expiry of the lease in the notice of termination. In these circumstances, the procedure[43] in which the applicants' proprietary interest had been terminated was incompatible with their right to the peaceful enjoyment of their possessions.

In Chapter 6 on The Right to Housing some cases are referred to in which the Court goes very far in its protection of tenants in their petitions against landlords, cf. e.g. *Mellacher v. Austria* and *James v. the United Kingdom*.[44] When choosing to protect the tenants the Court, however, at the same time accepts an interference with the landlords' possibilities of making a living by letting their property, and one might say that the right to housing is sometimes obtained at the expense of someone else's undisturbed right to have a business of his own. As long as such interferences affect strong and wealthy rent gougers' unscrupulous exploitation of supposedly weaker and less affluent tenants, one might be prepared to consider this a manifestation of the will of the Welfare State to carry into effect a just housing policy, and the Court has repeatedly held that the Contracting Parties are allowed an even very wide margin of appreciation in such issues.

This was also the point of departure in the case *Hutten-Czapska v. Poland*[45] about one of around 100,000 landlords in Poland who were affected by a restrictive system of rent control, which originated in laws adopted under the former communist regime. The rent control system imposed a number of restrictions on landlords' rights by setting a ceiling on rent which was so low that the landlords could not even recoup their maintenance costs, let alone make a profit. Moreover, the Polish authorities were authorised by decree to assign flats in privately-owned buildings to particular tenants.

---

[43] Cf. Chapter 10, Section 3 about the phenomenon *proceduralisation*.

[44] Cf. *James and Others v. the United Kingdom*, Judgment of 21 February 1986 and *Mellacher and Others v. Austria*, Judgment of 19 December 1989.

[45] *Hutten-Czapska v. Poland*, Judgment of 19 June 2006

On several occasions the Polish Constitutional Court had found the legislation unconstitutional, but the subsequent amendments made were not to the satisfaction of the applicant. The applicant complained under Article 1 of Protocol No. 1 that the situation amounted to a continuing violation of her right to the enjoyment of her possessions not only because she was unable to derive any income from her property but also because she could not regain possession and use of her property.

The Court –sitting as a Grand Chamber – agreed with the assessment of the applicant's situation set out in the Court's Chamber judgment.[46] Like the Chamber the Court found that "the authorities imposed a disproportionate and excessive burden on her, which cannot be justified by any legitimate interest of the community [....]."[47] The Court added:

> The Grand Chamber agrees with this assessment of the impugned situation. It would, however, add that, as established above, the violation of the right of property in the present case is not exclusively linked to the question of the levels of rent chargeable but, rather, consists in the combined effect of defective provisions on the determination of rent and various restrictions on landlords' rights in respect of termination of leases, the statutory financial burdens imposed on them and the absence of any legal ways and means making it possible for them either to offset or mitigate the losses incurred in connection with maintenance of property or to have the necessary repairs subsidised by the State in justified cases [....].[48]

Thus, unlike *Mellacher v. Austria* and *James and Others v. the United Kingdom*, the Court chose to give priority to the interests of landlords over the general housing policy and thereby indirectly also over the interest of tenants. The fundamental question in this case was who was to bear the burden of the "the malfunctioning of Polish housing legislation",[49] and the Court's answer will necessarily have a bearing on the Polish authorities' choices with regard to housing policy and with regard to resource allocation. In this context it should be noted that the case was chosen by the Grand Chamber Court as a "pilot case" for determining the general issue of the compatibility of the Polish legislation with the ECHR. As the case revealed the existence of an underlying systemic problem, it is not surprising that the Court chose to emphasise that consideration for protection of tenants could be taken care of in other ways. cf. the quotation above. However, with reference to Article 46 and the previous case *Broniowki v. Poland*[50] the Court found it necessary to state as follows:

---

[46] *Hutten-Czapska v. Poland*, Judgment of 22 February 2005.

[47] *Hutten-Czapska v. Poland*, Judgment of 19 June 2006, para. 223 with reference to para. 188 of the Chamber Judgment.

[48] *Ibid.*, para. 224.

[49] *Ibid.*, para. 237.

[50] *Broniowski v. Poland*, Judgment of 22 June 2004.

> As regards the general measures to be applied by the Polish State in order to put an end to the systemic violation of the right of property identified in the present case, and having regard to its social and economic dimension, including the State's duties in relation to the social rights of other persons [....], the Court considers that the respondent State must above all, through appropriate legal and/or other measures, secure in its domestic legal order a mechanism maintaining a fair balance between the interests of landlords, including their entitlement to derive profit from their property, and the general interest of the community – including the availability of sufficient accommodation for the less well-off – in accordance with the principles of the protection of property rights under the Convention.
>
> It is not for the Court to specify what would be the most appropriate way of setting up such remedial procedures or how landlords' interest in deriving profit should be balanced against the other interests at stake; thus, under Article 46 the State remains free to choose the means by which it will discharge its obligations arising from the execution of the Court's judgments [....].[51]

In this way the Court emphasises its respect for the domestic legislature with regard to policy choices while at the same time leaving no doubt that the "reasonableness-test" was not passed.[52]

6 *Claims for Salary*

In a discussion of work-related rights under the ECHR and its Protocols it would seem fair also to touch upon the issue of remuneration of work performed and of claims for pensions deriving from employment contracts. However, there is little to say. With regard to pension claims aspects of the issue is already covered by the presentation in Chapter 8 on The Right to Social Cash Benefits, and there is hardly anything to be gained from a separate discussion of employment-related pension rights.

Unlike the ESC/RESC, the ECHR does not include the right to a fair remuneration,[53] and despite the dynamic interpretation of what "falls within the ambit" of the various provisions of the ECHR and its Protocols, it is not likely that e.g. differential treatment of men and women with regard to remuneration for equal work could be examined under Article 14 unless of course remuneration can be considered an aspect of private life. After the entering into force of Protocol No. 12 the Court could deal with this issue, but it remains to be seen, how the Court's case law will develop in that respect.

---

51 *Hutten-Czapska v. Poland*, Judgment of 19 June 2006, para. 239.

52 The parties later reached a friendly settelemt, cf. Judgment of 28 April 2008. Cf. also *Megadat. Com SRL v. Moldova*, Judgment of 8 April 2008 concerning withdrawal of an operating license.

53 Cf. Article 4 of the ESC/RESC.

Remuneration, however, may be a decisive factor in the assessment under Article 4 of the ECHR.[54] Apart from that it is hard to think of protection of minimum demands with regard to remuneration under the ECHR or its Protocols. What can be said at the present stage is that such demands, whether or not deriving from a contractual relation, may be protected under Protocol No. 1 as "possessions", if the demand in question is "sufficiently established to be enforceable".[55] In *Smokovitis and Others v. Greece* the applicants – who were working on a temporary basis – had demanded a supplement to their salary in the form of a research allowance. This research allowance had been established by a first instance civil court and appealed against when Parliament enacted a law according to which the allowance in question only applied to permanent staff. The ECtHR noted that domestic courts had several times found that the research allowance applied to all staff, and that they had therefore created a "legitimate expectation" that they would have found in favour of the applicants.[56]As there was nothing to justify legislation with retrospective effect, the Court found a violation of Article 1 of Protocol No.1.[57] This theory of "legitimate expectations" has been confirmed in later cases, cf. e.g. *Mykhaylenky and Others v. Ukraine* in which judgment was awarded in favour of the applicants with regard to recovery of salary arrears and other payments from their former employer, a State-owned company which had performed construction work at Chernobyl.[58]

7 *Occupational Issues and the Application of Article 6*

According to the Court's established case law Article 6 extends to disputes over civil rights and obligations "which can be said, at least on arguable grounds, to be recognised under domestic law [....]".[59] The issue as to when a dispute within the sense of Article 6 exists is not to be pursued further in this context. Rather, as is the case with regard to social cash benefits, cf. Chapter 8, Section 4, the delimitation of the expression "civil rights" in Article 6 has had an impact on the procedural protection of occupational rights understood in a broad sense, and the purpose of this section is to analyse how the interpretation of this provision has developed.

54 As indicated above in Section 2, I have, however, chosen not to deal with Article 4.

55 Cf. *Stran Greek Refinereries and Stratis Andreadis v. Greece*, Judgment of 9 December 1994, para. 59 about a sum awarded by arbitration.

56 *Smokovitis and Others v. Greece*, Judgment of 11 April 2002, para. 32.

57 Cf. similarly about pension claims, *Vasilopoulou v. Greece*, Judgment of 21 March 2002.

58 Cf. *Mykhaylensky and Others v. Ukraine*, Judgment of 30 November 2004.

59 Cf. e.g. *O v. the United Kingdom*, Judgment of 8 July 1987, para. 54.

It is not contested that Article 6 may apply to disputes between a private employer and his employees for example with regard to the termination of employment.[60] Moreover, in disputes between private parties and public authorities the Court has held from the outset that it is not conclusive whether the public authority in question has acted as a private person or in its sovereign capacity. In ascertaining whether a case concerns the determination of a civil right, only the character of the right at issue is relevant.[61] Nor does the fact that the activity in question may be subject to supervision effected by the authorities deprive it of its private law character.[62] All that is relevant under Article 6 of the Convention is the fact that the object of the cases in question concerns the determination of rights of a private nature, and the Court's case law provides numerous examples of applicability with regard to such rights. Thus, a large number of judgments have been pronounced concerning difficulties with regard to the obtainment or revocation of permissions and licences for the exercise of certain professions.[63]

Of greater interest in this context is whether or to which extent rights may be recognised as civil rights in the sense of Article 6 even though they are classified in domestic law as public rights. According to the Court's established case law this must be determined by reference to the *substantive content and effects* of the right rather than its legal classification, and in the exercise of its supervisory functions the Court must take account of the *object and purpose* of the Convention and of the national legal systems of the other Contracting States.[64] This issue has proved to be particularly complicated as regards disputes between public sector employees and their conditions of employment, and the development of law has hardly found its final stage.

The original position of the Court was that disputes relating to conditions of employment in the public sector fell outside the scope of Article 6. Thus, the Court has held that "disputes relating to the recruitment, employment and retirement [....] are as a general rule outside the scope of Article 6 [....]."[65] However, met with claims for old age pension and disability pension of respectively a former judge and a carabiniere the Court recalled the *Feldbrügge* judgment and held as follows:

---

60 Cf. e.g. *Buchholz v. Germany*, Judgment of 6 May 1981 and *Obermeier v. Austria*, Judgment of 28 June 1990.

61 *König v. Germany*, Judgment of 28 June 1978, para. 90.

62 *Ibid.*, para. 92.

63 For more recent case law cf. Pieter van Dijk and Mark Viering (rev.) in Pieter van Dijk et. al. (eds.) *Theory and Practice of the European Concention on Human Rights*, 4th Edition, 2006, pp. 524–528.

64 Cf. originally in *König v. Germany*, para. 89.

65 Cf. *Giancarlo and Francesco Lombardo v. Italy*, Judgments of 26 November 1992, paras. 16 and 17.

> Notwithstanding the public law aspects pointed out by the Government, what is concerned here is essentially an obligation on the State to pay a pension [....] in accordance with the legislation in force. In performing this obligation the State is not using discretionary powers and may be compared, in this respect, with an employer who is a party to a contract of employment governed by private law.[66]

The Court, consequently, found that the pension rights of the applicants were to be regarded as civil rights within the meaning of Article 6 (1) thus recognising the differences between the Member States of the COE with regard to employment in the public sector. In some Member States teachers are employed as public sector employees whereas in others they belong to the group of private sector employees.[67] In this respect the development of law is quite similar to the one described in Chapter 8 concerning social cash benefits.

With regard to public sector employees' salary disputes and other financial disputes related to employment the Court has similarly deviated from its original position that public sector employment issues as a general rule fall outside the scope of Article 6. Thus, the Court has attempted to apply the criterion "pecuniary interest" but has faced considerable difficulties indeed in making a distinction between cases in which the pecuniary interest had a direct character and those in which the pecuniary interest was of an indirect character.

In *Neigel v. France* the applicant had brought proceedings to secure not only reinstatement in a municipal position as a short-hand typist but also payment of her salary. The Court held that the applicant's primary claim to be reinstated related to "the recruitment, careers and termination of service of civil servants."[68] Moreover, the Court chose to couple the issue of reinstatement with that of salary thereby enabling itself to distinguish the applicant's pecuniary interest from the interests of the applicants in the above-mentioned pension cases. The Court held as follows:

> As to her claim for payment of the salary she would have received if she had been reinstated, the Court notes that an award of such compensation [....] is directly dependent on a prior finding that the refusal to reinstate was unlawful [....].[69]

This judgment was pronounced by seven votes to one. The dissenting judge designated the reasoning as "sweeping, thin" and did in fact anticipate the later course of events, cf. below on the *Pellegrin* judgment, by presenting the view that a distinction should be made between different categories of public servants. Hence, she argued that only posts in the public service involving a certain degree of responsibility ought to be excluded from the protection of Article 6.[70]

---

[66] *Ibid.*

[67] Cf. also *Massa v. Italy*, Judgment of 24 August 1993.

[68] *Neigel v. France*, Judgment of 17 March 1993, paras. 43 and 44.

[69] *Ibid.*, para. 44.

[70] *Ibid.*, Dissenting opinion of Judge Palm.

Case law, however, developed gradually. In a number of judgments from 1997, the Court recognised that Article 6 applies if a public sector employee is involved in a dispute concerning "a purely economic right"[71] or an "essentially economic" one provided that the dispute does not call into question the authorities' discretionary powers.[72] Thus, if a dispute – as in the case *De Santa v. Italy* – concerns the level of salary laid down in the collective agreements, Article 6 applied. However, if – as in the case *Spurio v. Italy* – the salary claim was coupled with a dispute concerning promotion, the Court held that the issue of promotion related to the applicant's career, and that the claim for payment of the difference in salary was "directly dependent on a prior finding that the employer had acted unlawfully [....]."[73] A dissenting judge advanced arguments similar to those put forward by the dissenting judge in the *Neigel* case, namely that a distinction ought to be made between "the lowest office cleaner with only menial duties" and "the highest official who has, for instance, the power to exercise public authority." The dissenting judge, moreover, emphasised the differences between the Contracting States with regard to the choice between public v. private employment of employees performing public services. He concluded that the Court's interpretation of Article 6 would lead to dissimilar protection despite similarity of duties and called for an autonomous reinterpretation of the provision.[74]

In *Huber v. France* concerning a school teacher who was sent on compulsory sick leave Article 6 was similarly declared inapplicable. However, this time four out of nine judges expressed their dissenting opinions along the same line as the two dissenting judges in *Neigel v. France* and *Spurio v. Italy*. One dissenting judge added that the distinction between disputes concerning pecuniary interests and non-pecuniary interests "comes very close to being completely arbitrary" and recalled the background to the provision. He stated as follows:

> The Court's narrow interpretation of Article 6, which means that disputes on the "recruitment", "careers" or "termination of service" of civil servants are outside Article 6, is motivated only by the fact that historically governments have sought to avoid interference by courts of law in the sensitive relationship between authorities and their civil servants. The narrow interpretation therefore becomes *absolutely meaningless* in situations where the national law as in this case permits such interference by giving the civil servant access to the national court (author's emphasis).[75]

[71] Cf. *De Santa v. Italy, Lapalorcia v. Italy and Abenavoli v. Italy*, Judgments of 2 September 1997, paras. 18, 21 and 16, respectively.

[72] Cf. *Nicodemo v. Italy*, Judgment of 2 September 1997, para. 18.

[73] *Spurio v. Italy*, Judgment of 2 September 1997, para. 19.

[74] *Ibid.*, Dissenting Opinion of Judge Pekkanen, paras. 3–4.

[75] *Huber v. France*, Judgment of 19 February 1998, Dissenting opinion of Judge Foighel, para. 8.

The criterion relating to the economic nature of a dispute was finally abandoned in *Pellegrin v. France* about the termination of a public sector employment contract according to which the applicant was responsible for drawing up the budget of State investment in Equatorial Guinea. In this case the Court – sitting as a Grand Chamber – referred to the above-mentioned cases among others and admitted that the case law "contains a margin of uncertainty for Contracting States as to the scope of their obligations under Article 6 § 1 in disputes raised by employees in the public sector over their conditions of service."[76] The Court acknowledged that this criterion "leaves scope for a degree of arbitrariness, since a decision concerning the "recruitment", "career" or "termination of service" of a civil servant nearly always has pecuniary consequences."[77] Moreover, the Court went along with the dissenting judges in the previous mentioned cases and recognised the need to establish "an autonomous interpretation of the term "civil service" which would make it possible to afford equal treatment to public servants performing equivalent or similar duties in the States Parties to the Convention, irrespective of the domestic system of employment and, in particular whatever the nature of the legal relation between the official and the administrative authority [....]."[78]

The Court accordingly decided to apply a *functional criterion* according to which:

> the only disputes excluded from the scope of Article 6 § 1 of the Convention are those which are raised by public servants whose duties typify the specific activities of the public service in so far as the latter is acting as the depositary of public authority responsible for protecting the *general interests* of the State or other public authorities [author's emphasis].[79]

As manifest examples excluded from the scope of Article 6 the Court mentioned activities provided by the armed forces and the police. Moreover, the Court clarified that all disputes concerning pensions come within the ambit of Article 6 "because on retirement employees break the special bond between themselves and the authorities [....]."[80] By applying this criterion to the actual case the Court found Article 6 not applicable as the tasks assigned to the applicant gave him considerable responsibilities in the field of the State's public finances.

The functional criterion contributed to the protection of the majority of public employees whose functions do not relate to the *general interests* of the

76 *Pellegrin v. France*, Judgment of 8 December 1999, para. 60.

77 *Ibid.*

78 *Ibid.*, para. 63.

79 *Ibid.*, para. 66.

80 *Ibid.*, para. 67.

State such as e.g. caretakers for State schools, administrative assistants in the social services, academic university staff, administrative assistants in (lowest grade) in the Civil Service and secondary school teachers.[81] The criterion "the exercise of powers conferred by public law" narrowed the field of uncertainty, and the exceptions to the safeguards afforded by Article 6 (1) have been interpreted restrictively.[82] Still, the functional criterion is not precise either, and it has been suggested that Article 6 should have a wider area of applicability.

Not until *Vilho Eskelinen and Others v. Finland*, however, did the Court widen its interpretation of Article 6 in a dispute concerning wage supplements of five police officers and one office assistant. The Court argued as follows:

> The present case, however, highlights that the application of the functional criterion may itself lead to anomalous results. [....] As noted above, *Pellegrin* expressly mentioned the police as a manifest example of activities belonging to the exercise of public authority, thus excluding a whole category of persons from the scope of Article 6. On a strict application of the *Pellegrin* approach it would appear that the office assistant applicant in the present case would enjoy the guarantees of Article 6 § 1, whereas there is no doubt that the police officer applicants would not. This would be so irrespective of the fact that the dispute was identical for all the applicants.[83]

The Court went on by stating that it is:

> particularly striking that, taken literally, the "functional approach" requires that Article 6 be excluded from application to disputes where the position of the applicant as a State official does not differ from the position of any other litigant, or, in other words, where the dispute between the employee and the employer is not especially marked by a "special bond of trust and loyalty."[84]

Therefore, the Court found is necessary to further develop the functional criterion and emphasised that many countries allow civil servants to bring claims

---

[81] Cf. e.g. *Procaccini v. Italy*, Judgment of 30 March 2000, *Lambourdière v. France*, Judgment of 2 August 2000, *Castanheira Barros v. Portugal*, Judgment of 26 October 2000, *Büker v. Turkey*, Judgment of 24 October 2000, *Devlin v. the United Kingdom*, Judgment of 30 October 2001 and *Volkmer v. Germany*, Admissibility decision of 22 November 2001.

[82] Cf. e.g. *Frydlender v. France*, Judgment of 27 June 2000, para. 40. The case concerned an official employed under an individual contract by the Economic Development Department of the Ministry for Economic Affairs who was posted to the economic development office in New York as head of a section for the promotion of French alcoholic beverage. The French Government submitted that the applicant was a member of the diplomatic corps, and that he had to be excluded from the scope of Article 6 duc to the fact that he had responsibility for safeguarding the general interest of the State or other public bodies. The Court, however, found Article 6 applicable.

[83] *Vilho Eskelinen and Others v. Finland*, Judgment of 19 April 2007, para.51

[84] *Ibid.*, para. 53.

before courts also concerning recruitment and dismissal, and that EU law has a broad perception of judicial control. The Court also relied on the ECHR, Articles 1 and 14 according to which "everyone within [the] jurisdiction" of the Contracting States must enjoy the rights and freedoms in Section 1 "without discrimination on any ground."

The Court noted that the applicants, according to the national legislation, had the right to have their claims for allowances examined by a tribunal, and that it must primarily be for the Contracting States to identify those areas of public service where the individual interest must give way and recapitulated as follows:

> Firstly, the State in its national law must have expressly excluded access to a court for the post or category of staff in question. Secondly, the exclusion must be justified on objective grounds in the State's interest. The mere fact that the applicant is in a sector or department which participates in the exercise of power conferred by public law is not in itself decisive. In order for the exclusion to be justified, it is not enough for the State to establish that the civil servant in question participates in the exercise of public power or that there exists, to use the words of the Court in the *Pellegrin* judgment, a "special bond of trust and loyalty" between the civil servant and the State, as employer. It is also for the State to show that the subject matter of the dispute in issue is related to the exercise of State power or that it has called into question the special bond. Thus, there can in principle be no justification for the exclusion from the guarantees of Article 6 of ordinary labour disputes, such as those relating to salaries, allowances or similar entitlements, on the basis of the special nature of relationship between the particular civil servant and the State in question. There will, in effect, be a presumption that Article 6 applies. It will be for the respondent Government to demonstrate, first, that a civil-servant applicant does not have a right of access to a court under national law and, second, that the exclusion of the rights under Article 6 for the civil servant is justified.[85]

This criterion is indeed preferable to the functional one which led to strange results, and is had the advantage of being relatively precise. It leaves to the States themselves to limit judicial control to the extent it is necessary but demands that they are in fact able to demonstrate that the exclusion of the right is justified. In that way the Court reserves the right to have the final say and yet leaves more latitude to the Contracting States. One must assume that the potential for more reinterpretations of Article 6 with regard to civil servants is limited if existing at all. Yet the cases referred to illustrate how new facts have called for an evolutionary interpretation of the provision. Thus the reading of Article 6(1) has gone through a hermeneutic development during which the historic explanation for exempting public sector employees in

[85] *Ibid.*, para. 62.

a present-day context becomes "absolutely meaningless"[86] due to the fact that contemporary national law gives civil servants access to national courts.

8 *'Negative' Freedom of Association and the Right to Work*

Article 11 has in particular been invoked by workers whose jobs have been endangered because of their refusal to join a certain trade union, and case law on these so-called closed shop agreements has undergone a gradual development over the past 25 years. This development has been analysed on numerous occasions from a traditional freedom of association perspective, and I can hardly contribute to the voluminous literature on this point.[87] My aim in this context is another, namely to bring to light the social aspects of the 'negative' right to freely associate, and to point out how the ECtHR and the ECSR have gradually harmonised their interpretation of Article 11 of the ECHR and Article 5 under the ESC/RESC. Article 11of the ECHR runs as follows:

> Everyone has the right to freedom of peaceful assembly and to freedom of association with others, including the right to form and to join trade unions for the protection of his interests.
>
> No restrictions shall be placed on the exercise of these rights other than such as are prescribed by law and are necessary in a democratic society in the interests of national security or public safety, for the prevention of disorder or crime, for the protection of health or morals or for the protection of the rights and freedoms of others. This article shall not prevent the imposition of lawful restrictions on the exercise of these rights by members of the armed forces, of the police or of the administration of the State.

For the sake of comparison I quote also Article 5 of the ESC/RESC:

> With a view to ensuring or promoting the freedom of workers and employers to form local, national or international organisations for the protection of their economic and social interests and to join those organisations, the Contracting Parties undertake that national law shall not be such as to impair, nor shall it be so applied as to impair, this freedom. The extent to which the guarantees provided for in this article shall apply to the police shall be determined by national laws or regulations. The principle governing the application to the members of the armed forces of these guarantees and the extent to which they shall apply to persons in this category shall equally be determined by national laws or regulations.

86 *Huber v. France*, Dissenting opinion of Judge Foighel, para. 8.

87 Cf. e.g. Aalt Willem Heringa and Fried van Hoof (rev.) in P. van Dijk et al. (eds.) *Theory and Practice of the European Convention on Human Rights*, Intersentia 4th Edition, 2006, p. 831 ff., J.G. Merrils and A.H. Robertson, *Human Rights in Europe*, 4th Edition, 2001, Juris Publishing, Manchester University Press, p. 181 ff., Clare Ovey & Robin C.A. White, European Convention on Human Rigts, 4th Edition, 2006, Oxford University Press, p. 341 ff.

The following provision on the right to work in Article 1 (2) of the Appendix to the ESC/RESC is also of relevance to the issue of 'negative' freedom of association:

> This provision shall not be interpreted as prohibiting or authorising any union security clause or practise.

Already under the first Supervisory Cycle did the Committee of Independent Experts (now known as the ECSR) present its interpretation of Article 5 of the ESC. The Committee noted as follows:

> The Committee also noted that, in accordance with the appendix to the Charter, Article 5 does not rule on the admissibility of union security clauses or practises. The Committee considered, however, that any form of compulsory unionism imposed by law must be considered incompatible with the obligation arising under this Article of the Charter.[88]

The statement must be understood as if Article 5 is in fact 'neutral' with respect to closed shop agreements as the provision only concerns statutory demands concerning membership of a certain organisation, cf. the expression "imposed by law". However, after the judgment of the ECtHR in the case *Young, James and Webster v. the United Kingdom*[89] the Committee found it necessary to reassess the issue. The case concerned a closed shop agreement which was concluded between British Rail and three trade unions, providing that henceforth membership of one of those unions was a condition of employment. The three applicants, who had been employed prior to the agreement, failed to satisfy this condition. Therefore they were dismissed, and before the Court they claimed that the detriment suffered constituted a violation of Article 11 among others.

In this case, the Court was confronted with the fact that the very absolute wording of UDHR Article 20 (2), which reads that "no one may be compelled to belong to an association", deliberately was omitted from the ECHR. In this context the Court made the following general observation:

> Assuming for the sake of argument that, for the reasons given in the above-cited passage from the travaux preparatoires, a general rule such as that in Article 20 par. 2 of the Universal Declaration of Human Rights was deliberately omitted from, and so cannot be regarded as itself enshrined in, the Convention, it does not follow that the negative aspect of a person's freedom of association falls completely outside the ambit of Article 11 [....] and that each and every compulsion to join a particular trade union is compatible with the intention of that provision. To construe Article 11 [....] as permitting every kind of compulsion in the field of trade union membership would strike at the very substance of the freedom it is designed to guarantee [....].[90]

---

[88] COE, European Social Charter, *Committee of Independent Experts, Conclusions I*, 1970, at Article 5.

[89] *Young, James and Webster v. the United Kingdom*, Judgment of 13 August 1981.

When assessing the concrete events the Court attached importance to the fact that the applicants were faced with the dilemma either of joining the unions in question or of losing jobs for which union membership had not been a requirement when they were first engaged. The Court found that Article 11 provides for a certain protection with regard to the 'negative' right to organise and held as follows:

> However, a threat of dismissal involving loss of livelihood is a most serious form of compulsion and, in the present instance, it was directed against persons engaged by British Rail before the introduction of any obligation to join a particular trade union.
>
> In the Court's opinion, such a form of compulsion, in the circumstances of the case, strikes at the very substance of the freedom guaranteed by Article 11 [....]. For this reason alone, there has been an interference with that freedom as regards each of the three applicants.[91]

In light of the *Young, James and Webster case* the Committee of Independent Experts revised its interpretation of Article 5 of the ESC. The Committee held as follows:

> Without taking a stand on the question whether the Appendix to the Charter concerning Article 1, para. 2 is also applicable to Article 5, the Committee felt that even if this were the case, it would not follow either that the negative aspect of the freedom to organise would fall completely outside the scope of Article 5 or that an obligation to join a trade union would always be in conformity with the spirit of this provision.
>
> In accordance with the statement of the European Court of Human Rights in the above-mentioned case [....] it should be underlined that also as regards Article 5 of the Charter, to interpret this provision "as permitting every kind of compulsion in the field of trade union membership would strike at the very substance of the freedom it is designed to guarantee.[92]

In the following supervision cycle the Committee expressed it even stronger. Thus, the Committee added that:

> [....] no contracting party can fail to provide legal remedies or sanctions for practices which unduly obstruct the freedom to form or join trade union organisations, for otherwise the scope of the aforementioned provision of the Appendix would be excessively widened and situations incompatible with the fundamental freedom secured by Article 5 would be considered lawful.[93]

90 *Ibid.*, para. 52.

91 *Ibid.*, para. 55.

92 COE, European Social Charter, *Committee of Independent Experts. Conclusions VII*, 1981, at Article 5.

93 COE, European Social Charter, *Committee of Independent Experts. Conclusions VIII*, 184, at Article 5.

It follows that the Committee was of the general opinion that the ESC prohibits closed shop agreements, a position which is more far-reaching that that of the ECtHR in the case *Young, James and Websters*. However, in later judgments the Court has indeed attached importance to the opinion of the Committee and, in particular, taken into consideration whether or not the applicant in question was at risk of losing his livelihood.

Thus, in *Sibson v. the United Kingdom*, in which no violation was found, the Court attached importance inter alia to the fact that the applicant – unlike Young, James and Webster – was not faced with a threat of dismissal involving loss of livelihood. In this case the applicant had the possibility of going to work at a nearby location, to which his employers were contractually entitled to move him. Their offer to him in this respect was not conditional on his rejoining the union in question, and it was not established that his working conditions there would have been significantly less favourable than those at the original working place.[94]

In *Sigurjónsson v. Iceland* about compulsory membership of a specific private-law association for taxi-drivers the Court went somewhat further than in Young, James and Webster by stating that Article 11 "must be viewed as encompassing a negative right of association."[95] The Court saw no need to take a position whether "this right is to be considered on an equal footing with the positive right."[96] However, the Court recalled the status of the Convention as a living instrument which must be interpreted according to present-day conditions in the light of the following statement concerning the interpretation of the issue of a 'negative' right of association under a number of instruments one of them being the ESC:

> A growing measure of common ground has emerged in this area also at the international level. As observed by the Commission, in addition to the above-mentioned Article 20 para. 2 of the Universal Declaration [....]. Article 11 para. 2 of the Community Charter of the Fundamental Social Rights of Workers, adopted by the Heads of State or Government of eleven member States of the European Communities on 9 December 1989, provides that every employer and every worker shall have the freedom to join or not to join professional organisations or trade unions without any personal or occupational damage being thereby suffered by them. Moreover, on 24 September 1991 the Parliamentary Assembly of the Council of Europe unanimously adopted a recommendation, amongst other things, to insert a sentence to this effect into Article 5 of the 1961 European Social Charter [....]. Even in the absence of an express provision, the Committee of Independent Experts set up to supervise the implementation of the Charter considers that a negative right is covered by this

94 *Sibson v. the United Kingdom*, Judgment of 10 April 1993, para. 29.
95 *Sigurjónsson v. Iceland*, Judgment of 30 June 1993, para. 35.
96 *Ibid.*

> instrument and it has in several instances disapproved of closed-shop practices found in certain States Parties, including Iceland [....].
>
> Furthermore, according to the practice of the Freedom of Association Committee of the Governing Body of the International Labour Office (ILO), union security measures imposed by law, notably by making union membership compulsory, would be incompatible with Conventions Nos. 87 and 98 (the first concerning freedom of association and the right to organise and the second the application of the principles of the right to organise and to bargain collectively [....].[97]

In the concrete assessment as to whether Article 11 had been violated, the Court once again took into consideration – among other things – that a breach of the impugned membership was likely to bring about the revocation of the applicant's taxi-drivers licence. Thus, social considerations are indeed among the concerns of the Court in the evaluation of whether compulsory union member-ship is compatible with the Convention.

Social considerations were also reflected in *Gustafsson v. Sweden* although in a somewhat different manner. The case concerned a restaurant owner's refusal to be bound by a collective labour agreement either by joining an employer's association or by signing a substitute agreement. Hence, his restaurant was placed under a union blockade and a boycott was declared by the unions with the result that the restaurant owner suffered financial loss. The Court, sitting as a Grand Chamber, held that:

> the positive obligation incumbent on the State under Article 11 [....] including the aspect of protection of personal opinion, may well extend to treatment connected with the operation of a collective-bargaining system, but only where such treatment impinges on freedom of association. Compulsion which, as here, does not significantly affect the enjoyment of the freedom, even if it causes economic damage, cannot give rise to any positive obligation under Article 11.[98]

Moreover, the Court noted that the applicant "had not substantiated his submission to the fact that the terms of employment which he offered were more favourable than those required under a collective agreement."[99] In this context the Court attached importance to the special role and importance of collective agreements in the regulation of labour relations in Sweden. The Court recalled that:

> the legitimate character of collective bargaining is recognised by a number of international instruments, in particular Article 6 of the European Social Charter, Article 8 of the 1966 International Covenant on Economic, Social and Cultural Rights and Conventions nos. 87 and 98 of the International Labour Organisation (the first concerning freedom of association and the right to organise and the

---

[97] *Ibid.*

[98] *Gustafsson v. Sweden*, Judgment of 25 April 1996, para. 52.

[99] *Ibid.*, para. 53.

> second the application of the principles of the right to organise and to bargain collectively).[100]

Thus, from the wording of the judgment it seems as if the Court – when reaching the conclusion that Article 11 had not been violated – did indeed seek to take into consideration the needs and interests of those workers who benefit from the existence of a collective-bargaining system.[101] As pointed out by one of the dissenting judges, it is unclear, however, from the wording of the judgment whether the majority assessed the union's interests in relation to paragraphs 1 or 2 of Article 11.[102]

In the case of *Sørensen and Rasmussen v. Denmark* the Court discussed the distinction between the 'positive' and 'negative' aspects with regard to Article 11. The applicants complained that the existence of pre-entry closed-shop agreements and their application to them violated Article 11, and the Court put forward the following (hermeneutic) reflections:

> The Court does not in principle exclude that the negative and the positive aspects of the Article 11 right should be afforded the same level of protection in the area under consideration. However, it is difficult to decide this issue in the abstract since it is a matter that can only be properly addressed in the circumstances of a given case. At the same time, an individual cannot be considered to have renounced his negative right to freedom of association in situations where, in the knowledge that trade-union membership is a pre-condition of securing a job, he accepts an offer of employment notwithstanding his opposition to the condition imposed. Accordingly, the distinction made between pre-entry closed-shop agreements and post-entry closed-shop agreements in terms of the scope of the protection guaranteed by Article 11 is not tenable. At most this distinction is to be seen as a consideration which will form part of the Court's assessment of the surrounding circumstances and the issue of their Convention-compatibility.[103]

The Court reiterated that "the boundaries between the State's positive and negative obligations under Article 11 do not lend themselves to precise definition" and repeated that whether one chooses the 'positive' or the 'negative' approach the applicable principles are pretty much similar. What one has to do is to balance the competing interests between the interests of the community and those

---

100 *Ibid.*

101 In a later dismissal of a request for revision, the Court explains its position with respect to the disagreements concerning the terms of employment. Thus, the applicant produced evidence that the terms of employment, which were offered by him, were in fact more favourable. However, the Court dismissed the applicant's request by emphasising that "the Court had regard to the general interest sought to be achieved through the union action, in particular the special role and importance of collective agreements in the regulation of labour relations in Sweden", cf. *Gustafsson v. Sweden*, Judgment of 30 July 1998, para. 31.

102 *Gustafsson v. Sweden*, Partly dissenting opinion of Judge Jambrek, para. 5.

103 *Sørensen and Rasmussen v. Denmark*, Judgment of 11 January 2006, para. 56.

of the individual, and the Court did not find it necessary to consider whether the obligations in question belonged in a 'positive' or 'negative' category. The Court recognised that the Contracting States have a very wide margin of appreciation as to how the freedom of trade unions to protect the occupational interests of their members may be secured, but added that "where the domestic law of a Contracting State permits the conclusion of closed-shop agreements between unions and employers which run counter to the freedom of choice of the individual inherent in Article 11, the margin of appreciation must be considered reduced."[104] And the Court concluded its General Principles in the following way:

> In assessing whether a Contracting State has remained within its margin of appreciation in tolerating the existence of closed-shop agreements, particular weight must be attached to the justifications advanced by the authorities for them and, in any given case, the extent to which they impinge on the rights and interests protected by Article 11. Account must also be taken of changing perceptions of the relevance of closed-shop agreements for securing the effective enjoyment of trade-union freedom.
>
> The Court sees no reason not to extend these considerations to both pre- and post-entry closed-shop agreements.[105]

As to the concrete cases the Court considered that the applicants were in fact compelled to join a particular trade union. The Court admitted that both applicants were aware before taking up their respective jobs that an obligation existed to join the trade union in question, and that this was a condition for obtaining and retaining their employment. Had they denied they would not have been recruited. Moreover, both applicants were opposed to membership of the trade union in question for political reasons. The Court furthermore observed that Denmark had taken legislative attempts to eliminate entirely the use of closed-shop agreements, an attempt that reflected the trend which has emerged in the Contracting Parties, "namely that such agreements are not an essential means for securing the interests of trade unions and their members and that due weight must be given to the right of individuals to join a union of their own choosing without fear of prejudice to their livelihood. In fact, only a very limited number of Contracting States including Denmark and Iceland continue to permit the conclusion of closed-shop agreements [....]".[106]

The Court repeated the attitude of the ECSR in general and its criticism of Denmark in particular and referred to the Community Charter of the Fundamental Social Rights of Workers and to the Charter of Fundamental Rights of the European Union. The Court concluded as follows:

---

104 *Ibid.*, para. 58.

105 *Ibid.*

106 *Ibid.*, para. 70.

> In view of the above it appears that there is little support in the Contracting States for the maintenance of closed-shop agreements and that the European instruments referred to above clearly indicate that their use in the labour market is not an indispensable tool for the effective enjoyment of trade-union freedoms.
>
> In conclusion, taking all the circumstances of the case into account and balancing the competing interests at issue, the Court finds that the respondent State has failed to protect the applicants' negative right to trade union freedom.
>
> Accordingly, there has been a violation of Article 11 of the Convention in respect of both applicants.[107]

Mention should finally be made of *Evaldsson and Others v. Sweden*[108], who was one of five applicants employed by a construction company which was bound by a collective labour agreement concluded between a union and Swedish Construction Industries. Under the collective agreement the local union branch had the right to monitor salary payments and to be reimbursed for the costs involved on the basis of a fee of 1.5 percent of the worker's salary. The applicants were not members of any union and wanted to be exempted from paying the fee. They did not want to pay to an organisation with a political agenda which they did not support. In addition, it was impossible for the applicants to check how the money was spent. Before the ECtHR the applicants claimed that the deductions were in non-compliance with their rights under Article 1 of Protocol No. 1.

The Court agreed that the deductions amounted to interference, which was moreover in accordance with Swedish law. Having established that, the Court made a lengthy discussion of the issue of proportionality which is not to be repeated here. The Court noted that:

> only the actual cost of monitoring was to be covered by the fees. In these circumstances, the applicants were entitled to information which was sufficiently exhaustive for them to verify that the fees corresponded to the actual cost of the inspection work and that the amounts paid were also not used for other purposes. This was even more important as they had to pay the fees against their will to an organisation with a political agenda which they did not support
>
> Moreover, while the respondent State has to be given a wide margin of appreciation in the organisation of its labour market, a system which, as in the present case, in reality delegates the power to legislate, or regulate, important labour issues to independent organisations acting on that market requires that these organisations are held accountable for their activities. This requirement was particularly significant in the present case, where the relevant labour market organisations had concluded a collective agreement whose effects also extended to unorganised workers, obliging them to contribute financially to a particular

[107] *Ibid.*, paras. 75–77.

[108] The case does not concern ECHR Article 11, but Article 1 of Protocol No. 1.

> activity carried out by a trade union. In these circumstances, the Court finds that the State had a positive obligation to protect the applicants' interests.[109]

In conclusion, the Court found a violation of Article 1 of Protocol No. 1, "even having regard to the limited amounts of money involved for the applicants".[110] The decision was unanimous. However, one judge had a concurring opinion and focused on the reluctance of the applicants to contribute financially to "an organisation with a *political agenda which they did not support*".[111] According to this judge it would have been feasible to examine the case under Article 11.

The cases referred to illustrate how the perception of the 'negative' freedom of association has developed over the years concurrently with the decreasing influence of trade unions. Case law seems to give priority to the individual interests rather than the collective ones, although the balancing of the conflicting interests is carefully considered. Whether or not the development is to be welcomed is debatable, but that is not the issue here. It is a fact, though, that the interpretation of the two sister treaties, the ECHR and the ESC/RESC has been harmonised, and that both treaty bodies consider their sister treaty as a very relevant source of law. Once again, one can describe this development as a hermeneutic development.

9 *A Right to Collective Bargaining Under the ECHR?*

It is natural to continue the discussion of the formal freedom of association by asking what is the substantial content of this freedom, whether defined in 'negative' or 'positive' terms. One of the central issues in this context is whether the ECHR also provides for a right to collective bargaining and, if that is the case, what such a right implies. When analysing this issue, the Court has referred to Article 6 of the ESC/RESC which – unlike Article 11 of the ECHR – deals with this subject in great detail. Article 6 (1–3) runs as follows:

> With a view to ensuring the effective exercise of the right to bargain collectively, the Parties undertake:
>
> 1) to promote joint consultation between workers and employers;
> 2) to promote, where necessary and appropriate, machinery for voluntary negotiations between employers or employers' organisations and workers' organisations, with a view to the regulation of terms and conditions of employment by means of collective agreements;

---

[109] *Ibid.*, para. 63.

[110] *Ibid.*, para. 64.

[111] *Ibid.*, Concurring Opinion of Judge Fura-Sandström.

3) to promote the establishment and use of appropriate machinery for conciliation and voluntary arbitration for the settlement of labour disputes;

This provision formed part of the Court's reasoning in *National Union of Belgian Police v. Belgium*,[112] which concerned the issue as to whether a right of unions to be consulted comes within the scope of Article 11. The Court held this not to be the case:

> Not only is this latter right not mentioned in Article 11 [....] but neither can it be said that all the Contracting States in general incorporate it in their national law or practice, or that it is indispensable for the effective enjoyment of trade union freedom. It is thus not an element necessarily inherent in a right guaranteed by the Convention.[113]

What is interesting, however, is that the Court goes on to claim that the right to be consulted cannot be an element in the ECHR because it is dealt with in the ESC:

> In addition, trade union matters are dealt with in detail in another convention, also drawn up within the framework of the Council of Europe, namely the Social Charter of 18 Octobre 1961. Article 6 para. 1 of the Charter binds the Contracting States "to *promote* joint consultation between workers and employers". The *prudence* of the terms used shows that the Charter does not provide for a real right to consultation. Besides, Article 20 permits a ratifying State not to accept the undertaking in Article 6 para. 1. Thus it cannot be supposed that such a right derives by implication from Article 11 para. 1 [....] of the 1950 Convention, which incidentally would amount to admitting that the 1961 Charter took a *retrograde step* in this domain [author's emphasis].[114]

Thus, the Court is of the opinion, that the prudent expression *to promote* is chosen in order to underline that consultation is not a 'real right' but merely a policy statement. Moreover, the ESC allows for reservations with respect to Article 6. If one were then to assume that Article 11 of the ECHR provided for a 'real right' to consultation, this right would be more far-reaching than the one undertaken under Article 6 of the ESC. Accordingly, the coming into force in 1961 of the ESC would have amounted to a *retrograde* step.

The Court, however, admitted that the phrase "for the protection of his interests" in ECHR Article 11 shows that the Convention safeguards freedom to protect the occupational interests of trade union members by trade union action, the conduct and development of which the Contracting States must both permit and make possible:

---

[112] *National Union of Belgian Police v. Belgium*, Judgment of 27 October 1975.

[113] *Ibid.*, para. 38.

[114] *Ibid.*

> In the opinion of the Court, it follows that the members of a trade union have a right, in order to protect their interests, that the trade union should be heard. Article 11 para. 1[....] certainly leaves each State a free choice of the means to be used towards this end. While consultation is one of these means, there are others. What the Convention requires is that under national law trade unions should be enabled, in conditions not at variance with Article 11 [....] to strive for the protection of their members' interests.[115]

Hence, trade unions have a right "to be heard". This right, however, can be put into practice in a variety of ways, and States are left with a free choice of the means to be used. There is no obligation to consultation.

Against this background it comes as no surprise that the Court in *Swedish Engine Drivers' Union v. Sweden* reached the conclusion that Article 11 does not either entail a right for trade unions to conclude collective agreements. In this case the Court repeated the argumentation put forward in *National Union of Belgian Police* and added that the ESC "affirms the voluntary nature of collective bargaining and collective agreements."[116] In this respect the Court referred to the wording of Article 6 (2) of the ESC according to which the Contracting States "undertake to promote, where necessary and appropriate, machinery for voluntary negotiations between employers or employers' organisations, with the view to the regulation of terms and conditions of employment by means of collective agreements." As in *National Union of Belgian Police* the Court added that trade unions "should be heard". It is left to the Contracting States, however, to decide the way in which this requirement is to be implemented.

The conclusion that ECHR Article 11 does not guarantee either a right to consultation, to collective bargaining or to conclude collective agreements is based on an interpretation of Article 6 of the ESC. The reference to the ESC, however, seems not to be motivated by a wish to define the social and the civil element respectively of the right to organise. The Court rather seems to strive for a uniform interpretation of the two conventions, and in a certain sense the object is to deprive the ESC of a legal content in order to establish that the right to consultation, to collective bargaining and collective agreements is not either within the scope of the ECHR:

It forms part of the argumentation of the Court that Article 6 of the ESC has a means and ends-character. However, at the same time the Court admits that Article 11 of the ESCR to a certain extent has a similar character. Thus, the Court recognises that the Contracting States themselves have a very wide margin with respect to the choice of means by which they work towards the overall aim of

115 *Ibid.*,para. 39.

116 *Swedish Engine Drivers' Union v. Sweden*, Judgment of 6 February 1976, para. 39.

protecting the interests of the individual. In this specific context the method of regulation is of the same character as the one chosen in the ESC. Hence, when the Court deprives Article 6 of the ESC the character of 'real right', one could argue that something similar should apply to the right to organise under ECHR Article 11. However, the phrase "for the protection of his interests" is not entirely without legal content. Thus, the Contracting States can hardly completely disregard the obligation to strive for workers' right to protect their interests. Non-action would probably amount to a violation of Article 11. Even though the means are optional, the end – to protect the interests – is obligatory, and in this way the phrase does indeed have a legal content.

The Court does recognise the relevance of the ESC to the interpretation of the ECHR. However, it is worth noticing that the ESC's description of means and ends differs from that of the ECHR. What we witness is two different kinds of means-and-end regulation. Hence, in the ESC the end is rather precisely stated as "the effective exercise of the right to bargain collectively", "regulation of terms and conditions of employment by means of collective agreements", and "the settlement of labour disputes", whereas the ECHR refers to something more indefinite, namely "the protection of his interests." Collective bargaining is one among many possible means for the furthering of this end. Thus, what is described in Article 6 of the ESC as the end is recognised in Article 11 of the ECHR as an (optional) means, and the relevant match in the ESC is hardly Article 6, but rather Article 5 which – like Article 11 of the ECHR – aims at "the protection of their economic and social interests". The Committee of Independent Experts has repeatedly emphasised that observance of Article 6 of the ESC has respect for Article 5 as a necessary prerequisite. Article 6 has Article 5 as its basis.[117] Moreover, Article 6 of the ESC – unlike Article 11 of the ECHR – enumerates the means with which the Contracting States are to promote collective bargaining. Although the Contracting States to a certain extent are allowed to act at their discretion, cf. the expression "where necessary and appropriate", Article 6 of the ESC is more far-reaching that Article 11 of the ECHR.

In this light is appears logical that the ECtHR in the previously mentioned *Gustafsson* case, cf. above in Section 8 refers to the conventions on economic, social and cultural rights in support of its perception that union actions because of a restaurant owner's refusal to be bound by a collective labour agreement did not constitute a violation of the applicant's freedom of association. While the Court in *National Union of Belgian Police* and *Swedish Engine Drivers' Union* strives for a uniform interpretation of the ESC and the ECHR, the

---

[117] Cf. e.g. *Conclusions XIII-3*, 1996, at Article 6 and *The right to organise and to bargain collectively*, 2nd Edition, Human Rights. Social Charter monographs – No. 5, 2001, p. 56.

situation in *Gustafsson* seems different. Thus, the way in which the Court refers to the ESC seems to indicate that the Court (now) recognises that the ESC does in fact encompass a right to collective bargaining, and that the existence of this right justified the limitation of the applicant's freedom of action under Article 11 of the ECHR. It should be noted in this context that the perception of the Committee is that Article 6 of the ESC does encompass the right to collective bargaining. Thus, the Committee has held on several occasions that the lack of negotiating measures amounts to a violation of the ESC and in that way confirmed the legal relevance regulation in terms of means and ends.[118] The *Gustafsson* case, however, illustrates that the two provisions, ECHR Article 11 and ESC Article 6, are intertwined. Having recognised that ESC Article 6 encompasses a 'positive' right to collective bargaining for employers, among others, it follows naturally that the ECHR cannot include a 'negative' right not to enter into collective agreements.[119] The existence of the latter right would amount to a repulsion of the former.

That the Court has in fact changed its position with regard to the legal content of Article 6 of the ESC (and now also the RESC) is confirmed in *Wilson, National Union of Journalists & Others v. the United Kingdom.*[120] This judgment does, furthermore, constitute a good illustration of the application of the integrated approach because the Court leans on the ESCR's interpretation of Articles 5 and 6 of the ESC/RESC. The case concerned the fact that under British legislation an employer was permitted to use financial incentives to induce employees to relinquish important union rights such as the right to be represented by the union, the right of the union to negotiate, to be consulted and agree to terms and conditions of employment. This situation has been considered inconsistent with Articles 5 and 6 of the ESC/RESC and similarly been criticised by the ILO Committee on Freedom of Association as inconsistent with ILO Conventions No. 87 and 98.

The Court initially repeated its position from previous case law, namely that the expression "for the protection of his interests" has a legal content, and that the right to collective bargaining is one among other possible means in the safeguarding of the right "to be heard". The Court went on by recalling that it "has not *yet* been prepared to hold that the freedom of a trade union to make its voice heard extends to imposing on an employer an obligation to recognise a trade union [author's emphasis]."[121] The expression *yet* suggests – what case

[118] Cf. e.g. *The right to organise and to bargain collectively*, 2nd Edition, Human Rights. Social Charter monographs – No. 5, 2001, p. 49 ff.

[119] Cf. also *AB Kurt Kellermann v. Sweden*, Admissibility decision of 1 July 2003.

[120] *Wilson, National Union of Journalists & Others v. the United Kingdom*, Judgment of 2 July 2002.

[121] *Ibid.*, para. 44.

law clearly illustrates – that the interpretation is not final, and the Court does add that "[t]he union and its members must, however, be free, in one way or another, to seek to persuade the employer to listen to what it has to say on behalf of its members."[122] By referring to the conclusions from the Committee of Independent Expert and the ILO Committee on Freedom of Association, the Court concluded that:

> by permitting employers to use financial incentives to induce employees to surrender important union rights, the respondent State has failed in its positive obligation to secure the enjoyment of the rights under Article 11 of the Convention. This failure amounted to a violation of Article 11, as regards both the applicant trade unions and the individual applicants.[123]

Hence, since 1975 the Court has executed a volte-face in its interpretation of Article 11 of the ECHR. In National Union of Belgian Police and Swedish Drivers' Union from 1975 and 1976 the Court refused to accept that a right to consultation and to collective bargaining formed part of Article 11 by arguing that the ESC did not provide a 'real right' to collective bargaining, and that the ESC allows for reservation with respect to Article 6. Thus, if one were to assume that Article 11 of the ECHR provided a 'real right' to consultation and to collective bargaining, this right would be more far-reaching than the right undertaken under Article 6 of the ESC, and the adoption of the latter in 1961 would have amounted to a retrograde step. In the *Gustafsson* case it seems, however, as if the Court now recognises that the ESC does in fact encompass a right to collective bargaining, and in *Wilson, National Union of Journalists & Others* the Court goes even further. Thus, the Court seeks inspiration from Article 6 of the ESC – as interpreted by the Committee of Independent Experts – in its re-interpretation of Article 11 of the ECHR as now encompassing additional elements of a right to collective bargaining. The development illustrates an initial, although cautious, endeavour to perform an integrated interpretation of the two conventions, and provides the basis for an assumption that the last word has not yet been said with respect to a possible recognition of the right to collective bargaining under Article 11 of the ECHR.

10 *A Right to Collective Action Under the ECHR?*

The right to collective action is not mentioned in Article 11 of the ECHR. Article 6 (4) of the ESC /RESC, however, *recognises*:

---

122 *Ibid.*

123 *Ibid.*, para. 48.

> the right of workers and employers to collective action in cases of conflicts of interest, including the right to strike, subject to obligations that might arise out of collective agreements previously entered into.

Hence, this provision differs from Article 6 (1–3) in that it does not follow the means-and-end approach. Contracting States *recognise* that the right to collective action is to be respected, and the interesting question in this context is whether this provision has any impact on the interpretation of Article 11 of the ECHR. This issue arose in *Schmidt and Dahlström v. Sweden*[124] about two public employees who were members of trade unions which called for selective strikes. On the basis of a special clause in the collective agreement both members were denied the right to retroactivity of certain benefits on account of strike, even though they had not themselves been involved in the strikes. They claimed the denial of the benefits to be in non-keeping with Article 11 and, moreover, that the clause in question "tended to discourage them from thenceforth availing themselves of their right to strike, which is, in their submission, an "organic right" included in Article 11 [....]."[125]

The Court rejected the first argument by holding that Article 11 "does not secure any particular treatment of trade union members by the State, such as the right to retroactivity, for instance salary increases, resulting from a new collective agreement."[126] The Court added that such right is not enunciated in the ESC either. The Court rejected the second argument by referring to previous case law according to which each State is left with a free choice of the means to be used when safeguarding the freedom to protect the occupational interests of trade union members. The Court went on to say that the grant of a right to strike represents one of the most important rights, but not the only one. The Court added that:

> [s]uch a right, which is not expressly enshrined in Article 11 [....] may be subject under national law to regulation of a kind that limits its exercise in certain instances. The Social Charter of 18 October 1961 only guarantees the right to strike subject to such regulation, as well as to "further restrictions" compatible with its Article 31, while at the same time recognising for employers too the right to resort to collective action (Article 6 para. 4 and Appendix). For its part, the 1950 Convention requires that under national law trade unionists should be enabled, in conditions not at variance with Article 11 [....] to strive through the medium of their organisations for the protection of their occupational interests. Examination of the file in this case does not disclose that the applicants have been deprived of this capacity.[127]

---

[124] *Schmidt and Dahlström v. Sweden*, Judgment of 6 February 1976.

[125] *Ibid.*, para. 36.

[126] *Ibid.*, para. 34.

[127] *Ibid.*, para. 36.

Thus, the Court decided the case solely on the basis of Article 11 (1) with reference, however, to Article 31 of the ESC according to which such restrictions are allowed which are "prescribed by law and [....] necessary in a democratic society for the protection of the rights and freedoms of others or for the protection of public interest, national security, public health, or morals."

The Court could, however, have reached a similar conclusion on the basis of Article 11 (2), which is worded very much similar to that of Article 31 of the ESC, and it is not perfectly clear why the Court chose the above-mentioned approach. Nor is it clear why the Court chose to refer to the fact that Article 6 (4) and the Appendix of the ESC also recognise the right of employers to resort to collective action. The right of employees to collective action is still a right even though the ESC admits the same right to employers.

Again it seems as if the Court delimits the scope of Article 11 of the ECHR by hollowing out the scope of Article 6 of the ESC. However, the restriction clause in ECHR Article 11 (2) is hardly less far-reaching than that of Article 31 of the ESC, and the Committee of Independent Experts and later the ECSR has practiced Article 6 (4) quite extensively also with respect to public servants. In fact, the provision has been designated as a "landmark in international law" seen from the standpoint of the worker.[128]

In later case law, the Court has accepted that collective action concerns the occupational interests of union members, and that prohibition of strikes must be regarded as a restriction on the applicant's power to protect those interests. Such restrictions must accordingly be in compliance with the requirements of Article 11 (2) of the Convention.[129] Likewise, in *Federation of Offshore Workers' Trade Unions and Others v. Norway* about the imposition of compulsory arbitration and the termination of industrial action on Norwegian oil platforms, the Court "proceeded on the assumption that the first paragraph of Article 11 applied to the matter complained of, and that the impugned restriction amounted to an interference with a right guaranteed by it."[130] The Court, however, did not find that the restrictions imposed amounted to a violation of Article 11. Thus, the Court attached importance to serious consequences of a halt to activities with respect to economy, distribution and supply but emphasised that its decision:

> should not be taken as meaning that a system of compulsory arbitration for bringing lawful strikes to an end would be considered proportionate in all cases in which economic pressure is being exerted.[131]

---

[128] Cf. Donna Gomien et. al., *Law and practice of the European Convention on Human Rights and the European Social Charter*, COE Publ., 1996, p. 393.

[129] Cf. *Unison v. the United Kingdom*, Admissibility decision of 10 January 2002.

[130] *Federation off Shore Workers'Trade Unions and Others v. Norway*, Admissibility decision of 27 June 2002.

[131] *Ibid.*, ad 2. The Court's assessment.

The situation had been assessed differently by the ECSR, but the Court chose not to deal with the perception of the Committee. The above-quoted passage, however, indicates that other factual circumstances might lead the Court to another result.[132] Thus, the harmonisation of Article 11 of the ECHR with Article 6 of the ESC with respect to the issue of the right to industrial action is not as evident as it is with respect to the issue of negative freedom of association and the right to collective bargaining, cf. above. However, recent case law does not rule out the possibility of future harmonisation.

11 *Other Issues Relating to Freedom of Association*

Three Turkish cases concern some other aspects of freedom of association. In *Tüm Haber Sen and Çinar v. Turkey* a trade union for public sector contractual staff working in the communications field was dissolved on the ground that State employees could not form trade unions, and the applicants (Çinar was the former president of the trade union Tüm Haber Sen) claimed that the Turkish State had violated their rights under Article 11.

The Court departed from the expression "for the protection of his interests", cf. Article 11 (1). Thus, the Court underlined that a trade union "must thus be free to strive for the protection of its members' interests, and the individual members have a right, in order to protect their interests, that the trade union should be heard [....]."[133] Likewise the Court underlined that the Convention "makes no distinction between the functions of a Contracting State as holder of public power and its responsibilities as employer"[134], cf. Article 11 (2), which indicates that the State is bound to respect the freedom of assembly and association of its employees, subject to the possible imposition of "lawful restrictions" in the case of members of its armed forces, police or administration.

Accordingly, interference had taken place, and the issue before the Court was whether it had taken place in accordance with Article 11 (2). The interference had taken place in accordance with Turkish law, but the Court was not convinced by the Government's perception that the interference was "necessary in a democratic society." Moreover, the Court referred to ILO Convention

[132] Cf. also *Ahmet Imam and Others v. Greece*, Admissibility decision of 20 October 1997 and *the National Association of Teachers in further and higher education v. the United Kingdom*, Admissibility decision of 16 April 1998. In both cases, the Commission found that requirements on trade unions to reveal the names of members participating in a ballot before industrial action did not amount to a disproportionate interference with the unions' rights under Article 11. Both decisions are rather concrete, and it is not excluded that such requirement under different circumstances may constitute a violation of Article 11.

[133] *Tüm Haber Sen and Çinar v. Turkey*, Judgment of 21 May 2006, para. 28.

[134] *Ibid.*, para. 29.

No. 87, which was ratified by Turkey. According to Article 2 of that convention all workers, without any distinction between the public and private sectors, are secured the unrestricted right to establish and join trade unions, cf. Article 2 of the Convention.

Furthermore, although Turkey had not accepted Article 5 of the ESC/RESC the Court found it relevant to refer to this provision as well. According to the Committee of Independent Experts (and now the ECSR) Article 5 of the ESC affords all workers the right to form trade unions and applies to civil servants as well. It argued as follows:

> The Court can only subscribe to this interpretation by a particularly well-qualified committee. It also notes that Article 5 of the European Social Charter sets out conditions for the possibility of forming trade union organisations for members of the police and the armed forces. By converse implication this Article must be considered as applying without restriction to other categories of State employees.[135]

Accordingly, the Court found a violation of Article 11, which is hardly surprising. What is remarkable on the face of it, however, is that the Court applies Article 5 of the ESC/RESC although Turkey had not accepted that provision. On the other hand, one can argue that it would be even more remarkable if the Court interpreted Article 11 differently depending on whether or not the Contracting State in question had accepted Article 5 of the ESC/RESC. It is an unavoidable consequence of the integrated approach, and Article 5 of the ESC/RESC has in a way become part of ECHR Article 11.

Also, in *Demir and Baykara v. Turkey* the Court sitting as a Grand Chamber referred to Articles 5 and Article 6 of the ESC/RESC as a legal source in the interpretation of ECHR Article 11.[136] The situation resembled that of Tüm Haber Sen, and the Grand Chamber agreed with the applicants that the annulment of a collective agreement went contrary to Article 11.

In *Metin Turan v. Turkey* the Court sitting as a Chamber took for its basis that the applicant – who was a civil servant – was transferred to another region due to his participation in trade union activities. The Court did not find that the decision was necessary in a democratic society.[137] The judgment is referred to the Grand Chamber.

Another question is whether Member States have obligations to protect workers from being denied the right to membership of a trade union, or, if they are already members, from being excluded. Is the right to freedom of

---

135 *Ibid.*, para. 39.

136 *Demir and Baykara v. Turkey*, Judgment of 12 November 2008.

137 *Metin Turan v. Turkey*, Judgment of 14 November 2006.

association a collective right to associate together or does an individual have a right to be a member of a trade union after his own choosing. This question was originally raised in *Ernest Dennis Cheall v. the United Kingdom*[138] in which the applicant was excluded from a trade union at the request of the TUC (the Trades Union Congress) due to the fact that the acceptance of the applicant as a member of the trade union in question had taken place in contradiction with the "TUC Principles and Procedures", according to which a trade union has an obligation to enquire into previous trade union memberships of applicants. The case was declared inadmissible by the Commission which found as follows:

> The right to join a union "for the protection of his interests" cannot be interpreted as conferring a general right to join the union of one's choice irrespective of the rules of the union. In the exercise of their rights under Article 11, para. 1, unions must remain free to decide, in accordance with union rules, questions concerning admission to and expulsion from the union. The protection afforded by the provision is primarily against interference by the State.[139]

The Commission went on by emphasising that "the State must protect the individual against any abuse of a dominant position by trade unions [....]".[140] Such abuse might occur, for example, "where exclusion or expulsion was not in accordance with union rules or where the rules were wholly unreasonable or arbitrary or where the consequences of exclusion or expulsion resulted in exceptional hardship such as job loss because of a closed shop."[141]

The applicant's exclusion was, however, in accordance with the trade union's rules which were not found to be unreasonable. Moreover, the expulsion of the applicant did not involve loss of his job because of a closed-shop arrangement. Accordingly, the application was declared inadmissible.

The circumstances in *Associated Society of Locomotive Engineers & Firemen v. the United Kingdom* were somewhat different. In this case a provision in the British labour legislation prohibited trade unions from excluding a person or expelling a member wholly or to any extent on the ground that the individual is or was a member of a political party. Therefore the applicant trade union had been obliged to re-admit a former member who had been excluded due to his membership of the far right British National Party.

In this case the Court referred to the *Cheall case* and furthermore to the ECHR's perception of the conformity of British labour legislation with Article 5 of the ESC:

[138] *Ernest Dennis Cheall v. the United Kingdom*, Admissibility decision of 13 May 1985.

[139] *Ibid.*

[140] *Ibid.*

[141] *Ibid.*

> In that context, the European Committee of Social Rights [....] has given consideration on numerous occasions to sections 174–177 of the 1992 Act. Concern with the interference by section 174 in the right of trade unions to fix their own rules and choose their own members was expressed by the Committee in Conclusions XIII-3, p. 109; Conclusions XV-1 p. 629; and in November 2002, Conclusions XVI-1, p. 684 where it held:
>
> "Section 174 of the 1992 Act limits the grounds on which a person may be refused admission to or expelled from a trade union to such an extent as to constitute an excessive restriction on the rights of a trade union to determine its conditions for membership and goes beyond what is required to secure the individual right to join a trade union .....The Committee concludes that, in light of the provisions of the Trade Union and Labour Relations (Consolidation Act) 1992 referred to above (sections 15, 65, 174 and 226A) the situation in the United Kingdom is not in conformity with Article 5 of the Charter"
>
> In Conclusions XVII-1 (2004) it again concluded that the United Kingdom was not in conformity with Article 5 of the Charter as section 174 constituted an excessive restriction on trade unions' right to determine their membership conditions.[142]

The Court recognised that lawfulness was not an issue. Nor was it disputed that the aim of the relevant provision in British law aimed at protecting the rights of individuals. The Court, however held as follows with regard to the implications for the expelled person, Mr. Lee:

> [T]he Court is not persuaded however that the measure of expulsion impinged in any significant way on Mr Lee's exercise of freedom of expression or his lawful political activities. Nor is it apparent that Mr Lee suffered any particular detriment, save loss of membership itself in the union. As there was no closed shop agreement for example, there was no apparent prejudice suffered by the applicant in terms of his livelihood or in his conditions of employment. The Court has taken account of the fact that membership of a trade union is often regarded, in particular due to the trade union movement's historical background, as a fundamental safeguard for workers against employers' abuse and it has some sympathy with the notion that any worker should be able to join a trade union (subject to the exceptions set out in Article 11 § 2 in fine). However, as pointed out by the applicant, ASLEF represents all workers in the collective bargaining context and there is nothing to suggest in the present case that Mr Lee is at any individual risk of, or is unprotected from, any arbitrary or unlawful action by his employer. Of more weight in the balance is the applicant's right to choose its members. Historically, trade unions in the United Kingdom, and elsewhere in Europe, were, and though perhaps to a lesser extent today are, commonly affiliated to political parties or movements, particularly those on the left. They are not bodies solely devoted to politically-neutral aspects of the well-being of their members, but are often ideological, with strongly held views on social and political issues. There was no hint in the

---

142 *Case of Associated Society of Locomotive Engineers & Firemen (Aslef) v. the United Kingdom*, Judgment of 27 February 2007, paras. 23–24 and para. 39.

> domestic proceedings that the applicant erred in its conclusion that Mr Lee's political values and ideals clashed, fundamentally, with its own. There is no indication that the applicant had any public duty or role conferred on it, or has taken the advantage of state funding, such that it may reasonably be required to take on members to fulfil any other wider purposes.[143]

Thus, in the absence of any identifiable hardship suffered by Mr Lee or any abusive and unreasonable conduct by the applicant, the Court concluded that the balance had not been properly struck and that the case fell outside any acceptable margin of appreciation. Accordingly, there had been a violation of Article 11.[144]

12 *Future Prospects*

The ECHR does not include a provision on the right to work which one can invoke at the job centre. However, that does not imply that the ECHR is irrelevant when it comes to work-related rights, and case law illustrates how the ECHR e.g. gives a rather comprehensive protection against arbitrary dismissal. In addition, the Convention seems to give protection also with regard to the seeking of employment and also with regard to rights connection to the right to organise, collective bargaining and the right to collective action. Moreover, the ECtHR seems to strive for harmonisation with the ESC/RESC. Both conventions – the ECHR and the ESC/RESC – include relatively vague and imprecise provisions, which have, however, been interpreted as giving a relatively good protection of worker's rights. In this context it is particularly relevant to draw attention to the way in which the ECtHR has gradually given the ECHR a more 'positive' content by reading social elements into various of the Convention's provisions. The potential of the ECHR has hardly been utilised, and there is all the reason to believe that this development will continue – not in leaps but on a case to case basis. The interpretation of the ECHR has hardly reached its final stage and might never come to a halt. In perfect harmony with a hermeneutic interpretation of the ECHR work-related rights under the ECHR are 'unfinished' rights which are likely to bee influenced by new sets of facts and altering perceptions of work-related facts.

---

[143] *Ibid.*, para. 51.

[144] *Ibid.*, paras. 52–53.

Chapter 10

Socio-Economic Demands as Justiciable Rights – The Issue of Power Balance

1 *Initial Remarks*

The comprehensive case law referred to in Chapters 5 to 9 is illustrative of the fact that the ECHR encompasses socio-economic elements, and that it makes good sense to talk about the right to health, housing, education, social cash benefits and also of work-related rights under the Convention. Many of the decisions of the ECtHR have radical consequences for the Contracting Parties, not only with respect to administrative bodies' interpretation of domestic legislation, but also with respect to the legislature's liberty to freely adopt and uphold legislation. Moreover, many of the Court's decisions affect the possibility of the legislature and of the executive to freely take decisions regarding financial resources. As they are furthermore binding on the Contracting Parties, they are likely to have a stronger impact on domestic bodies than decisions from the ECSR, cf. Chapter 11 about The Relation between the ECHR and the ESC/RESC.

The Court's case law illustrates aspects of the phenomenon which has obtained the designation *legalisation*. We speak of increasing legalisation, which is often considered an unwelcome American influence, and it is a common perception that the balance between legislatures and courts – domestic or international – has been disturbed. Thus, the term legalisation has a somewhat negative connotation in that it is usually associated with undesirable politisation of the judiciary and thus impairment of the democratically elected legislature. This perception derives from a *majoritarian* supposition that legitimate lawmaking lies in the will of parliaments, the elected representatives of the sovereign people. Thus, it is often assumed that it is possible to uphold a well-defined division of powers between the legislature, the executive and the judiciary, and in the most extreme versions the judiciary is nothing more than "the mouth that pronounces the words of the law."[1] According to this perception,

[1] Charles Montesquieu, *The Spirit of the Laws* (1748), translated and edited by Anne M. Cohler, Basia Carolyn Miller and Harald Samuel Stone, Cambridge University Press, 1989.

the legitimate task of the judiciary is simply exhausted in the implementation of the legislature's will. This question of division of powers becomes even more critical with respect to case law from the ECtHR. Thus, in this context it is an *international* body which "deprives" domestic legislative bodies of part of their legislative power, and this phenomenon has given rise to considerable anxiety with regard to domestic self-government.

Proponents of socio-economic rights, however, extend a cordial welcome to the phenomenon as an expression of a strengthening of the legal status of individuals with respect to socio-economic demands. Many of the judgments referred to above in Chapters 5 to 9 make up valuable contributions in favour of the perception of socio-economic rights as *justiciable* rights in the sense that they can form the legal basis for the solution of individual disputes concerning socio-economic issues. That is also the case as regards the decisions from the ECSR, cf. below in Chapter 11. Socio-economic rights have waited a long time to be recognised as legal rights, and some will say that legalisation has a positive connotation when applied in this context. I myself am one of them.

Therefore, the present chapter is devoted to a general discussion of the compatibility of democracy and the justiciability of socio-economic demands irrespective of whether they are protected in civil and political rights instruments or socio-economic rights instruments. Are there reasons to profess democratic misgivings with regard to judicial review of socio-economic issues, and how do we understand the concept of democracy? The chapter supplements Chapter 4 about Theoretical and Methodological Considerations concerning the hermeneutic approach to human rights interpretation and vice versa; only the present chapter has its specific focus on the division of powers and the hermeneutic relations between the various bodies – domestic as well as international – involved with human rights implementation and interpretation.

As indicated above, the considerable anxiety with regard to judicial influence over what is considered political matters is particularly strong when the judicial body is not even a domestic body but an international or regional treaty body, in this case the ECtHR. An important aim in this context is, therefore, exactly that of discussing the issue of the division of powers between the ECtHR and domestic bodies. However, the basic questions with regard to division of powers are identical regardless of whether the judicial body is domestic or international, and the domestic discussion is, moreover, strongly related to the one which concerns the relation between domestic bodies and the ECtHR. All of the judgments of the Court have previously been dealt with by domestic courts, and although the margin of appreciation should be taken into consideration, domestic courts are to regard the case law of the Court as a very important source of law. Accordingly, it is difficult to separate the two issues. Nevertheless, I will begin by discussing the issues primarily from the domestic perspective before adding the international dimensions, cf. below in Section 3.

Finally in Section 4, I will address the issue of a possible delimitation or classification of the judicial elements of socio-economic demands.

2 *Division of (democratic) Powers at the Domestic Level*

2.1 *Initial Remarks*

The issue of judicial review is often discussed as an issue of review of statutes and their conformity not only with constitutional provisions but also with international human rights standards. The issue of division of powers review arises, however, in two different ways depending on whether the lawsuit concerns the *consistence* of a certain provision with human rights – whether protected in domestic constitutions or internal treaties – or merely the *application* of a certain provision in the case at hand. The first situation clearly concerns the division of powers between the legislature and the judiciary whereas the second often relates to the division of powers between the executive and the judiciary.

Although the two issues – human rights validity of legislative and administrative action respectively – are hardly entirely distinct, they differ at least in one sense. While judicial review of the concrete application of a statute might lead to the conclusion that human rights requirements have not been observed in the case at hand, the provision as such might be in full compliance. This has as an indirect implication that judicial review can be fully consistent with parliamentary supremacy, simply because the legislative intention is and has to be of a general nature, cf. above in Chapter 4 about Theoretical and Methodological Considerations. From a hermeneutic point of view, there is or should not be any (legislative) intention with regard to the concrete application, and it is a central aspect of the principle of division of powers that legislation has a general managerial purpose. If, however, the provision is set aside as not consistent with human rights, the legislative power has indeed been overruled.

Although the two categories of situations have common features, I will deal with them separately. Moreover, the issue of judicial reticence with regard to the review of the *application* of socio-economic provisions must be considered differently depending on the wording of the provision in question. I intend, therefore, to make a distinction between legal provisions worded with precision as individual rights and vague standards, maybe qualifying as *meta-rights*,[2] well aware of the fact that such a distinction oversimplifies the issue. A distinction between vague and precise standards may even seem to contradict the perception of the human rights obligation as a wave motion, cf. above in

[2] Amartya Sen, "The right not to be hungry" in P. Alston et al. (eds.), *The Right to Food*, 1984, pp. 69–81 (on 70). Cf. above e.g. in Chapter 1.2.

Chapter 2 about Typological and Terminological Considerations. However, the application of another terminology in this particular context of socio-economic rights is compatible with the wave metaphor after all, as the main part of the continuum belongs in the category of vague standards. Moreover, the precisely worded standards are not the ones to make up the biggest challenge with regard to the recognition of the democratic legitimacy of judicial review.

In Sections 2.2 and 2.3, I will deal with the issue of application of socio-economic standards, precise or vague, which, according to their wording, are in compliance with human rights standards in general. Issues relating to human rights may, nevertheless, arise either with regard to the interpretation of the provision in question or with regard to the exercise of discretionary powers of administrative authorities. Discretionary powers are not unlimited. Discretion, says Ronald Dworkin, "like the hole in a doughnut, does not exist except as an area left open by a surrounding belt of restriction",[3] and the belt of restriction in this context is human rights. In Section 2.4, I take up the issue of the democratic legitimacy of the judiciary when setting aside a certain statutory provision due to its non-compliance with human rights.

As the discussion of the notion of democracy is particularly relevant to this discussion, I have chosen to deal with this issue in the same context. The answers to many of the questions raised in this chapter may be dependent on how one defines democracy and perceives the relation between human rights and democracy. Are we to see democracy as a system of representative (popular) government or should we (also) consider democracy a system of (basic) rights and legal guarantees? I incline to the perception of democracy as a substantive concept. However, it is a fact that the perception of democracy as a formal concept, synonymous with majority rule is widespread, and at least outside of academic circles the issue debated is simply whether or not popularly elected judges can set aside majority rulings of parliamentarians. Hence, it seems relevant to begin by considering the issue from the perspective of democracy merely as procedure, as nothing more than the majority's power to impose its legislative decisions on the people. In Section 2.4 the perspective will be broadened. However, for the present purpose democracy may be understood as majority rule.

2.2 *Judicial Review of the Application of Legal Provisions Worded Precisely and as Individual Rights*

Rather few legal provisions leave no room whatsoever for legal interpretation, and the perception of Montesquieu that the judiciary is only to be "the mouth that pronounces the words of the law" is not very much to the point as a general

[3] Ronald Dworkin, "Is Law a System of Rules?" in Ronald Dworkin (ed.), *The Philosophy of Law*, Oxford University Press, 1977, p. 52.

rule of conduct. However, the issue of judicial review of the administration of legal provisions concerning socio-economic issues is rather uncomplicated as long as the provisions in question are worded in a precise manner giving the individual a right to claim a certain benefit or service from the State. If the legal facts and the legal consequences are worded unequivocally, the legislature has left limited room for interpretation, let alone use of discretionary powers. Thus, if the legislature has decided that e.g. citizens can claim old-age pension by the age of 65, or that parents with children below the age of 3 have the right to a certain child benefit irrespective of the total income of the family, very few uncertainties arise with respect to the application of the provisions in question. Should administrative decisions not respect such provisions, they will be set aside as unlawful.

Benefits such as old-age pensions and child benefits involve expenditure, and implicit in the adoption of statutory provisions concerning such benefits lies a willingness to defray expenditure. Thus, budgetary implications are not as such a hindrance to the acceptance of the justiciability of socio-economic rights. The reluctance of citizens in at least some Member States of the COE to choose litigation as a means to enforce that type of socio-economic legal claims might have more to do with the fact that the addressees are often of modest means. Moreover, there is reason to believe that many such disputes find their solution within the administrative complaints system or through the agency of parliamentary ombudsmen.

In conclusion, statutes leaving little or no room for interpretation do not give rise to serious difficulties with regard to the issue of division of powers. The text speaks more or less for itself and even if the judiciary *adds* something when interpreting the concrete provision in a concrete context, the competence to do that may be considered to be implicit in the text, some would say *delegated* from the legislator. While not recognising the judiciary as "the mouth that pronounces the words of the law" some would argue that the judiciary acts *on behalf* of the legislator, thus "solving" the problem with regard to the democratic legitimacy of the law making.[4]

However, such considerations are of very limited practical use. Statutory provisions which leave limited or no doubt in each and every concrete context are few, and considerations as the above-mentioned give no answer to the fundamental question of the democratic legitimacy of judicial review in other respects.

2.3 *Judicial Review of the Application of Vague Legal Standards*

Most human rights obligations within the socio-economic sphere presuppose that States themselves have the responsibility to take the necessary

---

[4] Cf. Jan Fridthjof Bernt, 'The Significance of Autonomous Law in Modern Society?, *Kritisk Juss*, 2000, 193–206 (on p. 194).

implementation steps by means of domestic legislation. It is understood that the international obligation first and foremost is to be implemented by means of legislative or other regulatory measures[5] rather than judicial action. That appears from the ESC/RESC and even more clearly from the CESCR, which in Article 2 (1) includes the following phrase:

> Each State Party to the present Covenant undertakes to take steps, individually and through international assistance and co-operation, especially economic and technical, to the maximum of its available resources, with a view to achieving progressively the full realization of the rights recognized in the present Covenant by all appropriate means, *including particularly the adoption of legislative measures* [author's emphasis].

However, the legislature does not take a stand with regard to all socio-economic issues and, moreover, often chooses to apply a language which is as vague as the language of many international obligations. Domestic legislation within the socio-economic sphere is often worded with very little precision as an obligation for local and regional bodies e.g. to provide "the necessary number of day-care centres" or "the necessary means to live on",[6] thus apparently leaving it to these bodies to decide what is in fact necessary, and to make sure that the administration of domestic standards is not at variance with human rights obligations. The legislature's motives for choosing such vague language are dealt with below. One may question, however, the necessity of insisting on domestic legislation as an obligatory connecting link between international human rights obligations and domestic judicial review.

The perception of the legislature as an obligatory connecting link between vaguely worded human rights obligations on the one hand and administrative bodies' factual application of domestic standards on the other seems to lead to a kind of circularity in the argumentation regarding the possibilities and limitations of judicial review. It is argued that the judiciary should exercise considerable self-restraint when examining the application of standards which have substantial budgetary implications due to their lack of democratic legitimacy. However, when the legislature does not make full use of its democratic mandate to guide the administration on how to apply a certain statutory provision, a legal vacuum is created with which neither the legislature nor the judiciary has control. Rather, various professions with no democratic legitimacy whatsoever fill in the vacuum often within the framework of local self-government and within the limits imposed by financial constraint.

---

[5] Some human rights instruments presuppose legislation, others accept various kinds of regulatory measures even (collective) agreements between the social partners. For the sake of convenience, however, I apply the term 'legislation' in the following.

[6] Both examples are from Danish social legislation.

Admittedly, many of the professions working in the socio-economic sphere have developed codes of ethics many of which have a strong resemblance to human rights principles. However, history tells us that professional ethics and human rights do not always go hand in hand with budgetary weighing, and there is a risk that human rights and professional ethics will be set aside in the competition. The need for judicial review will have to be discussed in this light.

Before addressing this question one may ask why the legislature deliberately chooses to adopt legislation which is worded with limited precision thereby unavoidably reducing the possibilities to control the behaviour of local and regional bodies. Thus, a precise choice of words limits the needs and possibilities of local and regional bodies for administrative standard setting. Moreover, traditional considerations not only over legal security but also over management call for the legislature to make maximum use of its legislative powers. Precision limits the administrative leeway, and has the advantage that it is possible to reduce the subsequent recourse to examination by administrative complaints bodies and parliamentary ombudsmen.

Surely, the fact that vague and unclear standard setting is a very common phenomenon is neither due to a declared wish to reduce legal security for the individual nor to a wish to reduce the managerial effect of legislative standards. Rather, the expectation that the legislature is able to give precise directives for every imaginable legal problem is unrealistic. The law maker is not able to create a comprehensive system of legal norms that give adequate and exhaustive answers to each and every legal question, and that is not the purpose of legislation either. Jan Fridthjof Bernt speaks of *legislative optimism*, based on two assumptions:

> First that the law maker will be able to create a comprehensive system of legal norms which will give an adequate answer to all legal problems, and secondly that the legislative system is able to respond adequately and quickly to new needs or new political priorities which necessitate changes in the law[7]

Jan Fridthjof Bernt refers to both assumptions as unrealistic. He holds that it is an impossible task for the legislator to foresee and give precise directives for all possible legal problems and sees the legislative processes as commonly too slow and to inaccurate to serve as corrective tools when an established or presumed legal rule is considered obsolete.[8]

With regard to the first assumption it might be added that practical and technical circumstances may be a hindrance to a precise regulation of many issues. Within the socio-economic sphere the needs may appear in a variety of

[7] Jan Fridthjof Bernt, *Ibid.*, p. 195.

[8] *Ibid.*

ways and, similarly, they can be relieved in many different ways and at changeable standards. In addition, the technological development provides for an increasing number of new possibilities, not least with regard to health care, and often there is no other choice but that of leaving it to professionals to create the law on a step-by-step basis.

Financial considerations might also have an influence on the choice of language in statutory provisions. Some tasks within the socio-economic field are so resource demanding that the legislature may be tempted to leave it to local self-governing bodies to determine the standards with due consideration to local needs and local capacity, even if it would in fact be possible to give rather precise directives. In that way responsibility can be passed on to local bodies, while the legislature remains free to criticise the local authorities' discretion. In that context is has been pointed out that it may be advantageous for the State to 'get rid of' resource-demanding tasks under the pretext of promoting local self-government.[9]

In that context it seems relevant to refer to another tendency which has been identified in some countries in recent years.[10] What I refer to is the (bad) habit of passing restrictive legislation which is at the very edge of violating human rights but at the same time leaving the responsibility to keep within the limits of human rights to law-applying bodies. The legislation in question is typically open to the use of discretionary powers. However, the legislator gives no advice whatsoever on how to use the discretion. The legislator simply assumes in the preparatory works that the provisions in question will be applied in accordance with human rights obligations without, however, guiding law-applying bodies on how to avoid any violation of human rights.

Administrative bodies in the first instance are often not very knowledgeable with regard to human rights, and many people abstain from using existing remedies and put up with the initial decision in-stead. Moreover, considering the fact that the legislation in question is often worded in a way which indirectly proposes a very restrictive scope of application the risk (or chance?) of (un)intentional human rights violation is appreciable. However, if law-applying bodies do in fact have the necessary knowledge about human rights and choose to apply the provision in question in compliance with human rights, the legislature should not regard it with suspicion and consider whether or not the law has been disregarded. The legislature has expressly wanted an application

9 This issue is dealt with by Jan Fridthjof Bernt in "Kan kommunalt selvstyre og retssikkerhed forenes?" (The compatibility of legal security and local self-government) in *Lov og rett*, 1994, pp. 67–92 (on p. 89).

10 Cf. e.g Ida Elisabeth Koch and Jens Vedsted-Hansen, "International Human Rights and National Legislatures – Conflict or Balance" in *Nordic Journal of International Law*, Vol. 75, Issue 1, pp. 3–28.

of the legislation in compliance with human rights obligations despite the restrictive wording of the provision in question.

Thus, the wording of many socio-economic rights in vague and imprecise terms makes it hard to tell what the intention of the legislature was. The perception of the judiciary as "the mouth that pronounces the words of the law" becomes meaningless. The legislature has (deliberately) given up and left it to the professions to create the law on a case-by-case basis. The legislature *asks* for interpretation, and to claim that the judiciary interferes with the legislature by setting certain limits to the law making of the executive professions is accordingly ill founded. The legislature is to lay down the *general* guidelines, whereas responsibility for the *concrete application* falls under the executive. Dworkin's distinction between *concept* and *conception* might elucidate the fundamentally different character of these two activities:

> The contrast between concept and conception is here a contrast between levels of abstraction at which interpretation of the practice can be studied. At the first level agreement collects around discrete ideas that are uncontroversially employed in all interpretations; at the second the controversy latent in this abstraction is identified and taken up.[11]

While most human rights principles are undisputed or unchallenged at the abstract level (concept), disagreements will typically occur when these concepts are to be applied at the concrete level (conception). One thing is agreeing on a text; extending or applying the text in a concrete context is another. However, the law does not come into being without this interpretative process. The rule is merely a text – a combination of words – the meaning of which must be arrived at through interpretation. What characterises law is exactly this interplay between text, facts and the law-applying body or person, and the meaning of the text must furthermore be determined in the actual legal and social context within which it is interpreted.

This does not imply that (executive and) judicial bodies should not show respect for the fact that the budgetary competence first and foremost lies with political bodies – a consideration which is particularly important with regard to resource-demanding rights. However, all rights have costs,[12] and the distinction between norm application and resource allocation cannot be upheld to the full. To a certain extent they are two sides of the same coin, and democracy cannot function if the tripartite division of powers is to be understood as a water-tight distinction, cf. above in Chapter 4, Theoretical and Methodological Considerations about the hermeneutic relationship between the three powers.

---

[11] Ronald Dworkin, *Law's Empire*, Fontana Press 1986, p. 71.

[12] Stephen Holmes & Cass Sunstein, *The Cost of Rights: Why Liberty depends on Taxes*, W.W. Norton & Company, 1999, Chapter 1.

This conception of the relation between text and application and between legislative and judicial bodies is reflected e.g. in the well-known decisions of the Constitutional Court of South Africa in the *Grootboom* case and the *Treatment Action Case (TAC)*, both cases in which the *vertical* movement of the hermeneutic circle was decisive for the result.[13] The cases illustrate that it makes limited sense to talk about an *abstract* interpretation of the right to housing and the right to health in Articles 26 and 27 of the South African Constitution. What could be derived from the two provisions was general principles on the need for the housing and health policy to be *comprehensive*, *flexible* and *balanced*. The precise legal content of the provisions, however, found its expression in the concrete application i.e. in the encounter with concrete factual circumstances: a housing policy that provided no measures for those in desperate need of housing (*Grootboom*) and a prohibition to distribute a life-saving drug – offered free of charge by the pharmaceutical company – to new born babies of HIV infected women (*TAC*).

From this follows that a comparison between *concept* and *conception*– between legislation and application – is similar to a comparison between apples and oranges. Only to a certain extent does it make sense to discuss who has the final say – the legislature or the judiciary – since their rationality is not the same. The legality requirement known e.g. from criminal law cannot be satisfied, and the demand for legal security is of a different character in as much as the regulation does not relate to interferences. Under these circumstances, the role of the judiciary is not to be regarded a mechanic application of full-fledged norms. The judiciary is to function as an active, creative participant in the law-making process without which neither past and present nor norm and fact can interact coherently. To a certain extent the legislature and the judiciary function within each their legal spheres, although both activities, legislation and application, are to show respect for the same basic human rights principles.[14]

It is therefore consistent with respect for the democratic legitimacy of the legislature that the judiciary undertakes the task of judicial review, although the democratic legitimacy of the judiciary – if any – derives exactly from the legislature. The legislature presupposes that enactment is administered in accordance with human rights principles, and how is this to be controlled if not by the judiciary? Judicial supervision of legislative respect for basic rights can therefore be regarded as a necessity for democracy, and the independence

---

13 *Government of the Republic of South Africa and Others v. Grootboom and Others*, CCT 11/00 of 4 October 2000 (Constitutional Court of South Africa) and *Minister of Health and Others v. Treatment Action Campaign and Others*, CCT 8/02 of 5 July 2002 (Constitutional Court of South Africa).

14 For a more extensive analysis of these issues cf. e.g. Ida Elisabeth Koch, "The Justiciability of Indivisible Rights" in *Nordic Journal of International Law*, 2003, Vol. 72, No. 1, pp. 3–39.

of the judiciary together with the fact that courts do not act on their own motion weakens a supposition for partiality and politicisation. It is not for the judiciary, but for the individual citizen to decide when and why litigation is to occur, and it is for the parties to decide which arguments are to be presented to the court. Furthermore, the obligation to give reasons for its decisions provides considerable guarantee that the judiciary does not act *ultra vires*.

2.4 *Judicial Review of the Human Rights Compliance of Statutory Provisions*

2.4.1 *Initial Remarks*

As indicated above, the distinction between judicial review of the *application* of statutory provisions and judicial review of the provisions *as such* is often blurred. Concrete decisions may well have a general impact according to the demands of the situation. However, even unclear boundaries may sometimes be helpful, and the most difficult question to answer when discussing the issue of democracy and division of powers is indeed whether or not judicial review of the human rights compliance of statutory provisions as such is in compliance with democracy.

Thus, it cannot be explained away that judges are not democratically *elected* in the same way as parliamentarians, and that they do not represent the people in the traditional sense of the term. They do not group themselves in political parties, and they do not plunge into campaigns for their points of view. In COE Member States judges are typically *appointed*, and they are expected to be politically independent when conducting the legal tasks that are entrusted to them. It is hard to avoid the question how to justify that a group of not popularly elected judges have the competence to invalidate acts of parliament. How does one reconcile judicial review and democracy? There are several answers.

Before turning to this issue allow me a brief comment on the somewhat idealised picture of democracy that we like to pay tribute to. We often picture popularly elected politicians as the ones who take the initiatives, as people with a perfect overview over human rights case law and who deal with draft laws in all particulars. However, that is not the way politics works. Parliamentarians are not the ones who are at the helm. Rather, public officials in the ministries are the ones who have the overview and the knowledge, and they are also the ones who take the initiatives. Human rights issues are usually not discussed in parliaments. They have been settled previously in the ministries and one should not underestimate the importance of governmental power.

2.4.2 *A Representative Basis for Judicial Review*

Is has been argued that judicial review has democratic features after all. As regards constitutional review it has been asserted that the legitimacy lies in the fact that the legal basis for judicial review – the Constitution itself – is adopted by the people and/or its elected representatives. This perception was presented by Mr. Chief Justice Marshall in the famous US judgment from 1801, *Marbury v. Madison*, in the following way:

> That the people have an original right to establish, for their future government, such principles as, in their opinion, shall most conduce to their own happiness is the basis on which the whole American fabric has been erected. The exercise of this original right is a very great exertion; nor can it nor ought it to be frequently repeated. The principles, therefore, so established are deemed fundamental. And as the authority, from which they proceed, is supreme, and can seldom act, they are designed to be permanent.[15]

If the Constitution includes a human rights catalogue it may furthermore be contended that these rights have a greater democratic support than ordinary legislation, and a somewhat similar argumentation may be put forward with regard to human rights treaties. International human rights are not forced upon States. Rather, States themselves have positively decided to be bound by a certain set of norms, the observance of which is furthermore monitored by international bodies. When accepting to be bound by the ECHR, parliaments of the COE Member States have accepted to be bound not only by the substantial provisions of the Convention but also by the concrete decisions of the ECtHR. Thus, it could be argued that what restricts majority rule is not the existence of judicial review *per se*, but *human rights* – as part and parcel of the notion of democracy – whether deriving from domestic constitutions or international treaties. This line of arguing will be dealt with in further detail below in Section 2.4.4.

The people – the demos – referred to in this argument, however, is often a previous generation, and it seems somewhat strained to argue that this is where one is to find the democratic legitimacy of judicial review. That would correspond to an acceptance of being ruled by the dead. The people or their elected representatives must be entitled to change their minds, and if judicial review were to find its legitimacy in the people, it would have to be the existing people or their elected representatives.[16] If one were to attach any importance to the argument, it would be necessary to presume that the actual people or their elected representatives tacitly express their continuous support for the choices of previous generations by not taking initiatives to alter the state of law.

Most importantly, however, it should be emphasised that the norms subject to discussion – whether found in constitutions or in international human

---

[15] U.S. Supreme Court, *Marbury v. Madison*, 5 U.S. 137 (1803).

[16] L. B. Tremblay, "The legitimacy of judicial review: The limits of dialogue between courts and legislatures" in *International Journal of Constitutional Law*, Vol. 3, Issue 4, 2005, pp. 617–648 (on p. 621).

rights treaties – are vague and indeterminate. Thus, when arguing that judicial review finds its legitimacy in the popular will, one needs to remember that this will is most uncertain. The advice of Napoleon that a constitution should be "short and obscure" has indeed been followed not only in constitution making but also in the drafting of human rights treaties. Human rights catalogues in most constitutions and most human rights treaties are worded with little precision, and the above argument about the people's consent proves incoherent. With the expression of L. B. Tremblay it would "require constitutional norms to be carved in a democratic stone, but the text looks like an empty shell."[17] The assumption that basic rights can or should be literally applied without it being necessary for the executive or the judiciary to interpret the legislative *message* is without foundation in reality. Thus, the commitment to the rule of law does not provide a satisfactory justification of judicial review.

Robert Alexy's point of departure is that "[t]he only way to reconcile constitutional review with democracy is to conceive of it too, as representation of the people",[18] and he introduces the notion of *argumentative representation.* For judicial arguments to be representative from his point of view "a sufficient number of people must, at least in the long run, accept these arguments for reasons of correctness."[19]Accordingly, there are two fundamental conditions of true argumentative representation. These are:"1) the existence of sound or correct arguments, and 2) the existence of rational persons, that is persons who are able and willing to accept sound or correct arguments for the reason that they are sound or correct."[20] Robert Alexy holds that "[c]onstitutional review can be successful only if the arguments presented by the constitutional court are sound and only if a sufficient number of members of the community are able and willing to exercise their rational capacities:"[21]

> *If these conditions are fulfilled,* the answer to the question, raised above, as to why purely argumentative representation shall have priority over representation based on election and re-election is no longer difficult [author's emphasis].[22]

An outstanding question is, however, *if these conditions are fulfilled.* The first condition may not give rise to misgivings. The second condition, however, builds on a construction of "constitutional persons", who may exist in theory but not necessarily in practice. Most people have very little contact with the work of

[17] L. B. Tremblay, *Ibid.*, p. 622.

[18] Robert Alexy, "Balancing, constitutional review, and representation", *International Journal of Constitutional Law*, Vol. 3, Issue 4, 2005, pp. 572–581 (on p. 578).

[19] *Ibid.*, p. 580.

[20] *Ibid.*

[21] *Ibid.*

[22] *Ibid.*

the judiciary, and the idea of argumentative representation as a general answer to the question seems to me to be of greater theoretical than practical interest.

2.4.3 *Institutional Dialogue as Legitimising Judicial Review*

Another attempt to defend the legitimacy of judicial review from a democratic perspective relates to the question of who has the last word: the judiciary or the legislature? The argument is that even though the judiciary has the competence to strike down legislation it would always be possible for the legislature to reverse, modify or even avoid the decisions, taken by the judiciary. Admittedly, this is in many situations a valid argument. The judicial decision will tend to be 'negative' in the sense that it does not prescribe in 'positive' terms the legislation to be adopted. The judiciary will restrict itself to pointing out the unacceptable situation leaving it to the legislature to consider in which way to comply. Thus, when amending the legislation according to a judicial decision the legislature responds to the point of view of the judiciary. This response will often be satisfactory from a human rights point of view, thus settling the dispute to the satisfaction of both bodies: the judiciary and the legislature.

Moreover, the entire litigation process has been considered a dialogue between the judiciary and the legislature, and a whole theory of *institutional dialogue* has developed explaining how judicial review and democracy are in fact compatible.[23] Thus, it is argued that the judiciary and the legislature participate in a dialogue as regards the balancing of constitutional principles and public policies, a dialogue which has the effect of enhancing the democratic process, rather than denying it. Not only do the judiciary and the executive (the government) communicate during the legal process with a view to enlightening the disputed issues in the best possible way. The two branches also interact in the decision making. Thus, while the judiciary has the competence to evaluate whether or not the legislation in question is in compliance with human rights obligations, the government (and parliament) are often left with a wide scope when having to decide in which way the judicial decision is to be carried out. Proponents of the theory of institutional dialogue claim that judicial review would rarely raise "an absolute barrier to the wishes of the democratic institutions."[24] Rather, they would argue as follows:

> In the end, if the democratic will is there, the legislative objective will still be able to be accomplished, albeit with some new safeguards to protect individual rights and liberty. Judicial review is not a "veto over the politics of the nation", but rather the beginning of a dialogue as to how best to reconcile the individualistic values

[23] *Ibid.* with references and critical remarks.

[24] Cf. Peter W. Hogg and Alison Thornton in Peter W. Hogg & Allison A. Bushell, *The Charter Dialogue Between Courts and Legislatures (Or Perhaps the Charter of Rights Isn't Such A Bad Thing After All)*, Osgoode Hall, 1997, pp. 75–124 (on p. 81).

> of the Charter with the accomplishment of social and economic policies for the benefit of the community as a whole.[25]

Thus, judicial review is considered legitimate from a democratic perspective because the interaction between the two branches has the effect of making them somewhat accountable to one another. In this way the division of powers between the various bodies is not to be seen as a strict demarcation of territories but rather as 'positive' and democratic co-operation aiming at better protection of human rights.

The theory of institutional dialogue is of Canadian origin and has emerged conceptually out of the experience of Canadian constitutionalism under the Canadian Charter of Rights and Freedoms with its general and very far-reaching limitation clause and its extensive override clause.[26] Nevertheless, the idea that dialogue and democracy are closely intertwined is a commonly accepted perception, and institutional dialogue may occur wherever (domestic or international) judicial bodies have the competence to asses the human rights compliance of legislative work.

However, the interaction or dialogue between branches during a legal process hardly confers the necessary democratic legitimacy on the practice of judicial review. It has been asserted – and rightly so from my point view – that the dialogue or communication between the two branches – the legislature and the executive – does not aim at taking a collective decision, and that the "mere fact that judges, in constitutional cases, listen to the government and attend to its arguments does not necessarily mean that a deliberative dialogue is going on between the courts and the legislatures."[27] Moreover, whereas government and legislature are to find *general* political solutions to societal issues, the task of judges is to make *concrete* legal decisions. This does not necessarily prevent the branches from communicating, but to some extent they speak each their own language and have each their methodology and rationality. Thus, judicial review is governed by legal methodology and takes place in *concrete* cases according to judicial rules of procedure. Judges are e.g. to give reasons for judgments and decisions[28] and by governing the dialogue this "doctrine of judicial responsibility"[29] sets its own limits to legal decision making.[30]

---

[25] *Ibid.*, p. 105.

[26] The Canadian Charter of Rights and Freedoms, Articles 1 and 33. Cf. http://laws.justice.gc.ca/en/charter/index.html.

[27] Luc L. B. Tremblay, *Ibid.*, p. 635.

[28] ECHR Article 45 is worded as follows: "Reasons shall be given for judgments as well as for decisions declaring applications admissible or inadmissible."

[29] Luc. L. B. Tremblay, *Ibid.*, p. 634 ff.

[30] The limitations following from the doctrine of judicial responsibility may remove, however, some of the misgivings one might have with regard to judicial review and democracy understood as majority rule.

The legislative process is of course also governed by procedural rules. However, these rules are different rules putting limited restraint on the legislature with regard to substance, and even if one expects government and parliament to comply with human rights obligations, it is a fact that the legislature's task is different from that of the judiciary. The legislature is to find *general* political solutions to societal questions and problems.

The interaction between the branches should not be underestimated. However, there are cases in which there is very little room for dialogue, and "the doctrine of judicial responsibility" sometimes requires that the judiciary has to reach a decision, which leaves little or no room at all for revision or modification.[31] It does happen that parliaments adopt legislation contravening human rights, and it does happen that the specific legislative aim cannot be pursued in any other way without violating human rights. The judiciary sometimes *has* the last word, and the legislature will have to comply. The countermajoritarian viewpoint prevails.

However, that does not imply that the separation of powers between the branches can be delineated precisely. As already indicated above in Chapter 4 about Theoretical and Methodological Considerations it is hardly possible, let alone desirable, to make a sharp distinction between the legislature, the judiciary and the executive. When trying to delineate the area of competence of each of the three powers, regard should be had to that of the two others and vice versa. It is an illusion to separate powers completely. Thus, when considering the tripartite division of powers from a hermeneutic perspective, each element should be considered part of a greater whole – the democratic system as such – which in turn must be understood in terms of the elements; the legislative, the executive and the judicial powers. A hermeneutic community is, however, not necessarily identical with a decision-making community or a dialogue forum.

2.4.4 *Democracy and Human Rights – A Substantial Concept of Democracy*

If democracy is merely perceived of as a system of representative (popular) government, it might be difficult to accept the legitimacy of judicial review setting aside legislation as inconsistent with human rights. Thus, if one departs from this perception of democracy as nothing but free election and majority rule it is not difficult to follow the majority conclusion of e.g. the Norwegian democracy and power study according to which the domestic and international legalisation of politics leads to the withering or disintegration of representative government.[32]

---

31 Provided of course that the legal basis does not provide for override clauses like Article 33 in The Canadian Charter of Rights and Freedoms.

32 Cf. e.g. NOU 2003:19, *Makt og demokrati. Sluttrapport fra Makt-og demokratiutredningen*, Statens forvaltningstjeneste, Informationsforvaltning, 2003, p. 57 ff.

On the other hand, if a principle of legislative supremacy is understood to presuppose absolute judicial obedience to statute, it has as an implicit consequence an acceptance of the tyranny of the majority. Furthermore, the view deprives basic rights of their status as guidelines or limitations to the legislative power. Everything becomes debatable, and human rights seem to lose their *raison d'être.*

However, democracy is not necessarily identical with the rights of the majority.[33] Rather, a qualified concept of democracy presupposes respect for human rights,[34] sometimes defined exactly as limitations of majority action. Kaarlo Tuori goes as far as designating the majoritarian view as "a vulgar conception of the relationship between the courts and democracy."[35] Moreover, the ECtHR has several times stated that

> [....] democracy does not simply mean that the views of a majority must always prevail: a balance must be achieved which ensures the fair and proper treatment of minorities and avoids any abuse of a dominant position.[36]

When accepting this perception of democracy as the point of departure, the electoral unaccountability of the judiciary no longer serves as a restraint for judicial review. On the contrary one might argue in favour of judicial review exactly *because* judges are not accountable to the *majority*. Courts are accountable to the *people* – although not democratically elected – and function as a protective mechanism against the abuse of majority rule. Adjudication is therefore not to be regarded as an expression of judicial display of forces but rather as a protective measure.

Thus, in the discussion of human rights and democracy one has to take as a point of departure that human rights are meant exactly as barriers or bounds to political decision making, and that they would be deprived of their *raison d'être*, if judicial bodies were not to uphold them. Moreover, as already indicated, human rights treaties are not forced upon States but agreements entered into voluntarily with a view to limiting the free display of forces and establishing obligations to take certain measures for the protection of human rights.[37]

---

[33] Cf. David Beetham, *Democracy and Human Rights,* Polity Press, 2000, p. 18ff.

[34] Beetham sees the connection between democracy and human rights as an intrinsic rather than extrinsic one, in the sense that "human rights constitute a necessary *part* of democracy", *Ibid.* p. 92. In this context Beetham's human rights concept is synonymous with civil and political rights. However, according to Beetham, "a democratic society, then, requires both the institutions of private property and free exchange, *and* the guarantee of basic economic rights, if it is to be founded upon a general consent", *Ibid.*, p. 102.

[35] Kaarlo Tuori, *Critical Legal Positivism*, Ashgate, 2006, p. 233.

[36] Cf. e.g. *Sørensen v. Denmark and Rasmussen v. Denmark*, Judgment of 11 January 2006, para. 58 with reference to previous case law.

[37] Admittedly, an issue with regard to division of powers arises because of the wording of many human rights in imprecise terms. Human rights norms must to be subject to interpretation

The fact that democracy and human rights are closely interlinked has also found expression e.g. in the Preamble to the UDHR from 1948. It emphasises that it is "essential, if man is not to be compelled to have recourse, as a last resort, to rebellion against tyranny and oppression, that human rights should be protected by the rule of law." Similarly, in the preamble of the ECHR the States Parties consider the UDHR and reaffirm "their profound belief in those fundamental freedoms which are the foundation of justice and peace in the world and are best maintained on the one hand by an effective political democracy and on the other by a common understanding and observance of the human rights upon which they depend."

Even though it is not expressly said in the Preamble to the ECHR that effective human rights protection requires a democratic system of government, the ECtHR seems to have interpreted the Preamble as if it did. The Court has held e.g. that the Convention is "an instrument designed to maintain and promote the ideals and values of a democratic society",[38] and that "[d]emocracy thus appears to be the only political model contemplated by the Convention and, accordingly, the only one compatible with it."[39]

When discussing the issue of human rights and democracy it is of course also important to mention the limitation clauses in the ESC/RESC and the ECHR[40] according to which interferences with the rights protected under the Conventions shall be in accordance with the law and *necessary in a democratic society* for the consideration of various interests such as the economic well-being of the country, the protection of health or morals or the protection of the rights and freedoms of others. Moreover, the foundation of a State on the belief that it should be "a democracy capable of defending itself"[41] has been recognised in several judgments as creating a legitimate aim of an interference or differential treatment of an individual citizen:[42]

---

and their legal content will necessarily have to be established continuously in case law. The distinction between law application and law making therefore seems blurred. However, when interpreting human rights norms, judicial bodies must take into consideration that their task is different from that of the legislature, and that an acceptance of judicial review as a necessary corrective to majority rule does not legitimise any judicial law-making activity whatsoever.

[38] Cf. *Kjeldsen et al. v. Denmark*, Judgment of 7 December 1976, para. 53.

[39] Cf. *United Communist Party of Turkey and Others v. Turkey*, Judgment of 30 January 1998, para. 45.

[40] Cf. ESC article 31 (1), RESC Article G (1) and e.g. ECHR Paragraph 2 to Articles 8–11.

[41] Cf. Ida Elisabeth Koch and Jens Vedsted-Hansen, "International Human Rights and National Legislatures – Conflict or Balance?" in *Nordic Journal of International Law*, Vol. 75, Issue 1, pp. 3–28 (on p. 6).

[42] Cf. e.g. *Vogt v. Germany, Judgment of 26 September 1995* and *Sidabras and Džiautas v. Lithuania*, Judgment of 27 October 2004. Both judgments are referred to in greater detail in Chapter 9 about Workers' Rights under the ECHR.

> In view of the very clear link between the Convention and democracy [....] no one must be authorised to rely on the Convention's provisions in order to weaken or destroy the ideas and values of democratic society. Pluralism and democracy are based on a compromise that requires various concessions by individuals or groups of individuals, who must sometimes agree to limit some of the freedoms they enjoy in order to guarantee greater stability of the country as a whole [....].[43]

The interdependence between human rights and democracy, however, goes further. Thus, some of the provisions of the ECHR are not only best *maintained* by effective political democracy, as it is expressed in the Preamble to the ECHR. Rather, they are *preconditions* for democracy. Thus, some civil-political rights such as freedom of expression, of assembly and association and the duty of States Parties to hold free elections are important ingredients in the introduction and preservation of democracy without which the concept loses its intention.[44]

The link between democracy and socio-economic rights is usually regarded as much weaker than the link between civil-political rights and democracy, if recognised at all. However, one might argue that the prospects of democracy are poor if the population is impoverished and illiterate, thus unable to make use of its participatory rights. One might also remember that the growth of the Western Welfare State has to a wide extent served as a safeguard of democracy. Likewise, labour-related issues have attracted the attention of the international community due to the fact that conditions of labour may involve "such injustice hardship and privation to large numbers of people as to produce unrest so great that the peace and harmony of the world are imperilled."[45] The passage resembles the one from the Preamble to the UDHR in which the General Assembly emphasises that "it is essential, if man is not to be compelled to have recourse, as a last resort, to rebellion against tyranny and oppression, that human rights should be protected by the rule of law." Finally, it may be argued that the wording of the second paragraph of e.g. Articles 8–11 of the ECHR seems to presuppose that *democracy* may necessitate the interference with civil and political rights for the consideration of *social* demands. Thus, democracy may have a substantial content. Kaarlo Tuori holds as follows:

> Constitutional basic rights and human rights confirmed in international treaties impose restrictions on the power of the legislature and other state organs and bring thus into effect the law's self-limitation. In addition, both at the national and at the international level, institutional arrangements have been created to guarantee compliance with the Constitution and/or international human-rights

[43] *Refah Partisi and Others v. Turkey*, Judgment of 13 Februar 2003, para. 99.

[44] Cf. ECHR Articles 10 and 11 and Article 3 (a) of Protocol No. 1.

[45] Preamble to the Constitution of the International Labour Organisation, 1919, para. 2.

> agreements in the enactment, application and enforcement of the law. In this regard we can speak of *legal practices specialised in the self-limiting function of the law.*[46]

This perception of law as self-limiting is shared by Henning Koch, who in an article about the right of resistance defines substantial democracy in the following way:

> Substantial democracy (in a legal sense) is defined as a societal arrangement in which political democracy under judicial control 1) must be limited due to respect for certain ethical/political ideas and 2) must exercise its competence with a view to realising these values [my translation from Danish].[47]

In the following discussion, I will take my point of departure in a substantial perception of democracy.

3 *The ECHR as the Custodian of Substantial Democracy*

Departing from a substantial perception of democracy indeed makes it easier to defend the integrated approach of the ECtHR. Yet, an issue with regard to division of powers does arise because of the wording of many human rights in imprecise terms. That pertains particularly to the socio-economic elements of human rights, which are, moreover, often rather resource demanding.

Thus, the need for interpretation of human rights norms may create the impression that the Court interferes with domestic political matters. It is often argued that the Court's very dynamic interpretation of the Convention and its Protocols has widened the scope of the Convention and that the Contracting Parties' sovereign powers have been restricted to a degree which was unpredictable at the time of the conclusion of the treaty. And it *is* true that the Court has gone very far. The Court has indeed developed a very dynamic style of interpretation – not least in the protection of what has become known as 'positive' rights under the Convention. Nor does the Court recognise the classical distinction between 'positive' and 'negative' rights or socio-economic rights and civil-political rights, and it has dealt with issues that are traditionally regarded as belonging under another human rights convention – namely the ESC/RESC. The perception that the ECHR is only about non-interference with certain rights has been abandoned long ago. The Court deals with 'positive' obligations as independent obligations and recognises that the obligation not to interfere may require 'positive' measures. There is no water tight division

---

[46] Kaarlo Tuori, *Ibid.*, p. 229.

[47] Henning Koch, "Modstandsret – en europæisk demokratiforestilling" in Henning Koch og Anne Lise Kjær (eds.) *Europæisk retskultur – på dansk*, Thomson Publ., 2004, p. 101.

between economic, social and cultural rights and civil and political rights – as the Court held back in the seventies[48] – or as it is expressed in a number of more recent judgments:

> The boundaries between the State's positive and negative obligations do not lend themselves to precise definitions.[49]

Not least Article 8 about the right to protection of home, family life and private life has been subject to a very dynamic protection alone or in particular in conjunction with the non-discrimination clause in Article 14. The Court has gone very far in accepting issues as falling 'within the ambit' not only of Article 8 but also of Article 1 of Protocol No. 1 about the right to property. Various child benefits, parental benefits and other cash benefits have been considered falling 'within the ambit' of Article 8 or Article 1 of Protocol No. 1, and in some cases the Court has found that these articles in conjunction with Article 14 were violated, cf. Chapter 8 about The Right to Social Cash Benefits under the ECHR.

It appears far reaching, but if these differences were not reflected in the interpretation of what falls under the scope of the concept of e.g. possession, it would in fact have as a consequence that e.g. a heavily taxed Dane would enjoy less protection under the ECHR than a person from a country with a tradition for privately-funded social benefit schemes and a much lower level of taxation. In this way the equality principle has an impact also on the interpretation of the notion of possession.

This very dynamic interpretation of Article 14 has been the subject of criticism.[50] It has been asserted that the interpretation is incompatible with the wording and the context of Article 14, and it has been suggested that the Court retreats from this reading of the article and moreover from the wide recognition of 'positive' obligations. However, to me it would seem a bit strange if today we were to criticise an interpretation which goes back to 1970 as far as the recognition of 'positive' obligations is concerned and to 1968 as far as the interpretation of Article 14 is concerned. Moreover, the interpretation has been repeated time and again, and I would be inclined to say that the interpretation was recognised by the States Parties many years ago, and that the criticism is simply raised too late in the day.

Without the doctrine about 'positive obligations' we are left with the classical distinction between 'negative' and 'positive' rights as belonging in each

48 *Airey v. Ireland*, para. 26. Cf. above in Chapter 2 about Typological and Terminological Considerations.

49 E.g. *Pibernik v. Croatia*, para. 65.

50 Cf. Jens Elo Rytter, "Går menneskeretsdomstolen for vidt? – fortolkning og retsskabelse i Strasbourg." (Is the Human Rights Court going too far ?– Interpretation of Law-making in Strasbourg) in *Juristen* 2006, pp. 9–19.

their treaty, and in this context it is worth noticing the wording of the Convention. Article 1 and also Article 14 apply the term *secure* about the nature of the obligation and, moreover, speak of *rights* and freedoms. The terms *secure* and *rights* have a rather 'positive' ring.[51]

I do not find it surprising either that Article 14 is applicable if the subject matter 'falls within the ambit' of one of the substantial articles of the Convention. Otherwise, we would have to ask what Article 14 is all about. If we do not accept the interpretation, Article 14 is nothing more than an explanation of how we are to understand the expressions 'no one' or 'everyone' in the substantial articles of the Convention.

But of course one can ask whether the Court goes too far, and one may particularly ask how the integrated approach harmonises with traditional perceptions of division of powers? If one takes as a point of departure the dichotomous perception of the two sets of rights, it would seem as if the Court when applying the integrated approach goes far beyond the scope of the Convention. Thus, it could be argued and probably will be argued sooner or later that the Court interferes with the very socio-economic rights that many Contracting States have not been willing to recognise as legal rights within the framework of the ESC/RESC or the CESCR. As such the integrated approach might be subjected to even stronger criticism than the one which has otherwise fallen to the Court's share with regard to respect for domestic legislatures and with regard to setting the triviality threshold for what should be considered a human rights violation. Thus, it cannot be explained away that the Court's case law bears heavily upon the competence of the Contracting Parties with regard to resource allocation not only in concrete cases with manageable consequences but also at the general level.

On the face of it, such criticism seems justified. However, a description of the Court as neglectful of the primary competence of the domestic legislature in matters of resource allocation is misleading. Thus, case law leaves no doubts that the Court entrusts the Contracting Parties with an even very wide margin when financial interest are at stake. The Grand Chamber's judgment in the *Hatton* case concerning the balancing of the economic interest of the United Kingdom in night flying to and from Heathrow Airport and the suffering of the local population from sleep disturbances is indeed an illustration of this reticence.[52]

Likewise, a wide margin is recognised if a common ground has not been established with respect to the disputed issue. Thus, in the *Petrovic* case

---

[51] The limitation clauses to e.g. Articles 8–11 also make a distinction between *rights* and *freedoms*.

[52] About *the Hatton cases*, cf. Chapter 5 about The Right to Health under the ECHR, Section 2.3.

concerning fathers' right to paid parental leave the Court did *not* find that the applicant's rights under Article 8 in conjunction with Article 14 had been violated for the exact reason that there was no common standard at the material time as regards parental leave allowance for fathers. The *Stec* case about social rights as possession in the sense of Article 1 of Protocol No. 1 also provides a very good illustration of the Court's reticence in such resource-demanding cases, cf. above in Chapter 8 about The Right to Social Cash Benefits under the ECHR. One of the main reasons for the Court's not finding a violation was "the extremely far-reaching and serious implications, for women and for the economy in general [....]."[53] Such matters fall within the State's margin of appreciation.

Moreover, the Court seems to be very meticulous not to solve the entire question as to how a certain right is to be interpreted and implemented in order to adjudicate the particular case. The Court tries to be as concrete as possible. In the *Niedzwiecki* case about differential treatment between holders of different categories of residence permits with regard to child benefits the ECtHR emphasises that:

> The Court is not called upon to decide *generally* to what extent it is justified to make distinctions, in the field of social benefits, between holders of different categories of residence permits. Rather it has to limit itself to the question whether the German law on child benefits *as applied in the present case* violated the applicant's rights under the Convention [author's emphasis].[54]

In general, case law leaves no doubts that the ECtHR entrusts the Contracting Parties with an even very wide margin of appreciation in cases concerning general policies such as social, economic and environmental planning. The Court has repeatedly held that national authorities are generally better placed to take into account local needs and economic possibilities, and it would be fair to say that the margin of appreciation tends to widen the more 'positive' the obligation and the more vital the economic interest of the Contracting Party. Likewise, a wide margin is recognised if a common ground has not been established with respect to the disputed issue.

In this context it would also be relevant to mention another development in the Court's practice, namely that of putting greater emphasis on procedural protection. There is a tendency not least in cases concerning interferences in family life under Article 8 that the Court focuses on whether the measures complained of have been decided and implemented in accordance with adequate standards of administrative and judicial procedures. In cases where such procedures have *not* been applied e.g. if the affected family members have not

---

[53] *Stec and others v. the United Kingdom*, Judgment of 12 April 2006, para. 65.

[54] *Niedzwiecki v. Germany*, para. 44

been involved in the decision-making procedure this is often considered a violation *per se* without the Court finding it necessary to scrutinise the substantive basis of the interference. We see the same tendency under Articles 2 and 3 not least in Turkish cases about killings, disappearances, torture and inhuman treatment in which the Court has found that failure of the Turkish authorities to conduct an adequate investigation of alleged violations in itself is enough to constitute a violation of the Convention.[55]

Sometimes this approach is necessary because of difficulties with establishing what the factual circumstances were. However, it happens that the Court applies the approach even if it *is* possible to clarify the factual circumstances. That may be due to the heavy case load placed on the Court, but the phenomenon – proceduralisation – may also be perceived of as a way of granting States an extra margin of appreciation so to say. It might be a mechanism of exercising judicial self-restraint and emphasising the *domestic* responsibility for the effective protection of human rights.[56]

But procedural failure may of cause also lead to an intensified examination, and there may be cases in which the Court goes very far and maybe too far. However, there may also be cases in which the Court does not go far enough. I suppose that we can all of us think of cases that we dislike for one reason or the other.

The most pertinent question, however, is of course whether we can say something in general about where to draw the line.[57] What is the yardstick? Indeed, the Vienna Convention on the Law of Treaties is a good point of departure, but it should be recalled that the ECHR has a special status compared to international law as such because it is a human rights treaty with its own control machinery. According to Article 31 about the general rules of interpretation

1. A treaty shall be interpreted in good faith in accordance with the ordinary meaning to be given to the terms of the treaty in their context and in the light of its object and purpose.
2. The context for the purpose of the interpretation of a treaty shall comprise, in addition to the text, *including its preamble* and annexes [author's emphasis]:

Admittedly, the Vienna Convention puts emphasis on the *ordinary meaning*. But it is a mistake to claim that the purpose of the Convention and the context do not come into play before we are done with the wording. Rather, Article 31

55 Cf. Ida Elisabeth Koch and Jens Vedsted-Hansen, *Ibid.*

56 *Ibid.*

57 I have previously dealt with this issue, cf. *Human rights: A conflict between positive individual and collective democratic interests?*, Boom Juridische uitgevers, 2008, pp. 7–45.

speaks of the ordinary meaning to be given to the terms of the treaty *in their context and in the light of its object and purpose.*

Thus, what is relevant is the wording – the ordinary meaning – in a context and included in this context is the Preamble. And the ECtHR has chosen to place considerable emphasis on the purpose of the treaty and has, on that basis, gradually developed the style of interpretation that we know today. When speaking about the Vienna Convention on the Law of Treaties it is also relevant to emphasise that in Article 31 (3) it mentions as part of the context:

> (b) any subsequent practice in the application of the treaty which establishes the agreement of the parties regarding its interpretation;
> (c) any relevant rules of international law applicable in the relations between the parties.

Hence, (b) reflects the fact that the Court's interpretation is evolutionary rather than revolutionary, i.e. that the Court builds its decisions on previous case law. And with regard to (c) I might add that one of the relevant rules which is applicable in the relations between the parties is exactly the ESC/RESC to which the Court refers quite often – not least in cases concerning the interpretation of Article 11 about the freedom of assembly and association. It happened most recently in the judgment *Rasmussen and Sørensen v. Denmark,*[58] i.e. the judgment which did away with closed shop clauses on the private Danish labour market, cf. Chapter 9 about Work-Related Rights under the ECHR. Also this judgment has been criticised for being too far reaching because the wording of Article 11 according to the preparatory works of the Convention deliberately deviates from UDHR Article 20 according to which

> Everyone has the right to freedom of peaceful assembly and association. *No one may be compelled to belong to an association* [author's emphasis].

However, the ECSR – the primary body monitoring the States Parties' compliance with the ESC/RESC – has for many years held the viewpoint that closed shop agreements are in non-keeping with Article 5 of the ESC/RESC which is the social counterpart to ECHR Article 11. One can say that the two bodies are now in agreement with regard to the interpretation of the two provisions as regards closed shop agreements. In that context it is less interesting that ECHR Article 11 is deliberately formulated differently from Article 20 of the UDHR. According to the Vienna Convention's Article 32, preparatory works belong in the category of "supplementary means of interpretation."

Finally, if we were to accept the perception that the Court has gone very far and maybe too far in its interpretation of the Convention, the question would have to be raised whether the States Parties have accepted the Court's

58 *Rasmussen and Sørensen v. Denmark.*

interpretation in connection with the later adoption and ratification of a series of Protocols. I am thinking primarily of Protocol No. 11 about the restructuring of the control machinery. In the Preamble one will find the following reasoning:

> Considering the urgent need to restructure the control machinery established by the Convention *in order to maintain and improve the efficiency of its protection of human rights and fundamental freedoms*, mainly in view of the increase in the number of applications and the growing membership of the Council of Europe [author's emphasis];

The passage may be read as if the Contracting Parties affiliate themselves with the Court's previous interpretation and that they want the Court to proceed by protecting human rights in the same way as it has done until now.

All things considered, I do not find the normative development within the COE to be a threat to democracy. On the contrary, international human rights obligations must be seen as part of the foundation of democracy, and this fundamental function of human rights in democracy presupposes the current interpretative evolution of these norms, as illustrated by the hermeneutic and integrated approach gradually developed over the years by the ECtHR.

4 *Justiciable Socio-Economic Elements of Human Rights*

4.1 *Introductory Remarks*

The integrated approach to human rights protection proves that the classical dichotomous perception of the two sets of rights, socio-economic rights and civil-political rights is misleading. However, integration does not by magic dissolve the boundaries between the two sets of rights, nor does it provide us with definite answers in regard to the justiciability issue. The fact that social elements of civil rights can be considered justiciable by applying a hermeneutic – and thereby integrated – approach does not necessarily entail the justiciability of *social* rights when they appear alone. He who cannot link his need to a civil right – because he is *only* hungry, homeless or sick – cannot invoke the integrated approach, and even *if* a link to a civil right can be established, a certain nearness or proximity must be required for the integration to be legally acceptable.[59] Considerations in regard to coherence and integration – as core

[59] Cf. e.g., *Botta v. Italy*, Judgment of 24 February 1998 about a disabled man's asserted right to gain access to the beach and the sea. The Court found that the right asserted "concerns interpersonal relations of such broad and indeterminate scope that there can be no conceivable direct link between the measures the State was urged to take in order to make good the omissions of the private bathing establishment and the applicant's private life", cf. para. 35.

elements in hermeneutic thinking – do not imply that 'anything goes'. The *legal community's communicative qualification norm* sets its own limits for the creativity of the legal analysis. However, in this specific context the communicative qualification norm does not have a very distinct content even if we delineate the analysis to COE Member States. COE Member States have rather different traditions of constitutional protection, and even within the EU there are different opinions with regard to the justicability of socio-economic rights.

However, judicial bodies influence one another, and what we witness these years is in fact a transnational dialogue on the issue of justiciability not only between legal scholars but also between judicial bodies worldwide.[60] A speculative answer might be that adjudication of socio-economic rights is no longer an entirely domestic issue. Judicial bodies influence one another, and one cannot exclude that the acceptance of justiciability in one context will have an indirect bearing in other contexts, as it contributes to the gradual softening of the strict categorisation of rights as belonging either in the socio-economic or the civil-political sphere. Judge Albie Sachs from the South African Constitutional Court may be right when predicting that 21st-century jurisprudence will "focus increasingly on socio-economic rights."[61] Therefore, I intend to try to present some general remarks about the issue of justiciability and division of powers with regard to socio-economic rights.

4.2 *From 'Rechtsstaat' Paradigm to Welfare State Paradigm*

When discussing these issues one might take into consideration at which end of the continuum the obligation in question belongs, cf. the notion of waves of duties referred to in Chapter 2 about Typological and Terminological Considerations. Thus, there is a difference between asking for *protection* of something already existing such as a house or a job and asking for the *provision* of the same good. Neither of the two demands is entirely cost free. However, protecting someone against illegal eviction is usually less resource demanding than providing someone with housing.

When moving along the continuum towards an increasingly active and resource-demanding obligation we sooner or later leave the '*Rechtsstaat*' or *Rule of law paradigm* and move to a *Welfare State paradigm*.[62] Within this

---

[60] Modern technology has provided us with valuable tools for taking this dialogue further on its way, cf. e.g. www.echr-net.org, which includes a database of legal jurisprudence on economic, social and cultural rights.

[61] A. Sachs, "Social and Economic Rights: Can they be made Justiciable?" 53 *Southern Methodist University Law Review*, 2000, Issue 4., pp. 1381–1391.

[62] Cf. also Ida Elisabeth Koch, "The Justiciability of Indivisible Rights" in *Nordic Journal of International Law*, 2003, Vol. 72, Issue 3, pp. 3–39.

paradigm, the point of departure is no longer that the right was originally (fully) enjoyed, but rather that the right is not enjoyed for one reason or the other. The provision of socio-economic rights to those who have nothing implies that States take active and resource-demanding steps with the view to enabling them to enjoy these rights, and it goes without saying that this obligation is normally the most resource demanding.

The *Welfare State obligation* is also the one that raises most difficulties when discussing the division of powers between the judiciary and the legislature, and the apparent lack of attention to traditional concerns of division of powers that seems to be part of the integrated approach can probably be explained. The obligatory link of the social need to a civil right limits the budgetary consequences of the integrated approach, and the very *concrete* character of the integrating judicial decisions will often exempt judicial bodies from taking a stand on issues such as the existence of a *general* minimum core right to housing or health care – issues that are traditionally regarded as core issues for democratically elected politicians.[63] Moreover, even though civil rights encompass (social) elements, they have their centre of gravity at the less demanding end of the continuum whereas it is the other way around as regards socio-economic rights. Accordingly, it is clear that the accepted justiciability of civil rights cannot automatically be 'transferred' to social rights. The issue of division of powers is particularly important as regards the socio-economic rights which require active resource-demanding measures.

As indicated in Chapter 2 about Typological and Terminological Considerations the issue today is not *whether* judicial bodies have a say in disputes concerning resource- demanding issues but *where* to draw the line between judicial and legislative powers when the disputed measures are resource demanding and the legal basis vaguely worded. Case law from various parts of the world provides an abundance of proof that socio-economic rights are justiciable to some extent and the issue is rather whether or not it is possible to say something more specific about the justiciable elements.

4.3 *Identification of Possible Justiciable Socio-Economic Elements*

In Chapter 4 about Theoretical and Methodological Considerations, I take the view that law must be seen as 'unfinished', as being in constant motion reflecting an ever-increasing part of a complex and changeable factual reality. Also, the perception of interpretation as application, which leads in fact to an amalgamation of law and facts, indirectly suggests that it is hardly possible to

[63] I deliberately say "*often* exempts the Court ", since some of decisions do in fact have a general character. By way of example, some of the decisions referred to in Chapter 8 on The Right to Social Cash Benefits under the ECHR have far-reaching budgetary implications.

categorise the situations in which a judicial body is ready to consider a certain right or element of a right justiciable. Moreover, the rejection of *dichotomies* and *trichotomies* to the advantage of *waves of duties* in Chapter 2 about Typological and Terminological Considerations contradicts the assumption that justiciable elements can be captured in neat categories. Furthermore, the five chapters on various socio-economic elements of the ECHR do not leave an unambiguous picture. Given the fact that the factual reality is highly complex and changeable it would seem illogical if law was unambiguous and static.

Nevertheless, it is presently commonly recognised that human rights encompass justiciable elements of a socio-economic character, and the question as to which are exactly these justiciable socio-economic elements has not been exhausted. Some speak of minimum core rights as justiciable rights together with the prohibition against discrimination, whereas it is more uncertain whether the obligation to progressively realise economic, social and cultural rights, cf. e.g. CESCR Article 2(1) is justiciable. The ICESCR, however, has identified a number of rights in the CESCR as justiciable. Thus, in a general comment the Committee establishes that a number of rights under the Covenant such as equal rights of men and women, the right to equal remuneration, trade union rights and the right to primary education are justiciable:

> In addition, there are a number of other provisions in the International Covenant on Economic, Social and Cultural Rights, including articles 3, 7 (a) (i), 8, 10 (3), 13 (2) (a), (3) and (4) and 15 (3) which would seem to be capable of immediate application by judicial and other organs in many national legal systems. Any suggestion that the provisions indicated are inherently non-self-executing would seem to be difficult to sustain.[64]

In a later general comment about the domestic application of the Covenant, the Committee adds that most socio-economic rights encompass justiciable dimension, without, however, indicating what kind of dimensions:

> While the general approach of each legal system needs to be taken into account, there is no Covenant right which could not, in the great majority of systems, be considered to possess at least *some significant justiciable dimensions*. It is sometimes suggested that matters involving the allocation of resources should be left to the political authorities rather than the courts. While the respective competences of the various branches of government must be respected, it is appropriate to acknowledge that courts are generally already involved in a considerable range of matters which have important resource implications. The adoption of a rigid classification of economic, social and cultural rights which puts them, by definition, beyond the reach of the courts would thus be arbitrary and incompatible with the principle that the two sets of human rights are indivisible and interdependent. It would also drastically curtail the capacity of

[64] CESCR *General Comment No. 3*, The nature of States parties' obligations (Art. 2, par.1), 14 December 1990, para. 5.

> the courts to protect the rights of the most vulnerable and disadvantaged groups in society [author's emphasis].[65]

While I perfectly agree that socio-economic rights encompass justiciable dimensions, I find the reasoning of the Committee rather poor. The Committee seems to presuppose exactly what is to be proven, namely that the notion of indivisibility has a legal content. Something similar goes for the last part of the explanation concerning the protection capacity of the courts. The justiciability discussion is exactly about the issue whether or not courts are to enforce socio-economic rights for the benefit of the most vulnerable and disadvantaged groups in society.

Although I am sceptical from the outset, I will try to follow along the lines of some of those who have tried to capture the notion of justiciability in categories with a view to increasing the protection of socio-economic demands.

It is indeed true that quite many cases concern the denial of socio-economic rights on the basis of one of the prohibited grounds of discrimination. Case law from domestic courts and from international treaty bodies is so convincing that one might group these cases as a specific category. The HRC, the ECtHR and also domestic courts bodies examine allegations of discrimination on a regular basis and judging from case law the examination is quite thorough.[66] The possible budgetary consequences for the States Parties do not seem to cast a damper on the intensity of the examination. In this context is has been argued that the legislative reply to established human rights violations because of discrimination is 'down equalising' i.e. decreasing the service or benefit in order not to increase the total expenses and yet be able to provide the rights and services to a wider group. However, this avenue may often not be open due to legitimate expectations, political considerations and also prohibitions against retrogressive action.

As another possible category, it has been discussed whether or not judicial bodies will be able to establish the minimum core of a right in the sense of a minimum decency threshold. A question in this context is whether this minimum standard is to be understood as a global standard common for all UN Member States or whether domestic standards should be established reflecting the economic situation of the country in question.[67] The ICESCR seems to take

---

65 CESCR *General Comment No. 9*, The domestic application of the Covenant, 3 December 1998, para. 10.

66 Cf. the examples in Chapter 8 on The Right to Social Cash Benefits under the ECHR.

67 Cf. B.A. Andreassen et al., "Assessing Human Rights Performance in Developing Countries: The Case for a Minimal Threshold Approach to the Economic and Social Rights" in B.A. Andreassen and A. Eide (eds.), *Human Rights in Developing Countries* 1987/1988, 1988, Akademisk Publ. pp. 333–355.

its point of departure in a global definition of minimum core rights. Thus, in an early general comment the Committee holds as follows:

> On the basis of the extensive experience gained by the Committee, as well as by the body that preceded it, over a period of more than a decade of examining States parties' reports the Committee is of the view that a minimum core obligation to ensure the satisfaction of, at the very least, minimum essential levels of each of the rights is incumbent upon every State party. Thus, for example, a State party in which any significant number of individuals is deprived of essential foodstuffs, of essential primary health care, of basic shelter and housing, or of the most basic forms of education is, prima facie, failing to discharge its obligations under the Covenant. If the Covenant were to be read in such a way as not to establish such a minimum core obligation, it would be largely deprived of its raison d'être.[68]

Against this understanding it has been countered that a global standard is of limited practical importance to Western Welfare States and the obligation in Article 2 (1) of the CESCR can easily be interpreted as a relative obligation containing also a demand for domestic minimum standards, cf. the expression "to the maximum of its available resources." However, the Committee is hardly in a position to establish exactly what should be the minimum core right to health, housing and social cash benefits in each and every Member State, and one should hardly expect any guidelines from the Committee to that effect. In its concluding observations the Committee has chosen a very cautious friendly dialogue approach. The Committee speaks of progressive realisation, of minimum core rights and non-discrimination as not being subject to progressive realisation, but is usually only *concerned* – maybe even *deeply concerned*. However, the Committee seldom speaks of violations and many States Parties pay no attention to its recommendations. Rather, in the reporting procedure the Committee encourages the States Parties to establish minimum thresholds themselves. E.g. in a Concluding Observations about Denmark the Committee express the following regrets:

> The Committee regrets the absence of disaggregated statistical data on the extent of poverty in the State party's report, particularly among refugees and the immigrant population, and notes that *the State party has yet to adopt an official poverty line*, which would enable the State party to define the extent of poverty and to monitor *and evaluate progress in alleviating poverty* [author's emphasis].[69]

Thus, CESCR Article 2 (1) may be understood as imposing an obligation on each State Party to define its own national minimum standard, and maybe one can say that the Committee has also delegated to the domestic level the competence to monitor that the standard is observed. The obligations deriving

[68] CESCR *General Comment No. 3*, The nature of States parties obligations (Art. 2, par.1), 14 December 1990, para. 10.

[69] *Concluding Observations of the CESCR : Denmark*, 14 December 2004, para. 20.

from CESCR Article 2 are relative and comparisons of the protection level should not be made *among* States but rather *within* States, depending on the resources available and depending on actual demands. It is crucial to separate the lack of commitment from that of incapacity, and the conventional cross-national comparisons should be replaced by cross-temporal assessments, i.e., assessments of the situation in the country against its own past.

In this context it would be relevant to mention the more operational approach of the ECSRs. The following passage is from one of the most recent conclusions concerning the Danish *starting allowance*, a social cash benefit paid at a very low rate to primarily refugees and immigrants:

> The Committee notes from Eurostat that the poverty threshold in Denmark defined as 50 % of median equivalised income corresponded to about 808 € per month in 1999.
>
> [....]
>
> In view of the poverty threshold referred to above and taking into account that the starting allowance falls below this threshold for several of the target groups concerned, the Committee considers this allowance to be inadequate when assessed in isolation. However, pending further information on the value of supplementary benefits [....] it reserves its position as to the conformity of the situation.[70]

Thus, here we have a regional poverty threshold which takes into consideration that the income levels in COE countries are very different. I suppose that similar common regional and maybe even global thresholds could be established with regard to other rights as well, although I assume that a numerical formula would be difficult to establish with regard to at least some socio-economic rights. However, here we are approaching an issue which is beyond my knowledge.[71]

I have no knowledge either about the extent to which governments throughout the world have established such minimum standards or decency thresholds. Domestic judicial bodies, however, have not been very keen on establishing minimum core rights positively in the sense that they have hesitated to define the exact level of a certain right. E.g. the South African Constitutional Court in *Grootboom* did not find itself in a position to define the minimum core right to housing and chose instead to undertake a reasonableness review resulting in the conclusion that the initiatives taken to solve the South African housing

[70] *Conclusions XVII-1 (Denmark)*, 2004, at Article 13.

[71] Cf. e.g. Paul Hunt, "State Obligations, Indicators and Benchmarks, and the Rights to Education" in *Human Rights Law and Practice*, 1998, Vol. 4, No. 2, pp. 109–115, Katarina Tomasevski, "Indicators" in Asbjørn Eide et al. (eds.), *Economic, Social and Cultural Rights – A Textbook*, 2nd Revised Edition, Martinus Nijhoffs Publ, 2001, pp. 531–562.

problem were inadequate. One can say that the court recognised the legal relevance of Amartya Sen's notion of *metarights*[72] when concluding that the measures taken to pursue the goal – that everyone has the right to have access to housing – were not reasonable as required under Article 26 (2) of the South African Constitution.[73] Budgetary constraints may have the implication that individuals cannot be given the right to housing. However, they still have the right "to have *policies* p *(x)* that genuinely pursue the objective of making the right to *x* realisable", *x* in this case being housing.

This understanding is reflected in several cases from the Constitutional Court of South Africa in which the Court has found certain measures inadequate to address e.g. the rights of the most disadvantaged[74] without, however, involving itself in subsequent policy considerations, and the approach might very well be followed by other States as the reasonableness requirement must be considered an inherent part of human rights law in general. The reasonableness approach, however, need not be a metarights approach. One example is the Norwegian Supreme Court's judgment in the *Fusa* case concerning the validity of a decision limiting the amount of home care and domestic help to a disabled senior citizen.[75] The Norwegian Supreme Court recognised that Fusa Municipality had far-reaching discretionary powers as far as the extent of the service was concerned. However, despite the fact that the municipal economy was overstretched, the Supreme Court found that the municipality was obliged to respect a certain minimum level of social services. The Supreme Court, however, did not define this minimum. The message sent was more like: "This is not good enough. Try again". Thus, the Norwegian Supreme Court understood its role as that of determining whether the right to social services had been violated and left to the municipality the choice of determining which means to remedy the situation would be the most appropriate.

The reasonableness test can be regarded as a manifestation of the possibility of judicial bodies' review of rights subject to progressive realisation. In this sense the reasonableness test can be considered a stronger proof of the justiciability of socio-economic rights than the one claiming that adjudication is only relevant with regard to minimum core rights and the prohibition against discrimination since these demands are not subject to progressive realisation. However, when discussing a situation in terms of progressive realisation one usually presumes that there is a (not very well-defined) minimum threshold and that progress is made *beyond* the level of this minimum. The homeless

[72] Cf. Amartya Sen, *Ibid.*

[73] *Government of the Republic of South Africa and Others v. Grootboom and Others*, para. 32ff.

[74] C.f. also *Minister of Health and Others v. Treatment Action Campaign and Others.*

[75] Supreme Court Judgment of 25 September 1990, reported in *Rettstidende* (Norwegian Legal Magazine) 1990, p. 874ff.

people in the *Grootboom* case were in a desperate situation having literally no roof over their heads, and it is hard to think of a more desperate housing problem than the one that befell these people. Hence, if the *Grootboom* case – in which absolutely nothing was done for the homeless people – is to be read as an illustration of what progressive realisation requires, one cannot avoid asking 'what is left' for the minimum core obligation. It is hard to do less for homeless people than what was done in *Grootboom*.

However, the reasonableness review may be compatible with the notion of minimum core rights. Only, it requires that progressive realisation is not perceived of as something that comes after or builds upon the minimum core standard of the right in question. Rather, the progressive realisation must be understood as beginning with nothing, passing by the minimum threshold and proceeding until the right is fully realised, if that moment ever occurs. When establishing that the measures taken are not reasonable, the judicial body in question may at the same time be of the perception that the measures fall below the minimum threshold without, however, defining it 'positively'. The choice of the reasonableness aproach is probably first and foremost due to a preference for establishing what is *not* good enough rather than embarking on the policy choices as to what *is*. In this way it is possible to obtain a balance between basic social values and concrete policy choices and express recognition of and respect for the tasks of the legislature.

Another issue, however, is whether it is expedient to apply a minimum core approach to justiciability. Bruce Porter is probably right when arguing as follows:

> By contrast, a minimum core approach to justiciability tends to divorce rights claims from individual circumstances and unique interests that may be at stake. It shifts the focus of a claim from the particular relationship between a rights claiming community and government to a more abstract debate about quantifiable universal entitlements and minimum obligations of governments to all citizens, in which a court is understandably reluctant to engage.[76]

The reasonableness standard on the other hand gives room for a more contextualised and hermeneutic approach to human rights violations which prevents the particular of the individual case from being squeezed into preconceived perceptions and strict categories. Moreover, the reasonableness standard has the advantage that it also captures the essence of non-discrimination. Thus a differential treatment is discriminatory if it does not have an "objective and reasonable justification", which in turn may be the case if it does not pursue a

---

[76] Bruce Porter, "The Crisis of ESC Rights and Strategies for Addressing It" in John Squires et al. (eds.), *The Road To A Remedy – Current Issues in the Litigation of Economic, Social and Cultural Rights*, UNSW Press, 2005, pp. 43–69 (on p. 52).

legitimate aim" or if there is no "reasonable relationship between the means employed and the aim sought to be realised."[77]

Hence, it might be advantageous to give up trying to classify the justiciable elements of vague and resource-demanding rights and content oneself with an overall reasonableness standard. The indicators or 'bearing points' one will have to search for and apply in order to do full justice to the particularities of the individual case vary from case to case and the justiciable elements of a certain right can hardly be categorised or classified on a general basis. As already discussed in Chapter 2 about Typological and Terminological Considerations human rights obligations are neither dichotomous nor trichotomous but rather to be captured in Waldron's metaphor: waves of duties. It may disturb our sense of order and desire to classify. However, the quality of human rights protection will hardly suffer.

[77] Cf. e.g., *Abdulaziz, Cabales and Balkandali v. the United Kingdom*, Judgment of 28. May 1985, para. 72. See also Appendix to Article E of the RESC according to which "a differential treatment based on objective and reasonable justification shall not be deemed discriminatory."

Chapter 11

The Relation between the ECHR and the ESC/RESC

1 *Initial Remarks*

In previous chapters I have illustrated how and why the ECtHR by applying an integrated hermeneutic approach to human rights interpretation has been able to read a variety of socio-economic elements into the substantial provisions of the ECHR. Moreover, I have drawn attention to the fact that the Court on several occasions has chosen an interpretation of the ECHR which harmonises with the sister treaty body, the ECSR's interpretation of the ESC/RESC.

The time has now come to address the reverse relation namely that of the impact of the ECHR on the interpretation of the ESC/RESC. Thus, as already indicated in Chapter 1 the notion of indivisibility can easily be understood as something more than the protection of socio-economic demands under conventions primarily protecting civil-political rights. It might also make sense to talk about the protection of civil-political demands under socio-economic rights. In addition, it might be worth while touching upon the issue of overlapping protection between the two treaties and considering which of the two gives the better protection. Moreover, as the two treaties are both COE bodies, thus having their roots in the same legal culture and tradition, it seems relevant to analyse the style of interpretation of the ECSR in order to see to which extent this body and the ECtHR do in fact belong to the same legal community, cf. Chapter 4 about the legal community's communicative qualification norm.

Arguably, this exercise has greater theoretical than practical interest. Civil and political rights are already given judicial protection under the ECHR and the CCPR, and one might not expect that protection under the collective complaints procedure to the ESC/RESC would add much to the already existing judicial protection. However, it cannot necessarily be taken for granted that the protection of civil-political demands is always better under the ECHR than the ESC/RESC.

As indicated in Chapter 1 case law under the collective complaints procedure[1] is rather sparse at the present stage. As of 1 January 2009, 53 cases have been lodged. Most of them have been declared admissible, and as of the same date, 39 cases had been considered on their merits. Making comparison with the overwhelming amount of case law under the ECHR would be completely reckless, and a lack of balance in the presentation is unavoidable. It follows that the present chapter can only give a very cautious, tentative and provisional idea of where the ECSR is heading.[2]

2 *The ECSR's Style of Interpretation*

The ECSR did not initiate its examination of cases under the collective complaints procedure by presenting its overall view on human rights interpretation. However, already in case No. 1 about the prohibition of child labour under Article 7 the ECSR established that:

> the *aim* and *purpose* of the Charter, being a human rights protection instrument, is to protect rights *not merely theoretically, but also in fact*. In this regard it considers that the satisfactory application of Article 7 cannot be ensured solely by the operation of legislation if it is not *effectively* applied and rigorously supervised [....] [author's emphasis].[3]

Thus, the *aim and the purpose* of the Charter is to provide an *effective human rights protection* which takes into consideration the factual circumstances, and

[1] In 1995, the Council of Europe adopted a Protocol Providing for a System of Collective Complaints, ETS No. 158. This Protocol came into force in 1998 and as of 7 October 2008, 14 of the Member States who have ratified either the original Charter from 1961 or the revised Social Charter from 1996 have accepted to be bound by the Collective Complaints Procedure. According to this procedure various organisations are entitled to submit complaints. i.e. international organisations of employers and trade unions, other international NGOs with consultative status under the COE and representative national organisations of employers and trade unions. The same applies to other national NGOs with particular competence, if the State in question has declared that it recognises this right. Finland is to my knowledge the only country to have made such a declaration.

[2] For literature about the ESC/RESC and the collective complaints procedure, cf. e.g. David Harris and John Darcy, *The European Social Charter*, 2nd. Edition, Transnational Publishers Inc., 2001 and Robin R. Churchill and Urfan Khaliq, "Violations of Economic, Social and Cultural Right, The Current Use and Future Potential of the Collective Complaints Mechanism of the European Social Charter" in Mashood A. Baderin and Robert Mccorquodale (eds.), Economic, Social and Cultural Rights in Action, 2007, Oxford University Press, pp. 195–240.

[3] Complaint No. 1/1998 by the *International Commission of Jurists against Portugal*, Decision of 9 December 1999, para. 32 with reference to Conclusions XIII-3.

the passage fits neatly into the style of interpretation of the ECtHR. A similar statement was made in case No. 6.[4]

In case No. 8, to which I shall return later, the Quaker Council for European Affairs claimed that the duration of civilian service was in con-compliance with Article 1 (2) of the Charter about the right of the worker to earn his living in an occupation freely entered upon. The Greek Government recalled that Article 4 (3)(b) of the ECHR about forced labour expressly excludes all military service and any other alternative service from the scope of the protection. The Committee responded to this argument in the following way:

> The Committee states in response that it takes account of Article 4 para 3 b) of the European Convention on Human Rights when interpreting Article 1 of the European Social Charter. Accordingly, the obligation to perform military service or, for conscientious objectors, the obligation to perform civilian service instead of military service cannot, as such, be considered a form of forced labour, contrary to Article 1 para. 2.[5]

Thus, the Committee – like the ECtHR – applies an integrated approach, taking into account the very much similar provision under the ECHR when interpreting Article 1(2) of the Charter.

Similarly, in case No. 13 about discrimination with regard to education the ECSR observes that Article E of the RESC "is almost identical to the wording of Article 14 of the European Convention on Human Rights."[6] Accordingly, the Committee leans on the interpretation of the ECtHR in the following way:

> As the European Court of Human Rights has repeatedly stressed in interpreting Article 14 and most recently in the Thlimmenos case [....] the principle of equality that is reflected therein means treating equals equally and unequals unequally.[7]

In this way the Committee subscribes to the interpretation of Article 14 of the ECHR and recognises that Article E of the Charter also encompasses indirect discrimination. The Committee adds that:

> [....] indirect discrimination may arise by failing to take due and positive account of all relevant differences or by failing to take adequate steps to ensure that the rights and collective advantages that are open to all are genuinely accessible by and to all.[8]

---

[4] Complaint No. 6/1999 by the *Syndicat national des professions du tourisme against France*, Decision of 10 October 2000, para. 26.

[5] Complaint No. 8/2000 by the *Quaker Council for European Affairs (QCEA) against Greece*, Decision of 25 April 2001, para. 22.

[6] Complaint No 13/2002 by *Autism – Europe against France*, Decision of 4 November 2003, para. 52.

[7] *Ibid.*

[8] *Ibid.*

Moreover, as from case No. 11 the Committee structures the decisions in a way which is closer to that of the ECtHR with subsections named: 'Procedure', 'Submissions of the participants in the procedure', 'Relevant domestic law', 'As to the law' and 'Conclusion'.[9]

Notions such as *proportionality* and *margin of appreciation* appear in early case law from the Committee. E.g. the issue in case No. 12 was whether a compulsory so called wage monitoring fee was in compliance with the right not to join a trade union under Article 5 of the Charter, an issue which could also arise under ECHR Article 11. The majority of the Committee concluded that monitoring fees did not entail compulsory unionism. The majority set forth some general remarks about the issue, but claimed not to be in a position to verify the use of the fees and in particular to verify to what extent the fees were *proportional* to the costs of the service carried out and to the benefits for the workers. They concluded as follows:

> The Committee considers therefore that it is for the national courts to decide the matter in the light of the principles the Committee has laid down on this subject or, as the case may be, for the legislator to enable the courts to draw the consequences as regards the conformity with the Charter and the legality of the provisions at issue.[10]

The Committee, however, reserved the right "to supervise the situation in practice through the reporting procedure and, as the case may be, the collective complaints procedure."[11] Although not applying the term *margin of appreciation*, the approach of the Committee clearly indicates the recognition of this notion.[12]

In a separate opinion two Committee members agreed that States Parties should enjoy "a wide margin of appreciation in their choice of the means to be employed"[13] when seeking to achieve a proper balance between the competing interests in the labour market. They even referred to case law from the ECtHR, namely *Gustafsson v. Sweden*. However, by applying another typical term of the ECtHR, they concluded that "the monitoring fee does not *strike at the very substance* of the right not to join a trade union as protected by Article 5."[14]

---

[9] Cf. Complaint No. 11/2000 from *European Council of Police Trade Union against Portugal*, Decision of 21 May 2002.

[10] Complaint No. 12/2002, the *Confederation of Swedish Enterprise against Sweden*, Decision of 15 May 2003, para. 42.

[11] *Ibid.*, para. 43.

[12] Already in *Quaker Council for European Affairs (QCEA) against Greece* the Committee subscribes to the notions of proportionality and margin of appreciation, cf. paras. 24–25.

[13] *Confederation of Swedish Enterprise*, Separate opinion of Mr Konrad Grillberger and Mr Matti Mikkola.

[14] *Ibid.*

Case No. 14 was the opportunity for the ECSR to make some general remarks about interpretation of the Charter. The case concerned foreign nationals unlawfully resident in the country for less than three months, and the International Federation of Human Rights Leagues (FIDH) claimed that it was a violation of Articles 13 and 17[15] of the Charter that these foreign nationals were entitled only to medical treatment for emergencies and life threatening conditions. The matter subject to interpretation was the Appendix to the RESC which reads as follows:

> 1. [....] the persons covered by Articles 1 to 17 and 20 to 31 include foreigners only in so far as they are nationals of other Parties lawfully resident or working regularly within the territory of the Party concerned, subject to the understanding that these articles are to be interpreted in the light of the provisions of Articles 18 and 19.
>
> This interpretation would not prejudice the extension of similar facilities to other persons by any of the Parties.

When deriving the legal content from this provision the Committee took as its point of departure Article 31 (1) of the Vienna Convention on the Law of Treaties according to which a treaty "shall be interpreted in good faith in accordance with the ordinary meaning to be given to the terms of the treaty in their context and in the light of its object and purpose." The Committee continued as follows:

> The Charter was envisaged as a human rights instrument to complement the European Convention on Human Rights. It is a living instrument dedicated to certain values which inspired it: dignity, autonomy, equality and solidarity. The rights guaranteed are not ends in themselves but they complete the rights enshrined in the European Convention of Human Rights.
>
> Indeed, according to the Vienna Declaration of 1993, all human rights are "universal, indivisible and interdependent and interrelated" (para. 5). The Committee is therefore mindful of the complex interaction between both sets of rights.
>
> Thus, the Charter must be interpreted so as to give life and meaning to fundamental social rights. It follows inter alia that restrictions on rights are to be read restrictively, i. e. understood in such a manner as to preserve intact the essence of the right and to achieve the overall purpose of the Charter.[16]

The passage illustrates that the Committee is a strong advocate of an integrated (hermeneutic) approach to human rights interpretation and places strong emphasis on basic values. The Committee goes on as follows:

---

[15] Article 13 is about the right to social and medical assistance. Article 17 is a general provision on the rights of children.

[16] Complaint No. 14/2003 by the *International Federation of Human Rights Leagues (FIDH) v. France*, Decision of 8 September 2004, paras. 27–29.

> The restriction attaches to a wide variety of social rights in Article 1–17 and impacts on them differently. In the circumstances of this particular case, it treads on a right of fundamental importance to the individual since it is connected to the right to life itself and goes to the very dignity of the human being. Furthermore, the restriction in this instance impacts adversely on children who are exposed to the risk of no medical treatment.
>
> Human dignity is the fundamental value and indeed the core of positive European human rights law – whether under the European Social Charter or under the European Convention of Human Rights and health care is a prerequisite for the preservation of human dignity.[17]

Thus, human dignity requires active and resource-demanding measures under the ECHR and the ESC/RESC, and the Committee concluded its interpretation of the Appendix by stating that "legislation which denies entitlement to medical treatment to foreign nationals within the territory of a State Party, even if they are there illegally, is contrary to the Charter."[18]

With regard to the alleged violation of Article 13 the Committee expressed its doubts. Given the existence of a form of medical assistance, the Committee concluded that France did not violate Article 13. With regard to Article 17, however, the Committee referred to the CRC which "protects in a general manner the rights of children and young persons, including unaccompanied minors, to care and assistance."[19] Hence, with regard to children the Committee found that because of the three months' residence requirement, and the limited amount of medical care (emergencies and life threatening conditions) the situation was not in conformity with Article 17.

This interpretation of the Charter is indeed far reaching, and it is not surprising that some members of the Committee distanced themselves from the decision. They claimed that the Vienna Convention does not support an interpretation in contradiction to the explicit wording of the Charter.[20]

Fortunately, I do not have to take sides. I do, however, endorse the underlying interpretative principle that Article 31 (1) of the Vienna Convention does allow for an interpretation beyond the wording, cf. above in Chapter 4. Furthermore, I consider the case a very good illustration of the Committee's wish to apply a similar style of interpretation as that of the ECtHR. As a curiosity, I can add that as from case No. 14 and onwards the Committee – like the ECtHR – applies the Latin abbreviation *v.* in stead of *against*. Thus, the name of the case is *International Federation of Human Rights Leagues (FIDH) v. France.*

---

[17] *Ibid.*, paras. 30–31.

[18] *Ibid.*, para. 32.

[19] *Ibid.*, para. 36.

[20] *Ibid.*, Dissenting opinion of Mr. Stein Evju joined by Mrs Polonca Koncar and Mr Lucien Francois and Dissenting opinion of Mr Rolf Birk.

Also, in case No. 15 about itinerant Roma people and their right to housing under Article 16 of the Charter,[21] the ECSR developed further its integrated approach. The Committee emphasised that "the right to housing permits the exercise of many other rights – civil and political as well as economic, social and cultural rights."[22] Moreover, the Committee underlined that Article 16 of the Charter "contains similar obligations to Article 8 of the European Convention of Human Rights."[23] And even though Article 16 of the Charter has a far more 'positive' content than Article 8 of the ECHR, the Committee nevertheless found it relevant to bring the following quotation from the Connors case,[24] referred to above in Chapter 6:

> The vulnerable position of gypsies as a minority means that some special consideration should be given to their needs and their different lifestyle both in the relevant regulatory framework and in reaching decisions in particular cases [....]. To this extent, there is thus a positive obligation imposed on the Contracting States by virtue of Article 8 to facilitate the gypsy way of life [....].[25]

The emphasis on the ECHR is all the more notable as the ECtHR in the Connors case and the other cases about Roma people did *not* find a violation of Article 8 of the ECHR, whereas the ECSR in the present and other similar cases established that Article 16 of the Charter was violated. Thus, by applying a kind of reasonableness test[26] the Committee concluded that "Greece had failed to take sufficient measures to improve the living conditions of the Roma" and that "a significant number of Roma are living in conditions that fail to meet minimum standards [....]".[27] Thus, the estimate that 100,000 Roma live in sub-standard housing was corroborated by information from other bodies,[28] and it was not "convincingly denied by the Government."[29]

---

21 Article 16 runs as follows: "With a view to ensuring the necessary conditions for the full development of the family, which is a fundamental unit of society, the Parties undertake to promote the economic, legal and social protection of family life by such means as social and family benefits, fiscal arrangements, provision of family housing, benefits for the newly married and other appropriate means."

22 Complaint No. 15/2003 by *European Roma Rights Center v. Greece*, Decision of 8 December 2004, para. 24.

23 *Ibid.*, para. 25.

24 *Connors v. the UK*, Judgment of 27 May 2004, para. 84.

25 Complaint No. 15/2003, *European Roma Rights Center v. Greece*, Decision of February 2005, para. 20.

26 Cf. Chapter 10.4.3.

27 *Ibid.*, para. 42.

28 Speaking of integration, these 'other bodies' referred to in a footnote in para. 40, were the ICESCR, the UN Committee against Torture and ECRI (the European Commission against Racism and Intolerance), all of whom have expressed concern about the way in which Greece has dealt with the housing situation of Roma people in Greece.

29 *Ibid.*, para. 40.

The integrated approach of the ECSR continues in a series of complaints about corporal punishment of children all lodged by the World Organisation against Torture under Article 17 of the Charter. According to its wording Article 17 does not specifically forbid corporal punishment. However, under Article 17 (1) (b) the Contracting Parties undertake to take all appropriate measures including the establishment or maintenance of appropriate institutions or services "to protect children and young persons against negligence, violence or exploitation."

In the first case No. 17 regarding the situation in Greece, the Committee recalled its interpretation of Article 17 in the General Introduction to Conclusions XV-2 (Vol. 1, 2001) [....] and went on as follows:

> The Committee furthermore recalls that the Charter is a living instrument which must be interpreted in light of developments in the national law of member states of the Council of Europe as well as relevant international instruments.[30]

Thus, once again the Committee reminds us that the Charter – like the ECHR – is a living instrument, and the international instruments of relevance to the interpretation of Article 17 of the Charter in particular are the following:

a. Article 19 of the United Nations Convention on the Rights of the Child and case-law as interpreted by the Committee on the Rights of the Child;[31]
b. Article 3 of the European Convention on Human Rights as interpreted by the European Court of Human Rights (*inter alia* Tyrer v. the United Kingdom, 1978, as regards judicial birching of children, Campbell and Cosans v. the United Kingdom, 1982, as regards corporal punishment inflicted at school and A v. the United Kingdom, 1998, as regards parental corporal punishment);[32]

The Committee, moreover, referred to the following soft law instruments in its interpretation of Article 17 of the Charter:

c. Recommendation No. R (93) 2 on the medico-social aspects of child abuse adopted by the Committee of Ministers on 22 March 1993; Recommendation No. R (90) 2 on social measures concerning violence within the family adopted by the Committee of Ministers on 15 January 1990; Recommendation No. R (85)4 on violence within the Family adopted by the Committee of Ministers on 26 March 1985;

[30] Complaint No. 17/2003, by *World Organisation against Torture ("OMCT") v. Greece*, Decision of 7 December 2003, para. 31.

[31] For information about the interpretation of Article 19, cf. e.g. Sharon Detrick, *A Commentary on the United Nations Convention on the Rights of the Child*, Martinus Nijhoff Publishers, 1999.

[32] Complaint No. 17/2003, *Ibid.*

d. Recommendation 1666 (2004) "Europe-wide ban on corporal punishment of children" adopted by the Parliamentary Assembly on 24 June 2004.

On this basis the Committee concluded that its case law "is to the effect that the prohibition of all forms of violence must have a legislative basis."[33] With regard to the concrete situation in Greece the Committee concluded by ten votes to three that Greek legislation did not explicitly and effectively prohibit corporal punishment of children, and that Greek legislation did not comply with the requirements of the Charter.

In case No. 18 concerning the situation in Ireland the Committee developed further its interpretation of Article 17 of the Charter conceivably in order to convince the members of the Committee who had dissenting opinions in the case concerning Greece. The Committee held as follows:

> As to Article 17 of the Revised Charter, the wording of Article 17§1 b, *inter alia* specifically mentions protection from "violence". The Committee therefore has to interpret the meaning of this provision and define its scope and the precise rights it guarantees to individuals. The Committee also considers as the European Court on Human Rights has done in respect of the European Convention on Human Rights, that a teleological approach should be adopted when interpreting the Revised Charter, i.e. it is *necessary to seek the interpretation of the treaty that is most appropriate in order to realize the aim and achieve the object of the treaty, not that which would restrict to the greatest possible degree the obligations undertaken by the Parties.*
>
> The Committee sets out its reasoning on the substance of the issue below, but by way of preliminary remarks the Committee recalls that when it stated the interpretation to be given to Article 17 in 2001 [....], it was influenced by an emerging international consensus on the issue and notes than since this consensus is stronger. As regards its reference to the UN Convention on the Rights of the Child, the Committee recalls that this treaty is one of the most ratified treaties, and has been ratified by all member states of the Council of Europe including Ireland, and therefore it was entirely appropriate for it to have regard to it as well as the case law of the UN Committee on the Rights of the Child [author's emphasis].[34]

The emphasised part of the quotation stems from case law of the ECtHR.[35] Thus, the Committee endorses the teleological approach of the ECtHR and reminds us that case law of the CRC must be taken into consideration given the fact that the CRC is one of the most ratified – if not *the* most ratified – of all human rights Conventions.

---

33 *Ibid.*, para. 32.

34 Complaint No. 18/2003, *World Organisation against Torture ("OMCT") v. Ireland*, Decision of 7 December 2004, paras. 60–61.

35 Cf. *Wemhoff v. Germany*, Judgment of 27 June 1968, As to the law, para. 8.

For some reason or other the above passage was not repeated in the three following cases. In one of the cases the Committee found a violation of the Charter,[36] in the two others no violation was found.[37]

The limited case law under the collective complaints procedure makes it difficult to conclude on the style of interpretation of the ECSR. However, so far it seems as if the Committee and the ECtHr do in fact belong to the same legal community, and the collective complaints procedure has given the ECSR the opportunity to develop further as a judicial body. Both treaty bodies consider their treaties living instruments aiming at providing effective human rights protection, and they both apply a contextual, integrated approach including other human rights instruments when relevant. Also, it seems as if the ECSR has really aimed at becoming the sister body of the ECtHR by referring to the ECHR whenever relevant, and that the Committee has subscribed to the interpretative principles developed over the years by the ECtHR.

3 *Overlapping Protection between the ECHR and the ESC/RESC*

3.1 *Introductory Remarks*

Although the protection of social rights under the ECHR is quite comprehensive, it is clear that it cannot match the protection under the ESC/RESC. There are indeed cases in which the ECSR can provide a much better protection under the Charter than the ECtHR can do on the basis of the ECHR. Complaint No.14 about the right of illegal immigrants to health care services may serve as one example.[38] The Roma cases about the right to housing may serve as another.[39] However, there is a considerable overlap between the two treaties, and the present section seeks to identify some of this overlap. I intend to take my point of departure in case law from the collective complaints procedure and subsequently consider whether the same or a similar protection could be obtained on the basis of the ECHR.

---

[36] Complaint No. 21/2003, *World Organisation against Torture ("OMCT") v. Belgium*, Decision of 7 December 2007.

[37] Complaint No. 19/2003, *World Organisation against Torture ("OMCT") v. Italy*, Decision of 7 December 2004 and Complaint No. 20/2003, *World Organisation against Torture ("OMCT") v. Portugal*, Decision of 7 December 2004.

[38] Complaint No. 14/2003 by the *International Federation of Human Rights Leagues (FIDH) v. France*, Decision of 8 September 1999.

[39] Cf. e.g. Complaint No. 15/2003, *European Roma Rights Center v. Greece*, Decision of 8 December 2004 and Complaint No. 27/2004 *European Roma Rights Center v. Italy*, Decision of 7 December 2005.

3.2 *Work-Related Rights*

It is commonly known that the ESC/RESC gives a comprehensive protection with regard to workers' rights to just conditions of work, safe and healthy working conditions, a fair remuneration, the right to organise and the right to bargain collectively.[40] The Contracting Parties are under an obligation to take a variety of active measures for the benefit of workers – some of which have far-reaching budgetary consequences – and it is beyond doubt that the ECHR does not come anywhere near to the ESC/RESC with regard to the safeguarding of workers' rights.

There is, however, a considerable overlap in the protection of the two conventions. The issue of the right to organise and the right to collective bargaining has already been touched upon in Chapter 9, and the issue of forced labour will be touched upon below in Section 4. A few other cases, however, are worth mentioning in order to delineate some of the (possible) overlapping areas of the two conventions with regard to work-related issues.

In case No. 9/2000[41] *Confédération Française de l'Encadrement CFE-CGC v. France* the complainant argued i.e. that the French regulation on working hours for managerial staff was in non-compliance with Article 2 (1) of the RESC according to which the Contracting Parties undertake to provide for reasonable daily and weekly working hours. According to the structure of the French working hours' regulation, the weekly rest period must be for 35 consecutive hours in addition to the daily rest period of at least 11 hours. However, there was no specific limit to weekly working time, the implication being that the managerial staff could risk working for up to 78 hours a week. The ECSR held as follows:

> The Committee is of the view that this length of working time is manifestly excessive and therefore cannot be considered reasonable within the meaning of Article 2 para. 1 of the revised Social Charter.[42]

Case No. 10, *Tehy ry and SSTK ry against Finland* dealt with the issue of just conditions of work cf. Article 2 (4) of the ESC according to which the Contracting Parties undertake "to provide for additional paid holiday or reduced working hours for workers engaged in dangerous or unhealthy occupations as prescribed." The complainant alleged that Finland was in breach of this provision on the grounds that hospital personnel engaged in occupations

---

[40] Cf. ESC/RESC Articles 1–6.

[41] Complaint No. 9/2000, *Confédération Française de l'Encadrement CFE-CGC v. France*, Decision of 16 November 2001.

[42] *Ibid.*, para. 31.

where they are exposed to ionising radiation were no longer entitled to additional paid leave.

The Committee recalled that Article 2 (4) leaves to the Contracting Parties "a certain latitude in the choice of occupations to be classed as dangerous and unhealthy."[43] By referring to previous Conclusions the Committee, however, held that exposure to ionising radiation generally poses a health risk to workers and others. The Committee went on by referring to the point of view of the International Commission on Radiological Protection [the ICRP] that "even small radiation doses may produce some deleterious health effects" and that "stochastic (random) effects (such as the probability of cancer or genetic detriment) cannot be completely avoided because no threshold can be invoked for them."[44] With regard to the concrete situation the Committee recognised that "in Finland workers in the health sector in radiation-related occupations are exposed to doses of radiation well below the maximum limits stipulated in domestic legislation and agreed internationally [....]."[45] Nevertheless, the Committee concluded as follows:

> However in light of the evidence, in particular the current recommendations of the ICRP, the Committee considers that at present it cannot be stated that exposure to radiation even at low levels is completely safe. It finds no reasons to alter its case law, namely that work involving exposure to ionising radiation is covered by Article 2 para. 4. Therefore radiation-related work in the health sector in Finland must be considered as being dangerous and unhealthy within the meaning of Article 2 para. 4 of the Charter. This being the case, workers in this sector should be entitled to additional paid holidays or reduced working hours.[46]

Now, the question is whether it is likely that a parallel protection could be obtained e.g. on the basis of Article 8 of the ECHR on respect for private life. I do not see why not. The Court would hardly be as specific as the ECSR with regard to which measures should be applied to remedy the violation. However, it is worth noticing that the Committee's conclusion leaves a certain appreciation to the Member States, and considering the Court's case law concerning environmental health, it cannot be excluded that the Court would reach a somewhat similar conclusion, cf. above in Chapter 5.

A question can also be raised with regard to Complaint No. 6/1999. In this case the applicant alleged in its complaint that all the bodies offering guided tours within the remit of the Ministry of Culture and Communication, the museums of fine arts, the towns and regions belonging to the Villes et Pays

---

[43] Complaint No. 10/2000, *Tehy ry and STTK ry against Finland*, Decision of 17 October 2001, para. 20.

[44] *Ibid.*, para. 24.

[45] *Ibid.*, para. 26.

[46] *Ibid.*, para. 27.

d'Art et d'Histoire network, and the National Fund for Historic Monuments and Sites discriminate between, on the one hand, lecturer guides approved by these bodies and, on the other, interpreter guides and national lecturers with a state diploma. The SNPT further claimed that this discrimination resulted in a denial of the right to work for interpreter guides and national lecturers with a state diploma.[47]

As to the question whether the two professional categories were in comparable situations, the Committee noted that "approved lecturer guides and the interpreter guides and national lecturers with a state diploma are people qualified to conduct guided visits who have followed officially defined training, and who are entitled to a professional card such as is required to conduct tours in museums and historic monuments under the terms of the Act of 13 July 1992."[48]

The Committee also noted that the French Conseil d'Etat had ruled that the services rendered by lecturers to so-called "free" groups could not on the whole be regarded as differing significantly from, and are thus comparable to, those received by users of the visits organised by the Louvre Museum.[49] In this light the Committee found that the two categories were comparable categories for the purposes of Article 1 (2) of the RESC about the right to work. According to this provision the Contracting Parties undertake "to protect effectively the right of the worker to earn his living in an occupation freely entered upon." As to the assessment of whether the differential treatment was reasonable and objective the Committee answered this question in the negative. Accordingly, the differential treatment constituted discrimination in employment to the detriment of interpreter guides and national lecturers with a state diploma.

The facts of the case were a great deal more complicated and detailed than what appears from the above presentation. However, the issue here is only to give as much knowledge of the case which is necessary to consider the question as to whether or not similar facts could lead the ECtHR to a similar conclusion on the basis of e.g. Article 8 of the ECHR either alone or in conjunction with Article 14.

Against the background of the Court's case law on access to work, cf above in Chapter 9, there is hardly anything that would prevent the Court from dealing with similar issues. What was at stake was a simple question of non-discrimination, and accordingly, there seems to exist an overlapping protection between the two conventions also in this respect.

---

[47] Complaint No. 6/1999 by the *Syndicat national des Professions du tourisme against France*, Decision of 10 October 2000, para. 5.

[48] *Ibid.*, para. 27.

[49] *Ibid.*, para. 28.

3.3 *The Right to Education*

The ESC does not include the right to education. According to Article 17 of the RESC, however, the Contracting Parties undertake to take all appropriate and necessary measures designed:

> [....] to ensure that children and young persons, taking account of the rights and duties of their parents, have the care, the assistance, the education and the training they need, in particular by providing for the establishment or maintenance of institutions and services sufficient and adequate for this purpose;[50]

The right to education also applies to persons with disabilities which appears from the specific provision in Article 15 according to which the Parties undertake, in particular:

> [....] to take the necessary measures to provide persons with disabilities with guidance, education and vocational training in the framework of general schemes wherever possible or, where this is not possible, through specialised bodies, public or private;[51]

These provisions together with the non-discrimination clause in Article E of the RESC were challenged in Complaint No. 13/2002 by *Autism-Europe* which claimed that the de facto situation in France was in violation of the Charter because in practice, insufficient provision was made for the education of children and adults with autism "due to identifiable shortfalls – both quantitative and qualitative – in the provision of both mainstream education as well as in the so-called special education sector."[52]

The Committee described the underlying vision of Article 15 as one of "equal citizenship for persons with disabilities and, fittingly, the primary rights are those of "independence, social integration and participation in the life of the community". Securing a right to education for children and others with disabilities plays an obviously important role in advancing these citizenship rights."[53] With regard to Article E the Committee considered that disability was "adequately covered by the reference to "other status" ",[54] and – by referring to the *Thlimmenos case* about indirect discrimination, decided by the ECtHR[55] – found that the provision also prohibits indirect discrimination.[56]

---

50 Cf. RESC Article 17 (1).

51 Cf. RESC Article 15 (1).

52 Complaint No. 13/2002 by *Autism-Europe against France*, Decision of 4 November 2003, para. 16.

53 *Ibid*., para. 48.

54 *Ibid*., para. 51.

55 Cf. Chapter 9 about Work-related Rights under the ECtHR.

56 *Ibid*., para. 52.

In its assessment of the concrete case the Committee recalled that the implementation of the Charter requires the State Parties to take not merely legal action but also *practical action* to give full effect to the rights recognised in the Charter.[57]

While the French legislation may be in compliance with the Charter, the Committee considered:

> that the proportion of children with autism being educated in either general or specialist schools is much lower than in the case of other children, whether or not disabled. It is also established, and not contested by the authorities, that there is a chronic shortage of care and support facilities for autistic adults.[58]

Accordingly, the ECSR found a violation of Articles 15 (1) and 17 (1) whether alone or read in conjunction with Article E of the Charter.[59]

The question now is how the ECtHR would react if presented to a similar set of facts, if. e.g. a group of autists claimed that their right to education under Article 2 of Protocol No. 1 to the ECHR had been violated due to a shortage of educational facilities.

It is sometimes assumed that Article 2 of Protocol No. 1 relates to children and young persons, whereas adult education falls outside the scope of the provision. That point of view is probably doubtful, however, narrowing the question to children with autism it is more than likely that the Court would reach the conclusion that their rights had been violated. As appears from Chapter 7 the Contracting States have the competence to decide the setting up of a public education system, but is was presupposed when the Protocol was adopted that a public educational system was in fact set up in all COE Member States. That appears also from the wording of Article 2 to Protocol No.1, cf. the expression "[n]o one must be denied the right to education" and "[i]n the exercise of any function which it [the State, author's addition] assumes in relation to education and to teaching".[60]

The expression 'no one' indicates that discrimination with regard to education is prohibited i.e. that the educational system should also comprise children with disabilities. However, for children with disabilities special measures are required whether they are taught in ordinary schools or in schools for children with special needs. Their situation is significantly different from that of other children, and they must accordingly be treated differently. As to my knowledge the notion of indirect discrimination has not (yet) been recognised

---

57 *Ibid.*, para. 53.

58 *Ibid.*, para. 54.

59 Cf. also Complaint No. 41/2007, *Mental Disability Advocacy Center (MDAC) v. Bulgaria*, Decision of 3 June 2008 about education for children with intellectual disabilities.

60 Cf. Chapter 7, The Right to Education under the ECHR, Section 3.2.2.

under Article 2 (1) of Protocol No. 1, but it would seem very inconsistent to recognise the notion in one context and not in another. However, Article 2 of Protocol No. 1 may have to be read in conjunction with Article 14, cf. the reference to the *Thlimmenos case* referred to in Complaint No. 13 under the collective complaints procedure under the ESC/RESC. Mention should also be made of the Grand Chamber's judgment in *D. and H. and Others v. the Chech Republic*, referred to in detail in Chapter 7 about the Right to Education.[61]

A last case might be worth mentioning in the context of education. The very first complaint lodged by the International Commission of Jurists [the ICJ] claimed that the situation in Portugal with regard to child labour was in non-compliance with Article 7 (1) of the Charter. According to this provisions the Contracting Parties undertake:

> to provide that the minimum age of admission to employment shall be 15 years, subject to exceptions for children employed in prescribed light work without harm to their health, morals or *education* [author's emphasis];

It follows that one of the underlying reasons for this prohibition of child labour is the consideration for children's education. As to the definition of "prescribed light work" the Committee held as follows:

> The nature of the work is a determining factor. Work which is unsuitable because of the physical effort involved, working conditions (noise, heat, etc.) or possible psychological repercussions may have harmful consequences not only on the child's health and development, but also on its ability to obtain *maximum advantage from schooling* and, more generally, its potential for satisfactory integration in society [author's emphasis].[62]

The Committee noted that the statutory measures adopted in Portugal to implement Article 7 (1) were rigorous. Thus, any work – including light work – performed by children under the age of 15 was illegal. However, the Committee at the same time considered that "the satisfactory application of Article 7 cannot be ensured solely by the operation of legislation if this is not effectively applied and rigorously supervised."[63]

As to the factual situation the Government did not dispute that children under the age of fifteen actually perform work, and the Committee decided to rely on a 1998 statistical survey carried out in collaboration between the Portuguese Government and the ILO. It emerged from this survey that a significant number of children performed work several hours a day:

---

[61] *D. and H. and Others v. the Chech Republic*, Grand Chamber Judgment of 13 November 2007.

[62] Complaint No. 1/1998 by *the International Commission of Jurists against Portugal*, Decision of 9 September 1999.

[63] *Ibid.*, para. 32.

> The Committee observes lastly that, taking all sectors together, the duration of work declared exceeds that which may be considered compatible with children's health or schooling: 31.6% of the children concerned worked on average for more than 4 hours per day across all sectors. This percentage is particularly high in the construction sector and the manufacturing sector where, respectively, 66.6% and 42% of the children concerned worked on average for more than four hours per day. The Committee notes that *among the children aged between 6 and 14 years who performed paid work, just 68% attended school* [author's emphasis].[64]

The Committee did not find that the measures taken by the Portuguese Government to rectify the situation were satisfactory and concluded that the situation with regard to child labour in Portugal was in non-compliance with the Charter.

Now, the question is whether this situation could be dealt with under the ECHR, not as a question of child labour but as a denial of education for the 32% of the working children who did not attend school due to their work burden. I do not see why not. Admittedly, the children in question are not denied the right by the educational system but rather by their parents who keep them away from school for the sake of money. However, the authorities have an obligation to see to it that children's rights are not interfered with by third parties, cf. the notion of '*Drittwirkung*', and the situation can easily be construed as a denial of education. According to Article 2 (1) of Protocol No. 1, no one shall be denied the right to education, and when authorities do not enforce this right, there is a violation of the Protocol.

There is no case law from the ECtHR about child labour. However case law about the right to education in general, cf. Chapter 7, supports this perception.

4 *Civil-Political Dominance in Socio-Economic Rights*

4.1 *Initial Remarks*

Above in Section 3, I have tried to argue that some of the cases decided by the ECSR under the collective complaints procedure attached to the ESC/RESC could as well have been decided by the ECtHR under the ECHR. These cases illustrate that the traditional 'positive/negative' thinking is false, that the ESC/RESC is also about the obligation not to interfere and that the potential of the ECHR has not yet been made use of. According to the dichotomous perception of human rights one would assume that the ECHR gives a better protection with regard to interferences than the ESC/RESC. However, that is not

[64] *Ibid.*, para. 37.

necessarily the case, and the issue will require closer scrutiny. Arguably, such scrutiny is difficult as case law under the two treaties is not entirely comparable. The ECtHR rules in concrete cases and in principle the rulings apply only to the facts of the case at hand. The decisions of the ECSR, on the other hand, have a general character. Still, it might be possible to deduce something from case law of the two bodies. I have focused on two issues. The first is corporal punishment of children. The second is conscientious objectors and forced labour.

4.2 *Corporal Punishment of Children*

In Section 2, I have already referred to a series of cases decided by the ECSR on the issue of corporal punishment of children, and I shall turn directly to case law under the ECHR. Not all of the cases concern education specifically but I have chosen to deal with the subject more broadly.

The most relevant provision under the ECHR with regard to corporal punishment of children is Article 3 according to which "no one shall be subjected to torture or to inhuman or degrading treatment or punishment", cf. e.g. *Tyrer v. the United Kingdom*, *Costello-Roberts v. the United Kingdom* and *A v. the United Kingdom.*[65] Also, Article 8 about the right to private life may have relevance with regard to corporal punishment cf. the just-mentioned *Costello-Roberts* case and also *Campbell and Cosans v. the United Kingdom.*[66] Thus, the right *not* to be punished corporally belongs in both conventions although the three relevant articles, Articles 3 and 8 of the ESCR and Article 17 of the ESC/RESC are worded differently.

In the *Tyrer* case the applicant – a 15 year-old boy who had committed a crime – was sentenced to three strokes of a birch on the bare posterior in accordance with the relevant criminal legislation. The punishment was administered three weeks after the sentence in a police station where he was held by two policemen. This was considered "degrading" in the sense of Article 3. The ECtHR, however, took for its basis that in order for punishment to be degrading the humiliation or debasement involved must attain a particular level of severity and must in any event be other than the usual element of humiliation inherent in any punishment.[67]

The case *Campbell and Cosans* was about the use of corporal punishment in two State schools in the United Kingdom. It appeared from the case that teachers are "by virtue of their statute as teachers, invested by the common law with

[65] *Tyrer v. the United Kingdom, Costello-Roberts v. the United Kingdom* and *A v. the United Kingdom.*

[66] *Campbell and Cosans v. the United Kingdom.*

[67] *Tyrer v. the United Kingdom*, para. 30.

power to administer such punishment in moderation as a disciplinary measure."[68] In the two schools concerned the corporal chastisement took the form of striking the palm of the pupil's hand with a leather strap called a "tawse". However, in the concrete case neither of the pupils was strapped. The Court recognised that the mere threat of torture, inhuman or degrading treatment or punishment may in itself be in conflict with Article 3. However, the risk of being strapped with a tawse, as described above, could not, according to the Court, amount to degrading treatment within the meaning of Article 3.[69]

In the *Costello-Roberts* case a seven-year-old schoolboy was given three "whacks" on his buttocks through his shorts with a rubber-soled gym shoe. The punishment was administered after a three-day wait by the headmaster of a private (independent) school. According to the law private schools were free to use corporal punishment as a disciplinary measure if the punishment was "reasonable."[70] Moreover, the Government contended that it was clear from domestic legislation that "the Secretary of State has no power to refuse to register an independent school on the ground that corporal punishment is administered there and that any refusal to register a school on this ground would be open to legal challenge by the school concerned."[71]

The Court had "certain misgivings about the automatic nature of the punishment and the three-day wait before its imposition [....]."[72] However, compared to the circumstances of the *Tyrer case* the Court did not consider that the minimum level of severity had been attained and, accordingly, no violation of Article 3 had been established.

The applicant furthermore alleged that his corporal punishment had given rise to a breach of his private life under Article 8, and the Court stated as follows:

> The Court does not exclude the possibility that there might be circumstances in which Article 8 art. 8) could be regarded as affording in relation to disciplinary measures a protection which goes beyond that given by Article 3 [....]. Having regard, however, to the purpose and aim of the Convention taken as a whole, and bearing in mind that the sending of a child to school necessarily involves some degree of interference with his or her private life, the Court considers that the treatment complained of by the applicant did not entail adverse effects for his physical or moral integrity sufficient to bring it within the scope of the prohibition contained in Article 8[....]. While not wishing to be taken to approve in any way the retention of corporal punishment as part of the disciplinary regime of a

---

68 *Campbell and Cosans v. the United Kingdom*, para. 12.

69 *Ibid.*, paras. 25–31.

70 *Costello Roberts v. the United Kingdom*, para. 15.

71 *Ibid.*, para. 18.

72 *Ibid.*, para. 32.

> school, the Court therefore concludes that in the circumstances of this case there has also been no violation of that Article (art. 8).[73]

Thus, while not finding that the United Kingdom had violated the Convention, the Court, nevertheless, felt a certain desire to distance itself from the use of corporal punishment in its conclusions under both articles.

The last case which is worth mentioning in this context is the case *A v. the United Kingdom* about a stepfather who hit his nine-year-old stepson with a stick. A paediatrician who examined the boy considered that "the bruising was consistent with the use of a garden cane applied with considerable force on more than one occasion."[74] The stepfather was charged with assault occasioning actual bodily harm but found not guilty by a jury. It appeared from the case that:

> [i]n criminal proceedings for the assault of a child, the burden of proof is on the prosecution to satisfy the jury, beyond a reasonable doubt, *inter alia* that the assault did not constitute lawful punishment.
>
> Parents or other persons *in loco parentis* are protected by the law if they administer punishment which is moderate and reasonable in the circumstances. The concept of "reasonableness" permits the courts to apply standards prevailing in contemporary society with regard to the physical punishment of children.[75]

The Court considered that the treatment reached the level of severity prohibited. Moreover the Court found that the obligation to "secure to everyone [....] the rights and freedoms" deriving from Article 1 in conjunction with Article 3 requires States Parties to take measures to protect particularly children from ill-treatment administered by private individuals:

> The Court recalls that under English law it is a defence to a charge of assault on a child that the treatment in question amounted to "reasonable chastisement" [....]. The burden of proof is on the prosecution to establish beyond reasonable doubt that the assault went beyond the limits of lawful punishment. In the present case, despite the fact that the applicant had been subjected to treatment of sufficient severity to fall within the scope of Article 3, the jury acquitted his stepfather, who had administered the treatment [....].
>
> In the Court's view, *the law did not provide adequate protection* to the applicant against treatment or punishment contrary to Article 3 [....]. In the circumstances of the present case, the failure to provide adequate protection constitutes a violation of Article 3 of the Convention [author's emphasis].[76]

---

73 *Ibid.* para. 36.

74 *A. v. the United Kingdom*, para. 9.

75 *Ibid.*, para. 14.

76 *Ibid.*, paras. 23–24.

Thus, the circumstances of the case made it necessary for the Court to phrase its conclusion in general terms. However, what amendments were to be made to the then existing law is entirely up to the domestic authorities, and the judgment cannot be interpreted as if corporal punishment as such is in nonconformity with the ECHR. The issue as to what is the permissible level of physical rebuke remains open.[77]

Considering the fact that the ECHR is a living instrument, one may ask, however, for how long the Court can uphold this interpretation. As the ECSR rightly points out in Complaint No. 18 with reference to Conclusions from 2001 "it was influenced by an emerging international consensus on the issue and notes that since this consensus is stronger."[78] The ECtHR usually follows the trends in the COE Member States, and it is more than possible that the most recent case law is already outdated. However, the Court has not – as the ECSR – had a chance to reconsider the issue. At any rate it seems as if the ESC/RESC at present gives children a better protection against corporal punishment than does the ECHR.

Thus, according to the interpretation of Article 17 of the ESC/RESC the provision requires that domestic legislation bans corporal punishment of children at home, in prisons and in educational institutions. In the first cases the Committee required an explicit ban. In two later cases regarding the situation in Italy and Portugal the Court, however, relaxed the requirements. In neither of the cases did the law explicitly forbid corporal punishment. However, case law from the Italian Court of Cassation and the Portuguese Supreme Court seemed to prove that the legislation was to be interpreted as forbidding the use of corporal punishment,[79] and the Committee accepted that as a satisfactory legislative basis.[80] A new case, however, was lodged concerning the situation in Portugal by *World Organisation Against Torture* that asked the Committee to confirm that Article 17 requires an explicit statutory ban on all corporal punishment and degrading punishment or treatment of children. The Committee held that domestic law must prohibit and penalise all forms of violence and concluded as follows:

---

[77] The Commission specifically stated that "this finding does not mean that Article 3 is to be interpreted as imposing an obligation on States to protect, through their criminal law, against any form of physical rebute, however mild, by a parent of a child", cf. *Commission Report*, adopted on 18 September 1997, para. 55.

[78] Complaint No. 18/2003, *World Organisation against Torture ("OMCT") v. Ireland*, Decision of 7 December 2004, para. 61.

[79] Complaint No. 19/2003, *World Organisation against Torture ("OMCT") v. Italy*, Decision of 7 December 2004, para. 22 and Complaint No. 20/2003, *World Organisation against Torture ("OMCT") v. Portugal*, Decision of 22 January 2005, para. 16.

[80] *Ibid.*, para. 49.

> The relevant provisions must be sufficiently clear, binding and precise, so as to preclude the courts from refusing to apply them to violence against children.
>
> Moreover, states must act with due diligence to ensure that such violence is eliminated in practice.
>
> The conclusion to be drawn from the Supreme Court's decision of 5 April 2006 is that Portuguese law does not include such provisions, even though this was the interpretation that had been drawn from a previous decision of that court. In addition, the Government has not supplied information to show that the measures in practice are likely to result in the eradication of all forms of violence against children.[81]

It is difficult to compare the two conventions with regard to the protection of children against corporal punishment. However, the ESC/RESC seems to be able to compete with the ECHR despite the fact that these conventions first and foremost are regarded as conventions for the protection of economic, social and cultural rights.

4.3 *Conscientious Objectors and Forced Labour*

The issue of the length of substitute civilian service for conscientious objectors as compared to military service has also been dealt with under both the ESC/RESC and the ECHR, however, with differing results. Under the ECHR, in 1987, the applications were declared inadmissible by the ECtHR as manifestly ill-founded whereas the ECSR in 2001 found that the ESC/RESC had been violated.

Thus, in two Dutch cases from 1987, *N.C. Van Buitenen against the Netherlands* and *G.G. against the Netherlands*[82] the applicants who were both conscientious objectors invoked Article 4 of the ECHR about compulsory labour in conjunction with Article 14 because they had to spend around 18 months doing substitute civilian service whereas the normal duration of military service was 14 months.

According to Article 4 (3) (b) of the ECHR the term "forced or compulsory labour" does not include "any service of a military character or, in the case of conscientious objectors in countries where they are recognised, service enacted instead of compulsory military service; [....]." The Commission found, however, that although the Netherlands was not obliged to recognise the applicants as conscientious objectors, their complaints nevertheless fell within the ambit of Article 4. The Commission also found that there was a differential treatment

[81] Complaint No. 34/2006, *World Organisation against Torture (OMCT) v. Portugal,* Decision of 22 January 2007, paras. 20–22.

[82] *N.C. Van Buitenen against the Netherlands* and *G. against the Netherlands,* Admissibility decisions of 2 March 1987.

but had regard to the reasons given by the Dutch courts, viz. that "substitute civilian service is generally considered as less ardous and that there was a need to avoid refusal of military reason for that reason."[83]Moreover, the Commission found that the additional time the applicants had to serve was "reasonably proportional to the different nature of the two different services"[84] and declared the applications manifestly ill-founded and as such inadmissible.

In Complaint No. 8/2000 the *Quaker Council for European Affairs (QCEA)* lodged a complaint with the ECSR claiming that Greece did not ensure satisfactory application of Article 1 (2) of the ESC/RESC according to which the Contracting Parties undertake "to protect effectively the right of the worker to earn his living in an occupation freely entered upon."

The QCEA claimed that alternative civilian service was 18 months longer than normal military service which varies between 18 and 21 months. The QCEA contended that "imposing a length of service twice that of military service is disproportionate and, furthermore, deprives young adults of a career for up to 39 months."[85] The Greek Government, not surprisingly, contended that civilian service does not come within the scope of Article 1 (2) of the Charter and referred to Article 4 (3) (b) of the ECHR. The Committee stated in response:

> [....] that it takes account of Article 4 para. 3 b) of the European Convention on Human Rights when interpreting Article 1 para. 2 of the European Social Charter. Accordingly, the obligation to perform military service or, for conscientious objectors, the obligation to perform civilian service instead of military service cannot, as such, be considered a form of forced labour, contrary to Article 1 para. 2. The Committee further states that conscientious objectors who perform alternative civilian service are not workers who earn their living in an occupation freely entered upon within the meaning of Article 1 para. 2 of the Charter.
>
> The Committee considers, however, that alternative civilian service may amount to a restriction on the freedom to earn one's living in an occupation freely entered upon. Such a situation comes therefore within the scope of Article 1 para. 2 of the Charter. It is accordingly for the Committee to determine whether, in the present case, the conditions and modalities for the performance of alternative civilian service, compared to military service, constitute a disproportionate restriction on the freedom guaranteed by Article 1 para. 2 of the Charter.[86]

The Committee went on accepting the viewpoint of the Government that alternative civilian service is less onerous than military service and that the

---

[83] *Ibid.*, The Law, para. 1.

[84] *Ibid.*

[85] Complaint No. 8/2000 by the *Quaker Council for European Affairs (QCEA) against Greece*, Decision of 25 April 2001, para. 8.

[86] *Ibid.*, paras. 22–23.

Contracting Parties "indeed enjoy a certain margin of appreciation in this area."[87] The Committee, however, attached importance to the duration of civilian service and stated as follows:

> The Committee considers that these 18 additional months, during which the persons concerned are denied the right to earn their living in an occupation freely entered upon, do not come within reasonable limits, compared to the duration of military service. It therefore considers that this additional duration, because of its excessive character, amounts to a disproportionate restriction on "the right of the worker to earn his living in an occupation freely entered upon", and is contrary to Article 1 para. 2 of the Charter.[88]

This "excessive character"[89] of the additional duration amounted to a disproportionate restriction of the right of the worker to earn his living in an occupation freely entered upon, as it is stated in Article 1(2) of the Charter. Accordingly, the Committee concluded by 6 votes against 3 that the situation in Greece was in non-conformity with the Charter.

One dissenting committee member claimed that the ESC/RESC does not cover conscientious objectors' service exacted instead of compulsory military service, and asserted that there "is no doubt that this kind of service is neither a case of compulsory labour according to Article 4 para. 3 lit. b of the European Convention on Human Rights, nor according to Article 1 para. 2 of the European Social Charter."[90]

Thus, at the face of it the ESC/RESC gives a better protection with regard to the length of alternative civilian service than the ECHR. However, that is not necessarily the case, and the dissenting Committee Member is hardly right if he finds that the issue undoubtedly falls outside the scope of the ECHR. In 1987, the ECtHR recognised that the issue fell within the ambit of Article 4 (3) (b) of the ECHR. However, when applied in conjunction with Article 14 no violation was found. The factual circumstances in the two Dutch cases from 1987 were, however, quite different from the factual circumstances in the case which was decided by the ECSR. In the Dutch cases the duration of the alternative service was 18 months in all and the two applicants served 3–5 months longer than ordinary military service. In the case about the *Quaker Council* for *European Affairs* the difference between the ordinary and alternative service was 18 months and the total duration of alternative service was up to 39 months. If the ECtHR were to make a decision on the basis of similar facts under Article 4 (3) (b) of the ECtHR, one cannot entirely exclude that the Court would come

87 *Ibid.*, para. 24.
88 *Ibid.*, para. 25.
89 *Ibid.*
90 *Ibid.*, Dissenting opinion of Mr. Rolf Birk, para. 2.

to a similar conclusion namely that the differential treatment between military service and civilian service was disproportional. Until now, however, conscientious objectors seem to be better protected by the ESC/RESC.

5 *Closing Remarks*

The purpose of this chapter has been to illustrate that the notion of indivisibility is not only about the protection of socio-economic elements under the ECHR but also about the protection of civil-political elements under the ESC/RESC. Moreover, a few civil-political rights actually seem to be better protected under the ESC/RESC than under the ECHR. The indivisibility of human rights "cuts both ways", and in this way the chapter seems appropriate as a prelude to the closing discussion in Chapter 12 about the most adequate framework for the protection of human rights as indivisible rights.

Chapter 12

Concluding Forward-looking Observations

1 *Initial Remarks*

It has been the aim of this work to explore how in particular the ECtHR perceives of the notion of human rights as indivisible, interrelated and interdependent. Not that the Court deliberately has been working with the express purpose of examining this notion. On the contrary, the Court has simply dealt with a great number of cases brought before it by numerous individuals from the COE Member States. However, some of these cases encompass facts belonging in the socio-economic sphere.

The examination illustrates that the Court has no rigid perception of the ECHR and its Protocols as belonging to a particular category of human rights. The Court seems willing to argue for the abolition of the classical categorisation of human rights as belonging in (at least two) different categories if that is what it takes to provide proper, effective and up-to-date human rights protection. The Court seems to dissociate itself from the perception of human rights as either 'positive' or 'negative', and an understanding of human rights as appearing in generations is not reflected in the Court's case law either. Waldron's perception of human rights obligation as *waves of duties* seems to come closer to the Court's perception of the States' human rights obligations towards individuals, cf. Chapter 2. Not that the Court sees no difference between various human rights provisions. It does indeed, and it should be repeated that the Court has a cautious approach to issues which have a bearing on policy choices, in particular those which have budgetary implications. However, is has become increasingly evident that a separation of human rights in civil-political rights and economic, social and cultural rights respectively can not be upheld.

Thus, the notion of human rights as indivisible rights does have *legal* implications, and case law illustrates that judicial are bodies obliged or authorised to take into consideration the complexity of 'real life' when making assessments of human rights compliance under the ECHR. Craig Scott's concern that the inter-treaty textual relations might create *ceiling effects*[1] in the sense that a treaty body's reference to human rights commitments in a legal instrument other than its own can be used as a means not to expand but to limit the meaning, and thus the scope, of the protection does not seem to be reflected at least in the Court's recent case law. On the contrary, the Court's reference to human rights commitments in a legal instrument other than the ECHR seems to be used to widen and not to narrow the perspective, and the potential of the integrated approach is hardly exhausted. What is worth mentioning in this context is also that the ECSR in its interpretation of the ESC/RESC often refers to the Court's case law, cf. Chapter 11, and the tendency seems to be that the two treaty bodies, the ECtHR and the ECSR are keen on harmonising their interpretation of the two treaty systems.

Thus, case law over the years from the ECtHR and the ECSR brings to light the interconnectedness of the two sets of rights, and the question is what could or should be the legal and institutional consequences of this development if any. If human rights are indivisible, interrelated and interconnected, how is it possible to uphold a legal and institutional machinery dealing with the two kinds of rights as if they were separate rights? Before dealing with that issue some further remarks are, however, to be made about the added value of hermeneutics.

2 *Returning to the Issue about the Added Value of Hermeneutics*

I suggested in Chapter 4 that a hermeneutic perspective on human rights might bring the integration further on its way because it arranges in an ordered whole a series of interpretative principles developed in legal theory and practice. Looked at in this way the added value of hermeneutic thinking is what it does for the *structuring* and *fixing of the order of priority* of – not necessarily consistent – legal principles and traditions. The relevance of the individual interpretative principle – the detail – is to be considered in terms of the whole and *vice versa*, and the right interpretative approach is the one that contributes in the best possible way to maintaining or even improving coherence in the human rights system. Therefore, one might say that the hermeneutic situation does not only concern the relations between text, context and interpreter and the relations between the legislative, executive and judicial powers, but also the relation between various interpretative principles and traditions.

Moreover, applying a hermeneutic perspective to human rights makes it superfluous to speak of social rights *permeating* the civil rights norm system – as

[1] Cf. Chapter 3.

Craig Scott did originally[2] – suggesting that what permeates into the ECHR does not really belong there. The designation might be misunderstood as indicating that treaty bodies by applying an integrated approach are working near the limits of their mandate or even overstepping their mandate by borrowing norms from another treaty. A hermeneutic approach makes it more relevant to speak of civil rights as encompassing social elements and *vice versa*, e.g. that the social component in a civil right is an inherent element to be activated in the encounter with the relevant facts rather than an alien substance borrowed from another convention. This way of expressing the relation is probably also in keeping with Craig Scott's later understanding of effective human rights protection:

> The key point is that making rights effective, by way of interpreting rights to have social and economic dimensions that place positive duties on the state, need not proceed from borrowing from rights that already have a recognized legal pedigree as social and economic rights. Instead, effective human rights protection can, and should, be a result of contextual interpretative analysis of what is needed to make a right truly a right of "everyone" [....].[author's emphasis].[3]

Contextual interpretative analysis is indeed crucial for the understanding and for the development of the integrated approach, and the emphasis on context in the quotation corresponds very well to what hermeneutics would refer to as the vertical interpretative movement, cf. above in Chapter 4. The perception of interpretation as application, which leads in fact to an amalgamation of law and facts, is perhaps the best illustration of the added value of hermeneutics in the understanding and development of the integrated approach, and there is every reason to keep Gadamer's words in mind:

> A law does not exist in order to be understood historically, but to be concretized in its legal validity by being interpreted. Similarly the gospel does not exist in order to be understood as a merely historical document, but to be taken in such a way that it exercises its saving effect. This implies that the text, whether law or gospel, if it is to be understood properly – i.e., according to the claim it makes – must be understood at every moment in every concrete situation, in a new and different way. *Understanding here is always application* [author's emphasis].[4]

However, the introduction of other aspects of hermeneutic thinking in the understanding of the integrated approach provides a *general framework of understanding* encompassing other interpretative principles as they have been

2 Craig Scott, "The Interdependence and Permeability of Human Rights Norms: Towards a Partial Fusion of the International Covenants on Human Rights", *Osgoode Hall Law Journal*, Vol 27, No. 4, 1989, pp. 769–878.

3 Craig Scott, "Reaching Beyond (Without Abandoning) the Category of Economic, Social and Cultural Rights" in *Human Rights Quarterly*, Vol. 21, Issue 3, 1999, pp. 633–660 (on p. 641).

4 Gadamer, *Ibid*., p. 309.

developed over the years by the Court. The necessity of considering the detail in terms of the whole and *vice versa*, cf. above in Chapter 4 about the hermeneutic circle, not only allows for but *requires* the application of a broader range of legal sources in the interpretation of the ECHR, i.e. also sources which are traditionally considered in relation to conventions protecting economic, social and cultural rights. Moreover, the horizontal structure of the hermeneutic circle reflects very well the notions of *dynamic interpretation*, *present-day-conditions* and *living instrument*, cf. above in Chapter 4, and also the notion of pre-understanding contributes to a better understanding of how and why legal interpretation changes corresponding to changes in the pre-understanding of the legal community. The various elements of hermeneutic thinking – as elements of a *greater* whole – contribute in each their way to an understanding of the Court's approach and lay down guidelines for future evolutionary integrative steps. Thus, the study of cases which have either been declared inadmissible or in which no violation of the ECHR has been found indicates that the potential of the integrated approach is far from being exhausted. Thus, the Court has not entirely ruled out that the right to be provided with an apartment or to have a life-saving drug free of charge be protected under the convention.[5]

Consciousness of hermeneutic thinking widens the horizon of the interpreter in that it becomes part of pre-understanding thus allowing for new questions to be posed and new answers to be given. By way of example, the traditional pre-understanding of socio-economic rights as nothing but policy statements discards a number of questions which might lead to a more nuanced understanding of the normative character of these rights and their relation to civil and political rights. The Court's perception of socio-economic demands seems much more nuanced.

Thus, it should be recalled that Ricoeur does not understand the interpretative process as a *dialogue* between interpreter and text. Rather, he conceives of text as disengaged from spoken language, cf. Chapter 4. The text, according to Ricoeur, is dumb; it does not respond to our questions, and the relation between writing and reading is not identical to the relation between speaking and hearing. Ricoeur prefers to see the inscription as something that gives *semantic autonomy* to the text:

> [W]hat writing fix is not the event of speaking but the "said" of speaking",[6] and the "said" assumes greater importance than the act of speaking. When written down,

---

[5] Cf. e.g. *Marzari v. Italy*, Admissibility decision of 4 May 1999, *Nitecki v. Poland*, Admissibility decision of 21 March 2002. Cf. also *Calvelli and others v. Italy*, Judgment of 17 January 2002 about appropriate health care.

[6] Paul Riceour, *Interpretation Theory: Discourse and the Surplus of Meaning*, Texas Christian University Press, 1976, p. 27.

> the meaning of the text and the intention of the author cease to coincide. A distance between the text and its author has been established, and hermeneutics accordingly begins where the dialogue ends.[7]

> Writing, in effect, assures the triple autonomy of the text which characterises it: autonomy with regard to the reader and his intentions; autonomy with regard to the initial situation of the discourse and from every social-cultural conditioning affecting that situation; and autonomy with regard to the initial hearer and the original audience [....].[8]

3 *A Protocol to the ECHR Concerning Socio-Economic Rights – Historical Remarks*

The Court's case law – and also case law from the ECSR – brings to light the interconnectedness of the two sets of rights, and the question is what could or should be the legal and institutional consequences of this development if any. If human rights are indivisible, interrelated and interconnected, how are we to proceed with a legal and institutional machinery presupposing that the two sets of rights are separate rights?

The notion of human rights as indivisible rights has long since been recognised by the COE, and the issue as to whether (certain) socio-economic rights should be directly protected under the ECHR or otherwise be given stronger protection is certainly not a new one. On the contrary, history tells us that the political bodies under the COE on a number of occasions have discussed the regrettable inferior role of these rights, and considered how one should address the issue of giving them a stronger protection.

The course of events up until 1990 is described by Klaus Berchtold who begins his review by referring to COE Consultative Asssembly Recommendation 583 (1970).[9] The Consultative Assembly recommended the drafting of a protocol to the ECHR including some socio-economic rights. However, the initiative was eventually rejected by the Committee of Ministers who concluded that the preparation of such a protocol was neither desirable nor expedient.

In 1978, the Parliamentary Assembly adopted a new recommendation concerning the drafting of a protocol concerning the possible inclusion of certain socio-economic rights under the ECHR monitoring system.[10] This proposal

---

7 *Ibid.*, p. 32.

8 Paul Ricoeur, "Ethics and Culture" in *Political and Social Essays*, collected and ed. by David Stewart and Joseph Bien, 1974, p. 259.

9 Klaus Berchtold, "Council of Europe activities in the field of economic, social and cultural rights" in Franz Matscher (ed.) *The Implementation of Economic and Social Rights, National, International and Comparative Aspects*, N. P. Engel Verlag, 1991, p. 355 ff.

10 COE, Parliamentary Assembly, Recommendation 838 (1978) of 27 September 1978.

was initiated by the Committee of Ministers' Declaration on Human Rights[11] leaving open, however, the issue as to whether the strengthening of the protection of socio-economic rights was to be implemented via the ECHR monitoring system or by other appropriate means.

After intensive and lengthy discussions – and in the light of the initiatives with regard to the re-launching of the ESC as the RESC – the project was eventually shelved. The reluctance as to including socio-economic rights under the ECHR was due to concerns with regard to the work load of the Commission and the Court as well as scepticism concerning the justiciability of socio-economic rights.

On the occasion of the 50th anniversary of the UDHR, the Committee of Ministers of the COE adopted, on 10 December 1998, a declaration in which the Governments of the Member States of the Council of Europe reaffirmed "the need to reinforce the protection of fundamental social and economic rights [....] all of which form an integral part of human rights protection".[12]

Furthermore, in 1999 the Parliamentary Assembly of the COE recommended that the Committee of Ministers:

> i. carry out a survey to ascertain which of the social rights guaranteed by the constitutions of member states, and considered as enforceable by national courts, might be added to the rights protected by the provisions of the European Convention on Human Rights;
> ii. carry out a survey to ascertain which of the rights guaranteed by the European Social Charter and the revised European Social Charter could be considered enforceable and be added to the rights protected by the provisions of the European Convention on Human Rights;
> iii. consult the European Court of Human Rights in order to ascertain which of the social rights could be considered as already guaranteed by the Convention, in the light of its case-law;
> iv. draft an additional protocol to the European Convention on Human Rights, on the basis of the above-mentioned surveys, with a view to guaranteeing as a first stage some of the following rights:[13]

The rights referred to were more or less the same rights as those encompassed by the ESC/RESC, and the recommendation led the Steering Committee for Human Rights (the CDDH) to set up a Working Group on Social Rights to examine issues in relation to the possible protection of social rights within the framework of the ECHR. The Working Group held a number of meetings and

[11] COE, Committee of Ministers, Declation on Human Rights of 27 April 1978.

[12] COE, Committee of Ministers, Declaration on the occasion of the 50th anniversary of the Universal Declaration of Human Rights, 10 December 1998.

[13] COE Parliamentary Assembly, Recommendation 1415 (1999), Additional protocol to the European Convention on Human Rights concerning fundamental social rights.

submitted its final report to the CDDH in May 2005. It appears from the Working Group's Activity report for the CDDH[14] that opinions differed as regards the possible continuation of the reflections concerning the adoption of a protocol to the ECHR concerning socio-economic rights. Against this background the CDDH held that:

> it was obvious that such an activity would have no political support at the present time. The question raised was that of whether or not the CDDH experts considered it useful to keep the subject of social rights and the ECHR on their agenda, in one form or another.[15]

Eventually, it was decided simply to follow the developments concerning protection of socio-economic rights at the national, regional and global level, and a "rapporteur" was appointed with this end in view.[16] Accordingly, the issue has been put in cold storage for the time being, and one might conclude that the COE Member States suffer from disintegration with regard to a stronger protection of socio-economic rights.

Against the background of the discussions within the COE during the last 30 years, the prospects of an adoption of a protocol to the ECHR concerning socio-economic rights do not seem bright. The weak protection of socio-economic rights has been remedied to some extent by the entering into force of the collective complaints procedure under the ESC/RESC and of course by the integrated approach of the ECtHR, which has been the primary subject for examination in the present work. However, the COE has not taken the full consequence of the recognition of human rights as indivisible rights which has been central in the discussion over the years.

The issue, however, has not been completely shelved, and the developments within the EU and the UN may very well serve as a guarantee that the discussion is going to continue also in the COE – maybe after a pause. Thus, the adoption and possible entering into force of a Protocol to the CESCR concerning an individual complaints procedure is likely in the long term to have an impact also on the discussion within the COE. Similarly, if the Lisbon Treaty enters into force with its reference to the Charter of Fundamental Rights[17] it might have a knock-on effect on the developments within the COE. Thus, the Charter includes socio-economic rights into the rights catalogue[18] and refers

---

[14] COE, *Report of 18 May from Working Group on Social Rights* (GT-DH-SOC) (2005)007.

[15] COE, *Report of 29 June 2005 from the Steering Committee for Human Rights*, CDDH(2005)009, Section 5.4, para. 17.

[16] *Ibid*, Section 5.4, paras. 20 and 21.

[17] Cf. The Consolidated Version of the Treaty on European Union of 18 April 2008, Article 6, according to which the Charter shall have the same legal value as the treaty.

[18] The Charter of Fundamental Rights of the European Union, adopted on 7 December 2000.

in the Preamble specifically to the principle of human rights as indivisible rights and to constitutional traditions and international obligations including the ESC/RESC. It seems reasonable, therefore, to consider the concerns of some Member States with regard to the entrusting of the Court to ensure that socio-economic rights are respected.

4 *Considerations on a Protocol to the ECHR about Socio-Economic Rights*

There is no need to go further into the issue of socio-economic rights as justiciable rights. It has been dealt with quite extensively in Chapter 10, cf. above in Section 3, and the case law of the ECtHR and the ECSR, cf. Chapter 11, speaks for itself. It seems more and more artificial to insist on the non-justiciability of socio-economic rights, and it appears a bit hypocritical to deny justiciability and at the same time insist on indivisibility. The Court has recognised that elements of socio-economic rights are justiciable rights or that facts of a socio-economic character have relevance in the adjudication process. Moreover, case law from the ECSR indicates that civil-political demands have relevance also for the protection under the ESC/RESC.

I have furthermore argued in Chapter 10 that no issue with regard to the division of powers between the judiciary, the legislature and the executive need to arise because of the ECtHR's integrative approach to human rights protection. If democracy is perceived of as a substantive concept, judicial supervision of the legislature's and the executive's respect for human rights can be considered a necessary precondition for the maintenance and upholding of democracy within COE Member States. The normative development within the COE cannot be considered a threat to democracy, and the hermeneutic and integrated approach of the ECtHR and the ECSR confirms that socio-economic demands are in fact to some extent justiciable.

It is true that socio-economic rights have received better protection after the adoption of the Protocol on a collective complaints procedure, cf. Chapter 11. Also the integrated approach of the ECtHR contributes to the respect for these rights. At the same time, however, the present arrangement for the protection of socio-economic rights seems inconsistent in the long run. There is an increasing overlap between the two monitoring systems, and it might be about time to consider what should be the consequence, if any, of the development, which confirms that human rights are in fact indivisible, interrelated and interdependent.

One possibility is, of course, to leave everything the way it is. Its does no harm to the protection of socio-economic rights that the COE operates with two bodies which feel responsible for the protection of (aspects of) socio-economic rights. There is all the more reason to continue as up to now since both the ECtHR and the ECSR seem eager to harmonise their interpretations of the ECHR and the ESC/RESC. The parallel protection might even contribute to an increasing protection of socio-economic rights inasmuch as the two monitoring bodies maintain a dialogue on how to interpret overlapping provisions of the ECHR and the ESC/RESC.

Another way forward is to adopt a protocol to the ECHR concerning the protection of socio-economic rights as it has been considered on several occasions. That solution is indeed likely to strengthen the protection of socio-economic rights since the ECHR monitoring system is very much stronger that that under the ESC/RESC. On the other hand, entrusting the Court with the handling of individual complaints concerning socio-economic issues might gradually undermine the work of the ECSR with regard to collective complaints, a development which is not promising at all. The collective complaints procedure has its limitations, but indeed also its advantages as it offers the possibility of dealing with a certain issue in a more general manner.

Considerations with regard to order speak for the abolition of the whole ESC/RESC system together with the adoption of a protocol to the ECHR including the same or similar provisions. That would imply a recognition of the justiciability of socio-economic rights, and free the Court from considerations with regard to the treaty-crossing character of its activities. At the same time it would function as the guarantee that socio-economic rights are regarded with the same respect as civil-political rights. The logical consequence, however, would be the abolition of the whole reporting system under the ESC/RESC, which is not desirable either. On the contrary, the reporting system has its own raison d'être inasmuch as its purpose is to overview the general state of law, and it might even be argued that the reporting system ought to be extended to covering also the rights presently encompassed by the ECHR and its Protocols.

The time has hardly come to embark on such a comprehensive reform of the monitoring system under the COE. The political will is non-existent for the time being, and the matter probably deserves much greater consideration than has been given in this context. Moreover, the Court is overburdened already as it is, and reforming the COE monitoring system along the lines delineated would indeed require resources. On the other hand, in the long run it will probably be necessary to consider what should be the consequences of the development in the protection under the two treaty systems, and it seems to me difficult and artificial to uphold the view that socio-economic rights should be given less and a different protection than civil-political rights. For the time being, therefore, there is every reason to follow carefully how the two monitoring bodies, the ECtHR and the ECSR, administer their tasks towards a greater respect for the notion of the indivisibility, interrelation and interconnectedness of human rights.

5 *Final Remarks*

These final concluding remarks are meant as an encouragement to continue the discussion about the justiciability of human rights, the issue of division of powers and the notion of human rights as indivisible rights. Much more is undoubtedly to be said, and I will look forward to following the continued discussion about these issues, which are indeed in focus for the time being. However, I will end here by quoting Gadamer for the last time. He writes as follows in the afterword to Truth and Metdods:

But I will stop here. The ongoing dialogue permits no final conclusion. It would be a poor hermeneuticist, who thought he could have, or had to have, the last word.[19]

[19] Gadamer, *Ibid.*, p. 579.

European Court of Human Rights: List of Judgments

A v. the United Kingdom, Judgment of 23 September 1998
Abdulaziz, Cabales and Balkandali v. the United Kingdom, Judgment of 28. May 1985
A. O. v. Italy, Judgment of 30 May 2000
Abenavoli v. Italy, Judgment of 2 September 1997
Acimovic v. Croatia, Judgment of 9 October 2003
Aerts v. Belgium, Judgment of 30 July 1998
Airey v. Ireland, Judgment of 9 October 1979
Akdivar and Others v. Turkey, Judgment of 16 September 1996
Aleksanyan v. Russia, Judgment of 22 December 2008
Alexandridis v. Greece, Judgment of 21 February 2008
Allard v. Sweden, Judgment of 24 June 2003
Margareta and Roger Andersson v. Sweden, Judgment of 25 February 1992
Ashingdane v. the United Kingdom, Judgment of 28 May 1985
Kjartan Asmundsson v. Iceland, Judgment of 12 October 2004
Associated Society of Locomotive Engineers & Firemen (Aslef) v. the United Kingdom, Judgment of 27 February 2007
Azinas v. Cyprus, Judgment of 20 June 2002
Beard v. the United Kingdom, Judgment of 18 January 2001
Beck, Copp and Bazeley v. the United Kingdom, Judgment of 22 October 2000
Belgium Linguistic case, Judgment of 23 July 1968
Bellini v. Italy, Judgment of 29 January 2004
Bensaid v. the United Kingdom, Judgment of 6 February 2001
Bilgin v. Turkey, Judgment of 16 November 2000
Bizzotto v. Greece, Judgment of 15 November 1996
Boicenco v. Moldova, Judgment of 11 July 2006
Botta v. Italy, Judgment of 24 February 1998
Bouamar v. Belgium, Judgment of 29 February 1988
Brand v. the Netherlands, Judgment of 11 May 2004
Broniowski v. Poland, Judgment of 22 June 2004
Brumarescu v. Romania, Judgment of 28 October 1999

Brumarescu v. Romania, Judgment of 23 January 2001
Bruncrona v. Finland, Judgment of 16 November 2004
Buchholz v. Germany, Judgment of 6 May 1981
Buckley v. the United Kingdom, Judgment of 25 September 1996
Büker v. Turkey, Judgment of 24 October 2000
Burdov v. Russia, Judgment of 7 May 2002
Calvelli and Others v. Italy, Judgment of 17 January 2002
Campbell and Cosans v. the United Kingdom, Judgment of 25 February 1982
Castanheira Barros v. Portugal, Judgment of 26 October 2000
Chapman v. the United Kingdom, Judgment of 18 January 2001
Connors v. the United Kingdom, Judgment of 27 May 2004
Costello-Roberts v. the United Kingdom, Judgment of 25 March 1993
Coster v. the United Kingdom, Judgment of 18 January 2001
Cyprus v. Turkey, Judgment of 10 May 2001
Cvijetic v. Croatia, Judgment of 26 February 2004
D v. the United Kingdom, Judgment of 2 May 1997
D.G. v. Ireland, Judgment of 16 May 2002
D. H. and Others v. the Czech Republic, Judgment of 7 February 2006
D. H. and Others v. the Czech Republic, Judgment of 13 November 2007
D.P. and J.C. v. the United Kingdom, Judgment of 10 October 2002
Darby v. Sweden, Judgment of 23 October 1990
Demades v. Turkey, Judgment of 31 July 2003
Demir and Baykara v. Turkey, Judgment of 12 November 2008
De Santa v. Italy, Judgment of 2 September 1997
Devlin v. the United Kingdom, Judgment of 30 October 2001
Deumeland v. Germany, Judgment of 29 May 1986
Dikme v. Turkey, Judgment of 11 July 2000
Doğan and others v. Turkey, Judgment of 29 June 2004
Dougoz v. Greece, Judgment of 6 March 2001
Dulas v. Turkey, Judgment of 30 January 2001
Dybeku v. Albania, Judgment of 18 December 2007
E and Others v. the United Kingdom, Judgment of 26 November 2002
Elci and Others v. Turkey, Judgment of 13 November 2003
Erkalo v. the Netherlands, Judgment of 2 September 1998
Evaldsson and Others v. Sweden, Judgment of 13 February 2007
Fadeyeva v. Russia, Judgment of 30 November 2005
Feldbrügge v. the Netherlands, Judgment of 29 May 1986
Ferrazzini v. Italy, Judgment of 12 July 2001
Fredin v. Sweden, Judgment of 18 February 1991
Freimann v. Croatia, Judgment of 24 June 2004
Frydlender v. France, Judgment of 27 June 2000
Gaskin v. the United Kingdom, Judgment of 7 July 1989

Gaygusuz v. Austria, Judgment of 16 September 1996
Gillow v. the United Kingdom, Judgment of 24 November 1986
Giunta v. Italy, Judgment of 13 July 2000
Glasenapp v. Germany, Judgment of 28 August 1986
Glass v. the United Kingdom, Judgment of 9 March 2004
Golder v. the United Kingdom, Judgment of 21 February 1975
Moreno Gómez v. Spain, Judgment of 16 November 2004
Christine Goodwin v. the United Kingdom, Judgment of 11 July 2002
Gorodnichev v. Russia, Judgment of 24 May 2007
Grande Oriente d'Italia di Palazzo Giustiniano, Judgment of 31 May 2007
Grant v. the United Kingdom, Judgment of 23 May 2006
Guerra et al. v. Italy, Judgment of 19 February 1998
Gustafsson v. Sweden, Judgment of 25 April 1996
Gustafsson v. Sweden, Judgment of 30 July 1998
Guzzardi v. Italy, Judgment of 6 November 1980
H. v. France, Judgment of 24 October 1989
Haase v. Germany, Judgment of 8 April 2004
Hatton and Others v. the United Kingdom, Judgment of 2 October 2001
Hatton and Others v. the United Kingdom, Judgment of 8 July 2003
Hertel v. Switzerland, Judgment of 25 August 1998
Hobbs, Richards, Walsh and Geen v. the United Kingdom, Judgment of 14 November 2006
Hokkanen v. Finland, Judgment of 23 September 1994
Huber v. France, Judgment of 19 February 1998
Hutchison Reid v. the United Kingdom, Judgment of 20 February 2003
Hutten-Czapska v. Poland, Judgment of 22 February 2005
Hutten-Czapska v. Poland, Judgment of 19 June 2006
I v. Finland, Judgment of 17 July 2008
Immobiliare Saffi v. Italy, Judgment of 28 July 1999
Ivanova v. Bulgaria, Judgment of 12 April 2007
James and Others v. the United Kingdom, Judgment of 21 February 1986
Johnson v. the United Kingdom, Judgment of 24 October 1997
K and T v. Finland, Judgment of 12 July 2001
Kalashnikov v. Russia, Judgment of 15 July 2002
Keegan v. Ireland, Judgment of 26 May 1994
Keenan v. the United Kingdom, Judgment of 3 April 2001
Kerojärvi v. Finland, Judgment of 19 July 1995
Khokhlich v. Ukraine, Judgment of 29 April 2003
Khudobin v. Russia, Judgment of 26 October 2006
Kjeldsen, Busk Madsen and Pedersen v. Denmark, Judgment of 7 December 1976
König v. Germany, Judgment of 28 June 1978
Kolanis v. the United Kingdom, Judgment of 21 June 2005

Kosiek v. Germany, Judgment of 28 August 1986
Koua Poirrez v. France, Judgment of 30 September 2003
Kucheruk v. Ukraine, Judgment of 6 September 2007
Kudla v. Poland, Judgment of 26 October 2000
Kutic v. Croatia, Judgment of 1 March 2002
Kuznetsov v. Ukraine, Judgment of 29 April 2003
Kyrtatos v. Greece, Judgment of 22 May 2003
Lambourdière v. France, Judgment of 2 August 2000
Lapalorcia v. Italy and *Abenavoli v. Italy*, Judgments of 2 September 1997
Leander v. Sweden, Judgment of 26 March 1987
Le Calvez v. France, Judgment of 29 July 1998
Lee v. the United Kingdom, Judgment of 18 January 2001
Lemke v. Turkey, Judgment of 5 June 2007
Francesco Lombardo v. Italy, Judgment of 26 November 1992
Giancarlo Lombardo v. Italy, Judgment of 26 November 1992
Loizidou v. Turkey, Judgment of 18 December 1996
Luczak v. Poland, Judgment of 27 November 2007
Lunari v. Italy, Judgment of 11 January 2001
Lustig-Prean and Beckett v. the United Kingdom, Judgment of 27 September 1999
Marinković v. Croatia, Judgment of 21 October 2004
Massa v. Italy, Judgment of 24 August 1993
Matos e Silva v. Portugal, Judgment of 16 September 1996
McGlinchey and Others v. the United Kingdom, Judgment of 29 April 2003
Megadat. Com SRL v. Moldova, Judgment of 8 April 2008
Mellacher and others v. Austria, Judgment of 19 December 1989
Melnik v. the United Kingdom, Judgment of 28 March 2006
Mennito v. Italy, Judgment of 5 October 2000
Mentes and Others v. Turkey, Judgment of 28 November 1997
Metin Turan v. Turkey, Judgment of 14 November 2006
Mocarska v. Poland, Judgment of 6 November 2007
Morsink v. the Netherlands, Judgment of 11 May 2004
Mouisel v. France, Judgment of 14 November 2002
Mürsel Eren v. Turkey, Judgment of 7 February 2006
Mykhaylensky and Others v. Ukraine, Judgment of 30 November 2004
N. v. the United Kingdom, Judgment of 27 May 2008
Nasri v. France, Judgment of 13 July 1995
National Union of Belgian Police v. Belgium, Judgment of 27 October 1975
Neigel v. France, Judgment of 17 March 1993
Niedzwiecki v. Germany, Judgment of 25 October 2005
Niemietz v. Germany, Judgment of 16 December 1992
Nicodemo v. Italy, Judgment of 2 September 1997
O v. the United Kingdom, Judgment of 8 July 1987

Obermeier v. Austria, Judgment of 28 June 1990
Okyay and Others v. Turkey, Judgment of 12 July 2005
Olsson v. Sweden (I), Judgment of 24 March 1988
Olsson v. Sweden (II), Judgment of 27 November 1992
Orhan v. Turkey, Judgment of 18 June 2002
López Ostra v. Spain, Judgment of 9 December 1994
Ahmet Öskan and Others v. Turkey, Judgment of 6 April 2004
Open Door and Dublin Well Women v. Ireland, Judgment of 29 October 1992
P., C. and S. v. the United Kingdom, Judgment of 16 October 2002
Paskhalidis and Others v. Greece, Judgment of 19 March 1997
Peers v. Greece, Judgment of 19 April 2001
Pellegrin v. France, Judgment of 8 December 1999
Perkins and R. v. the United Kingdom, Judgment of 22 October 2002
Petrovic v. Austria, Judgment of 27 March 1998
Pibernik v. Croatia, Judgment of 4 March 2004
Pincová and Pinc v. the Czech Republic, Judgment of 5 November 2002
Poltoratskiy v. Ukraine, Judgment of 29 April 2003
Popov v. Russia, Judgment of 13 July 2006
Posti and Rahko v. Finland, Judgment of 24 September 2002
Powell and Rayner v. the United Kingdom, Judgment of 21 February 1990
Price v. the United Kingdom, Judgment of 10 July 2001
Procaccni v. Italy, Judgment of 30 March 2000
Prodan v. Moldova, Judgment of 18 May 2004
Prokopovich v. Russia, Judgment of 18 November 2004
Rainys and Gasparavicius v. Lithuania, Judgment of 7 April 2005
Refah Partisi and Others v. Turkey, Judgment of 13 February 2003
Rieme v. Sweden, Judgment of 22 April 1992
Runkee and White v. the United Kingdom, Judgment of 10 May 2007
Salesi v. Italy, Judgment of 26 February 1993
Sampanis and Others v. Greece, Judgment of 6 June 2006
Schirmer v. Poland, Judgment of 21 December 2004
Schmidt and Dahlström v. Sweden, Judgment of 6 February 1976
Schouten and Meldrum v. the Netherlands, Judgment of 9 December 1994
Schuler-Zgraggen v. Switzerland, Judgment of 24 June 1993
Scollo v. Italy, Judgment of 28 September 1995
Scozzari v. Italy, Judgment of 13 July 2000
Selçuk and Asker v. Turkey, Judgment of 24 April 1998
Selmouni v. France, Judgment of 28 July 1999
Sibson v. the United Kingdom, Judgment of 10 April 1993
Sidabras and Džiautas v. Lithuania, Judgment of 27 July 2004
Sigurjónsson v. Iceland, Judgment of 30 June 1993
Antonio Siena v. Italy, Judgment of 11 March 2004

Silva Rocha v. Portugal, Judgment of 15 November 1996
Smith, Jane v. the United Kingdom, Judgment of 18 January 2001
Smith and Grady v. the United Kingdom, Judgment of 27 September 1999
Smokovitis and Others v. Greece, Judgment of 11 April 2002
Sørensen and Rasmussen v. Denmark, Judgment of 11 January 2006
Spadea and Scalabrino v. Italy, Judgment of 28 September 1995
Spurio v. Italy, Judgment of 2 September 1997
Stambuk v. Germany, Judgment of 17 October 2002
Stec and Others v. the United Kingdom, Judgment of 12 April 2006
Steel and Morris v. the United Kingdom, Judgment of 15 February 2005
Stjerna v. Finland, Judgment of 25 November 1994
Străin and Others v. Romania, Judgment of 21 July 2005
Tysiac v. Poland, Jugdment of 20 March 2007
Stran Greek Refinereries and Stratis Andreadis v. Greece, Judgment of 9 December 1994
Stretch v. the United Kingdom, Judgment of 24 June 2003
Süßmann v. Germany, Judgment of 16 September 1996
Swedish Engine Drivers' Union v. Sweden, Judgment of 6 February 1976
Tarariyeva v. Russia, Judgment of 14 December 2007
Taskin and Others v. Turkey, Judgment of 10 November 2004
Thlimmenos v. Greece, Judgment of 6 April 2000
Timishev v. Russia, Judgment of 13 December 2005
Tre Traktörer Aktiebolag v. Sweden, Judgment of 7 July 1989
Tüm Haber Sen and Çinar v. Turkey, Judgment of 21 May 2006
Tyrer v. the United Kingdom, Judgment of 25 April 1978
Tysiac v. poland, Judgment of 20 March 2007
United Communist Party of Turkey and Others v. Turkey, Judgment of 30 January 1998
Valsamis v. Greece, Judgment of 18 December 1996
Van Raalte v. the Netherlands, Judgment of 21 February 1997
Varićak v. Croatia, Judgment of 21 October 2004
Vasilopoulou v. Greece, Judgment of 21 March 2002
Velikovi and Others v. Bulgaria, Judgment of 9 July 2007
Velosa Barreto v. Portugal, Judgment of 21 November 1995
Vilho Eskelinen and Others v. Finland, Judgment of 19 April 2007
Vo v. France, Judgment of 8 July 2004
Vogt v. Germany, Judgment of 26 September 1995
Wemhoff v. Germany, Judgment of 27 June 1968
Wessels-Bergervoet v. the Netherlands, Judgment of 4 June 2002
Willis v. the United Kingdom, Judgment of 11 June 2002
Wilson et al. v. the United Kingdom, Judgment of 2 July 2002
Wilson, National Union of Journalists & Others v. the United Kingdom, Judgment of 2 July 2002

Winterwerp v. the Netherlands, Judgment of 24 October 1979
Witold Litwa v. Poland, Judgment of 4 April 2000
X v. France, Judgment of 31 March 1992
X v. the United Kingdom, Judgment of 5 November 1981
X, Y and Z v. the United Kingdom, Judgment of 22 April 1997
Yakovenko v. Ukraine, Judgment of 25 October 2007
Yilderim, Hüseyin v. Turkey, Judgment of 3 May 2007
Young, James and Webster v. the United Kingdom, Judgment of 13 August 1981
Z v. Finland, Judgment of 25 February 1997
Z and Others v. the United Kingdom, Judgment of 10 May 2001
Zeman v. Austria, Judgment of 29 June 2006

European Court of Human Rights: List of Admissibility Decisions

AB Kurt Kellermann v. Sweden, Admissibility decision of 1 July 2003
Ahmet Imam and Others v. Greece, Admissibility decision of 20 October 1997
Arcila Henao v. the Netherlands, Admissibility decision of 24 June 2003
B v. the United Kingdom, Admissibility decision of 12 October 1983
Cheall, Ernest Dennis, v. the United Kingdom, Admissibility decision of 13 May 1985
Erikson v. Italy, Admissibility decision of 26 October 1999
Family H v. the United Kingdom, Admissibility decision of 6 March 1984
Federation off Shore Workers' Trade Unions and Others v. Norway, Admissibility decision of 27 June 2002
40 mothers v. Sweden, Admissibility decision of 9 March 1977
G. against the Netherlands, Admissibility decision of 2 March 1987
Larioshina v. Russia, Admissibility decision of 23 April 2002
Marzari v. Italy, Admissibility decision of 4 May 1999
Nasimi v. Sweden, Admissibility decision of 16 March 2004
National Association of Teachers in further and higher education v. the United Kingdom, Admissibility decision of 16 April 1998
Ndangoya v. Sweden, Admissibility decision of 22 June 2004
Nitecki v. Poland, Admissibility decision of 21 March 2002
Pancenko v. Latvia, Admissibility decision of 28 October 1999
Powell v. the United Kingdom, Admissibility decision of 4 May 2000
Salkic and Others v. Sweden and Admissibility decision of 22 June 2004
Skender v. the Former Republic of Macedonia, Admissibility decision of 22 November 2001
Stec and Others v. the United Kingdom, Admissibility decision of 6 July 2005
Unison v. the United Kingdom, Admissibility decision of 10 January 2002
N.C. Van Buitenen against the Netherlands and *G. against the Netherlands*, Admissibility decisions of 2 March 1987
Van der Lans, Adriana C. Goudswaard, Admissibility decision of 22 September 2005
Volkmer v. Germany, Admissibility decision of 22 November 2001

Wessels-Bergervoet v. the Netherlands, Admissibility decision of 3 October 2000
Wiggins v. the United Kingdom, Admissibility decision of 8 February 1978
X v. the Netherlands, Admissibility decision of 20 July 1971

The European Committee on Social Rights: List of Decisions

Complaint No 13/2002 by *Autism – Europe against France*, Decision of 4 November 2003
Complaint No. 9/2000, *Confédération Française de l'Encadrement CFE-CGC v. France*, Decision of 16 November 2001
Complaint No. 12/2002, the *Confederation of Swedish Enterprise against Sweden*, Decision of 15 May 2003
Complaint No. 11/2000, *European Council of Police Trade Union against Portugal*, Decision of 21 May 2002
Complaint No. 39/2006, *European Federation of National Organisations Working with the Homeless (FEANTSA) v. France*, Decision of 5 December 2007
Complaint No. 15/2003, *European Roma Rights Center v. Greece*, Decision of February 2005
Complaint No. 27/2004 *European Roma Rights Center v. Italy*, Decision of 7 December 2005
Complaint No. 1/1998 by the *International Commission of Jurists against Portugal*, Decision of 9 December 1999
Complaint No. 14/2003 by the *International Federation of Human Rights Leagues (FIDH) v. France*, Decision of 8 September 2004
Complaint No. 41/2007, *Mental Disability Advocacy Center (MDAC) v. Bulgaria*, Decision of 3 June 2008
Complaint No. 6/1999 by the *Syndicat national des professions du tourisme against France*, Decision of 10 October 2000
Complaint No. 8/2000 by the *Quaker Council for European Affairs (QCEA) against Greece*, Decision of 25 April 2001
Complaint No. 10/2000, *Tehy ry and STTK ry against Finland*, Decision of 17 October 2001
Complaint No. 17/2003, by *World Organisation against Torture ("OMCT") v. Greece*, Decision of 7 December 2003
Complaint No. 18/2003, *World Organisation against Torture ("OMCT") v. Ireland*, Decision of 7 December 2004

Complaint No. 20/2003, *World Organisation against Torture ("OMCT") v. Portugal*, Decision of 22 January 2005
Complaint No. 34/2006, *World Organisation against Torture (OMCT) v. Portugal*, Decision of 22 January 2007
Complaint No. 21/2003, *World Organisation against Torture ("OMCT") v. Belgium*, Decision of 7 December 2007
Complaint No. 19/2003, *World Organisation against Torture ("OMCT") v. Italy*, Decision of 7 December 2004

Bibliography

Alexy, Robert "Balancing, constitutional review, and representation", *International Journal of Constitutional Law*, Vol. 3, Issue 4, 2005.

Andreassen, B.A. et al. "Assessing Human Rights Performance in Developing Countries: The Case for a Minimal Threshold Approach to the Economic and Social Rights" in B.A. Andreassen and A. Eide (eds.), *Human Rights in Developing Countries* 1987/1988, 1988, Akademisk Publ.

Arambulo, Kitty *Strengthening the Supervision of the International Covenant on Economic, Social and Cultural Rights – Theoretical and Procedural Aspects*, Hart Intersentia, 1999.

Beetham, David *Democracy and Human Rights*, Polity Press, 2000.

Berchtold, Klaus "Council of Europe activities in the field of economic, social and cultural rights" in Franz Matscher (ed.) *The Implementation of Economic and Social Rights, National, International and Comparative Aspects*, N. P. Engel Verlag, 1991.

Bernt, Jan Fridthjof 'The Significance of Autonomous Law in Modern Society?, *Kritisk Juss*, 2000.

Bernt, Jan Fridthjof "Kan kommunalt selvstyre og retssikkerhed forenes?" (The compatibility of legal security and local self-government) in *Lov og rett*, 1994.

Bernt, Jan Fridthjof and David R. Doublet, *Vitenskapsfilosofi for jurister – en innföring*, Fagbokforlaget Vigmostad, 1998.

Bleicher, Joseph *Contemporary Hermeneutics – Hermeneutics as Method, Philosophy and Critique*, Routledge & Kegan Paul, 1980.

Bossuyt, Marc "La distinction entre les droites civils et politiques et les droits economiques, sociaux et culturel" in *Revue des Droits de l'Homme*, Vol. 8, No. 4, 1975.

Bradley, Anthony "The Convention Right to Education and the Human Rights Act 1998" in *European Human Rights Law Review*, 1999, Issue 4.

Bratt, Rachel G. and Michael E. Stone and Chester Hartman (eds.), *A right to housing: founda tion for a new social agenda*, Philadelphia, PA: Temple University Press, 2006.

Buyse, Antoine *Post-Conflict Housing Restitution. The European Human Rights Perspective, with a Case Study on Bosnia and Herzegovina*, Intersentia, 2008.

Cassese, Antonio "Prohibition of Torture" in R.St.J. Macdonal et al. (eds.) *The European System for the Protection of Human Rights*, Martinus Nijhoff Publ., 1993.

Cassese, Antonio "Are Human Rights Truly Universal?", in O. Savić (ed.), *The Politics of Human Rights*, Verso, 1999.

Chapman, Audrey R. "Core obligations related to the right to health" in Audrey Chapman et al. (eds) in *Core Obligations: Building a Framework for Economic, Social and Cultural Rights*, Intersentia, 2002.

Churchill, Robin R. and Urfan Khaliq "Violations of Economic, Social and Cultural Right, The Current Use and Future Potential of the Collective Complaints Mechanism of the European Social Charter" in Mashood A. Baderin and Robert Mccorquodale (eds.), *Economic, Social and Cultural Rights in Action*, 2007, Oxford University Press.

Clapham, Andrew "The 'Drittwirkung' of the Convention", in R. St. J. Macdonald, F. Matscher and H. Petzold (eds.), *The European System for the Protection of Human Rights*, Martinus Nijhoff Publ., 1993.

Coomans, Fons "Discrimination and Stigmatisation regarding Education: The Case of the Romani Children in the Czech Republic" in Willems (ed.), *Developmental and Autonomy Rights of Children: Empowering Children, Caregivers and Communities*, Intersentia, 2002.

Cowie, A.P. (Chief Editor) *Oxford Advanced Learner's Dictionary of Current English*, Oxford University Press, 1989, 4th Edition.

Cranston, Maurice *What are Human Rights?* The Bodley Head, 1973.

Daintith, Terence "The constitutional protection of economic rights" in *International Journal of Constitutional Law*, Vol. 2, Issue I, 2004.

Dallmayr, Fredc "Hermeneutics and the Rule of Law" in Drucilla Cornell et al. (eds.), *Deconstruction and the Possibility of Justice*, 1992.

Detrick, Sharon *A Commentary on the United Nations Convention on the Rights of the Child*, Martinus Nijhoff Publishers, 1999.

Doublet, David R. *Rett, Vitenskap og Fornuft*, Alma Mater 1995.

Drzewicki, Krzysztof "The Right to Work and Rights in Work" in Asbjørn Eide et al. (eds.) *Economic, Social and Cultural Rights – A Textbook*, 2nd Revised Edition, 2001.

Dworkin, Ronald "Is Law a System of Rules?" in Ronald Dworkin (ed.), *The Philosophy of Law*, Oxford University Press, 1977.

Dworkin, Ronald *Law's Empire*, Fontana Press 1986.

Eide, Asbjørn and Allan Rosas in Asbjørn Eide et al. (eds.) *Economic, Social and Cultural Rights – A Textbook*, Martinus Nijhoff Publ., The Hague, 2001.

Eide, Asbjørn "Universalization of human rights versus globalization of economic power" in Fons Coomans et al. (eds.), *Rendering Justice to the Vulnerable:Liber Amicorum in Honour of Theo van Boven*, Kluwer Law International, 2000.

Eide, Asbjørn "Realization of Social and Economic Rights and the Minimum Threshold Approach" in *Human Rights Law Journal*, 1989 Vol. 10, No. 1–2.

Eide, Asbjørn and Allan Rosas "Economic, Social and Cultural Rights: A Universal Challenge" in Asbjørn Eide et al. (eds.) *Economic, Social and Cultural Rights – A Textbook*, 2nd revised Edition, Martinus Nijhoff Publishers, 2001.

Gadamer, Hans-Georg *Truth and Method*, 2nd Revised Edition, 1989.

Gammeltoft-Hansen, Hans et al., *Forvaltningsret* (Administrative law), 2nd Edition, 2002.

Gloppen, Siri "Kampen for sosiale rettigheder – er rettsalen riktig arena?" ("The struggle for social rights – is the court the right arena?") in *Mennesker & Rettigheter, Nordic Journal of Human Rights*, Vol. 21, Issue 1, 2003.

Gomien, Donna et. al. *Law and practice of the European Convention on Human Rights and the European Social Charter*, Council of Europe Publishing, 1996.

Gulddal, Jesper and Martin Møller "Fra filologi til filosofi – introduktion til den moderne hermeneutik" in *Hermeneutik. En antologi om forståelse* ("From philology to philosophy – Introduction to modern hermeneutics" in Hermeneutics, An anthology on understanding), Jesper Gulddal and Martin Møller, Gyldendal 1999.

Harris, David and John Darcy *The European Social Charter*, 2nd. Edition, Transnational Publishers Inc., 2001.

Heringa, Aaat Willem and Leo Zwaak (rev.) in P. van Dijk et al. (eds.), *Theory and Practice of the European Convention on Human Rights*, 4th Edition, Intersentia, 2006.

Heringa, Aalt Willem and Fried van Hoof (rev.) in P. van Dijk et al. (eds.) *Theory and Practice of the European Convention on Human Rights*, Intersentia 4th Edition, 2006.

Holmes, Stephen and Cass R. Sunstein, *The Cost of Rights: Why Liberty Depends on Taxes*, W.W. Norton and Company, 1999.

Hulsen, Peter "Back to Basis: A Theory of the Emergence of Institutional Facts" in *Law and Philosophy* Vol.17, Issue 3, 1998.

Hunt, Paul "State Obligations, Indicators and Benchmarks, and the Rights to Education" in *Human Rights Law and Practice*, 1998, Vol. 4, No. 2.

Koch, Henning "Modstandsret – en europæisk demokratiforestilling" in Henning Koch og Anne Lise Kjær (eds.) *Europæisk retskultur – på dansk*, Thomson Publ., 2004.

Koch, Ida Elisabeth and Jens Vedsted-Hansen, "International Human Rights and National Legislatures – Conflict or Balance" in *Nordic Journal of International Law*, Vol. 75, Issue 1.

Koch, Ida Elisabeth "Social Rights as Components in the Civil Right to Personal Liberty: Another Step forward in the Integrated Human Rights Approach" in *Netherlands Quarterly*, Vol 20, No. 1, 2002.

Koch, Ida Elisabeth "The Justiciability of Indivisible Rights" in *Nordic Journal of International Law*, 2003, Vol. 72, No. 1.

Koch, Ida Elisabeth *Behandling som alternativ til frihedsstraf – samspillet mellem kriminalretten og social- og sundhedsretten* (Treatment as an alternative to imprisonment – the interlink between criminal law and social and health law), JØP Publ., 1995.

Koch, Ida Elisabeth *Human rights: A conflict between positive individual and collective democratic interests?*, Boom Juridische uitgevers, 2008.

Koch, Ida Elisabeth "Dichotomies, Trichotomies or Waves of Duties?" in *Human Rights Law Review*, Vol. 5, Issue 1, 2005.

Koch, Ida Elisabeth "Social Rights as Components in the Civil Right to Personal Liberty" in *Netherlands Quarterly*, Vol. 20, No. 1, 2002.

Koch, Ida Elisabeth "Boligrettigheder – Beskyttelse af sociale rettigheder gennem indgreb i civile rettigheder" (Housing Rights – Protection of Social Rights by means of Interferences in Civil Rights) in *MENNESKER & RETTIGHEDER, Nordic Journal for Human Rights*, No. 4, 2001.

Krause, Katarina "The Right to Property" in Asbjørn Eide et al. (eds) *Economic, Social and Cultural Rights – A Textbook*, 2nd. Revised Edition, 2001.

Leckie, Scott "Violations of Economic, Social and Cultural Rights" in Theo C. van Boven et al. (eds.), *The Maastricht Guidelines on Violations of Economic, Social and Cultural Rights*, SIM Special No. 20, Netherlands Institute of Human Rights, 1998.

Liebenberg, Sandra "The Protection of Economic, and Social Rights in Domestic Legal Systems" in Asbjørn Eide et al. *Economic, Social and Cultural Rights – A Textbook*, Martinus Nijhoff Publ., 2001.

Merrils, J.G. and A.H. Robertson, *Human Rights in Europe*, 4th Edition, 2001, Juris Publishing, Manchester University Press.

Montesquieu, Charles *The Spirit of the Laws* (1748), translated and edited by Anne M. Cohler, Basia Carolyn Miller and Harald Samuel Stone, Cambridge University Press, 1989.

Nowak, Manfred "The Right to Education" in Asbjørn Eide et al. (eds.) *Economic, Social and Cultural Rights – A Textbook*, Martinus Nijhoff Publ., The Hague, 2001.

Opsahl, Torkel "The Convention and the right to respect for family life, particularly as regards the unity of the family and the protection of the rights of parents and guardians in the education of children" in *Privacy and Human Rights*, Manchester University Press, 1973.

Ovey, Clare and Robin C.A. White, *European Convention on Human Rigts, 4th Edition*, 2006, Oxford University Press.

Palmer, Stephanie "AIDS, Expulsion and Article 3 of the European Convention on Human Rights" in *European Human Rights Law Review*, Issue 5, 2005.

Porter, Bruce "The Crisis of ESC Rights and Strategies for Addressing It" in John Squires et al. (eds.), *The Road To A Remedy – Current Issues in the Litigation of Economic, Social and Cultural Rights*, UNSW Press, 2005.

Ravlo, Line "I hvilken utstrekning er økonomiske, sosiale og kulturelle rettigheter sikret i den europæiske menneskerettighedskonvention?" ("To which extent does the ECHR encompass economic, social and cultural rights?") in *Retfærd*, Vol. 25, Issue 97, 2002.

Riceour, Paul *Interpretation Theory: Discourse and the Surplus of Meaning*, Texas Christian University Press, 1976.

Ricoeur, Paul "Ethics and Culture" in *Political and Social Essays*, collected and ed. by David Stewart and Joseph Bien, 1974.

Ricoeur, Paul "The Hermeneutical Function of Distanciation" in *Philosophy Today*, Vol XVII, Issue 2–4, 1973.

Ryssdall, Rolf "The Coming of Age of the European Convention on Human Rights" in *European Human Rights Law Review*, Vol. 18, Issue 1, 1996.

Rytter, Jens Elo "Går menneskeretsdomstolen for vidt? – fortolkning og retsskabelse i Strasbourg." (Is the Human Rights Court going too far? – Interpretation of Law-making in Strasbourg) in *Juristen* 2006.

Sachs, A. "Social and Economic Rights: Can they be made Justiciable?" 53 *Southern Methodist University Law Review*, 2000, Issue 4.

Samuel, L. *Fundamental Social Rights: Case law of The European Social Charter 78*, Council of Europe, 1997.

Scheinin, Martin "Justiciability and the Indivisibility of Human Rights" in John Squires et al. (eds.), *The Road to a Remedy: Current Issues in the Litigation of Economic, Social and Cultural Rights*, Australian Human Rights Centre, The University of New South Wales.

Scheinin, Martin "Sociala rättigheter som mänskliga rättigheter" ("Social Rights as Human Rights") in *Nordisk Administrativt Tidsskrift*, 3/1994.

Scheinin, Martin "Economic and Social Rights as Legal Rights" in Asbjørn Eide et al. (eds.), *Economic, Social and Cultural Rights: A Textbook*, Martinus Nijhoff, 2nd Edition, 2001.

Scott, Craig "The Interdependence and Permeability of Human Rights Norms: Towards a Partial Fusion of the International Covenants on Human Rights" in *Osgoode Hall Law Journal*, Vol 27, No. 4, 1989.

Scott, Craig "Towards the Institutional Integration of the Core Human Rights Treaties" in *Giving Meaning to Economic, Social and Cultural Rights*, Isfahan Merali & Valerie Oosterveld (eds.), University of Pennsylvania Press, 2001.

Scott, Craig "Reaching Beyond (Without Abandoning) the Category of Economic, Social and Cultural Rights" in *Human Rights Quarterly*, Vol. 21, Issue 3, 1999.

Sen, Amartya "The right not to be hungry" in P. Alston et al. (eds.), *The Right to Food*, 1984.

Sepúlveda, Magdalena in *The Nature of the Obligations under the International Covenant on Economic, Social and Cultural Rights*, Hart Intersentia, 2003.

Shue, Henry *Basic Rights: Subsistence, Affluence and U.S. Foreign Policy*, Princeton University Press, 2nd Edition, 1996.

Steiner, Henry J. and Philip Alston in *International Human Rights in Context*, 2nd Edition, Oxford University Press, 2000.

Toebes, Brigit "The Rights to Health" in Asbjørn Eide et al. (eds.) *Economic, Social and Cultural Rights – A textbook*, 2nd Revised Edition, Martinus Nijhoff Publishers, 2001.

Tremblay, L. B. "The legitimacy of judicial review: The limits of dialogue between courts and legislatures" in *International Journal of Constitutional Law*, Vol. 3, Issue 4, 2005.

Tuori, Kaarlo *Critical Legal Positivism*, Ashgate, 2006.

van Boven, Theo C. et al. (eds.) *The Maastricht Guidelines on Violations of Economic, Social and Cultural Rights*, SIM Special No. 20, Netherlands Institute of Human Rights, 1998.

van Dijk, Pieter and Mark Viering (rev.) in Pieter van Dijk et. al. (eds.) *Theory and Practice of the European Concention on Human Rights*, 4th Edition, 2006.

van Dijk, P. and G.J.H van Hoof *Theory and Practice of the European Convention on Human Rights*, Kluwer Law International, 3rd Edition, 1998.

van Hoof, G.J.H. "The Legal Nature of Economic, Social and Cultural Rights: a Rebuttal of Some Traditional Views" in P. Alston et al. (eds.), *The Right to Food*, Martinus Nijhoff Publ.,1984.

van Rijn, Arjen (rev.) in P. van Dijk et al. (eds.) *Theory and Practice of the European Convention on Human Rights*, 4th Edition, Kluwer Law International, Intersentia, 2006.

Vasak, Karel "A 30-year Struggle: The Sustained Efforts to Give Force of Law to the Universal Declaration of Human Rights" in *Unesco Courier*, November 1977.

Vermeulen, Ben in P. van Dijk et al. (eds.) *Theory and Practice of the European Convention on Human Rights*, 4th Edition, Intersentia.

Vierdag, E. W. "The legal nature of the rights granted by the International Covenant on Economic, Social and Cultural Rights" in *Netherlands Yearbook of International Law*, Vol. IX, 1978.

Waldron, Jeremy "Homelessness and the issue of freedom" in *Liberal Rights, Collected Papers 1981–1991*, Cambridge University Press, 1993.

Jeremy Waldron, "Two sides of the coin" in *Liberal Rights: Collected Papers, 1981–1991*, Cambridge University Press, 1993.

Wildhaber, Luzius "Right to Education and Parental Rights" in R. St.J. Macdonald et al. (eds.), *The European System for the Protection of Human Rights*, Martinus Nijhoff Publ, 1993.

Wildhaber, Luzius "Protection against Discrimination under the European Convention" in *Baltic Yearbook of International Law*, Vol. II, 2002.

Wittgenstein, Ludwig *Philosophical Investigations*, translated by G. E. M. Anscombe, 1953, 3rd edition, 1967.

Index

www.ingramcontent.com/pod-product-compliance
Lightning Source LLC
LaVergne TN
LVHW081514300926
849161LV00006B/1175
9789004160514